WHY OCCUPY A SQUARE?

JEROEN GUNNING
ILAN ZVI BARON

Why Occupy a Square?

*People, Protests and Movements
in the Egyptian Revolution*

OXFORD
UNIVERSITY PRESS

OXFORD

UNIVERSITY PRESS

Oxford University Press, Inc., publishes works that further
Oxford University's objective of excellence
in research, scholarship, and education.

Oxford New York
Auckland   Cape Town   Dar es Salaam   Hong Kong   Karachi
Kuala Lumpur   Madrid   Melbourne   Mexico City   Nairobi
New Delhi   Shanghai   Taipei   Toronto

With offices in
Argentina   Austria   Brazil   Chile   Czech Republic   France   Greece
Guatemala   Hungary   Italy   Japan   Poland   Portugal   Singapore
South Korea   Switzerland   Thailand   Turkey   Ukraine   Vietnam

Published by Oxford University Press, Inc
198 Madison Avenue, New York, New York 10016

Published in the United Kingdom in 2014 by C. Hurst & Co. (Publishers) Ltd.

www.oup.com

Library of Congress Cataloging-in-Publication Data is available for this title
Why Occupy A Square
People, Protests and Movements in the Egyptian Revolution
Gunning, Jeroen and Baron, Ilan Zvi
9780199394982

Printed in India
on Acid-Free Paper

CONTENTS

ACKNOWLEDGEMENTS

This book would not have been possible without the generous help of many. First of all, we wish to thank Robin Coningham, Pro-Vice Chancellor of the Faculty of Social Sciences and Health at Durham University, for providing funding for our fieldtrip in 2011 and for granting a double period of research leave for Gunning in 2012–13. Lorraine Holmes, as always, was invaluable in navigating the ethical and insurance quagmire that is fieldwork these days. We would like to thank Nouran Aly, Khalil al-Anani, Fouad Marei and Ahmed Tohami for briefing us thoroughly before our fieldtrip, sharing their personal insights as close observers of the uprising and introducing us to their social networks in Cairo. We are immensely grateful to all those participants in the uprising who gave generously of their time to answer our questions with passion and probity; your palpable sense of commitment was humbling. We are particularly grateful to Elisa Wynne-Hughes for showing us around Tahrir Square, introducing us to some of her networks and acting as translator on the occasions we needed one. Immense thanks go to Nouran (Aly) for her tireless work on the protests table, scanning three years of *al-Masry al-Youm* articles for reports of large protests, and for her insightful analysis in her Master's thesis on the prelude to revolution. A host of people provided feedback on drafts and oral discussions of our argument, without which the book would not have been what it has become: Khalil al-Anani, Nouran Aly, Angharad Closs-Stephens, Jérome Drevon, Gennaro Gervasio, Vivienne Matthies-Boon, Caelum Moffatt, Emma Murphy, James Piscatori, Andrea Teti, Noa Vaisman and the Contextualising Conflict group at the Durham Global Security Institute. The comments from our two anonymous reviewers were similarly incisive and enormously helpful. Any errors, misinterpretations and omissions are of course our responsibility alone. Carrie Wickham went beyond the call of collegial friendship to organise, while in the midst of moving house, access to the uncorrected proofs of her forthcoming book on the Muslim Brotherhood, besides offering additional details. Thanks also go to Eric Crahan and Eric Henney at Princeton University Press for authorising access to Carrie's book. We are immensely grateful to our copy editor, Tim Page, who did a brilliant job knocking the manuscript into final shape with a hawk's eye for erring detail; and to Michael Dwyer whose support, patience and flexibility have been crucial to seeing this project come to fruition. Finally, this book would not have been possible without the continued love and support of our families.

INTRODUCTION

We are the ones controlling the streets today, not the regime. I feel so free—
things can't stay the same after this.

Ahmed Ashraf, a 26-year-old bank analyst
(quoted in the *Guardian* 2011a)

It was 29 January 2011. Amira (Interview 2011), a reporter for the
opposition newspaper *al-Masry Al-Youm*, was walking down from her
office to Tahrir Square. The usually crowded streets around Cairo's
busiest square were empty. No cars or busses, just people making their
way to the Square. It was the day after Tahrir had been occupied by
Egypt's largest protest movement in years, and the reporter had flown
back hurriedly from her posting in Germany to be with her friends at
this critical juncture in Egypt's political history. She had been following the protests online from the first demonstrations on 25 January.
When the Mubarak regime had shut down the internet on 27 January,
she had panicked as she could no longer follow her friends and check
on their fates. She had booked the next flight back while her friends
were battling the police during the 'Friday of Rage.'

As Amira approached the Square on the morning after, she noted seeing military trucks, but no police. The Square was surrounded by makeshift barricades, behind which the protesters had created a temporary
camp. At the entrance to the Square was a woman wearing a *niqab*
[Islamic veil], holding a placard saying 'Down with Mubarak.' The
women looked at each other and for a moment they smiled. For the first
time, the reporter—a staunch secularist—felt a connection with a reli-

gious co-citizen. Tahrir had created a space where the usual divisions no longer held, at least for the duration of the Square's occupation.

Between 25 January and 11 February 2011, Egypt experienced an unprecedented mass protest that grabbed the world's imagination. A non-violent protest directed against the Mubarak regime set in motion a train of events that resulted in the overthrow of one of the longest serving authoritarian rulers in the world. On 25 January, tens of thousands of Egyptians, most with no prior experience of activism, took to the streets to join the hardened activists who had called for the demonstration to demand an end to police abuse, a higher minimum wage and political reform. Protests began in Cairo's 'informal areas', in the narrow alleyways criss-crossing these un-planned urban sprawls, rather than in the city's main squares and boulevards, where the police were waiting. Bursting out of the alleys in their thousands, the protesters outnumbered the police, briefly occupying Tahrir Square for the first time since 2003.

The police cleared the Square with brute force after midnight on that first day, and for the next two days the police violently tried to suppress the small groups of protesters that ventured outside. On Friday, 28 January, activists called for a second mass protest, and Egyptians responded in their hundreds of thousands. After Friday prayers, crowds surged through Egypt's main cities, from Alexandria to Luxor, advancing on the security cordons sent to hem them in. Despite the largely peaceful nature of the protests, fierce battles raged where police and protesters met. As the day progressed, square after square fell to the protesters, and as evening came the police fled in disarray, outnumbered and demoralised. Nationwide, more than 1,000 protesters had been reported wounded and dozens killed (Aljazeera 2011f; *Guardian* 2011c).

As the police slunk away, the army stepped in. Unlike in Bahrain, Libya, Yemen or Syria, the army largely refrained from attacking the protesters, a few initial tense confrontations notwithstanding. Tahrir Square became the symbolic centre of the protests. For fourteen days, the protesters stayed, refusing to leave until President Hosni Mubarak stepped down. Withstanding repeated attacks by thugs and Mubarak supporters, they created what came to be called the 'Republic of Tahrir', a thriving micro-cosmos of a different vision of society.

By 11 February, Mubarak was forced to resign by the Supreme Council of the Armed Forces (SCAF), itself under pressure from the ongoing protests, which had now moved into the industrial sector, and international actors, and with its own interests to secure. Nevertheless, in eighteen days the protesters had achieved what until then had seemed unthinkable: the removal of their authoritarian president, whose thirty-year-old regime had been likened to that of the pharaohs for its longevity and apparent imperviousness to protests. They also succeeded in creating a model of protest that continues to reverberate through Egyptian politics—and elsewhere.

How are we to make sense of these events? Can we find an explanation for why they occurred when they did, and in the way that they did? Can we explain their timing (why 25 January, and not earlier or later), their focus (why, for instance, did they combine a focus on police violence with demands for raising the minimum wage) and who participated (not just students, but workers, members of the lower middle classes and members of the elite)? How did the protests come about? Why did they attract so many who had hitherto been too afraid of police violence? How did these people overcome their fear in the face of vicious violence, detention and death? How were they able to outmanoeuvre the police? Was this really a 'leaderless revolution', as so many pundits claimed at the time? What role did Facebook, Twitter and the internet play? Were these as central as many claimed they were? How did the protests affect the way that public space was perceived?

Conceptualising the 'January 25 Revolution'

How we conceptualise the events of January–February 2011 impacts not only the questions we ask, but also the answers we find. First, was this in fact a revolution? Said differently, what conceptual terrain best provides an explanatory framework for understanding, evaluating and describing these eighteen days? If we call it a revolution as opposed to a rebellion, riot, protest or uprising, we provide a potential normative structure to our analysis but we also suggest a specific method of analysis and an underlying set of theories. Yet it is not at all clear what concept best explains these events. For example, if we describe the events as a revolution, then one could expect a fundamental structural shift in Egypt's systems of governance or in its social relations, neither of which, at the time of writing, is clearly the case. However, the participants in the events saw themselves as participating in a revolution.

Second, if this was not strictly a revolution, then is it more helpful to think of the events in terms of a mass protest carried out by a social movement? Social movements feature heavily in the literature on revolutions, and many of those involved in the events in Egypt describe themselves as members of numerous overlapping movements. Yet, as the significant fluctuations in popular support for the revolution after 11 February 2011 suggests, the extent to which those involved in the protests were meaningfully part of a movement, rather than simply an isolated (though subsequently recurrently repeated) protest event, is questionable. Also, a social movement lens presupposes a level of organisation and planning that is belied by the spontaneity of much of what happened.

Third, while the revolt was an internal matter, it also had clear international dimensions. One of the triggers that contributed to bringing people out on 25 January was the overthrow of the regime in Tunisia eleven days earlier. Some of the tactics employed had been the product of exchanges between local activists and transnational movements such as the Global Justice Movement, and many of the socio-economic grievances that contributed to the protests were products of global economic trends (although local economic dynamics were arguably more influential). The revolution was supported through the continuous broadcasting of the revolt by Aljazeera and other satellite stations, and through the discussion and broadcasting of events on social media worldwide. Moreover, the events in Egypt were part of a wider demand for change across the Middle East and were influenced by the foreign policies adopted by regional powers. The successes in Tunisia and in Egypt were key to the changing regional dynamics unleashed by what became known as the Arab Spring, and served as (idealised) templates for protest movements globally. The revolution also revealed the deep hypocrisy of Western foreign policy toward the region, with its advocacy of human rights on the one hand and its propping up of autocrats against protest movements in the service of oil and regional stability on the other.[1] The erosion of Mubarak's domestic legitimacy was in no small part due to his (perceived) role as the local enforcer of US regional policy towards Israel (and later Iraq).

The international reach and impact of the events confirms Fred Halliday's (1999) argument that revolutions matter for international relations. Yet it is not clear how helpful the discipline of International Relations (IR) is in actually explaining the revolution. IR does offer a variety of intellectual approaches, some of which can help to illuminate international aspects of the revolution, such as the global food crisis or the way other states responded to the revolution (although different IR approaches are often incommensurable with each other or contradictory). But it remains deeply influenced by a spatial politics of sovereignty that is misleading in its obsession with the state and the international system of states. This is unhelpful both in understanding the local dynamics at work in Egypt and in understanding the transnational grassroots linkages that, among many local factors, fed into the revolt. Moreover, as has been argued elsewhere (Booth 2007), IR can be seen as primarily derivative of other theories, and as such it is often more useful to go to the source. IR has, nevertheless, influenced us. The framework adopted in this book is influenced by post-positivist approaches in IR, and our approach to theory is influenced by the Critical Theory-inspired Welsh School of Security Studies. Beyond that, however, our categories of analysis are taken from other fields.

Fourth, the revolution was also very much about the politics of, and the contestation over, space. Tahrir Square became a spatial symbol of protest, both locally and globally, infused with new practices with revolutionary connotations (though interpreted differently in different global locations). At stake here is how we think of space in relation to politics. Whether the space is defined in terms of the polis or in terms of modern sovereignty, our language of political life is infused with assumptions about political space. Yet in Egypt what seems to have happened was the creation of a political space that, according to some key assumptions in modern political theory, could not have been 'political' in that it was neither sovereign nor, at least for fourteen of the eighteen days, effectively part of a state (although we would dispute this particular definition of 'political'). The protesters made use of spaces in innovative ways, chose to act in some locations as opposed to others, and changed the meaning and practices of key public spaces. It is not possible to understand the revolt without taking into account both how these spaces influenced the protests, and how the protesters reclaimed certain public spaces and then redefined them, re-inscribing them with new practices. But this in itself tells us little about how the protests came about.

A Revolution?

Those involved in the protests self-referentially called what they were doing a revolution. Insofar as the revolution defined itself by demanding a new Egypt (which not all protesters did to the same extent), the events had revolutionary intent. As Halliday (1999: 140) argues, 'revolutions are, above all, projects that claim to introduce something 'new' and which legitimate themselves by this'. However, this revolution was not directly about taking control of the state, which, according to Halliday (1999: 143), is one crucial part of any revolution. For many of the protesters the revolution was primarily about forcing Mubarak to resign. There was no revolutionary guard, so to speak, poised to take over the state, nor was there a coherent collective strategy for, or agreement about, establishing a new system of governance.

The uprising was successful in overthrowing Mubarak, but, at the time of writing, it has not succeeded in fundamentally refashioning the Egyptian state. There are certainly revolutionary elements to what happened. Clearly, the protests did foster a new public political space, drawing in a variety of new political actors, but whether or not this development is enough to warrant the analytical description of it being a 'revolution' is uncertain.

What is considered a 'revolution' is about convention, and, writing as academics, we follow academic convention. As Halliday (1999: 47) writes:

definitions of revolution are, like all definitions in social science, conventional: revolutions are not … objectively given 'things', waiting to be unearthed or identified like the objects of natural science. They are phenomena which human subjects choose to group, on the basis of criteria of significance and recurrence, into one category rather than another. The strength of such a definition is that it allows for the identification of a discrete set of historical events which can be studied in their own right …

Halliday (1999: 45–6) argues that in the period between the 1960s and 1980s, the literature on revolution provided a set of three distinctions. First, revolutions are different from rebellions, revolts and even a coup. Second, there is a distinction between political and social revolutions. Third, revolutions are 'moments of rupture and transition within social systems'.

These three features are clearly identifiable in Theda Skocpol's work on the subject, on whose work Halliday draws. Skocpol (1979: 4) writes:

Social revolutions are rapid, basic transformations of a society's state and class structures; and they are accompanied and in part carried through by class-based revolts from below. Social revolutions are set apart from other sorts of conflicts and transformative processes above all by the combination of two coincidences: the coincidence of societal structural change with class upheaval; and the coincidence of political with social transformation.

According to Skocpol, social revolutions are distinct from rebellions, which do not result in structural change. Furthermore, social revolutions are distinct from political ones in that 'political revolutions transform state structures but not social structures, and they are not necessarily accomplished through class conflict. What is unique to social revolution is that basic changes in social structure and in political structure occur together in a mutually reinforcing fashion' (1979: 4–5).

According to Skocpol's definition, the revolution in Egypt was a rebellion, with some elements of political transformation thrown in (if we stick with the problematic notion that the political concerns the state). It was not social because there was no major class shift, even though shifts in class fortunes mattered, both before and after the revolution. It was not political in Skocpol's sense because there was (at the time of writing) no fundamental transformation of state structures. Mubarak may have stepped down, but the military and many from among the old elite remain. Nevertheless, there was clearly something revolutionary about what happened. There has been a political transformation in the creation of new political spaces, identities and networks, and, significantly, in people's attitudes towards political participation and the state security apparatus. But the structures of state are largely unchanged, and it remains to be seen how deep this transformation is across society.

Within a Skocpolian framework, the Egyptian revolution was not a revolution. Yet it is insulting and methodologically dubious to reject participants' self-understanding. Consequently, it is appropriate in this case to retain the term revolution, but to suffix it. In view of ongoing events, what happened in Egypt can more accurately be described as an 'arrested revolution'. Moreover, the situation in January 2011 can be meaningfully described as a 'revolutionary situation', regardless of the outcome of the events. The question then becomes how it became revolutionary.

One way out of the 'revolution question' is Jack Goldstone's (1991: 10–11) list of eight 'constituent elements' that can be found in different combinations in revolutions and state breakdowns more generally. The question then becomes not whether something is a revolution, but which elements of state breakdown occurred:

(1) widespread elite or popular belief that the state is ineffective, unjust, or obsolete, producing widespread loss of confidence in, or allegiance to, the state; (2) elite revolt against the state; (3) popular revolts ... against state or elite authority; (4) widespread violence or civil war; (5) a change in political institutions; (6) a change in the status and power of traditional elites; (7) a change in basic forms of economic organization; (8) a change in the symbols and beliefs that justify the distribution of power, status, and wealth.

In our case, we are looking at a situation where (1), (2), (3) and to some extent (8) occurred, with elements (4), (5), (6) and (7) not being particularly relevant. Whether this is a revolution becomes a moot point, as what we are trying to explain is how, in vectoral terms, [1,1,1,0,0,0,0,1]—or (1), (2), (3) and (8)—occurred, with each digit indicating whether the corresponding constituent element, from 1 to 8, is absent (0) or present (1). Such a perspective is particularly helpful in trying to find comparative cases with similar dynamics.

Halliday and Skocpol are both influenced by Marxist structural thinking. The distinction that Skocpol draws between political and social revolutions is shaped by this perspective. Halliday's differentiation between revolution and other forms of political upheaval follows from this same distinction, although he recognises the difficulty in sustaining such a dichotomy. Nevertheless, both these thinkers raise the importance of structural change, as do most theorists of revolution.

Structure is important. As we show in Chapters 3–4, long-term structural changes underpinned and influenced the January 25 revolution, and one cannot give an adequate explanation without taking these into consideration. The literature on revolutions provides some insightful analysis of what structural strains cause a revolution to take place, and we will draw on this (though mostly within the context of social movement theory).

However, this overly structural approach is problematic. As Anthony Giddens (1986) argues, structures and agents cannot, and indeed should not, be understood to exist independently of each other but are mutually constitutive. To be sure, the Egyptian revolution, however unfinished, was in part caused by structural strains giving rise to grievances and by structural shifts providing new threats and opportunities, but the uprising was also contingent on the active mobilisation of new pools of citizens, the painstaking innovation of tactics, the (re-)formulation of grievances and the conscious establishment of links between hitherto unconnected protest networks. To bring these acts by agents into clearer focus, we need to look beyond the classical literature on revolutions.

INTRODUCTION

A Social Movement?

To bring the process of mobilisation behind the revolution into focus, we adopt a social movement theory framework, which is related to the literature on revolutions (consider, for example, Charles Tilly's seminal *From Mobilization to Revolution* (1978)). There is no single, agreed-upon definition of what a social movement is. Definitions range from those seeing movements as 'the actors of central conflicts in society, embodying fundamental oppositions regarding the direction of the historical process' (Touraine in Diani and McAdam 2003: 5–6) to those conceiving of movements as 'little more than expressions of preferences, that movement organizations are supposed to mobilize and turn into real action' (McCarthy and Zald in Diani and McAdam 2003: 6).[2] The definition we adopt is by Donatella della Porta and Diani (1999: 16), who define a social movement as a collection of '(1) informal networks, based (2) on shared beliefs and solidarity, which mobilize about (3) conflictual issues, through (4) the frequent use of various forms of protest'.

According to Cyrus Zirakzadeh (2006: 4), there are (at least) three characteristics to a social movement. First, social movements are concerned with transforming the prevailing social structures. They are driven by an idea of an alternative order and have the basic means to at least attempt to build this new order. Second, social movements are typically diverse, mobilising people from a wide variety of social and economic backgrounds. What sets them apart from institutionalised politics is that they usually represent those without the social prestige or wealth to have their interests 'routinely articulated or represented in the political system'. Third, social movements typically use 'confrontational and disruptive' tactics as well as those available within the legal system. Specifically, as Snow, Soule and Kriesi (2004: 11) clarify, social movements usually act 'outside of institutional or organizational channels'.

The term 'social' is misleading, since social movements are profoundly political.[3] The movements are social in the sense that they are not organs or products of state institutions, although their aims are political since they challenge power relations (including, often, the state). The distinction between social and political suggested by the term 'social movement' is a product of the intellectual history of understanding the modern state, and the dominant position which the state has come to occupy in social science's imagination. It is based on an (artificial) distinction between state and society, between the political and the social—the same distinction that separates sociology (with its presumed focus on society) from political science (with its presumed focus on the state). In the case of the Egyptian revolution, as in so many political events, this distinction is unhelpful, as the protests— a challenge to the regime (and thus political in the narrow sense of action pertaining to the state)—were rooted in the practices of what could be described as social movements.

If by social movements we mean a collection of networks, linked through shared beliefs and solidarity, which challenge the status quo through the frequent use of protest tactics, the January 25 revolution itself is not a social movement, since it lacked continuity and a sufficient level of shared identity. Although the protesters shared an aversion to Mubarak and the police, and developed a sense of solidarity towards each other during those eighteen days, they shared little else. Many did not belong to protest networks, and their 'membership' of the revolutionary movement was temporary. In addition, those present held a wide variety of (often conflicting) political beliefs, as has subsequently become starkly evident in the deep divisions running between the different protest networks.

Rather, the revolution can be better understood as a series of interlinked protest events constituting an episode (McAdam, Tarrow and Tilly 2001: 28–32) within a larger, ongoing conflictual situation, involving a coalition of networks and temporarily mobilised non-activists. To be sure, many of the protest networks behind the revolution were part of social movements, ranging from the pro-democracy movement to the workers' and Palestinian solidarity movements. Although they held different ideological beliefs, they shared a protest identity and a set of tactics, forged through years of acting together. A significant number of the non-activists who joined in would have been sympathisers of these broader movements. But most would not have been part of these movements in any meaningful sense. During the uprising, a revolutionary identity was formed among the protesters. But this identity has proved ephemeral; only if it becomes embedded and is sustained beyond the revolutionary moment can we speak of a social movement.[4]

To classify the uprising as a (revolutionary) protest episode does not mean that we cannot use social movement theory to analyse it. Social movement theories have been used to explain phenomena ranging from single protest events to transnational movements spanning decades. What they enable us to do is to make grassroots actors, their networks and the mechanisms by which they mobilise and affect social and political change central to our analysis, while maintaining a focus on the broader political and economic context within which they are dialectically situated. Because social movement 'theory' consists of a number of competing analytical traditions, it offers a rich seam of tools, from the focus on resources and organisational dynamics of resource mobilisation theorists, to the focus on ideas and beliefs of framing theories, to the focus on broader contextual factors of political process and political opportunity structure theorists.[5]

Since what we are interested in are the actors who prepared the ground for the revolution, we will focus specifically on the 'networks' that drove the protest events. Networks are integral to social movements. 'For all their differences,' Diani and McAdam (2003: 6) write, the numerous contending definitions prevalent in social movement theory 'all accommodate network mechanisms within their broader frameworks.' 'Networks' are here defined as 'sets of nodes, linked by some form of relationship', or 'tie', which occurs when two nodes (individual or organisational) are linked (directly, indirectly, intensely, weakly or in multiple ways) (Diani and McAdam 2003: 6–7).[6] Networks have boundaries, but these can be porous and overlapping (for instance, various activists belonged both to the Palestinian solidarity networks and the subsequent pro-democracy networks). They help in 'the mobilization and allocation of resources', 'the production and circulation of information' and 'the circulation of meaning and mutual recognition' (Diani and McAdam 2003: 10), and are at the heart of the relational mechanisms (such as brokerage) and cognitive mechanisms (e.g. shifts in awareness, identity or commitment) that are central to movement dynamics (McAdam, Tarrow and Tilly 2001: 26–7). Because our focus is on networks protesting against the current power-holders (whether these be the regime, industry bosses or local administrators), we use the term 'protest networks'.

The main insight we take from social movement theory is its emphasis on meso-level explanations, which bridge the divide between structure (and its concomitant macro/structural explanations) and agency (and micro/individual explanations) (Diani and McAdam 2003: 4). One popular way to explain protest movements, particularly prevalent among revolutionary studies, has been to look at the structures in politics and society. When these come under increasing strain—for instance, when inequality between different classes increases dramatically—society is 'ripe' for protests; the higher the strains, the more intense the grievances, the more likely it is that there will be a revolt.

One obvious flaw in this argument, and one that social movement theory was quick to point out, is that grievances do not necessarily lead to protests. If engaging in protest means death or detention, then potential activists will think twice before going out, especially if success is far from guaranteed. If opposition groups are routinely suppressed, marginalised or co-opted, it is difficult to build a protest momentum, let alone a protest narrative that identifies the problem, classifies it as a remediable injustice and proposes an action plan. Under such circumstances, most citizens will accept the regime and its claims to legitimacy, however grudgingly. For a structural strain to produce a revolutionary situation, it needs to be interpreted as such. Structural strain by itself cannot explain why protests occur in authoritarian settings. For that, we need to look at whether there are opportunities to protest and whether there are sufficiently well-organised networks able to interpret strains as unjust and remediable and to organise and resource any protests.

The notion of structural strains is captured within social movement theory by the notion of political opportunity structure (the mainstay of the political process model) (cf. McAdam 1982: 40–3; Kitschelt 1986).[7] How the state's security forces deal with protest, whether people have legitimate institutional channels to influence policies and what constellation of classes supports the state or has the resources to protest (both of which are affected by long-term socio-economic changes)—all these factors shape how protests unfold. Key here is not simply what types of structures prevail, but how these structures are interpreted and how these interpretations change over time.

This is where social movement theory departs from structural explanations, bringing in a focus on agency through the notions of movements, networks and mechanisms.[8] Movement actors interpret the situation through changing (and often contested) sets of frames: from injustice frames; to diagnosis and protest frames; to prognosis, action and motivational frames. Through mechanisms such as 'attribution of threat and opportunity, social appropriation [of, for instance, existing networks or frames], framing of the dispute, and arraying of innovative forms of collective action' (McAdam, Tarrow and Tilly 2001: 28), movement actors seek to mobilise people. These frames are developed and spread through the networks that make up the movement. Structures impact protest behaviour indirectly, through the constraints and opportunities they impose and the way these are interpreted by both movement actors and the general population, which in turn is affected by the relative strength of regimes versus opposition networks and how well each succeeds in making their interpretation resonate with the general population. How activists and the general population interpret structures is influenced by the structures they inhabit and the way they experience them, which in turn is a function of both where they are placed in these structures (for instance, whether they are poor or rich) and how they, their friends and their families view these structures (for instance, whether they feel they have been cheated by the system, which in turn is influenced by prevailing cultural tropes and practices).

Part I of this book takes its cue from these insights, starting with an analysis of the protest networks that emerged in the decade prior to 2011, the interpretive frames they deployed and the tactics they developed. We then move to an analysis of the broader structural context, and how this context shaped, and was interpreted by, the protest movements.

A Spatial Revolution?

Our understanding of politics is constrained by what counts as political space. 'Once upon a time,' Warren Magnusson (1996: 75) observes, 'it seemed as if the most important political issues could be contained quite effectively within the spaces defined by the state system.' Yet the events in Egypt cannot be contained within this framework. The protests were in a very fundamental sense a contestation between protesters and state authorities over the use and meaning of public space, and the occupation of Tahrir Square constituted a re-inscription of the practices and meanings associated with the Square. These practices were outside of the realm of (state) sovereign politics, as there was no central coercive authority, no hierarchical structure rooted in the state on the Square itself. While the ultimate goal of the protests was the resignation of Mubarak, it was not about taking over the state (except through refashioning the way state power was allocated). The practices developed within the Square, moreover, constituted an experiment of people reinventing political organisation in the (de facto) absence of a state.

Politics happens in a variety of locations, spaces and times. To focus on sovereignty and its system is to ignore how politics is often not about sovereignty at all. Indeed, following Magnusson (1996: 91), 'one way of understanding politics is as the mode of activity that emerges when other forms of government fail'. In this regard, we seek to develop an understanding of what happened in Egypt during those eighteen days by reframing the political away from moments of sovereign authority (although we do not dismiss such moments) and toward an account of politics defined as people acting in concert.

Hannah Arendt also influences this account of politics. While her account of politics is at times unclear and is contested (cf. Benhabib 2003; Calhoun and McGowan 1997; Canovan 1978; 1995; Villa 2000), Arendt does suggest that there is an agonistic or combative character to political life. For Arendt, politics often involves conflict, although not violence, and requires the inevitable plurality of people participating in public life (Arendt 2005). For Arendt, political life and political space are both constituted by the activity of people acting in concert. Arendt suggests that an understanding of politics should not come from the foundations made possible by (state) sovereignty, but from the public practices of people, as they are inscribed in public spaces.

In *On Revolution*, Arendt (1965: 31) writes how 'freedom itself needed … a place where people could come together—the agora, the market-place, or the *polis*, the political space proper.' The networks of people who came together in Tahrir Square and elsewhere in Egypt to protest demonstrate precisely the kind of politics that Arendt explains. Indeed, the mostly non-violent character of the protests further attests to how this arrested revolution was exceptionally political. For, as Arendt argues, violence destroys politics (1970; 1965), and the power of the Egyptian people was that they acted in concert primarily without violence.

In this regard, politics is not enabled by sovereign conditions or spaces, but involves people forging networks of communication and cooperation geared toward a public life. This understanding of politics does not suggest that the state is unimportant or that sovereignty can be ignored. Rather, the focus is on human plurality, spontaneity and acting in public. It is the participation, the practices of self-help that matter more than the structural dynamics of sovereignty, even though politics take place within a sovereign state and the implications of the revolution will impact both Egypt and other sovereign states. Rather than 'seeing like a state', we propose 'seeing like a city', to use Warren Magnusson's play on James Scott's *Seeing Like a State*, focusing on the ways people come together in 'self-organization' through a 'multiplicity of political authorities in different registers at different scales' (2011: 168).

In order to understand the (ongoing) revolution, our analysis explores some of the spaces of the revolt, primarily Tahrir Square and its environs. The protesters did not just claim public spaces for political activities but produced political spaces, with new symbols and practices that challenged existing representations of space (Lefebvre 1991: 33, 38–9). The revolt's spaces were not the spaces of state sovereignty, and the politics of the revolt cannot, consequently, be understood according to the logic of sovereignty that favours fixed, clearly defined spaces. The protests began in locations ostensibly far removed from the familiar sites of sovereign high politics—in particular in Cairo's poorer informal quarters—and in doing so, inverted, however briefly, the relationship between centre and periphery, at least as understood vis-à-vis relations of power. They constituted what one might call a 'trial by space' (Lefebvre 1991: 416–17), a contest between opposing social forces over the values, meanings and practices associated with public space, and the practices developed on Tahrir Square were a mixture of existing practices imported from other spaces and occasions (such as religious festivals) and new practices, which could be called revolutionary in their content.

The spaces of the protest were also, significantly, online spaces, the spaces of cyberspace, of Facebook and Twitter. The political spaces of the revolt were closely tied to the growth of information and communication technology. In this sense, the uprising is part of what Manuel Castells (2000) calls network society and what Anthony Giddens (1986) calls late modernity. Both of these terms are attempts at providing a theoretical orientation around a diffuse and increasingly anarchic yet orderly process of a contemporary life contextualised by contemporary information technology.

This relationship between 'virtual space' and 'urban space' in the genesis of protest movements is highlighted by Castells (2012: 222), who, in his study of contemporary protest movements (including the Egyptian revolution), argues that:

While these movements usually start on the Internet ... they become a movement by occupying the urban space ... This hybrid of cyberspace and urban space constitutes a third space that I call the space of autonomy. This is because autonomy can only be insured by the capacity to organize in the free space of communication networks, but at the same time can only be exercised as a transformative force by challenging the disciplinary institutional order by reclaiming the space of the city for its citizens.

The January 25 revolution was an occupation of urban space profoundly intertwined with information technology, although we do not want to overemphasise the role of technology (Chapter 8). Much of the mobilisation occurred offline, and many of those protesting, particularly those from a poorer background, are unlikely to have had regular internet access. Furthermore, when the regime shut down the internet, the revolution not only continued but intensified as people went out on to the streets to check on friends and be part of the events. However, social media played a key role in creating online communities centred around 'resistance identities' (Castells 2004: 8) (though, prior to January 2011, not necessarily translated into offline activism), and, through informational cascades, a protest momentum that facilitated the mobilisation of thousands with no previous experience of street activism. It also served to report the revolution to the world through visceral eyewitness accounts on Twitter and Facebook, which in turn helped people to overcome their fear of police violence by exposing it.

Methodology

In adopting a social movement theory framework, we recognise that we privilege certain factors while downplaying others. Our decision to focus, for instance, on the interplay between protest networks and changing state–society relations was driven largely by perspectives developed within the social movement theory field. Since this field was developed in the Western hemisphere to study Western protest movements, in addition to downplaying or emphasising certain factors, there is the potential to impose meanings and logics on the Egyptian situation which derive from other, not necessarily comparable, situations. Class relations, for instance, are important in any situation, but because of the different trajectories followed by Egypt and the United States, the notions of 'working class', 'middle class' and 'trade union' are not necessarily transferable between these cases.

At the same time, we are heedful of the advice, given to one of our interviewees, when she posted on Facebook that she was about to meet us: 'Tell them not to write from an Orientalist point of view' (Anonymous, Interview 2011). To assume difference on the basis of Egypt being part of some imagined (and supposedly exotic and thus dangerous) 'Orient' is as perilous as to assume similarity unquestioningly. As Williams (1991: 303, 305) rightly pointed out in a different context, 'both sameness and difference can function as arguments that veil the structural differences' between those in different positions of power, thereby 'reinforc[ing] the status quo'. Williams's solution was to move beyond the notion of a single truth and embrace the existence of multiple truths and identities, enabling her to transcend the sameness–difference dichotomy by looking for sameness in difference and vice versa (echoing Jacques Derrida's notion of 'traces'). Writing about gender and race dynamics in the United States, she concluded:

claims of difference simply mean that *in some contexts* gender or race may shape (or even determine) one's outlook. This reformulation of difference, which we could call post-modern difference, avoids essentialism because it refuses to concede that race, gender—or, indeed, *any* given category—will always be determinative. It allows us to argue that, although race and gender may prove determinative *in some particular context*, this is a far cry from a reified "minority perspective" or "women's voice" that determines how a given individual will react in every situation. (Williams 1991: 307)

In our case, this means embracing the possibility of both sameness and difference, contingent on the particular context in which they manifest themselves.

Such a position affects how we use theory. While we reject the possibility of objectivity—as researchers we are always situated—and the practice of generating universal law-like theories on the basis of 'objective' (and thus decontextualised, comparable) data, we accept, with Marx Horkheimer (1992: 194, 208, 226–30), that social science can uncover 'regularities' in human activity (though subject to contingency). Following Robert Cox (1986: 244), 'regularities in human activities may indeed be observed within particular eras, and thus the positivist approach can be fruitful within defined historical limits, though not with the universal pretensions it aspires to'. Mechanisms and processes uncovered in 1960s North America may thus be relevant for Egypt in the 2000s; however, we cannot automatically assume similarity, and within similarity there may well be difference. Difference, meanwhile, is neither a harbinger of fundamental 'otherness' nor necessarily the product of some age-old, supposedly unchanging, local culture (as Orientalism and essentialism suggest). Rather, where difference is observed, we search for underlying mechanisms that might be similar. For instance, elections in the Middle East are more often influenced by family dynamics and patrimonial relations than in the United States, giving rise to different meanings and practices; but this does not mean that regime unresponsiveness to popular grievances is not a potential factor in movement mobilisation (particularly as, quite apart from local Egyptian discourses of empowerment, such discourses are central to the transnational protest movements of which numerous Egyptian activists were a part). Where difference persists, we reflect on why this may be the case (the persistence of religious identities in the Middle East, for example, is not necessarily some inherent trait but can be explained with reference to particular political, socio-economic and legal structures and practices), and then consider what it means in terms of our theorising about causal mechanisms, adapting our model as we proceed.

This approach also affects how we treat our findings. We purposely refrain from building a universal theory of revolutionary episodes on the basis of our findings, as we hold each episode to be unique and contingent. However, we do tentatively posit a number of underlying mechanisms that seem to explain why, how and when this particular revolutionary episode happened, and suggest that similar mechanisms may be at play in other revolutionary episodes—and, conversely, that if these mechanisms are absent, then this may be a pointer to why an otherwise similar situation did not result in mass protests. This is not the same as positing universal laws, as we do not claim that these outcomes are inevitable or that these mechanisms are necessary conditions. Different interpretations, traditions (political, cultural) and contexts may change the way otherwise apparently similar mechanisms operate; moreover, the mechanisms observed in Egypt may not be necessary at all to arrive at a similar outcome. In other words, there are multiple paths and possibilities.

Apart from drawing on social movement theory, our analysis has been profoundly influenced by the way Egypt's recent structural and network histories have been interpreted by academics, political commentators and our interviewees. The links we observe between the pro-democracy and the Palestinian solidarity movement were pointed out to us by many of our interviewees as well as by certain academics and commentators. Having talked with people who participated in both movements, there clearly were links. But the importance we accord them is in part derived from the importance conferred upon them by our interviewees and other social movement scholars studying this phenomenon, such as Rabab al-Mahdi. Similarly, where interviewees' accounts contradicted social movement theory insights, we took heed (for instance, our interviewees' insistence that the protests were to a large extent spontaneous, rather than organised, led us to rethink social movement theory's emphasis on organisation).

Our use of databases has likewise been shaped by this approach. We do not treat databases as objectively 'true'. Leaving aside that the measures are usually crude, often distorted (because of miscounting) and unrepresentative of the nuances and complexities of lived experience, they can at best be interpreted—tentatively and cautiously—as rough proxies for a particular technocratic understanding of changing socioeconomic circumstances. More fundamentally, their value for us is that, as constructs, they inform both general debates about protest and socioeconomic factors, and debates about Egypt's socio-economic status, thus indirectly influencing the views of both regime and opposition.

We are furthermore aware that the content of our interviews was shaped by the timing of our research visit and the (multiple) identities and histories of both those we spoke with and ourselves. As one interviewee noted, the criticism expressed by some of our interviewees towards the activists behind the revolution would have been affected by the larger, critical re-evaluation of the revolution and its outcome that was underway in May 2011. Had we interviewed the same interviewees in autumn 2011, when the revolution was being deeply contested and the economy had worsened considerably, or in January 2012, when the revolution again became a widely celebrated symbol of resistance, some of the more interpretative responses (for instance, about the relative impact of different social change processes or the efficacy of tactics) might well have been different, although others (such as responses concerning people's whereabouts or the networks they were part of) would have remained the same. Indeed, when Gunning revisited some of the interviewees in 2013, their interpretations of the efficacy of the revolution had changed considerably. Had we managed to secure interviews with non-activists from Egypt's lower classes, the emphasis of our analysis might similarly have altered.

The interviews were impacted by our conceptual lenses and histories (for instance, Baron's own experience of activism and Gunning's experience of having lived in Gaza), and by the histories and lenses of those we interviewed. Though they are therefore open to contestation and re-interpretation, they nevertheless constitute valuable evidence in that they reveal how these particular participants in the January 25 revolution responded to the questions we asked at that particular time. However much they are contextual, they are nevertheless eyewitness accounts.

What we present here is a contribution, by no means final, to an ongoing process of trying to explain and understand the Egyptian revolution, based on conversations between us and participants in the January 25 revolution, and our reading of internet commentators, tweets, Facebook entries, media and other reports, socio-economic databases and academic texts on Egypt's contemporary political and socio-economic history. By and large, we have adopted a constructionist approach, or what Ann Cunliffe calls a focus on 'betweeness', where meaning is seen as being created 'between research participants' (and between text and researcher). Occasionally, we strayed into deconstructionist territory, with its focus on 'otherness', unsettling taken-for-granted narratives (such as that the revolution was self-evidently non-violent), looking for the unsaid (for instance, that the links between the April 6 movement and the workers were rather tentative).

Central to this approach is that the analysis we present is open to revision, is time- and space-specific (new meanings will emerge in different contexts), and is intended to invite debate rather than foreclose it (Edkins 2005: 65–6; Cunliffe 2003). In this, we follow Paul Ricoeur (1981: 210–15), who likened the practice of social science to the judicial process, following a 'logic of probability' (challengeable, never final), rather than a 'logic of empirical verification'.

For this book, we interviewed over forty Egyptians who participated in the revolution, and a number of observers. The sample was chosen using a mixture of targeting and 'snowballing'. We identified those networks we believed to have been central to the revolution (a decision which was influenced by media representations of the revolution and conversations with numerous fellow academics and Egyptian students in our department from different ideological persuasions), and actively sought out people who could introduce us to these networks. We then asked people we already knew (mostly Egyptian students in Durham, fellow academics and activist friends) for introductions to those within their wider social networks whom they deemed important to our research, and followed any further leads that came out of interviews.

The resultant sample is not random, and thus unrepresentative in a quantitative sense. From a qualitative perspective, however, it crudely 'represents' a cross-section of people who participated in the revolution. It includes leading activists from most of the central protest networks behind the revolution (April 6 Youth Movement, Democratic Front, ElBaradei's National Association for Change, leftists associated with the workers' movement, human rights activists and the 'fathers' of the pro-democracy movement, Kefaya), as well as Islamists or Islamist sympathisers, and crucially, a number of non-activists who had taken to the streets for the first time. Among the latter, there were a disillusioned former activist, members of the higher middle classes (an employee of the Central Bank of Egypt and the owner of a boutique cooking school) and members of the state elite (young diplomats and a childhood friend of Suzanne Mubarak, whose husband had served in Sadat's Cabinet). In most cases, we interviewed multiple members of each of these networks, thus broadening the diversity of perspectives (although there was remarkable consensus on most issues). Our 'sample' is nevertheless small and there are crucial sectors 'unrepresented'; for instance, all our non-activist interviewees are middle class, and we did not manage to interview football supporters, workers (as opposed to lawyers representing workers) or Egyptians living on less than $10, $4, let alone $2 a day (corresponding, according to the African Development Bank (2011: 20), with 'lower middle class', 'floating middle class' and 'poor'). We also decided not to actively pursue interviews with Muslim Brothers as our focus was primarily on the more informal and by and large secular protest networks behind the revolution (see pp. 00–00 for our rationale for doing so).

Our interviews were semi-structured, enabling us to compare between interviews by asking similar questions, yet allowing interviewees to introduce or expand on topics they felt were significant. Because of the timing of our fieldtrip (May 2011), many of our interviewees saw our interviews as a formal opportunity to record their views on, and experiences of, the revolution (although some, such as Ahmed Maher, co-founder of April 6, had of course already participated in numerous interviews with journalists). Because we were academics, rather than journalists, this increased the sense of gravity of the occasion. We used open-ended questions to map the factors our interviewees identified as having motivated people to take to the street. We then interpolated this list with the list of factors produced by our theoretical model (derived from social movement theory, revolutionary studies, urban studies and studies of Egyptian contemporary history). Where our theoretical model differed, we included those factors only if they were supported by databases, contemporary political commentary or the secondary literature on Egypt.

Taking our cue from social movement theory, our main 'unit of analysis' is the protest network. However, adopting the integrated approach proposed by McAdam, McCarthy and Zald (1996), where relevant, we include a focus on individuals (including emotions), structures and events, and the interplay between these and the networks. Rather than concentrating on ideologies, we use the conceptual lens of 'frames', or '"schemata of interpretation" that enable individuals "to locate, perceive, identify, and label" occurrences within their life space and the world at large' (Goffman paraphrased in Snow et al. 1986: 464). In the absence of clear-cut, overarching ideologies driving the uprising, 'frames' better encapsulate the eclectic, fluid ways in which activists made sense of their world and sought to mobilise the masses.

Our early understanding of the revolution was profoundly affected by watching Aljazeera Live, the BBC, Sky News and numerous Aljazeera documentaries, as well as following Twitter's '#jan25', '#Egypt' and other relevant hashtags. It was this intense experience of following the experiences of Egypt's protesters up close that drew us into writing this book in the first place. Gunning, as a social movement theorist, was particularly moved by the way these small networks managed to mobilise thousands and by the way non-activist Egyptians managed to overcome their fear. Baron, as a political theorist with an interest in political spaces, was moved by the spontaneity of the protests, and the way the protesters created a radically different society in the midst of authoritarian Egypt. It was this difference between our perspectives that set the agenda for much of the book—although, for reasons of time and competing commitments, Baron's main contributions are concentrated in Chapters 7 and 8.

Our analysis was similarly influenced by our experience of walking around Tahrir Square on 27 May 2011, billed at the time as the 'Second Revolution', when many of the practices seen during the revolution were reproduced (from the security checkpoints at every entry point into the Square, to the chants, speakers' podia and food- and flag-selling on the Square).

Our focus on space is in part a product of our theoretical interest in space (particularly Baron's), and in part a product of our (intentionally pursued) spatial explorations of Cairo. Based at the Shepheard Hotel, just off Tahrir Square, we explored the surrounding area to gain a sense of its spatial layout and the practices associated with these spaces (both during 'normal' and during 'protest' times). For similar reasons, we walked from Dokki (part of greater Mohandessin) along Tahrir Street to Tahrir Square, retracing the route the protesters took on 25 January and crossing the two bridges that saw fierce fighting on the 28 January, just as we retraced the route of those who marched up Qasr al-Aini Street.[9]

Focus of the Book

This book seeks to explain why, how and when the 'January 25 revolution' happened. To be clear, our focus is not on how the regime collapsed or on the impact of the protests after Mubarak stepped down. The former needs far deeper research into the motives and interests of the key players in the regime, the army and the wider elite, and the pressures they faced from other states in the region and elsewhere (including the United States). The latter changes by the day and is a topic in itself. Rather, our focus is narrower: to understand how Egyptians were mobilised in January 2011, the role that hardened activists played in this, how novices overcame their fear, and how the 2011 events related to the structural and organisational changes of the prior decade.

More specifically, this book aims to answer the following interrelated questions. When speaking of revolutions, there is a temptation either to see a revolution as a spectacular anomaly, which breaks with the past, or as the inevitable outcome of a situation at breaking point (an argument which is usually only made retrospectively, with history reinterpreted to fit the eventual outcome). We want to steer clear from both these temptations by asking how the 'revolution', or rather the mass mobilisation and strikes that contributed to convincing the army to depose Mubarak, was made possible by the events, networks and actors preceding it (Chapters 1–2). How did the protest networks, which organised the initial demonstrations, come about? How did the revolution's tactics relate to the tactics developed by these networks in the decade prior to the revolution? What protest waves preceded the revolution? Can these earlier protests tell us something about who became involved in the 2011 protests?

The second set of questions flows from this and relates to the broader structure–agency debate in the social sciences. Analysis of political events remains too frequently divided between those favouring structural explanations and those focusing on people and networks. We are interested in how broader structural changes in Egypt's political and socio-economic make-up shaped the protest networks behind the revolution and how these networks in turn affected and interpreted these broader structural changes (Chapters 3–4). Can a combined structural–network analysis help us to explain why the protests happened in the way they did at the time that they occurred (and not earlier or later)? Our aim is thus to weave structural and agential analyses together in recognition of the way structure and agency are mutually constituted. Our approach has similar aims to what Giddens (1986) famously called 'structuration'. However, it does so by using a social movement theory framework instead.

Our third set of questions concerns the relationship between activists/planning and non-activists/spontaneity (Chapter 5). What role did the former play? What role the latter? What motivated non-activists? What role did non-violence and violence play, and who, if anyone, controlled tactics? Crucially, what made people with no experience of protesting, often with no links to protest networks, and a profound fear of the police combined with a deeply ingrained aversion to protest, decide to go out on to the street, in the full knowledge that they might be killed that day? We approach this sub-question by looking at how people overcame their fear of police violence (Chapter 6). Fear is typically what stops aggrieved people from protesting. Yet fear, and the processes by which it is overcome, remain woefully under-researched in political science.

Our fourth set of questions revolves around two themes that emerge from the overall analysis. One concerns the role of Information and Communications Technology (ICT). Much has been made of the role of Facebook and Twitter in the Egyptian revolution. Using a social movement approach, we ask what role this technology actually played by looking at both protest dynamics and protesters' profiles (Chapter 8). The other theme concerns the politics of space, or rather the way the use and meaning of public space, and in particular Tahrir Square, was challenged and changed during the revolution. Spatial arrangements profoundly affect how protests play out, and protests usually involve a challenge to the way space has been inscribed and ordered. Yet spatial analysis is only in its infancy in social movement theory and is frequently overlooked in Middle Eastern studies. Our focus on space is a contribution to furthering this debate in both these disciplines (Chapter 7).

Throughout, our interest is not in describing the events that took place. There are an increasing number of highly compelling and informative books of this nature. Rather, our focus is on analysis and in particular what insights from various theoretical models can help to make sense of the events and how they unfolded. The impetus behind this approach comes in part from the observation that Middle Eastern studies has historically suffered from a lack of engagement with theory and an overreliance on empirical data and descriptive narrative (cf. Tessler 1999; Teti 2007). While the field has improved in recent years, there is still an urgent need to strengthen its engagement with theory, and this book is a contribution. We are also motivated by the sense that political science, and in particular the field of IR, often remains overly abstract, venturing into 'empirics' primarily through quantitative methods or dipping into case studies merely to illustrate a theory, without allowing the case study to unfold within its own logic (Clifford and Marcus 1986). Here, we seek a dialogue between empirics and theory.

PART I

PRELUDE TO REVOLUTION

1

MOBILISING PROTEST NETWORKS I (2000–2006)

One theme dominating media descriptions of the January 25 uprising was that this was a 'leaderless revolution', a more or less spontaneous eruption, without serious organisation, triggered primarily by the removal of Ben Ali in Tunisia eleven days earlier. While pundits acknowledged that Facebook activists had played an important role and that these protests fed off earlier protests, the general tone is encapsulated by the *Christian Science Monitor*'s Christen Chick: 'Like the popular uprising this month in Tunisia, the protests were a public outpouring of anger that had no leader and will likely prove difficult for opposition parties to harness' (Chick 2011). Or take the assessment of Steven Cook, fellow at the Council on Foreign Relations: 'It's leaderless as far as I can tell' (quoted in Chick 2011).

A closer look suggests that this is far from the case. The uprising was neither leaderless nor spontaneous. Even though the popular response and the eventual outcome far exceeded the planners' expectations, the initial demonstrations had been meticulously planned, drawing on previously developed tactical and framing repertoires. Once Tahrir Square and other places had been occupied, the protesters' camps became microcosms of a new Egypt, with elaborate organisational structures developed in part by experienced activists and their networks. News streams covering the events were distributed by a large body of experienced bloggers and tweeters from the various established protest sectors. There was no towering leader, and the uprising was carried by masses of spontaneous protesters, but it was sustained by experienced 'facilitators', carrying out a range of activities, many of which had been honed over years of protests. In short, the events of January 2011 did not emerge out of nowhere, but were the culmination of a decade of increasingly intense and widespread activism, involving an ever-widening pool of activists and networks.

One of the reasons pundits initially concluded that this uprising was 'leaderless' lies in the habit of focusing overly on formal politics. To return to Chick, her conclusion rests on the argument that the organisations behind these events were apolitical ('while their demands were political, their organization was not') because they did not involve the opposition parties. Informal networks, by this reasoning, are not part of formal politics, and, consequently, often remain under the radar of observers, or are downplayed. It is no coincidence that diplomats, such as the Australian ambassador to Egypt in 2005–2008, Robert Bowker (Interview 2011), rated the pro-democracy movement at the time as politically somewhat insignificant. Nor is it a coincidence that iconic mass protests have often been explained away as 'spontaneous', whether it concerns the 1960 sit-in movement in the United States, the 1965 Watts Riots in Los Angeles (also known as the Watts Rebellion) or the first Palestinian Intifada. Yet it is precisely this notion—that informal pre-existing networks are crucial to understanding protest politics—that social movement theory has long championed. Thus a detailed network analysis of the 1960 sit-in movement shows that this particular protest wave had its roots in the convergence of a number of pre-existing networks, in the same way as the Watts Rebellion was sustained by informal networks that had grown out of preceding protest waves (Morris 1981; Theoharis 2006).

Some of the first questions a social movement analyst would ask are: What networks existed prior to the 2011 uprising? What role did these networks play, both in the lead-up to and during the protests? What experience, tactics, frames and resources did the members of these networks bring to the protests? In what way were the activists connected to each other? How did they become socialised into activism? Where did the tactics they used come from? How did their 'framing' of the situation evolve? What protest waves preceded the events of January 2011, and how did the networks, tactics, frames and people involved change as a result of these waves?

Networks, whether formal, informal, structured or fluid, have been found to be crucial to the emergence of social movements and protest events. One of the problems social movements face is that people are more likely to live with the status quo than rise up against it. Millions live in grossly unjust circumstances. Yet successful uprisings are few and far between. To mobilise, movements have to persuade people that their lot is not only unacceptable (injustice frames), but that it can be changed (action frames), and that the proposed tactics will achieve this change (motivational frames)—or, at least, that they are a better alternative than doing nothing and that the risk is worth taking (cf. McAdam 1982: 48–51; Benford and Snow 2000).

Two of the key contributions social movement theory has made to our understanding of protests (including revolutions) derive from the insight that grievances do not automatically flow from structural conditions, and that grievances alone are not sufficient to initiate or sustain protest. Grievances are produced not just by structural conditions but also by human interactions and interpretations and, in this, networks are crucial in exposing people to like-minded others, and providing the resources and opportunities necessary to translate grievances into action.

Networks are crucial in producing protest conditions in various ways. By bringing people together, they can provide a platform to develop a shared 'injustice frame', a diagnosis of what is the cause of the (shared) injustice, and a prognosis of what to do about it (an 'action frame'). 'Frames' play an important part in social movement theory. To quote the pre-eminent theorist of framing, David Snow (2004: 384):

Collective action frames, like picture frames, focus attention by punctuating or specifying what in our sensual field is relevant and what is irrelevant, what is "in frame" and what is "out of frame" ... But frames also function ... as articulation mechanisms in the sense of tying together the various punctuated elements of the scene so that one set of meanings rather than another is conveyed ...

Networks can help transform people's understanding of their experiences by discursively linking previously unrelated experiences to each other, and to a particular set of injustice, motivation and action frames. Everyday economic grievances, for instance, do not automatically give rise to calls for regime change. People may blame themselves or their employer, or they may see the system as inevitable and unchangeable.

Networks can also provide emotional incentives to act; for instance, through developing a collective identity they can help people overcome their fear by demonstrating that they are in it together and persuading them that, in acting together, they might succeed. More prosaically, networks provide resources (whether in the form of committed activists, offices or access to networks of professionals) and facilitate the dissemination of tactics and action frames. The greater the number and size of networks in a social movement, the more resources the movement can draw on, and the more likely it is that tactics and information about planned protests travel beyond the core group of activists. Consequently, of particular interest is the growth and breadth of linked networks, the strength of the links between networks and whether networks succeed in mobilising hitherto un-mobilised strata of society.

Of equal interest is the emergence of new tactics—which is often a by-product of the attempt by regime forces to suppress opposition activity, or of opposition groups noting new opportunities. Social movements often go through phases where membership and tactics remain static, until a mixture of events and new tactics triggers an expansion, which in turn leads to tactical innovation. A historical illustration is the American Civil Rights Movement, which saw a rapid expansion following the arrest of Rosa Parks in 1955 and the tactical and organisational innovation that subsequently ensued (cf. Morris 1981: 751–3). New tactics are also often a product of using public spaces and pre-existing institutions in different and novel ways. Churches, for instance, became a key political and organisational instrument in the Civil Rights Movement, just as student and professional organisations came to be harnessed in the service of civil rights activism.

The existence of a dense network of pre-existing protest groups or social networks thus appears to be a precondition for a sustained mass protest event to occur. The case of Tunisia may be seen as challenging this hypothesis, as there did not appear, at least at first sight, to be well-established opposition networks. In fact, research suggests that existing informal networks facilitated the rapid diffusion of protest frames, tactics and a collective identity to sustain the protests, including among trade unions and social media users (pre-existing networks do not, after all, have to be seasoned political protest networks but can be co-opted) (Breuer 2012; Lee and Weinthal 2011).

The existence of dense social networks does not inevitably result in a mass uprising. In addition, there are usually trigger events, which, under the right structural, organisational and ideational conditions, can galvanise the masses into action. However, by gaining a deeper understanding of the types of protest networks that have emerged, how they are linked, what types of frames and tactics they have used, and how they interact with the security forces and the political elite, one is in a better position to understand who the key players are behind the mass protests (and why not others), how it was possible to organise the protests, and why particular tactics and frames dominated. Why, for instance, were the 2011 demonstrations led by loose networks of youth activists, rather than by political parties or NGOs? Why was Ben Ali's fall in Tunisia interpreted as a call to protest against police abuse, rather than regime change per se? Where did the flash mob tactics come from, and how did the activists manage to mobilise beyond the middle classes? Why did earlier trigger events not lead to a full-scale revolt (although this requires more than an analysis of network dynamics)?

Networks do not exist in a vacuum, and some of these questions can only be answered by looking at the broader structural context. For instance, the focus on police abuse was in part a function of the broader turn towards a police state, and the ability to move beyond the middle classes was facilitated by the development of cross-class informal neighbourhoods in Cairo and elsewhere. In Chapters 3 and 4 we will address the structural context which provided the raw material for the opportunities, threats and resources perceived and acted upon by these networks. It is one of the core arguments of this book that actors and structures dialectically constitute each other, and that we can therefore not separate them. For clarity of argument, we have separated our analysis of structural factors from our analysis of network mobilisation. But in the following, it is important to keep in mind the dialectical relationship between the two.

Four Waves of Protest

The 2011 uprising can be traced back to 2000 through four consecutive protest waves,[1] each feeding off the previous wave(s), drawing in an ever-widening pool of activists and producing new tactics. We define a 'protest wave', following Sydney Tarrow's original definition of a 'protest cycle', as 'a phase of heightened conflict across the social system' (1998: 142). We use the term 'wave' rather than 'cycle' as the latter implies a 'periodically recurring sequence of phenomena', which is not necessarily the case in the phenomena referred to in Tarrow's definition (Koopmans 2004: 21). However, as with Tarrow's original conceptualisation, a protest wave can be said to occur when there is an acceleration in the diffusion of protest ideas and actions, in the evolution of new protest networks and in the innovation of protest frames and repertoires of action.

The four waves we refer to in the Egyptian case overlapped and fed off other, ongoing protest dynamics, so that one could speak of a single continuous wave, with ebbs, troughs and high tides. However, because the focus, frames, breadth and tactics of the dominant protests in each phase changed, it is analytically useful to treat them as four distinct waves. The first wave (2000–2004) was primarily driven by protests against US and Israeli policies in the region, although economic and political grievances played a contributory role. The second wave (2004–2006) constituted the first direct, organised popular challenge against the Mubarak regime, focusing on the 2005 elections and proposed constitutional amendments, with economic hardship and police brutality additional themes. The third wave (2006–2009) was driven predominantly by industrial disputes and economic hardship, although political motivations continued to matter, particularly among the newly emerged youth networks and those affiliated to the outlawed Muslim Brotherhood, the main opposition movement. This wave coincided with a series of protests triggered by regional and international events, chief among them the Danish cartoon controversy and events in Israel–Palestine and Lebanon. The fourth wave (2010–2011) centred again on challenging the regime in the upcoming general and presidential elections, with police brutality, economic hardship and regime attempts to increase sectarian tensions providing additional fuel. By January 2011, this wave had succeeded in combining most of the networks and grievances from the previous three waves.

Each wave was fuelled by various combinations of protest episodes following each other in different protest sectors. One protest sector revolved around regional events, and in particular the Arab–Israeli conflict and US policies in the region. A second sector revolved around the electoral cycle and focused in particular on the fraud, graft and corruption perpetrated by the regime. A third, overlapping protest sector focused on human rights, and especially human rights abuses by the security forces and the regime. A fourth sector revolved around industrial disputes and neighbourhood disputes. A fifth, more ad hoc protest sector concerned sectarian protests, although we will only touch on this briefly in the fourth wave.[2] Each of these protest sectors came with its own set of tactics, networks, drivers and temporal dynamics, although there was considerable overlap. Muslim Brotherhood activists, for instance, were active in all five sectors, though to different degrees, and tactics developed in one sector informed the tactics employed in another, as protesters diffused ideas, frames and tactics across different networks.

Interacting with these distinct protest sectors were three further sets of protest dynamics. One concerned religious sensibilities, and was usually triggered by international events, such as the Danish cartoon controversy surrounding cartoons depicting the Prophet Muhammad or the Pope's controversial Regensburg address. A second set of protests, usually described as 'bread riots', was driven by economic hardship, and in particular rising food prices. A third protest dynamic revolved around ongoing confrontations between football fans and the police. The first two sets consisted of disparate, ad hoc protest events, which, though comprising mobilisation, diffusion and organisation, typically involved large, spontaneous crowds. They fed into the sustained protest waves and sectors discussed above and often included seasoned activists. But they were not protest waves as such, as they were too disparate and disconnected.[3] The third set of protest dynamics, by contrast, was highly organised in the sense that they involved the hierarchical football fan clubs of Egypt, chief among them the Ultras. As they were driven by the logic and rhythm of football matches, they were distinct from the protest waves identified above. However, as we will see, the Ultras, and the experience they had gained over years of fighting the police, were to play an important part in the 2011 uprising (cf. Montague 2012).

In the first of our two chapters on the mobilising networks that sustained the revolution we will focus on the first two protest waves. Our focus will be on the emergence of the informal protest networks that evolved out of the first pro-Palestinian protests. Even though the Muslim Brothers played a role in these waves, the Brotherhood will not be the central focus of our analysis. The impetus for the revolution did not come from the Brotherhood, and in each of the four waves preceding the uprising the Brotherhood was typically a late-comer or on a parallel track. As such, for the purposes of our analysis, it was more a resource to be mobilised, a pre-existing network in need of rallying (and binding to one's cause), than a central player in the chain of events leading to the uprising. This is not to deny the contribution of the Brotherhood to sustaining an overall protest culture, the role played by individual Brothers who joined the protest networks we focus on or the crucial part played by the Brotherhood in mobilising tens of thousands on the first Friday of the uprising and in protecting the Square subsequently. In the years 2008–2010, for instance, the Brotherhood were identified as key participants in seventy-four of the 410 protests described in *al-Masry al-Youm* as having more than 500 participants (Appendix).[4] Although most of these were demonstrations in solidarity with Palestinians (forty-two), thirty-one focused on elections or police abuse.[5] In other words, they were part of the same broad protest waves described below, and some of these demonstrations were carried out in partnership with the protest networks that form the main subject of these chapters. There is a temptation to look at Egyptian politics through an Islamist lens, since the Brotherhood has dominated opposition politics for so long. But the impetus behind the revolution came from the informal, and largely secular, protest networks that our analysis focuses on.

Wave I: Palestinian Solidarity and Anti-Iraq War Protest Waves (2000–2004)

The first stirrings that can be directly related to the events of 2011 can be found in the autumn of 2000. Public activism was largely absent in the 1990s. Between 1992 and 1997, the regime was engaged in the brutal suppression of Islamist organisations, with profound effects on political life more generally. Political parties were severely circumscribed, professional syndicates were brought under government control and the security forces suppressed public activism. The Muslim Brotherhood, the largest opposition party, had been the target of concerted government repression in response to its growing influence since the 1980s, and by the late 1990s it sought to minimise confrontation with the regime (Wickham 2013: 76–81, 97ff.). Opposition activity was concentrated primarily in civil society organisations, such as the numerous human rights NGOs that had sprung up over the decade. But these organisations did not engage in street activism. As an anti-war protester lamented in 2003:

Public activism is a relatively new phenomenon because it was usually [met with] oppression in the past ... Apart from the 'formal' political parties, there [were] no other avenues of political activism. In the 1990s, we had the so-called civil society—which are the human rights organizations. However, it cannot be called a movement, because it was never part of their objective to enlarge themselves or bring in new activists. (Wael Khalil, quoted in A. Hassan 2003a)

A poignant illustration of the lack of public opposition was the fact that when Mubarak was elected (unopposed) in 1999, few dared to criticise or ridicule him publicly—in sharp contrast to the 2005 and 2010 elections.

With the outbreak of the al-Aqsa Intifada in Israel–Palestine in September 2000, the situation began to change with the start of the first wave of public protests. The main protests of this period were either in support of the Palestinians or (later) against the Iraq war, although the human rights and pro-democracy networks were also gaining momentum. Crucially, lawyers and other professionals started to become mobilised through their professional organisations, having been politically inactive for most of the 1990s (if 'political' is defined narrowly as that which concerns the state). The protests also brought elite activists together with Egypt's less well-off population. Two key contributions of this period were the linking of activists across ideological divides, and the reclamation of the street as a space for public protest. In addition, the protests contributed to breaking the activists' fear of police violence despite increasing intimidation from the regime.

Activists began to stage public protests in support of the Palestinian al-Aqsa Intifada from autumn 2000 onwards. There is a long tradition in Egypt of protests in solidarity with the Palestinians, involving activists from across the ideological spectrum, including Muslim Brothers, leftists and Arab nationalists (Abou-el-Fadl 2012). Already in the late 1980s a cross-party committee was established to coordinate protests in support of the first Intifada. Sporadic protests continued during the 1990s, but it was not until the 2000s that a more sustained protest wave emerged.

After the initial student protests died down in October 2000 (Schemm 2002), the protests remained largely limited to sit-ins and hunger strikes in locations that were not public: university campuses, NGOs or professional unions (*Al-Ahram Weekly* 2005a). In March 2001, for instance, a three-day hunger strike took place at the Lawyers' Syndicate in solidarity with the Palestinians (El Amrani 2002). However, during 2002, protests began to spill out from university campuses on to the street. In April, following Israel's incursion into Ramallah in the West Bank, an estimated 10,000 students broke through the security cordon around Cairo University to join the Popular Committee for Support of the Palestinian Intifada (PCSPI), an (unregistered) umbrella organisation of leftists, liberals and Islamists, to protest at the Israeli embassy—only to be beaten back by heavy-handed riot police (Schemm 2002; *Al-Ahram Weekly* 2005a). In Alexandria, 9,000 people gathered on the streets, led by what appeared to be leftist students, who had supposedly hijacked an 'ordered' Muslim Brotherhood demonstration—again, to be eventually beaten back by riot police, resulting in the death of a student (Schemm 2002). However, within two weeks, the security forces had succeeded in pinning the protests back to the various activist mosques and university campuses.

This first wave of street activism grew dramatically when the United States invaded Iraq, drawing in protesters from well beyond the usual student, professional and leftist worker circles that had hitherto driven the protests. In March 2003, Cairo was rocked by one of the largest political demonstrations in years, with a crowd of an estimated 50,000–55,000 gathering in front of al-Azhar Mosque (A. Hassan 2003b). On 20 March, Tahrir Square was occupied for a day by some 2,000 to 3,000 protesters (Schemm 2003; El Amrani 2003), with some estimates putting the number of protesters at 20,000 (*Al-Ahram Weekly* 2005a). A further 10,000 marched north of the Square along the Corniche on the following day. March 2003 saw a number of further demonstrations on campuses (10,000 demonstrated at Zagazig University, north of Cairo) (Leupp 2003), around Tahrir Square and in front of various key mosques, such as Sayeda Zeinab Mosque (A. Hassan 2003b).

By 2004, demonstrations of 1,000 or more were taking place regularly, although none matched the March 2003 protest. The first anniversary of the invasion of Iraq was marked by a crowd of 2,000 in Tahrir Square, followed by a number of smaller demonstrations in the weeks after. Immediately following these protests, the targeted killing of Palestinian Hamas leader Sheikh Ahmed Yassin on 22 March led to a new slew of protests, drawing 50,000 nationwide (Moustafa 2004). Events in Israel–Palestine thus served to reinforce the anger that the invasion of Iraq had generated, just as the invasion of Iraq fuelled anger at the Israeli treatment of Palestinians.

As demonstrations became larger, the regime's response became harsher. People were beaten up, with many suffering severe injuries.

Water cannons were used. Many were arrested and tortured; women were threatened with rape. Offices of organisers were raided, and following the March 2003 demonstrations, hundreds were arrested and beaten (A. Hassan 2003b; Schemm 2002, 2003; OMCT 2003a).

One of the results of this increased regime violence against largely non-violent protesters was a hardening of attitudes, and an explicit linking of events in Iraq with the behaviour of the regime itself.[6] 'Using brute force [to suppress demonstrations],' one protester commented, 'brings the enemy close to home' (A. Hassan 2003b). This linkage had already been fuelled by Mubarak's refusal to come to the aid of the Palestinians during the al-Aqsa Intifada. As early as April 2002, shouts of 'Mubarak, you coward, you are the client of the Americans' and 'We want a new government because we've hit rock bottom' could be heard at the Palestinian solidarity demonstrations, while leftist students had by then concluded that 'The road to Jerusalem runs through Cairo' (Schemm 2002).[7]

On 21 March 2003, these slogans became more explicitly focused on government change, with shouts of 'Leave, Mubarak, leave' becoming increasingly common, turning anger against the US invasion inwards against Mubarak (Leupp 2003; Schemm 2003; A. Hassan 2003b). Egypt came to be redefined through events in Iraq and Israel–Palestine, with slogans such as 'Baghdad is Cairo, Jerusalem is Cairo', and 'We want Egypt to be free, life has become bitter' (*Al-Ahram Weekly* 2005a). During the 21 March marches, a huge banner depicting Mubarak was torn down near Tahrir Square, reputedly the first time a Mubarak poster was torn down in protest (Baheyya 2006; Schemm 2003)—unthinkable even two years earlier. In July 2003, anti-war and Palestinian solidarity activists formed 'The 20 March Popular Campaign for Change' (a reference to the anti-war demonstration of 20 March), calling for a 'Struggle against despotism and dictatorship' and saying 'No to extension, no to hereditary succession' (a reference to the reputed plan to install Mubarak's son, Gamal, as Egypt's next president) (*Al-Ahram Weekly* 2005a)—a slogan that was to be taken up by the second protest wave. In September 2003, demonstrations marking the third anniversary of the outbreak of the al-Aqsa Intifada rapidly became anti-government protests (*Al-Ahram Weekly* 2005a). The following year, calls for Mubarak to leave—'Down, down with Mubarak' and 'Say to Mubarak, say to Sorour [Speaker of the People's Assembly], when will you get the hell out of here?'—were prominent during the protests marking the first anniversary of the invasion

(Moustafa 2004). This shift in framing was to prove seminal, as the next wave picked up this theme and made it its central demand.

Calls for Mubarak to leave were further fuelled by the economic situation, and in particular by an increasing awareness of the discrepancy between the wealth of the political elite and that of ordinary Egyptians. Particularly in the March 2004 demonstrations, protesters refocused their anger against the Iraq invasion on the regime's record of crony capitalism and corruption. One of the slogans—'Ahmed Ezz, living in luxury, tell us who is protecting you? Down with the monopoly of the steel mills!'—targeted the unpopular steel magnate, who was accused of using his positions in the ruling National Democratic Party (NDP) and the People's Assembly to extend his dominance of the Egyptian steel market. Another slogan, 'Corruption, corruption is filling the country—skyrocketing corruption! Where is justice? Justice is dead', focused on corruption more generally. 'They wear the latest fashions!', the ringleaders shouted, 'And we live ten to a room!' was the crowd's response. Illustrating both the deteriorating economic situation and the increase in protesters from less well-off backgrounds were slogans such as 'Atef [Abeid, prime minister of Egypt], a kilo of beans now costs six pounds! Atef, a kilo of meat is over thirty pounds! Atef, the people of Egypt [are forced to] eat bricks!' (all quotations from Moustafa 2004).

What these protests and slogans demonstrate is a classic pattern in social movement dynamics. One burning issue morphs into another as activists come to redefine their grievances and demands in light of events. As the regime clamped down harder, as the number of protesters increased, encompassing people from a wider variety of socio-economic backgrounds, and as political and economic changes affected an ever widening section of the population, what began as a protest against US and Israeli policies in the region became a protest against the regime itself. With its loyalty to US interests becoming increasingly apparent, the regime's legitimacy came under increased scrutiny. In the words of one of the organisers of the anti-war movement:

Our protest in Tahrir Square on the first day of the invasion was as much about anti-American policy as it was about the fact that our government was allowing this to happen with its blessings. And that opens the door for a variety of attacks about who we are and what we stand for as Egyptians. (quoted in Azimi 2005)

This process of altering the focus of the protesters' ire toward the regime was fuelled by the way the regime cracked down on the pro-

testers without being able to stop the protests, suggesting to the protesters that, despite the violence, the regime was no longer as fully in
control as it used to be. The weakening of the government's legitimacy—itself a product of long-term changes in the relationship
between regime and society (Chapter 3)—in turn opened up space for
its other manifold shortcomings to be brought to the fore, principally
its refusal to allow meaningful political participation, and its mishan-
dling of the economy.

This first wave saw some of the biggest protest crowds Egypt had
seen since the 1970s, leading some to believe that the Mubarak regime
was (already) on its last legs (Baheyya 2008b). While the protests succeeded in attracting more than 50,000 people, they did not achieve
their aims. The significance of these protests for our analysis thus lies
primarily in the way that they laid the foundations for the subsequent
waves, which they did in at least six ways.

First, the protests provided a unifying focal point for the ideologically and socially divided activists. Throughout the 1980s and 1990s,
but especially during the 1990s, the schism between secularists and
Islamists[8] had widened, as key secular ideologues had been hounded
out of Egypt or, in some cases, assassinated. Opinions were deeply
divided on how to oppose the Mubarak regime, and what alternative
system should be put in its place. The al-Aqsa Intifada provided a rallying call behind which all sides could unite. The Popular Committee
for the Support of the Palestinian Uprising, for instance, and later the
Popular Committee Opposing US Aggression Against Iraq, brought
together Arab nationalists, Marxists, Islamists, civil society and professional organisations, intellectuals, public figures and artists (A. Hassan
2003a). The anti-Iraq war demonstration of March 2003 on Tahrir
Square similarly brought together leftists, Nasserists, Islamists and
well-heeled liberal students (Schemm 2003). The various committees
behind the protests were fluid (partly because they were illegal and
constantly disrupted by imprisonment), but they laid the foundations
for the cross-ideological organisations that formed the backbone for
the explicitly anti-Mubarak protests that began in 2004.

Enabling this cross-ideological convergence was the fact that, al-
Aqsa Intifada aside, all ideological trends had undergone a process of
internal reflection, triggered by a variety of factors, from the end of the
Cold War and the transformation of the left in the Middle East, to the
repression experienced by the Muslim Brotherhood, the marginalisa-

tion of liberals during the 1990s and the emergence of a new genera-tion, less tainted by the historical animosity of the past and more connected to other youth (International Palestinian Solidarity Activist, Interview 2011; El-Hamalawy 2007). By the early 2000s, the idea of working across ideological divides was thus more readily embraced than it would have been in the early 1990s or late 1980s.

In addition, the crisis that the Muslim Brotherhood found itself in meant that younger Brothers were actively looking for external alli-ances. The Brotherhood leadership, in response to the repression of the 1990s, the repercussions of 9/11 and deaths among its top leadership, was practising strict self-restraint. Brotherhood students, who were growing increasingly impatient at seeing the initiative pass to the smaller leftist groups and wanted to act, thus had to look elsewhere, despite their earlier distrust of secular student activists. Cross-partisan alliances, moreover, were thought to facilitate recruitment and aid in evading the police, while for those leftists willing to cooperate (chiefly the Revolutionary Socialists), cooperation meant a marked reduction in harassment from the previously hostile Brothers. This early cooper-ation between secular activists and Brotherhood students, who ten years later would be among the group's reformist leadership, was cru-cial for subsequent cross-partisan collaboration, both in 2004–2005 and in 2008–2011 (Wickham 2013: 101, 155–7; El-Hamalawy 2007).

Concretely, the protests served to reconnect long-term activists who had become politicised in the student and workers protests of the 1970s, but who had become fragmented and had gone their separate ways in the intervening decades, following different ideological trends (see also Wickham 2013: 109). The founders of Kefaya, the organisa-tion at the heart of the 2004 wave, were among the anti-Iraq war and Palestinian solidarity protesters, and the experience of organising pro-tests together, in the face of fierce repression, helped to cement a bond of trust that was crucial for the next phase. In the words of George Ishak (Interview 2011), a Christian liberal, 'we were all working together in different events supporting the Palestinians and Iraqis ... These demonstrations made us very close. We had known each from the 1970s onwards, but from a distance.' Ahmed Shaaban (Interview 2011), a long-term leftist, similarly noted: 'Everyone was helping peo-ple in Palestine, that is the one thing that brought us together. Then the Iraq war happened and the protests to stop the war. These activities brought us together.' The groups that sprang up provided activists with 'space for continued contact and collaboration … offering opportunities for self-education in negotiation, tactics, and means of overcoming ideological divisions' (El-Mahdi 2009: 94–5). These in turn helped activists to 'gain a sense of changing boundaries for mass participation and street mobilisation', preparing the leadership of the subsequent pro-democracy wave.

Second, the protests helped to mobilise a new stratum of young activists (although compared to later waves, the number of new recruits was relatively small). As we will see in Chapter 4, by 2000, the population cohort of 15–20 year olds had reached a peak, and it was from this pool that new activists were mobilised. Significantly, a number of those who were central in sustaining the 2011 uprising became politically active at this time. Shadi Ghazali-Harb (Interview 2011a), a key figure in the Democratic Front Party and nephew of Osama Ghazali-Harb, the party's founder, became more actively involved in politics during this period. Omar Saad (Interview 2011), a journalist and revolutionary socialist, became involved in public protests in 2001. Nadim Mansour (Interview 2011), a leftist workers' rights lawyer working for the Egyptian Center for Economic and Social Rights—one of the organisations that formed a hub for the 2011 uprising—was drawn into political activism as a high school student, working with university students to organise pro-Palestinian demonstrations. He subsequently became active in the workers' movement, which had strong links with the pro-Palestinian Egyptian left. Islam Lutfi, one of the Muslim Brotherhood youth who participated in the 2011 uprising from the start, was a student leader at the time, as was Muhamad Qassas (Wickham 2013: 155–6). Although Lutfi and Qassas had already been mobilised by the Brotherhood, the Palestinian solidarity protests brought them into contact with the secular protest networks.

Third, the protests provided a platform for civil society organisations to become politically active. The Lawyers' Syndicate, which in the past had been a centre of oppositional activism (Schemm 2002), re-emerged as a hub for students from different universities and older, experienced opposition activists to meet, forge new bonds and discuss future strategy. As Paul Schemm (2002) observed at the time:

As the universities are riddled with informers and encircled by vigilant security, the [Lawyers'] syndicate grounds have become a kind of "liberated territory" for student activists. Here student leaders from different universities meet to get to know each other as well as activists from older generations. Students are coming not just from traditionally activist institutions like Cairo

University and Ain Shams University, but also from the polytechnic colleges and secondary schools.

Beyond helping in the mobilisation of students from well beyond the traditionally activist institutions, the Lawyers' Syndicate also provided oppositional space and institutional support for the protests. It hosted protest rallies on its premises, distributed leaflets, displayed banners and issued statements (*Al-Ahram Weekly* 2003).

The Journalists' Syndicate similarly became involved in the protests, holding 'a peaceful assembly to protest the war and Israeli action against Palestinians', and subsequently hosting a series of hunger strikes in protest against regime violence against the protesters (OMCT 2003b; *Al-Ahram Weekly* 2003). The Islamist-dominated Doctors' Syndicate helped to organise the first government-sanctioned rally (*Al-Ahram Weekly* 2003). Although the number of syndicates involved remained small, the creation of linkages between the street protests and these professional syndicates was as important to the development of the Egyptian opposition as the mobilisation of the churches, student and professional organisations had been to the US Civil Rights Movement.

Crucially, the protests did not succeed in mobilising the Muslim Brotherhood organisation[9] into street politics or creating strong links with the Brotherhood's leadership. Although Brotherhood students were actively involved, the Brotherhood as an organisation remained largely aloof, whether for fear of reprisal (the leadership was still reeling from the repression of the 1990s) or lack of leadership. Most of the demonstrations and hunger strikes of the early 2000s were carried out by the left. When the Brotherhood did become involved, most notably in 2003 in protest against the Iraq war, it did so explicitly without confronting the regime. The Brotherhood's largest 2003 demonstration, which came after a series of smaller demonstrations by the left, was government-sanctioned and did not involve anti-regime slogans, in sharp contrast to the demonstrations organised by the left. The size of the 2003 demonstration, which drew over 100,000 people, showed how much more muscle the Brotherhood had in comparison with the leftist protest networks. But it also showed the limitations of the Brotherhood, as it could not afford to antagonise the regime because it had so much more to lose. This in part explains why the left spearheaded the protests (Wickham 2013: 100–1).

Fourth, the protests strengthened links between Egyptian activists and the various transnational movements protesting against Israel's treatment of the Palestinians and against the Iraq war. In 2002, international activists came to Egypt for the Stop-the-War coalition's first Cairo Conference (stopwar.org.uk n.d.) in what was described as the first 'closing of ranks between international and regional activists in an Arab capital' (*Al-Ahram Weekly* 2005a). The brief occupation of Tahrir Square on 20 March 2003 was described by one of the activists present as 'our Seattle', a reference to the international protests against the World Trade Organization (WTO) in Seattle in 2000, and an indication of how some Egyptian protesters had come to identify with the wider Global Justice Movement (Leupp 2003). The Stop-the-War Cairo Conference became an annual event (stopwar.org.uk n.d.), enabling the diffusion of tactics (in both directions).

Fifth, the protests created a spiral of contention, which altered the risk perception and focus of both the protesters and the regime following a classic pattern found in social movement activism. Protests addressing issues that are not directly threatening to the regime are (marginally) tolerated because they function as a safety valve for the regime by focusing public anger outward. When the protests grow in frequency and numbers, the regime turns to increasingly brutal forms of repression to maintain control. However, by this stage in the protest episode, the protests have gained a degree of momentum; repression thus serves to radicalise rather than deter people, and pushes them towards the protest networks, which by now are more firmly established. The repression further serves to refocus the anger of protesters against the regime. As the episode unfolds, both the regime and the protesters are faced with changed risk calculations: the protesters are prepared to risk more, in part to protect what has already been achieved (the threat of losing something has been found to be a greater motivator than the desire to gain something) (Buechler 2004: 59), and the regime has to increase its repression to achieve its aims, but this results in further radicalisation of the protesters (cf. Hafez and Wiktorowicz 2004: 69–71). By the end of the episode, even if the regime has (at least temporarily) succeeded in suppressing the protests, a cadre of activists has been created with enhanced skills to protest and evade police repression, and with an increased level of grievances against the regime. Moreover, the focus of the protests has shifted, from an external threat to an internal challenge to the regime.

Finally, this first wave was a laboratory for tactical innovation, some of which indirectly fed into the 2011 uprising. Moving on from hunger strikes, sit-ins and campus demonstrations, the activists reclaimed the street as a site of protest, something that had not been done in any sustained way since the 1970s. They learned how to outwit security cordons and circumvent blockades—for example, by melting away and regrouping elsewhere (El Amrani 2003), a technique that was facilitated by text messaging which, together with e-mail, was central to spreading the word about the March 2003 occupation of Tahrir Square (Schemm 2003; El Amrani 2003). They learned to overwhelm the police with surprise surges in numbers arriving from different directions (Schemm 2003)—a technique that, adapted, was to prove central to the 2011 uprising.

The demonstrations also proved to be a dry run, and inspiration, for the 2011 occupation of Tahrir Square.[10] On 20 March 2003, demonstrators converged on Tahrir Square and occupied it. On subsequent days, they were prevented from returning to the Square, blocked by police lines and water cannons (A. Hassan 2003b). Yet, for twelve hours, protesters were masters of the Square. In the words of one observer:

Many I've met, young and old, had the same comment, coming from an old song written by Salah Jahin. They told me, *El sharei lena*—the street is ours. Even one young woman commented: 'I never understood what that meant, now I do.' The street was ours, and [we're] not finished yet, the days ahead are crucial, we can make Tahrir Intifada our own Seattle, and out of it comes a movement [that] can challenge those rulers and [their] falling regimes. (quoted in Leupp 2003)

This theme, of reclaiming the street as 'ours', was to be picked up again in subsequent waves, particularly in 2011. Similarly, the connection drawn with the Battle in Seattle of 1999 illustrates a recurring theme of how (at least some) activists understood their activities to be part of a transnational protest movement. The March 2003 demonstration, in particular, was seen as part of the global anti-war movement. As a participating student proudly (though not wholly accurately) observed: 'Cairo witnessed the strongest and most powerful demonstrations against the war in the Arab world' (Leupp 2003).[11]

This first wave was still a far cry from the 2011 uprising in terms of numbers and breadth of participating organisations. Yet it began a protest wave that, rippling across the decade, fuelled other waves, culminating in Tahrir Square in 2011. As tweeter 3arabawy reminded people on 8 February 2011: 'Remember: The origin of the Egyptian pro-democracy movement is the pro-Palestine and anti-War movements. The local and the regional r linked' (Idle and Nunns 2011: 183).

Wave II: Kefaya and the Movement(s) for Change (2004–2007)

In 2004 a movement called 'Enough' (Kefaya) was launched in response to many of the same issues that drove the 2011 protests. Similar to 2011, Kefaya was concerned with the oppressive political climate in Egypt; the apparent shift to family rule as Hosni Mubarak seemed to begin the process of transferring political power to his son, Gamal; the lack of human rights, rampant corruption, the absence of a transparent political system; and the need for economic reform. These were the key themes that animated the second wave.

This wave formally began in summer 2004 with the circulation of Kefaya's founding document, a 300-strong signature petition calling for 'democracy and reform to take root in Egypt' (Khorshid 2005). Kefaya, or, to call it by its proper name, the Movement for Change, was the first organisation whose primary aim was to challenge the Mubarak regime directly (S. Mansour 2009; El-Ghobashy 2005; Carnegie 2010). It was also the first to have formally brought together intellectuals, political leaders and youth activists from across the political spectrum in a sustained way (although the various Palestinian solidarity committees had laid the groundwork for this).

Kefaya emerged out of the pro-Palestinian and anti-Iraq war protests (see also El-Mahdi 2009), which had brought its leaders together from across the ideological spectrum. The protests had brought them into contact with the newly galvanised student movement, thus broadening their base while strengthening relations with some key professional syndicates, especially the Lawyers' Syndicate.

The Iraq war protests had triggered a debate among opposition activists which led to a paradigm shift. Until then, the focus had been on regional events, protesting the policies of the United States and Israel in the region. When the Mubarak regime so violently crushed the anti-Iraq war protests, the activists concluded that the key issue was not US policy, but the Mubarak regime itself, which was enabling the United States to carry out its policies. This reading was reinforced by the regime's lacklustre response to the suffering caused to Palestinians by the al-Aqsa Intifada.

However, what propelled Kefaya into action was a series of political reforms, which were believed to be preparing the way for Gamal

Mubarak's succession. Kefaya broke a taboo by publicly questioning the apparent monarchical-succession plans of the Mubarak regime. For most of the 1990s succession was not an issue. But in the early 2000s, concrete and very visible steps were taken to groom Gamal for succession (Chapter 3). In particular, the meteoric rise of Gamal to the NDP's top echelons was interpreted by opposition activists as an attempt to prepare the path for his succession (although Mubarak has continued to deny this). In 2004, events accelerated with the appointment of a number of Gamal's close friends and business associates to what came to be known as 'Gamal's Cabinet' (S. Mansour 2009: 206). At the same time, a number of Gamal's business associates were rising through the NDP's ranks (Brownlee 2007: 134).

This dual provocation—Gamal's meteoric rise and a Cabinet made up of businessmen, who, having benefited financially from their proximity to the regime, were now tasked with 'overseeing the very businesses they ran' (*New York Times* 2011d)—served as the direct trigger for the next wave of protests. It focused the opposition movement's attention on the question of succession, and thus brought together those who had come to call for Mubarak to leave as a result of the anti-Iraq war protest episode, and those who had long been part of the pro-democracy movement, including leading Islamists. As the Cabinet reshuffle raised questions about the regime's links with businessmen, it also galvanised the various constituencies opposed to corruption, crony capitalism and neoliberal reforms. A fourth constituency which was drawn in consisted of the human rights organisations which had become increasingly central to the opposition movement as a result of the brutal way the police had tried to suppress the anti-war protests.

The trajectory of Nora, a Youth for Change activist, one of Kefaya's affiliated organisations, illustrates both the linkages between the first and second wave, and the pivotal role Kefaya had in galvanising people into action. Nora began her activism in 2002 at Cairo University, where she joined a protest in solidarity with the Palestinians. She was tear-gassed, but within days she was back, organising a protest in solidarity with Yasser Arafat, whose compound in Ramallah was besieged by the Israeli army. She became disillusioned when Saddam Hussein's statue was torn down by American troops in 2003 and draped in an American flag. For two years, she withdrew from politics. What rekindled her earlier activism were the protests Kefaya organised against the 25 May 2005 referendum. Witnessing first-hand the brutality of the police and thugs who sexually harassed the women activists, she became one of Youth for Change's activist core (Azimi 2005). Kefaya was not the only movement sustaining the second wave. After its high point in 2005, other movements—such as Judges for Change and the workers' movements—continued to protest. Other groups were also active around this time, particularly the Palestinian solidarity movement and the Muslim Brotherhood, which threw its weight behind the pro-democracy protests with a series of protests involving tens of thousands, dwarfing Kefaya's demonstrations (although compared to the numbers seen during the funerals of the Brotherhood's Supreme Guides, these demonstrations were relatively small, suggesting it did not 'flex its full mobilizing power') (Wickham 2013: 111). However, unlike Kefaya, the Brotherhood did not directly attack the president.

Kefaya's main goal was constitutional reform and an end to Mubarak's rule. Its first public rally, a silent protest in front of the High Court, with mouths taped shut with yellow stickers with the word 'Kefaya' (colloquial Egyptian for 'enough') written on them, was 'the first rally ever convened solely to demand that Mubarak step down and refrain from handing over power to his son' (El-Ghobashy 2005). Kefaya's founding petition called for constitutional as well as economic reforms. In 2005, it called for the annulment of the controversial Emergency Law.

The significance of Kefaya was not that it achieved any of its stated end goals. It was successful in triggering a debate among a core group of politically active people about succession and constitutional reforms, and helped in the creation of a protest culture. With the assistance of the Muslim Brotherhood (Wickham 2013: 112), it succeeded in persuading the majority of Egyptians to boycott the referendum on the constitutional amendment that was intended to pave the way for Gamal's eventual presidency; instead of the government's projected 70 per cent turnout, only between 18 and 23 per cent of people voted (S. Mansour 2009: 210). However, Kefaya (and the Brotherhood) failed to change the outcome of the constitutional amendment or overturn the Emergency Law. It similarly failed in forcing Mubarak to resign or abandon his succession plans, or in significantly changing the make-up of parliament.

The number of people Kefaya mobilised remained relatively small, particularly compared to the tens of thousands mobilised during the first wave and the 50,000–70,000 the Brotherhood had rallied in May 2005 (Wickham 2013: 111). Most of its rallies attracted less than 100 people; its largest rallies involved a few thousand. While it succeeded in sustaining its campaign over two years, by 2007 Kefaya was, at least according to one of its prominent members, 'dead' (quoted in S. Mansour 2009: 212). International diplomats did not consider Kefaya very significant at the time. It was only when the judges became involved that diplomats such as Bowker (Interview 2011) began to pay attention.

Kefaya's key significance lay in carving out a domestic opposition space and creating a model for sustained protests. In the words of Ishak (Interview 2011), one of Kefaya's six founders, 'we achieved three things: we broke the culture of fear, we obtained the right to demonstrate without permit, and we obtained the right to criticise the president'. While the ground for these achievements had been prepared by the Palestinian solidarity and anti-Iraq war protests (see also El-Mahdi 2009: 92–3), Kefaya was an important pivot in the development of contemporary Egyptian protest culture. All of the activists we interviewed listed Kefaya as laying the foundation for a domestically oriented opposition movement. Kefaya brought many of these activists together for the first time, provided support for political debate, routinised activism and helped to introduce activists to a variety of protest tactics. The movement had a lasting impact by showing that demonstrations against the regime were possible. It also triggered a return to street politics for the Muslim Brotherhood, which, as the largest opposition movement, felt upstaged and was stung by criticisms from all sides for not doing more (Wickham 2013: 110).

Although the taboo of calling on Mubarak to resign had already been broken by the previous wave—a fact often overlooked by the literature on Kefaya (e.g. S. Mansour 2009; El-Ghobashy 2005; Carnegie 2010)—this was the first time that any organisation had explicitly set out to target the Mubarak regime (rather than protesters calling for the regime to go as part of protests against the war in Iraq or against Israeli policies). In the words of Shaaban (Interview 2011), one of Kefaya's founders, 'Kefaya brought people out on the street and encouraged them to criticise the system; this was new.'

During the previous wave, participating activists had already begun to overcome their fear of standing up against the regime, despite harsh repression. Even though activists knew that public protests routinely led to arrests, beatings, torture and occasionally rape, they continued to protest. The routinisation of protest under Kefaya contributed to the protesters' overcoming their fear (just as the Brotherhood's protests contributed to helping its activists' overcoming their fear). By regularly facing down the regime with others, the perceived threat was mitigated by the sense of belonging to a group that refused to back down and that supported its members. Whenever someone was arrested, Kefaya's network of human rights activists and lawyers would provide legal and moral support. When a protest rally in front of the Journalists' Syndicate on the day of the May 2005 referendum was brutally broken up by bussed-in thugs and police, and two women were sexually harassed, their clothes torn off, Kefaya began holding weekly vigils, every subsequent Wednesday, throughout the summer (S. Mansour 2009: 210).

In addition to carving out a domestic protest space and legitimising the call for regime change, Kefaya made at least five significant contributions. First, Kefaya brought together a wide spectrum of Egyptians within a formal framework: from Nasserists to Islamists, students to professionals, pro-Palestinian activists to human rights workers. The pro-Palestinian and anti-Iraq war protests had sown the seeds, but Kefaya created a sustained institutional framework for cross-partisan cooperation. By creating a horizontal and ideologically inclusive umbrella organisation, Kefaya departed sharply from the old-style politics of hierarchical parties with narrowly circumscribed ideologies (S. Mansour 2009: 206). This enabled those from different political parties, and those from beyond—such as student activists, civil society actors and activist professionals—to join together in opposition to Mubarak. The creation of a formal umbrella organisation, with branches nationwide and a national coordinating committee, facilitated the forging of links between the disparate and often fluid opposition hubs and between the more formal, structured syndicates and parties. Crucially, and preparing the way for the third wave, it established a platform for liberal middle-class activists and members of the independent workers' movement to create links, albeit tentative ones (Ishak, Interview 2011; N. Mansour, Interview 2011).[12]

The idea for Kefaya was born during Ramadan at the house of former Muslim Brother and founder of the (post-)Islamist Wasat Party, Abu al-'Ala Madi. However, the movement was dominated by secularists, and some of its most influential Islamists were former Muslim Brothers rather than Brotherhood stalwarts. Those Brothers who did join were mostly from the Brotherhood's more pragmatic middle-generation, and had joined as individuals. As an organisation, the Brotherhood kept its distance. It did participate actively in the protest wave by staging mass demonstrations and joining the boycott of the constitutional referendum. It also initiated a new modus operandi for its members by urging its followers not to bring their Qur'ans to protest events, and to focus on secular demands, rather than calling for Islam as the solution. This was a significant departure, and a dry-run, for the Brotherhood's self-consciously secular behaviour during the 2011 uprising. It also entered into a (short-lived) alliance with leftist groups (National Coalition for Reform and Change). But when its own interests dictated a different path, it turned its back on the boycott of the presidential elections, refocused on increasing its electoral gains and returned to a more overtly religious language (Wickham 2013: 108, 110–18; El-Hamalawy 2007).

The cross-partisan alliance Kefaya represented thus never fully included the Muslim Brotherhood, and certainly not its leadership, and the tensions that emerged in 2005 were in many ways the same as those that emerged in 2011 after the ousting of Mubarak. According to Wickham (2013: 115–17, 110–11), there were three key reasons for this failure to establish the type of enduring cross-partisan alliance that has been so crucial in democratic transitions elsewhere. One was the sheer difference in size between the Brotherhood and its secular counterparts, making it all but impossible for the Brotherhood to participate without dominating. A second was the inexperience among the Brotherhood's top echelons of collaborating with ideological others, and the doubts secular activists continued to have regarding the Brotherhood's readiness to accept equal rights for all, regardless of faith or behaviour. This stands in sharp contrast to the former and reformist Brothers who joined Kefaya after a long period of debate and dialogue, during which the secular activists and the Islamists learned to trust each other. A third reason was the regime's policy of divide and rule, which played on the fears of the secular groups of becoming targets by association with the Brotherhood. Conversely, the Brotherhood remained reluctant to confront the regime directly, fearful as it was of losing its extensive network of social, religious and educational institutions. Indeed, when it did join the boycott, it bore the brunt of the regime's repression, with between 800 and 2,000 members arrested (Wickham 2013: 112). Thus, as in the first wave, it was the small size and the informality of the protest networks that enabled them to spearhead the pro-democracy wave and be innovative.

Cross-partisan cooperation was more sustained at the student level. In 2005, Muslim Brothers and leftists founded the Free Student Union as an alternative to the official student union. Part of the impetus behind this initiative came from activists who had been students during the Palestinian solidarity protests and forged the first tentative cross-ideological links, but it was sustained through joint protests and sharing time in prison, which helped to create bonds of trust beyond politics (El-Hamalawy 2007; Wickham 2013: 156–7).

Second, Kefaya succeeded in expanding the number of professional syndicates linked to the pro-democracy cause. During the first wave of Palestinian solidarity and anti-war protests, some unions, such as the Lawyers' Syndicate, had become mobilised. But most activism took place outside the unions. Some, such as the Judges' Club, had become more active politically after a changing of the guard in the early 2000s. But their links with the wider protest movement were still tenuous. Under Kefaya's leadership, numerous unions were drawn into the struggle, providing much-needed resources and public legitimacy. Protests now regularly took place in front of professional unions, such as the Journalists' or Lawyers' Syndicates, offering limited protection.

The integration of pro-reform judges into the protest movement was particularly pivotal. From a social movement theory perspective, its significance lies in the fact that it constituted the first public alliance between the pro-democracy movement and a key part of the establishment. In other protest movements, elite alliances were often crucial for increasing their chances of success (as was famously argued in the case of the US Civil Rights Movement, although the importance of elite support has since been hotly questioned) (cf. Morris 1981). Securing the support of the judges was crucial in signalling both to the regime and the protesters, as well as to the international community more broadly, that the regime could no longer command the uncritical loyalty of the entirety of the political establishment.

Elements within the judiciary in Egypt had struggled for judicial independence from the executive branch of government since the 1960s (Brown and Nasr 2005). Under Nasser, the struggle for judicial independence was severely curtailed in what became known as 'the massacre of the judiciary', involving the dismissal of over 100 judges. Under Sadat and Mubarak, judges regained many of their privileges, but reformists chafed against continuing restrictions on their independence and saw these privileges as an attempt to buy-off their resistance. Tensions came to a head in the early 2000s when reformist judges protested against the election law, on the grounds that it made them complicit in electoral fraud by limiting their ability to guarantee electoral transparency, while making them legally responsible for ensuring transparency. In 2002, reformist judges gained control of the Judges' Club and stepped up their efforts to secure judicial independence and electoral transparency. This, aided by a number of court judgements protecting NGOs, and in particular human rights NGOs, against government repression (Bernard-Maugiron 2008b: 244–5), laid the foundation for future cooperation with the pro-democracy movement. Some NGOs, such as the Egyptian Organization for Human Rights (EOHR), which formed part of the pro-democracy movement, had long-standing links with the judiciary, further cementing the alliance between the judges and the pro-democracy movement in 2005–2006.

From 2005 through 2006, the Judges' Club organised a series of increasingly high-profile protests. It began with a series of emergency general assemblies to discuss the judges' role in monitoring the upcoming referendum and elections and to propose alterations to the law. It then escalated into sit-ins, silent protests and eventually a pro-reform camp in front of the Judges' Club, in Cairo, Alexandria and elsewhere. Students and other activists began to protest in solidarity with the judges as the confrontation with the regime intensified. Protest rallies proliferated when a judge was beaten in a police clampdown on the pro-reform camp, and after two judges were summoned to 'answer charges of defamation of a fellow judge' (Bernard-Maugiron 2008a: 1–4). The confrontation between judges and the regime thus became not just a symbol of the regime's weakening control over the judiciary but a rallying point for the wider pro-democracy movement, fuelling and sustaining it when Kefaya itself had begun to run out of steam.

Third, Kefaya spurned numerous sectorally based movements: Youth for Change, Students for Change, Doctors for Change, Journalists for Change, Writers and Artists for Change, Workers for Change and the March 9 movement for university independence, to name but a few (S. Mansour 2009: 207; Carnegie 2010). Kefaya widened mobilisation and routinised it, thus encouraging the development of spin-off protest groups. These groups in turn served to expand the number and variety of people involved in public protests. For example, Workers for

Change created links between the largely middle-class Movement for Change and the workers' movement, which was to prove vital for the third wave of protests. Youth for Change laid the foundation for many of the subsequent youth movements. The April 6 Youth Movement was founded in 2008 by activists who had cut their political teeth in the Youth for Change movement (Maher, Interview 2011). The Democratic Front Party likewise contained a number of activists from the original Youth for Change movement (Ghazali-Harb, Interview 2011a). Many of those supporting ElBaradei had similarly been Youth for Change activists. Youth for Change succeeded in mobilising a broader sector of youth than the anti-war movement preceding it, and Kefaya is generally credited with bringing youth into mainstream politics (Ishak, Interview 2011; Shaaban, Interview 2011; Maher, Interview 2011; Khalil Saeed, Interview 2011). Under its umbrella, Kefaya also helped to strengthen the relationship between the activist youth and the human rights NGOs, which would become crucial in the legal defence of imprisoned bloggers and activists during the third wave.

Fourth, by creating a broad organisational network, Kefaya was able to sustain prolonged protest episodes. The weekly protests following the brutal clampdown on the May 2005 referendum rally would have been impossible without such a level of organisation. Protests were supported by coverage in the affiliated opposition media, such as *al-Dustur* and *al-Masry al-Youm*. Bloggers exposed and disseminated human rights abuses. Organisational depth was strengthened by organisational breadth. Already in April 2005, Kefaya could mount simultaneous anti-regime demonstrations in fourteen major cities across Egypt (Carnegie 2010). This level of sustained and nationwide protest brought the opposition movement to a new level of organisation.

Fifth, Kefaya experimented with innovative tactics, moving from petitions to stay-at-home protests and in one instance involving masses of people sweeping brooms to demonstrate the need to clean up politics. The sweeping tactic, in particular, was a brilliant innovation, as it subverted the usual cat-and-mouse dynamic between demonstrators and security forces by making a violent police response look ridiculous (S. Mansour 2009: 209). Youth for Change was particularly adept at tactical innovation. It began to experiment with what some called 'vigilante street tactics'—'[taking] its message directly to the street', sending 'groups of two to four activists [to] visit public squares or parks, erect mini-exhibitions with flyers, and engage people on the street in impromptu discussion (their internal motto is *kilamateen wi bas* or 'two words is enough')', '[riding] public mini-buses, engaging potential supporters, hopping off as soon as they feel impending arrest (and they do get arrested)'. Building on the realisation of the anti-war activists regarding the importance of wresting control of the street away from the security forces, Youth for Change activists developed this theme further, creating a movement called 'The Street is Ours' [*al-shari' lena*] (Azimi 2005).

A further tactical innovation lay in Youth for Change activists actively seeking to relate Kefaya's abstract political vision to people's daily struggles for survival. As Khaled, one of the architects of the group's street tactics, put it:

Our job is to link young people's daily problems to the government, to explain to people that they have certain rights and someone has a responsibility to listen to their demands. The linkages are not intuitive to them. Our job is to uncover those links, to get the idea of reform on the table. (quoted in Azimi 2005)

Following a process known in social movement theory as 'frame bridging', Youth for Change activists recognised that the masses would not be mobilised unless they saw the linkage between their daily concerns and the toppling of Mubarak.[13] Activists preparing for 2011 drew on this innovation.

Youth for Change specifically began to target working-class areas such as Shubra and Sayeda Zeinab (Azimi 2005), actively trying to link the largely middle-class core of the Movement for Change with the concerns of the members of the working class. In this, they prepared the way for the third wave, which further cemented this embryonic link between the working and the middle classes, a link without which the 2011 uprising would not have succeeded.

Perhaps the most far-reaching contribution was the innovative use of information and communication technology (ICT), although groups such as the Egyptian People's Committee for Solidarity with the Palestinian Intifada and National Campaign Against the War on Iraq had already set up websites and started to use e-mailing lists in the previous wave (Bayat 2007: 183). In 2005, the use of ICT became especially important. Digital cameras and mobile phones were used to record plain-clothes police officers attacking protesters, videos or photos of which were then distributed through the internet. These technologies were similarly used by the anti-corruption group shayfeen.com (a play on 'we see you' as in: 'we are watching you'), which encouraged people to take videos of election irregularities or of officials molesting female protesters, for example, and then posting them on YouTube (Beyerle and Hassan 2009: 269–71). As Sherif Mansour (2009: 210) writes, 'Egyptians were particularly shocked; such actions are extremely shameful in Egyptian culture. This flagrant assault unified the opposition ...' (see also the discussion of moral shocks in Chapter 6).

Youth for Change and Kefaya were the first organisations to start using the internet interactively: Kefaya used the internet to gather signatures for its petition, and succeeded in collecting over 17,000 signatures (El-Ghobashy 2005). Given the novelty of the tactic, and the fact that only 7.5 per cent of Egyptians had internet access at the time, this was a phenomenal achievement (S. Mansour 2009: 208). Kefaya created a database of e-mail contacts that it used to distribute news and calls for action, and established an online forum, for which users, drawn from different groups ranging from Christians and Muslims to liberals and leftists, needed a username and password (Taema, Interview 2011).

The turn to internet-based mobilisation was both facilitated by, and served to encourage, the emergence of an active and influential blog-o-sphere. In the absence of a well-established independent media sector, internet blogs became the medium through which opposition activists communicated, exposing regime flaws and human rights abuses, developing strategies on how to oppose the government, and creating new action and injustice frames. Just as networks are crucial to the emergence of social movements by providing a space for developing goals, identities and tactics, internet blogs served this function in the evolution of the opposition movement.

Concluding Thoughts

In this chapter, we charted the (re-)emergence of the pro-Palestinian protest sector as it produced the first significant protest wave of the 2000s. It reclaimed the street as a protest site, united activists across ideological lines and began to transform a regional protest frame into a domestic one. In doing so, it laid the foundation for the Movement for Change at the heart of the second wave. This wave conclusively broke the taboo of challenging Mubarak's rule by making that its primary target. It consolidated the cross-ideological links established by the first wave and facilitated youth mobilisation by departing (to an extent) from the hierarchical culture of the political parties and triggering a slew of youth organisations, rallying hitherto un-mobilised youths. Professional syndicates were mobilised, and an embryonic nationwide network was established, capable of supporting a sustained protest campaign. Tactical innovations were introduced, including online mobilisation and grassroots activism linking everyday concerns with abstract political goals.

However, by 2006, the number of seasoned street activists was still relatively small. Aside from the Brotherhood's mass demonstrations, most political protests involved hundreds rather than thousands, and the early success of the anti-Iraq war demonstrations was not sustained. The failure of the Movement for Change to achieve political change, despite the support of elite figures such as activist judges, fuelled a decline in political protests. The decision of the Brotherhood to withdraw from the presidential boycott and to focus on increasing its electoral gains was a further blow to this protest wave. The subsequent clampdown on the Brotherhood in response to it gaining an unprecedented eighty-eight seats in parliament (more than four times the number of seats won in 2000) triggered a return to the self-imposed restraint seen during the early 2000s, as every attempt at mobilising its supporters in street protests was met with mass arrests. Moreover, the clampdown particularly targeted the reformists within the movement, strengthening the risk-averse, ideologically more rigid leadership (Wickham 2013: 120–3). With Kefaya all but defunct and the Brotherhood turning away from street protests and cross-partisan collaboration, the momentum shifted towards the parallel protest sector of the independent workers' movement. It was this movement, more than any other, which succeeded in creating a mass protest culture capable of challenging Mubarak, although it took the reinvigoration of the pro-democracy movement and a series of successive trigger events in 2010–2011 to channel this protest culture into a challenge against Mubarak.

2

MOBILISING PROTEST NETWORKS II (2007–2011)

In the previous chapter we traced the development of protest networks from the start of the pro-Palestinian protest wave to the protests demanding constitutional reform and an end to Mubarak's rule. In this chapter, we continue the story, starting with a crucial, but under-researched protest sector: the independent workers' movement. We then move on to the final protest wave of 2010.

Wave III: The Workers' Movement and April 6 (2007–2009)

The third wave of protests culminated in the 6 April 2008 strike in Mahalla El-Kubra, an industrial city in the Nile Delta, not far from Cairo. This strike was part of one of the longest protest episodes the country had experienced since the 1950s (Beinin in Said 2009). The episode began in December 2006, when 10,000 workers took to the town's square to demand their promised bonuses to supplement their wages, which were under strain from inflation and rising food prices (Chapter 4). On the following day, 20,000 workers joined the protests, and the company's mill compound remained occupied for four days (Beinin and el-Hamalawy 2007; Agbarieh-Zahalka 2008). Between December and September, when another strike brought the 24,000–27,000 workers to a standstill, an estimated 198,400 workers protested across the country, as the strikes spread to other sectors, including civil servants, metro drivers, cement workers, garbage-collectors and fishermen (El-Hamalawy 2008b). In December 2007, real estate tax-collectors staged a 55,000-strong strike, the largest that the country had ever experienced. In February 2008, the centre of gravity moved back to Mahalla as 20,000 workers and citizens took to the streets again (El-Hamalawy 2008b).

The next strike was called for 6 April 2008. Unlike previous strikes, political activists across the country—from Kefaya to the Democratic Front Party, the various youth movements and the numerous leftist organisations—joined forces to spread the call. Having made concessions to the strikers on previous occasions (though not necessarily honouring them), the government decided this time to pre-empt the strike. It arrested political activists across the country, blocked key protest sites such as Tahrir Square and the Bar Associations in Cairo, Alexandria and Gharbia, and bussed in security forces to Mahalla.

The planned strike in Mahalla was choked at the start by the police, and the nationwide protests did not materialise. But in the afternoon of 6 April demonstrators flooded the streets of central Mahalla, reputedly in response to the beating of an elderly woman. In the words of an activist who was there:

by the time of changing shifts at 3:30pm, workers were expected to start the planned demonstration, but nothing happened. Till an old woman got out in a narrow alley close to Al-Shon square and shouted 'where are the workers? Why are not they on [the] streets? Our life became bitter, we cannot feed our children', then the infamous police officer Haytham Al-Shamy stopped his car and started to beat up the old woman, accordingly other women in the street started to scream, we heard their screams in the square. Then, people started to chant 'Down with Hosni Mubarak'. The spark spread quickly and people got down to [the] streets and demonstrations started. As security forces intensively used gas bombs, people in narrow streets escaped the smoke that filled their houses by joining the demonstrations in the streets. ... The next day, 7 April, 100,000 demonstrated again calling for the release of the 350 people arrested the previous day. (A. Imam quoted in N. Aly 2011: 53–4)

While others put the number of protesters at 40,000 (cf. El-Hamalawy 2008a), it is clear that this was one of the biggest demonstrations the country had seen, and certainly the biggest in Mahalla until then.

The April 2008 protests had their roots in the ongoing industrial disputes between the independent workers' movement and their employers. Officially, workers could only join unions that belonged to the General Federation of Trade Unions (GFTU). The GFTU was government-controlled and, although strikes had become officially 'legal' in

2003, no strike prior to 2008 had been granted a permit, thus rendering all strikes de facto 'illegal' (Beinin and el-Hamalawy 2007).

Parallel to the GFTU and its predecessors, an independent workers' movement had emerged. Independent protests had begun as early as the 1930s in the Misr Spinning and Weaving Company in Mahalla, one of Egypt's flagship textile companies. Being at the heart of Egypt's modernisation drive, protests in Mahalla regularly triggered protests elsewhere in Egypt, and there is a long activist tradition, often running in families (Beinin and el-Hamalawy 2007).

Although there had been a constant trickle of protests through the years, 2004 marked the start of the workers' protest wave. In 2004, the number of protests across both public and private sectors tripled from eighty-six in 2003 to 266 and tripled again to 614 in 2007, remaining at that level through 2010 (Figure 2.1). Between 2004 and 2008, over 1,900 strikes took place involving an estimated 1.7 million workers (Solidarity Center 2010: 14). By contrast, overtly political protests decreased. In 2008, only twenty-nine of the 151 protest events reported by *al-Masry al-Youm* as involving more than 500 focused on political issues (including police abuse), against seventy-one championing economic and industrial themes. In 2009, this number dropped to ten, while economic and industrial public protests stayed at seventy-one (not including the 700 industrial disputes) (Appendix).

Activists trace this increase in protest activity to the influence of the previous protest waves. Shawky Solyman, a strike leader in Kafr Dawar, observed that while the word 'strike' was unthinkable in the minds of many during the 1990s, 'strikes became an established right

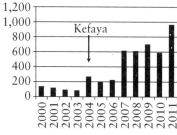
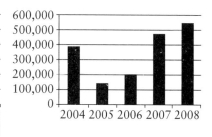

Figure 2.1: Estimated number of workers' protests in public and private sector (2000–June 2011) and number of protesters in both sectors (2004–2008) (Solidarity Center 2010: 16–18; Abdalla 2012: 2).[1]

for all workers' as a result of the activism of Kefaya and others (N. Aly 2011: 48). Joel Beinin and Hossam el-Hamalawy (2007a), veteran observers of the Egyptian workers' movement, similarly credit Kefaya's 'taboo-breaking demonstrations targeting President Husni Mubarak personally'. Writing separately, El-Hamalawy (2008a) emphasises the impact of the anti-Iraq war protests in '[breaking] the taboo surrounding criticisms of the regime' (see also the report by the Center for Socialist Studies, quoted in El-Mahdi 2009: 100–1).

The inspiration of the Movement for Change manifested itself in the names used by the various workers' networks themselves. In June 2007, a previously unknown group calling itself '7th of December Movement—Workers for Change' called for the unification of all workers to end 'corruption, tyranny, injustice, subjugation and humiliation and ... take back the rights, first among them freedom and democracy, from the thieves, robbers and hypocrites in this country ...' (note the focus on 'freedom and democracy', a central Kefaya theme, but not always central in the workers' movement) (Libcom.org 2007b). In April of the same year, a group calling itself 'Kafr el-Dawwar Workers for Change'—a direct offshoot of Kefaya (Beinin 2008: 228)—taking its cue from Kefaya, called for national cooperation to express solidarity with the Mahalla workers (Libcom.org 2007a; Beinin 2008: 235).[2]

The workers' protest wave was significant in numerous ways. It was the first time that the workers explicitly linked their struggle to regime change. Already in 2007, Beinin (2007) reported, 'important elements among the Mahalla strikers are now framing their struggle as a profoundly political fight with national implications. They are directly challenging the economic policies and political legitimacy of the regime of President Husni Mubarak.' One of the strike leaders, Muhammad al-'Attar, told a rally marking his release from prison: 'I want the whole government to resign ... I want the Mubarak regime to come to an end. Politics and workers' rights are inseparable. Work is politics by itself' (quoted in Beinin 2007). Occupied factories even began to be referred to as 'al-'ard al-moharara' [the liberated land] (A. Imam quoted in N. Aly 2011: 45).

The wisdom of linking industrial disputes to regime change was controversial, though. As Beinin (2007) noted:

Some remained hopeful that Husni Mubarak would intervene to compel the paying of bonuses ... perhaps banking on the regime's record of meeting economic demands in many of the strikes of the 2004–2007 wave. Others are more militant and identify the regime as their enemy. Twenty-three year old worker Karim al-Buhayri, who writes a widely read Arabic blog called Egyworkers, said, "Find us another society to live in. Or find us other rulers to rule us. Or find us our rights."

By 2008, protests were more overtly anti-regime (N. Mansour, Interview 2011). El-Hamalawy (2008a) reported:

[During the April 2008 strike] kids were chanting "Palestine style" as they threw rocks: "The revolution has come. The revolution has come." ... If you chanted "Down with Mubarak!" [in the 1990s] you would not necessarily find many people with the courage to repeat it after you. Now you find ordinary citizens, not political activists, chanting "Down with Mubarak!" and setting his pictures alight.

This framing shift was facilitated by the fact that the disputed bonuses had been promised by prime ministerial decree, rather than by individual employers in the public sector, where most of the strikes took place. Yet, as the above quotation from Beinin implies, the fact that the government did grant a series of concessions during 2006–2007 meant that it was by no means self-evident that the anti-regime frame would become dominant in 2008.

Although there is a long tradition among the left, from which many of the core workers' leaders came,[3] of seeing economic inequality as a political issue, workers had historically been reluctant to make this linkage. It seems that the frame bridging championed by Youth for Change, Ghad Party and Workers for Change activists, actively linking everyday economic grievances to regime change, contributed to this shift.

Ahmed Maher (Interview 2011), who would go on to become one of the founders of the April 6 movement, told us that he and the blogger community associated with Kefaya had started to support the workers' movement from 2006 onwards, spreading news about strikes, broadcasting worker's demands, facilitating links between different factories and cities. In their blogs, they tried to show that the problem lay with the regime rather than the factories and thus was political. But they also exhorted political activists to join the economic struggle. As Maher wrote after the 2008 strike, 'We should link politics with economic and social problems to show that our suffering is caused by a corrupt regime' (quoted in Shapiro 2009). Historically, an argument can be made that the success or failure of pro-democracy movements depends on whether they encompass both workers and members of the middle classes (cf. Rueschemeyer, Stephens and Stephens 1992). In this, the youth activists thus followed (a Marxist reading of) history.

However, the links between the workers and the pro-democracy movement remained tenuous, and many workers were sceptical of the latter's focus on regime change. When asked whether he had personal links with the workers' movement, Maher (Interview 2011) told us:

Yes, but I am a liberal, not from the left. To make links between economic and political demands, this was new to [the workers]. Through my links with the left [in the pro-democracy movement], I had links with the workers. A few understood it. Most did not.

The link between the largely liberal pro-democracy movement and the workers went through the Egyptian left, part of the middle-class milieu, many of whom had, exceptions notwithstanding, not been deeply embedded in the workers' movement.[4] The weakness of these links, coupled to the brutal response of the regime to the 2008 convergence of the pro-democracy and workers' movements, meant that the integration of these two movements stalled after April 2008, with important implications for the fourth protest wave. Consider the verdict of Nadim Mansour (Interview 2011), the workers' rights lawyer:

The links between the political activists and the workers were weak. The call for the strike was made by the workers. Then the political groups announced a set of political and socio-economic demands. It was ridiculous in a way because the workers suffered from the call for a general strike [because the regime's reaction was far more brutal than before and severely weakened the movement in Mahalla]. To an extent, it was a failure. The workers' movement was 'good' for the political groups because they had had trouble mobilising people and reaching the masses. The political groups tried to get the workers on board, but they failed.

Second, the workers' protests served to strengthen links between the workers and middle-class activists, temporarily re-galvanising the pro-democracy movement in the process. Left-wing middle-class activists had been involved in the workers' struggle for decades. But the 2008 Mahalla strikes marked the moment when liberal middle-class activists 'joined' the workers' struggle (however briefly and from a distance), forging organisational links between the workers and middle-class organisations such as Kefaya (which itself had been one of the catalysts for this development).

Kefaya, despite having been declared 'dead' by many, staged a solidarity protest in Cairo, in front of the Journalists' Syndicate, in support of the September 2007 strike in Mahalla (Beinin 2007); in 2008, it declared 6 April a 'Day of Popular Anger', calling for demonstrations across the country, just as Youth for Change and the youth wings of the Democratic Front Party and the Ghad Party did. In Mahalla itself, the success of the strikes led political activists back into the fray. For example, A. Imam, a member of the Democratic Front Party, recalled that 'We wanted to capitalize on that success to create a revolutionary momentum in Mahalla' (quoted in N. Aly 2011: 45). A Coordinating Committee of Parties and Political Forces was set up, and 'students, journalists and peasants' joined workers to protest against 'increasing prices and deteriorating living conditions', with numbers increasing from sixty to 1,000 within a month (N. Aly 2011: 45).

The tax-collectors' strike in December 2007 was a significant turning point as it brought white-collar workers into the until then largely blue-collar protest wave. It also showed people in Cairo that mass strikes were possible and achieved results (N. Mansour, Interview 2011). This trend continued after 2008 as more white-collar state employees were drawn into industrial disputes. A case in point was the 2009 strike by 'social and economic experts' at the Ministry of Justice against a change in working conditions (Said 2009).

The workers themselves aided this process through the extension of protest frames from a purely industrial focus to encompass the concerns of the wider pro-democracy movement. For instance, a statement by Mahalla workers, posted on the Egyworkers blog, called on:

people on 6 April to stand firmly against the danger that threatens all Egyptians and does not discriminate between workers, physicians or employees … The Egyptians are facing a "local colonialism" by businessmen spearheaded by Ahmed Ezz, Mohammed Abou El-Enein and others … Till when will we remain silent? … We should move to break the slavery chains and knock down the walls of humiliation. (quoted in N. Aly 2011: 51)

Third, the success and intensity of the protest wave encouraged independent workers to start establishing independent trade unions, thus consolidating their organisational strength. In 2008, the tax-collectors established the first independent union since the establishment of the official Egyptian Trade Union Federation almost sixty years before. The foundation for this union was the Higher Strike Committee, which negotiated a successful end to the property tax-collectors' strike of January 2008. Teachers, health technicians and pensioners followed suit and founded independent unions in 2010, while workers in the Public

Transport Authority and the postal service increased coordination, consolidating their underground networks throughout 2009 and 2010 (Alexander 2012).

Fourth, a number of previously apolitical actors were mobilised, broadening the pool of activists, and new networks emerged. In social movement terms, untapped 'sentient pools' were mobilised. This was particularly important as the two main political movements that had carried the previous wave, Kefaya and the Muslim Brotherhood, were both, for different reasons, largely absent from the political protest scene. Kefaya's supporters had become demoralised. The Brotherhood had refocused its energy on *da'wa*, its traditional activity of making society more pious by calling it to God, in response to the regime's brutal crackdown on the movement in the wake of its 2005 election success, which had in turn strengthened the conservative old guard. Thus as Wickham (2013: 120–3) concludes, 'from the Cairo Spring of 2005 to the Arab Spring of 2011, the Brotherhood rarely mobilized large numbers of supporters into the streets; the one major exception was the demonstrations it organized to protest Israel's incursion into Gaza in January 2009, which led to 1,200 arrests'.

The Brotherhood was not completely absent from the protests. Of the protests involving over 500 people documented by *al-Masry al-Youm* during 2008–2009, fifty-four were identified by the newspaper as Brotherhood protests. However, the vast majority (thirty-five) were Palestinian solidarity protests, and thus not focused on domestic issues.[5] In 2008, there were ten Brotherhood protests concerned with student and local elections and eight with police detentions. During 2009 there were only two other protests, and these were against police detentions. None of the domestic protests were large, by Brotherhood standards, and most were very localised. Thus the relative absence of the Brotherhood, combined with Kefaya's abeyance, meant that there was increased space for new movements to emerge.

The most visible of these new networks was the April 6 Youth Movement. This movement grew out of a Facebook page, set up to spread the call for nationwide protests in solidarity with the Mahalla strike. It was ostensibly the brainchild of Esraa Abd al-Fattah, a member of the liberal Ghad Party's youth wing, and Ahmed Maher, a member of Youth for Change, although others, such as the former coordinator of Youth for Change, Ahmed Salah (Interview 2011), also lay claim to having been a co-founder.

The April 6 Facebook page became a phenomenon almost overnight. In Maher's words:

The response was unbelievable. The first day 3000 people joined the page and they grew to 50,000 by 6 April. It was a new way for mobilizing. People joining the page were able to discuss new tactics and offer help and suggestions. The security did not figure it out; at that time they were totally ignorant about the new social media. (quoted in N. Aly 2011: 52)

Particularly interesting is the profile of those who joined: 'new, independent people, not activists', according to Maher (Interview 2011). Salah similarly noted:

The most important thing about these young people was their being not politicized. They had no links to political parties or forces. Politicized participants were one of the problems that caused the decline of YFC [Youth for Change] in 2006. The parties always get the best elements to work for their interests and not for the movement's goals. Facebook offered a new pool ... (quoted in N. Aly 2011: 55)

While the April 6 Youth Movement was a striking online success, its ability to get people out on to the street was less clear-cut. It is not known how many of the 76,000 who 'liked' the Facebook page went out to demonstrate in April 2008, but judging by the lack of demonstrations outside Mahalla, the numbers were small. Although the streets of Cairo and other major cities were quieter than usual (some claim that as many as a third of the population stayed at home) (S. Mansour 2010: 3), it is unclear how many people stayed at home as a direct result of April 6's calls, rather than other influences (Agbarieh-Zahalka 2008). What is clear is that April 6 did not succeed in organising a mass event again until 2010, and even then, the number of people mobilised remained small. Although Maher (Interview 2011) suggested that 1,000 of the 70,000 Facebook followers were interested in a 'real movement', most events only attracted a few dozen to a few hundred activists. Following Shapiro (2009):

A number of the events created last summer and fall by the April 6 Youth Movement did not succeed in the same way. Protests were typically attended by only a few dozen of the group's supporters and often shut down by the police before they even began. Back in July, Maher tried to organize a "flash mob" on the beach in Alexandria that would sing patriotic songs and fly a kite with the Egyptian flag painted on it. But on the day of the protest, Maher and his crew of about 30 young people were stopped by the police before they were even able to finish unfurling their kite.

April 6's attempts at mobilising people to commemorate the first two anniversaries of the 2008 strike were similarly unsuccessful (Carr 2009; BBC 2009, 2010b). A number of the April 6 activists we met in 2011 had been following the movement's Facebook page for months prior to the 2011 uprising. Yet most of them had not joined a street protest for fear of police brutality and arrest. Nevertheless, even though it was only after 25 January that they lost their fear of the police, they saw themselves as April 6 members well before 2011 (April 6 Cadres, Conversation 2011). Thus April 6's chief contribution lay in creating an online platform for mostly middle-class youth to become mentally engaged with the political struggle. By continuing to organise events, arrests and repression notwithstanding, it kept the protest culture alive, laying the foundation for the next wave of activism. In the words of Nora Younis, a blogger and April 6 activist, 'It's a rehearsal for a bigger thing ... Right now, we are just testing the power of each other' (Shapiro 2009).

A second 'sentient pool' that was galvanised consisted of non-activist citizens facing threats in their neighbourhoods. According to Nadim Mansour (Interview 2011), the Kefaya protests, and even more so the relentless wave of workers' strikes, had 'changed how people dealt with the public sphere'. Before, people would solve their grievances by getting around the system, where necessary through petty theft or bribery. Kefaya and the workers had shown that it was possible to challenge the authorities, that there was an alternative. Where previously similar levels of public unrest would have resulted in largely unorganised events such as bread riots (as by and large happened in 1977), now there was a well-established tradition of organised protests, capable of channelling everyday grievances into political demands. Of the 410 protests reported in al-Masry al-Youm as involving more than 500 protesters between 2008 and 2010, thirty-nine focused on neighbourhood issues, such as school closures or evictions (Appendix).

Parallel to the workers' movement, though feeding into and off it, the bloggers' 'movement' increased in size and importance. Although political bloggers had begun blogging as early as 2004, and blogging was an important part of the pro-democracy protest wave, it reached new heights during this third protest wave. Political blogs became one of the key sources of alternative and anti-regime information, and bloggers played a major role in highlighting police abuse. A number of them also supported, and broadcast the demands of, the workers' movement (Lim 2012; Al Malky 2007; Maher, Interview 2011). More-over, from 2006 onwards, Islamist blogs expanded exponentially. Cru-cially, those among the Brotherhood who spearheaded blogging were largely reformists, and thus both able and willing to establish links with secular bloggers (Al-Anani 2008; Wickham 2013: 125–6).

Fourth, and following from the previous, a major innovation was the enhanced use of the internet, and in particular Facebook. What enabled the April 6 movement to reach so many previously apolitical youths was Facebook. While Facebook had been around for some time, it was only in 2007 that political activists began to use the site intensively for organising protests and disseminating political mes-sages, and only in March–April 2008 that it became a major tool (Maher, Interview 2011; Eid, Interview 2011). This was in part because Facebook only reached a critical mass in 2008 (Figure 2.2). In addi-tion, Arabic-language internet facilities were on the rise (although this process had started earlier), making it an increasingly attractive medium for those who preferred Arabic (especially from the lower middle classes) (Abdulla 2007: 43–4).

In August 2007, when the Ghad Party's newspaper was banned, the party's vice chairman and long-time blogger, Wael Nawara, decided to turn to Facebook, creating two new pages, 'The Third Republic' and 'Egypt Remembers', to continue broadcasting his party's views and cri-tique the regime (APN 2008). In the same year, Esraa Abd al-Fattah,

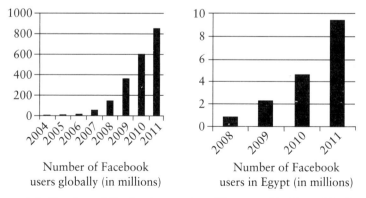

Number of Facebook
users globally (in millions)

Number of Facebook
users in Egypt (in millions)

Figure 2.2: Number of Facebook users in millions worldwide and in Egypt (Facebook n.d.; Burcher 2012; all figures in second graph refer to number of Facebook users in December of the relevant year).

who had become disillusioned with the hierarchy and bureaucracy of the party, turned to Facebook to organise protests. Her first attempt to mobilise 'around the opening of a movie about corruption and torture called "Heya Fawda" or "This Is Chaos"', resulted in 100 people turning up, and she began to use the site routinely (Shapiro 2009).

The networking facility of Facebook enabled April 6 to reach out to the thousands of youths already on Facebook who were (passively) concerned about the state of Egypt yet turned off by the inefficacy of existing political parties and the apparent lack of political options. Facebook's participatory features enabled April 6 to create a dynamic interactive platform for debate, innovation and organisation by inviting members to 'post comments or share news articles, videos or notes on the group's communal "wall"' (Shapiro 2009).

Facebook facilitated tactical and conceptual innovation through its participatory characteristics. It facilitated communication and in particular the spreading of 'system-critical frames' (McAdam 1982: 50). But pages such as April 6 also helped to mobilise people by linking their existing value systems to proposed actions, emphasising latent aspects of people's value systems (for instance by posting footage of police brutality or of successful strikes), and linking their broader concerns about, for instance, Gaza, to the need for regime change in Egypt.[6] However, Facebook was only one tool among many. Activists used blogs, text messages and flyers to spread the call for the April 2008 strike and much depended on face-to-face contacts. As Maher (Interview 2011) noted, the workers (and many others besides) did not have internet access; to engage them, one had to speak with them personally.

Facebook aside, blogs also became more effective, particularly as mobile phone technology improved. Phone videos of police brutality were posted online and spread through established blogger networks. Mohammed Khaled, for instance, posted a video of police torture on his blog. But as his blog was not widely read, he passed it on to Wael Abbas, one of Egypt's foremost bloggers, who asked people to identify the people in the video. The evidence thus gathered was used by lawyers, linked to the pro-democracy movement, and the police officers were convicted. This process, which was repeated in other cases, was facilitated by the links created between human rights NGOs, (youth) bloggers and the pro-democracy movement in the preceding two waves, and reinforced by human rights lawyers defending bloggers arrested by the regime (Eid, Interview 2011).

Fifth, as with the previous waves, this wave fuelled tactical innovation. Besides the technological innovations discussed above, offline tactics were improved on. A. Imam, for instance, recalled the learning that took place while he helped to organise demonstrations in Mahalla in December 2007:

We developed tactics to distribute fliers inviting people to the demonstrations. First, fliers should be divided into small groups. Second, targeted areas should be scanned before distribution. Third, when distributing, two activists watch the two ends of the street while [a further] two quickly pass fliers to people. The biggest challenge was overcoming my internal fear. The only thing that helped me was my deep conviction that I was doing the right thing. (quoted in N. Aly 2011: 46)

Prior to the April 2008 strike, activists similarly distributed flyers widely. In addition, they 'wrote on banknotes to promote the 6 April strike' (Maher paraphrased in N. Aly 2011: 52). Because of the new level of organisation, including online, the pool of people contributing to tactical innovation widened. The speed with which innovations were introduced in 2010 can be traced back directly to the expansion of the network of protesters during the third wave, and the increase in creative interactions this enabled.

By continuing to organise successful protests, many of them producing tangible results, new activists were able to overcome their fear of protesting. El-Hamalawy reported frequently hearing strikers say: 'We were encouraged to move after we heard of Mahalla.' Similarly, Shawky Solyman, the Kafr Dawar strike leader, said he was not afraid because 'we saw our peers striking in other companies and nothing happened to them' (both quoted in N. Aly 2011: 48).

One of the reasons so many were drawn into the protests was the fact that, at the start of this wave, the protests were not immediately suppressed and produced visible results. For much of 2007, the police, though present in large numbers, did not employ the type of violence routinely employed against pro-democracy, pro-Muslim Brotherhood or anti-Iraq war protests (Beinin and el-Hamalawy 2007; Beinin 2011b). Moreover, many of the strikes of 2006–2007 resulted in concessions from the government.

When the government's response became more heavy-handed, the protest wave had already gained momentum; rather than deterring, it galvanised people. In this, the protests followed a pattern familiar from social movement studies; when repression is applied reactively, mid-protest wave, when a protest dynamic has already been established and protest organisations have both mushroomed and gained organisational experience, and when such repression is indiscriminate in the people it targets, it tends to increase rather than deter protest (Hafez and Wiktorowicz 2004: 67–71).

The April 2008 Mahalla protests provide a poignant illustration of the role played by security forces in mobilising protesters. The beating of the old woman described above brought people out on to the streets. The teargas collecting in the narrow streets forced people out of their houses. The mass arrests triggered a demonstration the following day, calling for the release of the arrested.

In the same way, the arrest of Esraa Abd al-Fattah provided an immediate focus for the newly created Facebook group. April 6 followers replaced their profile pictures with a photo of Esraa with 'Free Esraa' written underneath. A member of April 6 heckled the prime minister at a meeting at Cairo University, calling for Esraa's release, and when Esraa was freed, it was shown live on television (Shapiro 2009), turning an otherwise relatively small organisation into a media sensation.

Equally importantly, the protests proved that the police were not all-powerful. Many of the activists who were arrested returned to activism as soon as they had been released. In Mahalla, protesters showed that they could beat back the police and remain in control of the square. Just as Kefaya had broken the taboo of criticising the president, the workers' wave helped tens of thousands of workers and non-activist citizens to overcome their fear.

In this, the protesters were helped by the media coverage that their protests received. As Nouran Aly (2011: 54), a young diplomat and participant-observer, concluded in her analysis of the decade leading up to the uprising:

Regardless of the results, images aired on TV of Mahalla confrontations, showing people fighting the retreating security forces and damaging Mubarak's pictures, deeply influenced Egypt's collective consciousness. These footages were more influential than any other framing processes undertaken by any change movement.

Gamal Eid (Interview 2011), director of the Arabic Network for Human Rights Information, similarly noted that the image that had become most famous was that of Mubarak's poster being torn down during the Mahalla strike.

In many ways, the 6 April strike was a precursor to the 2011 uprising. Like 2011, it involved a cross-section of workers, middle-class activists, students and housewives, and mobilised large numbers of people with no prior protest experience. As in 2011, reformists among the Muslim Brotherhood's youth had sought and eventually gained permission from their leadership to join the strike, a tradition they were to uphold during every subsequent anniversary of the strike (Wickham 2013: 157). Similar to 2011, the demonstrations involved the occupation of a city's main square—Mahalla, rather than Cairo— and they were directed at the Mubarak regime, rather than simply the workers' employers. Moreover, in many activists' minds the two events are linked. In the words of A. Imam, 'What happened in 25 January is an exact replication of what happened in Mahalla on 6 April [2008]' (quoted in N. Aly 2011: 54), although others downplayed this linkage (e.g. N. Mansour, Interview 2011).

A brief reflection on the differences between the two events can help to explain why the latter was so much more successful. The biggest difference between Mahalla 2008 and January 2011 was the geographical limitation of the demonstrations. In 2008, despite calls for a national strike, the protests were largely limited to Mahalla. Activists claimed that people had observed a nationwide strike, and many did indeed wear black, as requested. However, it is unclear whether people stayed at home out of solidarity or out of 'fear of getting caught in the crossfire between protesters and police' (*New York Times* 2008). Moreover, because the activists had called on people outside Mahalla to stay at home, they had scored an own goal, as they could neither prove the extent of their support, nor mount pressure on the regime by occupying public space (Chapter 7). Both the pro-democracy and workers' movements lacked experienced, nationally integrated networks (Beinin and el-Hamalawy 2007) able to stage nationwide street protests; the one opposition group which had such a capacity, the Muslim Brotherhood, kept itself out of the confrontation. This allowed the regime to focus all their attention on Mahalla and send in reinforcements, in sharp contrast to 2011, when security forces were stretched to breaking point by the spread of the protests. As A. Imam reflects, 'the only difference [between 2008 and 2011] was that on 6 April Mahalla was the only city challenging Mubarak; no demonstrations took place in other cities in Egypt. Mahalla people felt that Egypt let them down' (quoted in N. Aly 2011: 54). Strikingly, it was only in early 2010 that al-Masry al-Youm began to describe protests as 'nationwide' in our 2008–2010 survey of large protests, suggesting a scale shift between 2008 and 2010 (Appendix).

In 2008, the pool of seasoned, politicised activists was still relatively small. The workers' protests had succeeded in mobilising new strata of society, but most had not become seasoned activists. The middle classes, moreover, were still predominantly politically quietist. There was no credible alternative to Mubarak to rally around, such as ElBaradei. Facebook was still a relatively new phenomenon in Egypt, Twitter was still in its infancy in the Middle East,[7] and no equivalent to Khaled Said's murder had yet occurred to galvanise middle-class youths. There had been a number of well-publicised cases of police abuse. But none had resonated with the middle classes in the way that Khaled Said's death would, partly because as a mobilising tool Facebook was still in its infancy, but primarily because the abuses had involved the poor.

By 2008, moreover, the pro-democracy movement had run out of steam. It had failed to overturn the constitutional amendment that facilitated Gamal Mubarak's rise to power. Though the Muslim Brotherhood had secured an unprecedented eighty-eight seats in the 2005 election, the elections had been fraudulent and had returned a largely compliant parliament. Unlike in 2011, these defeats had led many to believe that change was unlikely to occur in the short term. There was no imminent presidential election to mobilise around, and the Brotherhood had withdrawn itself from political protests, focusing instead on *da'wa* and institutional politics for fear of reprisals and because its leadership was now in the hands of a risk-averse old guard. In short, because Mahalla occurred during the end phase of this particular pro-democracy wave, rather than during its ascendancy, it was far less likely to ignite a nationwide uprising.

While the workers continued to mount strikes throughout 2008 and 2009, their demands lost much of their overtly political edge. Strike leaders still recognised the inherent linkage between economic and political grievances, but the strikes limited their focus to economic and industrial demands (Said 2009). The pro-democracy movement, meanwhile, largely absented itself from these disputes, illustrating how fragile the links between the middle-class and workers' movements were. Groups such as the April 6 Youth Movement continued to call for an increase in the minimum wage on each subsequent anniversary of

April 6, in addition to calling for a new constitution. But between mid-2008 and early 2010, the pro-democracy movement only succeeded in mobilising small numbers, and much of the focus of activists was on regional events, such as the fate of Gaza. The Brotherhood in particular played a seminal role in organising demonstrations which protested against Israel's 2008–2009 invasion of Gaza, mobilising over 300,000 people throughout January 2009. While these protests kept the protest culture alive, they were ad hoc and reactive, and did not link back in a sustained way to the pro-democracy or workers' sectors (although members of these sectors would have participated). The regime's heavy-handed response to these protests, moreover, reinforced the risk-averse attitude of the Brotherhood's leadership, thus delaying a full return of the Brotherhood to the protest scene. Neither the Brotherhood nor the pro-democracy movement more broadly were wholly absent. In 2008, leaving aside Palestinian solidarity protests, twenty-nine of the 151 protests involving over 500 people (as reported in *al-Masry al-Youm*) concerned political issues or police abuse. In 2009, this number dropped to ten out of 129 (with only two on political issues).

However, the main locus of activism between 2006 and 2009 lay with the workers, who succeeded in mobilising substantially more people than either the anti-Iraq war protests or the pro-democracy movement had done. But because the links between them and the pro-democracy movement were limited, and because there were no sufficiently significant domestic political events to rally around, the ongoing workers' struggle failed to restart a sustained pro-democracy protest wave. It helped to maintain and promote a protest culture, but the trigger for the fourth wave had to come from elsewhere.

Wave IV: ElBaradei, Khaled Said, Elections and the Alexandria Bombing (2010–2011)

The fourth wave of protests began in earnest with the announcement by Mohammed ElBaradei—Nobel laureate and former head of the International Atomic Energy Agency (IAEA)—that he would stand for president in 2011. ElBaradei and his National Association for Change (NAC) served to bring together not just the existing pro-democracy organisations but a whole range of people with no history of activism. He was independent, with a track record of organisational competence, and perceived as being neither ideological nor autocratic. His international standing drew in members of the elite, many of whom had hitherto remained on the sidelines.

Like Kefaya before him, ElBaradei's campaign brought together members of the Muslim Brotherhood, the Communist Party, the liberal Ghad Party and the Democratic Front Party, among others. It also drew in the numerous youth groups, chief among them the April 6 Youth Movement. In addition, intellectuals of international fame, such as Alaa al-Aswani, flocked to his banner, as did company owners and IT specialists such as Khaled Haal (owner of an IT company which designed ElBaradei's website and online signature campaign) and Wael Ghonim (who would become one of the founders of the 'We Are All Khaled Said' Facebook page). As one NAC volunteer observed, 'We received more than 5000 curricula vitae, among these were PhD holders from world top universities and many others with impressive academic and professional backgrounds, they all wanted to see ElBaradei leading the change in Egypt' (A. Imam quoted in N. Aly 2011: 60). ElBaradei's campaign thus succeeded in uniting (and reinvigorating) a broader constituency than any group before. In the words of Khalil Saeed (Interview 2011), from the Democratic Front Party:

This was the first time lots of people from the opposition ... intellectuals, people who all the time fought each other ... all gathered because they trusted the man, his integrity, his· credibility. In 2009, there was nothing on the street, really, April 6 notwithstanding. ElBaradei changed this.

The one key oppositional sector which did not wholeheartedly join ElBaradei's campaign was the workers' movement (although one could say the same about the Muslim Brotherhood, which parted ways with ElBaradei over his election boycott). While workers' leaders supported ElBaradei's calls for political change, they insisted that economic change and workers' concerns were equally important, yet these were absent from ElBaradei's campaign (H. Fouad 2010). Some leftist leaders did publicly support ElBaradei (ElBaradei Association for Change 2010), but he did not succeed in building sufficiently strong bridges with the workers to make his campaign genuinely cross-class. Nevertheless, the continued mobilisation of the workers' movement, augmented by neighbourhood protests—in 2010 there were an estimated 584 industrial disputes (Abdalla 2012: 2), and of the 130 protest events reported in *al-Masry al-Youm* involving over 500 people, fifty-six concerned economic, industrial or neighbourhood issues (Appendix)—was pivotal in sustaining a protest culture among Egypt's lower classes, raising the susceptibility of thousands of non-activist Egyptians to the eventual call to revolution in January 2011 (the Brotherhood was similarly pivotal in mobilising the lower classes).

Calls for ElBaradei to stand for president had begun in August 2009, with the founding of the Facebook page 'El-Baradei Ra'isan' [ElBaradei for President]. By 19 February 2010, the date of ElBaradei's return to Egypt, the page 'had 65,775 followers and was growing at up to 2000 members per day' (N. Aly 2011: 59). When ElBaradei arrived, a crowd of over 1,000 (some put it at 4,000) (I. El-Amrani paraphrased in N. Aly 2011: 59) awaited him at the airport, despite a heavy police presence, roadblocks and security warnings to stay away (BBC 2010a).

The way the campaign was run showed the activist experience of those behind it, gained during preceding protest waves. According to one volunteer:

The campaign distributed booklets that helped people to participate in the event at minimum risk. For example, the booklets instructed people to go to the airport in groups not exceeding two or three persons, to take different designated routes and public transport, and to show no banners or flags on the way. (A. Imam quoted in N. Aly 2011: 60)

Another blogger noted, 'Versed in activist training seminars, [the campaign] trained 120 people to manage today's gathering at Cairo Airport. Each person will be responsible for maintaining [order], leading the welcoming committee, and organizing attendance' (El-Amrani quoted in N. Aly 2011: 59).

ElBaradei's chief contribution was to reignite hope that things could change. Here, finally, was a credible alternative to Mubarak, who had the ability to attract 1 million signatures for a manifesto for change (although this was with the considerable help of the Muslim Brotherhood, who were responsible for over at least half of these signatures) (al-Masry al-Youm 2011e, 2010b). Unlike the opposition candidates who had been 'allowed' to challenge the incumbent president in 2005, ElBaradei had no history in Egyptian politics under Mubarak and thus no local political baggage.

What gave ElBaradei's campaign added impetus was the realisation that if the campaign did not succeed, Egypt would be saddled with yet another autocrat, Gamal Mubarak. Although it was a punishable offence to question Mubarak's health, it had become obvious that he would not be able to stand for another term. In 2008, there were rumours that he had been at death's door and it was widely believed that Gamal would run for president in 2011 (though this was never officially confirmed) (*Daily News Egypt* 2010; *Washington Times* 2010). For many activists, this was the moment of truth: either they succeeded in preventing Gamal from running, or they had to put up with another thirty years of dictatorship. ElBaradei's drawing power was thus enhanced by the political context of the time.

However, ElBaradei was but one factor. What turned this initial wave of enthusiasm into a full-fledged protest wave was a series of subsequent events that came in rapid succession, affecting different sections of society, creating a momentum that brought ever more people into activism.

Less than seven weeks after ElBaradei's arrival came the anniversary of the April 2008 strike. A demonstration, planned by the April 6 Movement, was cut down brutally by the police (Ziada 2010). ElBaradei, typically, stayed away, but Ayman Nur, leader of the Ghad Party and presidential candidate in 2005, did join, despite the risk of police brutality. The event showed the youth supporting ElBaradei that their presidential candidate was not a natural protester and that, if protests were the way forward, they had to lead.

Exactly two months later, on 6 June 2010, a young middle-class man by the name of Khaled Said was pulled out of an internet café in Alexandria and brutally beaten to death by two policemen. The event sent shockwaves through the blogosphere, and in particular through the middle-class Facebookers and Twitterati. The details of his death and the motives of the policemen killing him were hotly disputed, ranging from (official) claims that he had died after swallowing a pack of marijuana (a story which did not fit the evidence) to (opposition) claims that he had video footage of two policemen 'dividing up the spoils of a drugs haul' (Elshaheed.co.uk n.d.; Schenker 2010; *al-Masry al-Youm* 2010a). Whatever the truth, his violent death, broadcast graphically through Facebook, blogs and Twitter, came to symbolise the predicament of all Egyptians. 'We Are All Khaled Said,' stated the website created by Wael Ghonim to commemorate Said and protest against torture and police brutality: 'Khaled … A story of many Egyptians' (Elshaheed.co.uk n.d.). Others called him 'everyman', with the implication that 'it could have been them' (*al-Masry al-Youm* 2011g).

This same sentiment was expressed in all our interviews: Khaled was like us; if he could be murdered for no apparent reason, none of us are safe. He was not a hard-core activist, and had lived his life in much the same way as other middle-class youths. While such police brutality was common in Egypt, Said's death struck a chord like no other before. 'Many of my friends,' Sally Samer (Interview 2011), a human rights activist, told us, 'well-educated people, started talking about being victims of such abuse. They were worried about their children. Everyone now began to focus on police brutality.' Before Said, there had been numerous instances of reported police brutality, but most involved members of the lower classes, Islamists or Bedouin. One of the most publicised incidents concerned the sodomising of micro-bus driver Emad al-Kebeer by policemen in 2007, evidence of which surfaced when the video the policemen took of themselves was posted on the internet (*al-Masry al-Youm* 2011f). But Kebeer was a micro-bus driver, and not middle class. Gamal (Interview 2011), a young diplomat, summed it up, saying: 'Police brutality was commonplace. The new thing about Khaled Said was that he somehow looked like us: people from the middle class who used the Internet, Facebook, young businessmen who went abroad. He was not an Islamist or a jihadist or a Bedouin.'[8]

For Samer's friends, 'the fact that [Said] was middle class was shocking ... If the attacked persons are poor, ... it cannot happen to me. Now, it can happen to me' (Samer, Interview 2011). Salah, the former April 6 leader (Interview 2011), similarly noted that the death of Said 'made [middle-class] people realise: we are not safe anymore. This is no longer about keeping quiet; it is no longer safe.'

Said's death served simultaneously to bridge, amplify and extend people's injustice frames. His death amplified feelings people had already harboured as a result of police harassment and growing alienation from the regime (Chapter 3). It brought together disparate experiences in one 'injustice frame', symbolising all that was wrong with Egypt. For many, it also served to extend their sense of injustice at police brutality into a belief that the regime had to change. The way 'We Are All Khaled Said' summarised the significance of his death sums up how it became both a symbol of what was wrong and a rallying cry to right it:

Khaled has become the symbol for many Egyptians who dream to see their country free of brutality, torture and ill treatment. Many young Egyptians are now fed up with the inhuman treatment they face on a daily basis in streets, police stations and everywhere. Egyptians want to see an end to all violence committed by any Egyptian Policeman. Egyptians are aspiring to the day when Egypt has its freedom and dignity back, the day when the current 30 years long emergency martial law ends and when Egyptians can freely elect their true representatives. (Elshaheed.co.uk n.d.)

Said's death, and the way it went viral, provided a catalyst for thousands with no history of political activism to become involved. A series of silent vigils were held to commemorate Said and protest against police brutality, each attracting thousands (*Al-Ahram Weekly* 2010; El-Amine and Henaway 2011). By January 2011, the pool of people with protest experience and a sense of belonging to a protest movement had grown substantially. This rapid mobilisation of hitherto quietist citizens did not happen wholly spontaneously (Chapter 5). As Ghonim describes in his autobiography, he and his co-administrator consciously devised protest events to draw 'Facebook followers' gradually into the struggle by helping them to overcome fear and build up a protest identity. Such developments were stimulated through anything from encouraging said 'followers' to identify themselves online as protesters and uploading photo and video footage, to asking them to participate in silent vigils and, ultimately, street protests.

The third significant event was the general election in November 2010. The election had been a central focus for ElBaradei's campaign—six of his National Association for Change's seven demands focused directly on making the elections freer and fairer, and the seventh, ending the state of emergency, was directed at creating an environment in which free and fair elections could take place. Most of the members of the NAC called for a boycott of the elections, with the notable exception of the Muslim Brotherhood, which sought to maintain its control of the eighty-eight seats it had won in the 2005 election. The pre-election period was highly charged, fuelling further protests and crackdowns. When the elections turned out to have been blatantly fraudulent, with police arresting opposition candidates, preventing voters from voting and intimidating civil society observers, the opposition organised further protests, although neither pre- nor post-election protests drew more than a few hundred activists at a time (Reuters 2010). Yet, despite their small size, these gatherings kept the protest culture alive, and, crucially, signalled to walkers-by and bystanders that this was the case (Abdel-Rahman, Interview 2011; Gamal, Interview 2011). Furthermore, the very fact that the elections were so blatantly fixed, with only fourteen out of 508 seats not affiliated to the ruling NDP, gave already active activists such as Samer (Interview 2011) the determination to step up their activism.

The fraudulent nature of the elections also convinced those parties that had participated of the futility of seeking reform through existing institutional means, uniting the otherwise fractured opposition. After the Brotherhood learned that it had lost all eighty-eight seats, it met with ElBaradei's NAC, Kefaya, the Wafd Party and the Democratic Front Party to 'coordinate strategy' and set up a 'parallel parliament' (Wickham 2013: 150). While the Brotherhood leadership remained wary of the secular protest networks, the 2010 election created the conditions for a rapprochement that would facilitate the eventual joining of forces in January 2011. Internally, moreover, the Brotherhood's decision to participate in the elections had exacerbated tensions between the conservative, risk-averse leadership and the reformists within the movement (Wickham 2013: 146–9, 142). Already disillusioned by the older leadership's attempts at manipulating internal elections and side-lining reformists in 2009, those in favour of reform had become further alienated, thus increasing the incentive to look outside the movement for allies. Although this was but a small and mostly urban-based group, it was members from this cohort that joined the secular protest networks in January 2011, providing a crucial bridge between the Brotherhood's leadership and the protest leadership.

The fourth galvanising event was the bombing of a church in Alexandria on 1 January 2011. The bombing, killing twenty-three and wounding nearly 100, came at a time of increasing sectarian tensions in the region, and triggered days of protests (*New York Times* 2011a; Reuters 2011). There is much that could be said about ongoing sectarian tensions, cross-sectarian collaboration and the place of Christians in Egypt. But what concerns us here is the way the bombing contributed to the overall protest environment. Although there were some incidents between Muslims and Christians, most of the clashes took place between furious Christians, joined by fellow Muslims, and the police. Almost immediately, Christians began to accuse the government of failing to protect them and turned their anger on the government. Crowds chanted 'Down with Mubarak' and 'Down with the military state.' A protester articulated what many apparently felt: 'The government is the reason this happened … They are the terrorists who attack us every day' (*New York Times* 2011a).

Sectarian tensions were held at bay by slogans such as 'Egyptians are one people' and 'Citizenship is the way out from the slide into sectarianism', and by placards bearing the Crescent and Cross logo that would become famous during the 2011 revolution (*New York Times* 2011a; *Elaph* 2011). While many of the protests involved predominantly Coptic Christians, there were key events including both Muslims and Christians, presaging the emphasis on Muslim–Christian unity during the January 2011 uprising. Many of the opposition leaders joined these protests, and thousands joined Copts in church services, pledging to act as 'human shields' against further attacks. According to AhramOnline (2011):

In the days following the brutal attack on Saints Church in Alexandria ... solidarity between Muslims and Copts has seen an unprecedented peak. Millions of Egyptians changed their Facebook profile pictures to the image of a cross within a crescent—the symbol of an "Egypt for All". Around the city, banners went up calling for unity, and depicting mosques and churches, crosses and crescents, together as one.

The pro-democracy movement rallied around the Christians and was galvanised by the attacks. 'We Are All Khaled Said', for instance, organised a vigil on 7 January 2011 to commemorate the victims of the attack. When Khalil Saeed (Interview 2011) took his son to the vigil, he recalls linking the church bombing to the death of Said: 'This is not just for Khaled, but also for the souls of the people killed in the Church.' April 6 and others helped to organise protests in the Christian neighbourhood of Shobra (*al-Masry al-Youm* 2011a).

Of particular interest to our overall analysis is that some of the demonstrations utilised tactics that were to be used during the January 25 revolution, indicating both the linkages between the Christian protests and the broader pro-democracy movement, and the way the Alexandria bombing protests set the scene for the larger protests only weeks after. Two protests are of particular interest: one in Shobra, a Cairo quarter not far from Tahrir Square, the other in front of the Ministry of the Interior, just off Tahrir Square. It was here that some of the new swarming and flash mob tactics, which April 6 and others had experimented with, were honed further and carried out on a mass scale (Chapter 5).

The 2010 protest wave was significant in a number of ways. Just as the previous waves had mobilised additional sectors of society, this wave's major contribution was to mobilise, or at least make politically aware, a significant section of the middle classes. The Palestinian solidarity and pro-democracy movements had been predominantly middle class (although the Brotherhood's election protests featured lower-class cadres as well), but these movements encompassed only a small, dedicated cadre of activists. The workers' movement had succeeded in mobilising hundreds of thousands over the period 2006–2009, but these were predominantly drawn from the working class (although from 2008 onwards, an increasing number of white-collar workers became involved). ElBaradei's contribution was to awaken a sizeable section of the middle class, as evidenced by the 1 million signatures his campaign gathered, with the help of the Brotherhood, for his demands for political reform. The death of Khaled Said then shocked the middle class, and in particular middle-class youth, into action. The protests against the 2010 election and the Alexandria bombing kept this mobilisation alive.

Second, the political protests of 2010 served both to mobilise Egyptians abroad and to increase links between the Egyptian protest movement and international movements. ElBaradei's campaign in particular galvanised diaspora Egyptians, but so did Said's death and the fraudulent 2010 elections. Samer (Interview 2011), for instance, recounted:

I have always been a human rights activist but I used to think politics was not an option. [Once ElBaradei came on to the scene], I became a member of the National Association for Change in London. ElBaradei boiled existing demands down to seven easily understandable demands. ... Egyptians abroad started to mobilise. ...

Egyptians abroad had always been marginalised. The only ones active [abroad] were the Muslim Brotherhood. ElBaradei galvanised us, so that we started fundraising, organising a Khaled Said event under Marble Arch in London. ... [The 2010 elections were a further factor as they were too blatantly fraudulent.] I came back not because I was called but because I felt there was activism. I did not believe that a revolution was about to happen ... but I wanted to be part of what was happening ... I wanted to be part of the ElBaradei campaign.

Omar Ashour (2010), an Egyptian academic in the UK, similarly noted that 'diaspora Egyptians are responding in a way they never have before to ElBaradei's message to them 'if you don't act and participate now, then do not complain tomorrow!' One of the reasons for this support was, following Ashour, the fact that:

ElBaradei and diaspora Egyptians understand each other. When ElBaradei speaks about "socialist democracy," for example, expatriate Egyptians do not conflate it with Nasser's Arab Socialism (now associated with demagoguery, military dictatorship, and economic failure). Rather, Egyptians who have lived in the United Kingdom, Canada, Austria, and Scandinavia understand well what ElBaradei means: a representative democracy, a social justice system, and a well-developed welfare state.

ElBaradei's demand to extend the right to vote to Egyptians living abroad also helped. In creating these transnational linkages and through targeted internet campaigns, the ElBaradei campaign prepared the ground for numerous ex-pats returning in January 2011 to join, support and strengthen the revolution, and facilitate mobilising support for the revolution abroad (a crucial resource) (Aljazeera 2011d).[9]

Parallel to this, the various protest networks intensified their links with international protest groups during 2009–2010, exchanging tactical innovations. April 6 activists went to Serbia to learn from the student movement Otpor! [Resistance] (Maher, Interview 2011; Fouad, Interview 2011; *New York Times* 2011e). They visited the United States to improve their technological skills, while a delegation from the Kenyan NGO Ushahidi visited Cairo to teach April 6 how to enhance their ability to report police abuse using mobile phones (Ishani 2011). In January 2010, Egyptian activists linked up with international activists coming to Egypt to protest against Israel's Gaza blockade, and discussed the tactic of 'flash mobs', which proved to be pivotal in outmanoeuvring the police on 25 January 2011 (Maher, Interview 2011). None of this is to deny that this was an Egyptian revolution, driven by local Egyptians, using tactics rooted in local dynamics. However, from a social movement theory perspective, the intensification of these transnational linkages and the resources this brought in terms of tactics and support is significant as it contributed to tipping the scales, however subtly, in favour of the protesters.

Third, this protest wave helped to create such a protest momentum that observers began to talk of an 'autumn of fury' (a reference to the period that led to Sadat's assassination). Zeinobia, a prominent blogger, wrote in October 2010: 'Strangely it is like history repeating in its own way and I wonder if the climax that we will witness Inshallah sooner or later is the end of a regime that shows all signs of weakness and fragility' (quoted in El-Amine and Henaway 2011). Hossam el-Hamalawy commented not long after on his much-read 3arabawy blog: 'No one knows when the explosion is going to happen, but it seems everyone I meet or bump into today feel[s] it's inevitable.' He reported a taxi driver saying: 'There will be another bread initfada [*sic*], like that of 1977. And this time we will burn the country down. We will not burn the cars, buses or shops. These are ours. No. We will burn them. We will burn this government. We will burn down the police stations.' (quoted in El-Amine and Henaway 2011)

By the end of 2010, *al-Masry al-Youm* had reported 130 protest events involving more than 500 people (not including industrial disputes, estimated at 584 for 2010 (Abdalla 2012: 2), or the many smaller protests). Of these, forty-seven focused on electoral reform, regime change or police abuse.[10] By contrast, although 2009 saw an equal number of large-scale protests (129), only ten focused on political issues, with the bulk revolving around economic/industrial (seventy-one) or regional issues (thirty-five). While the protests in 2010 were more sporadic, concentrated as they were around specific events, and thus less continuous than the economic, industrial and neighbourhood disputes of 2009 (Figure 2.3), they were far more visible, and thus had a greater impact on public debate. Moreover, if we discount the over 350,000 demonstrators mobilised against Israel's 2008–2009 invasion of Gaza during January–February 2009, as these protests did not feed into the other protests in a sustained way except through legitimising protest and giving people protest experience, the total (rough) estimate of protesters in 2009 was 182,850, compared to 257,050 in 2010, which indicated a 40 per cent increase (based on the estimates given in *al-Masry al-Youm*; the figure for 2008 was 271,450).Against an estimated 8,800 people participating in political and anti-police

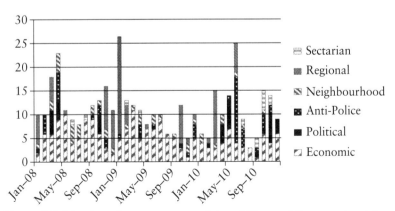

Figure 2.3: Number of protests reported by *al-Masry al-Youm* as involving over 500 people by category 2008–2010 (Appendix).

protests during 2009, a reported 77,300 did so in 2010, or nearly a tenfold increase (Appendix).[11]

None of the previous waves had produced this level of feverish expectation. In part, this was the result of the rapid confluence of events, each feeding into the next, and the success of this wave in broadening the protest pool. A key contribution of both ElBaradei's campaign and the series of vigils commemorating Said's death was that they had helped thousands of non-activists to overcome their fear of police brutality and retribution (Chapter 6). This in turn was facilitated by the fact that the three previous waves, in particular the last two, had served to normalise protest as a legitimate activity.

In 2010, moreover, the pro-democracy and workers' protest sectors were peaking together (see Figures 2.4–6 and Appendix). In the previous two waves, either the pro-democracy or the workers' movement had peaked, with the other playing a more limited role. In 2010, as the pro-democracy movement gained momentum, the workers' movement

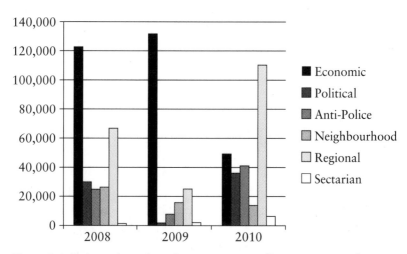

Figure 2.4: Estimated number of protesters annually per category of protest in protests numbering 500 or more, as reported in *al-Masry al-Youm* (Arabic) (2008–2010), excluding the Gaza protests of January–February 2009 (numbering 356,500). This chart does not include all of the 609, 700 and 584 strikes reported by Abdalla (2012: 2) for the years 2008, 2009 and 2010, unless they were reported as protest events by *al-Masry al-Youm*.

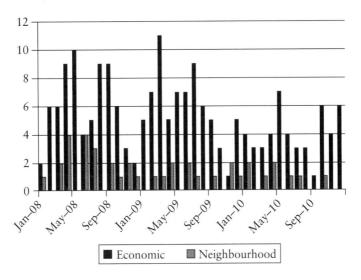

Figure 2.5: Number of protests reported by *al-Masry al-Youm* as involving over 500 people concerning economic/industrial or neighbourhood/local issues (Appendix).

continued full throttle, albeit on a parallel track. In addition, the latter had spurned a neighbourhood protest sector, which similarly continued to be active throughout 2010 (Figure 2.5). Although the lack of integration between the sectors limited what either could achieve during 2010, the heightened state of mobilisation across both facilitated mobilisation in January 2011. In addition, protests focusing on regional issues continued through the first half of the year, while sectarian tensions gave rise to protests in the second half. While neither were directed against the regime per se, both sets of protests fed into a general sense of unrest and a heightened level of mobilisation, particularly when they involved multiple networks.

In 2010, dissatisfaction with the regime was furthermore heightened by the confluence of a host of structural strains (Chapters 3–4). Food prices were rising again by the end of 2010, reaching levels not seen since April 2008 (the Mahalla strike). Unemployment was up, especially for university graduates, while poverty was on the increase. Inflation had reached 15 per cent by 2009. The regime's standing was low, particularly following the 2010 elections, while police brutality was becoming more indiscriminate, intense and exposed. Elite fissures had become more pronounced in the face of Gamal's expected succession in 2011. Thus even without the fall of Ben Ali in Tunisia, Egypt was approaching a near-perfect storm.

In addition, by 2010 the number of networks had reached a critical mass, able to sustain a prolonged protest wave (although such an argument can typically only be made retrospectively). Not only had the number and size of groups expanded, but second-order umbrella groups had sprung up, linking existing organisations. The Front to Defend Egypt's Protesters, for instance, grew out of the links between human rights NGOs such as the Egyptian Center for Economic and Political Rights, pro-democracy protesters and workers, and became a group in its own right, present at all protests from 2008 to offer legal services (Samer, Interview 2011; N. Mansour, Interview 2011). ElBaradei's National Association for Change was similarly a second-order umbrella organisation, linking existing groups such as the Democratic Front Party, April 6 and (elements of) the Brotherhood. More than Kefaya, which primarily brought individuals together from across the political spectrum, the NAC united groups in a loose organisational framework. The tentative links between April 6 and some of the Brotherhood youth, themselves facilitated by the earlier cross-partisan alliances in the Free Student Union and during the pro-Palestinian protests, had deepened, as expressed in the coming together on each subsequent anniversary of the 6 April strike. These links in turn reinforced relations between reformist elements among the Muslim Brothers and the NAC, and, after the elections, between the Brotherhood leadership, the NAC and the Democratic Front Party. The fact that the reformist Brotherhood youth was 'in regular contact with other members of their generation through social networking sites' (Wickham 2013: 141) and that Brotherhood bloggers shared the blogosphere with secular bloggers facilitated these tentative collaborations.

Fourth, the 2010 protest wave subtly changed the framing of the protests. It continued to play a role in bridging injustice frames, amplifying latent grievances and transforming quietist into activist frames, as previous campaigns had done, mobilising hitherto un-mobilised 'sentient pools'. But, as a late-riser in the decade-long waves of contention, much of the ground had already been prepared by early risers such as Kefaya (Lynch 2011: 304–5; N. Aly 2011: 62). Its main contribution was in amplifying the theme of police brutality, and bridging this to other key mobilisatory themes.

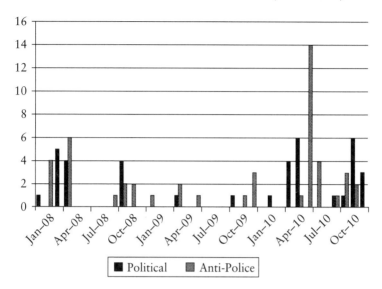

Figure 2.6: Number of protests reported by *al-Masry al-Youm* as involving over 500 people concerning political or anti-police issues (Appendix).

Where previous waves had focused, consecutively, on the regional situation, regime change and constitutional reform, and workers' rights, the overarching theme of political protests in 2010 became police brutality and an end to emergency law, although the other themes continued to be salient.

Police brutality had featured in all three previous protest waves and numerous protests were explicitly framed as protests against police brutality or arrests (see earlier charts). In 2007, for instance, eighteen of the eighty-seven events featuring over 100 protesters (not counting the 614 industrial protests) were protesting police brutality, arrests, house demolitions or student expulsions. But that number was dwarfed by the twenty-five demonstrations focusing on political reform (broadly conceived) and the twenty-five protests against economic conditions. In 2010, the theme of police brutality came to dominate among the non-industrial protesters (Figure 2.6); twenty-five of the 130 large-scale demonstrations reported in *al-Masry al-Youm*—or 19 per cent—were explicitly about police abuse or arrests, against 10 per cent and 6 per cent in 2008 and 2009 respectively. In addition to a demonstration protesting emergency law, the fourteen protests against the parliamentary elections also concerned police violence.

The 'We Are All Khaled Said' movement was triggered directly by police brutality. Three of ElBaradei's seven demands—'1. Ending the state of emergency; 2. The empowerment of the Egyptian judiciary to supervise the full electoral process; 3. Monitoring of the elections by local and international civil society organizations' (Ikhwanweb 2010a)—were concerned with police brutality and the abuses emergency law allowed.

One of the reasons that police brutality and emergency law became a central frame in 2010 was that 'state of emergency powers' were renewed for a further two years in May 2010. The increase in police violence during 2010 augmented its status as a central theme, as the regime sought to suppress the increasingly restive opposition, deepening the unifying experience among the different protest sectors, from pro-democracy activists, through workers and neighbourhood protesters to football supporters.[12]

The effect of police brutality becoming the overarching theme of the protests was that, apart from unifying different protest sectors, it increased the resonance between activists and the broader population. Police brutality was not abstract like regime change or constitutional reform, and ending it was something that many could sign up to. Many had experienced police brutality first-hand, as a result of policing practices becoming more indiscriminate and brutal, particularly from 2005 onwards (Chapter 3). Because the police were seen to be targeting everyone, including the law-abiding middle and lower classes, activists were able to argue that every citizen was at risk already, and that the situation had reached a point of no return. If you were at risk regardless of whether you demonstrated, and if you could be persuaded that the status quo was no longer tenable, the decision to go out and demonstrate would seem less risky.

The main framing challenge facing the Egyptian protesters in 2010 was to lower people's perception of risk, as popular dissatisfaction with the regime was already widespread (one of the preconditions for revolution). The police's indiscriminateness and the success of the protesters' mobilisation combined to do just that. Although the final trigger for the January uprising was the Tunisian revolution, it is no coincidence that the first protest was scheduled for Police Day, and framed primarily as a protest against police abuse. A rally against police brutality had already been on the books since December (Maher, Interview 2011; *Newsweek* 2011a); after Tunisia, it turned into what one analyst described as 'a mass rally against police brutality' (Naeem 2011).

Fifth, the 2010 wave further consolidated Facebook, Twitter, blogs and mobile phones as central mobilisatory tools. The April 6 Facebook page continued to have around 78,000 members, and was 'considered the most active' of the activist Facebook pages (Al-Shorfa.com 2010). The ElBaradei for President Facebook page had attracted some 240,000 members by May 2010, and its membership reportedly increased 'at a daily rate of around 5,000' (Al-Shorfa.com 2010). Within weeks of Khaled Said's death in June, 130,000 people had joined the 'We Are All Khaled Said' Facebook page. By January 2011, this number was approaching 380,000, and when it issued a call for a demonstration on 25 January 2011, 90,000 signed up within days (Daily Beast 2011; *New York Times* 2011b). The consolidation of Facebook as a key tool for the online activist community was facilitated by the fact that the number of Egyptians on Facebook had more than quintupled from 822,560 in December 2008 to 4,634,300 in December 2010 (Figure 2.2 above).

Twitter had likewise become a central mobilisatory tool.[13] Groups such as April 6 had been using it for some time, and when one of its members, Asmaa Mahfouz, went to protest the death-by-self-immolation of four Egyptians (in response to the self-immolation of Bouazizi in Tunisia the previous month) on 18 January 2011, her YouTube video condemning the low turnout went viral once it was advertised on Twitter (as well as on Facebook and numerous blogs) (Chitty 2011). Twitter was instrumental in securing the release of blogger Wael Abbas in June 2009 (New Tactics in Human Rights 2010). But Twitter came into its own in the lead-up to the 2010 elections, when it was used to pass on information, tactics, locations and warnings. It was particularly effective at alerting human rights organisations to arrests, enabling them to send lawyers to the relevant police station and securing the release of detainees before they were imprisoned and tortured (Ishani 2011).

A third technological contribution of this wave was the improved use of mobile phones to capture protests and police brutality. As Maryam Ishani (2011) records, Egyptian activists began seeking professional training in shooting high-quality video footage during demonstrations when they saw the poor quality of much of the footage coming out of the Iranian protests of 2009. 'Although compelling,' she writes, 'the images were often too shaky and confusing to be used by international media outlets, thus limiting their impact.' April 6 activists in particular received training from US and Kenyan NGOs, which was put to good use during the January 2011 uprising.

Facebook, video phones and Twitter played a central part in turning a tragedy such as Khaled Said's death into a mass protest episode. If reports claiming that Said had filmed policemen dividing up drugs are correct, the very fact that he had the tools to film such a scene and post it online was a catalyst in triggering this tragedy. His death went viral precisely because it was possible to broadcast pictures instantaneously, without government control, and because there was a vibrant internet community looking for, and spreading, information about police brutality. Many of those we interviewed commented that it was the graphic juxtaposition of the smiling, carefree face with the brutally deformed death mask that hit, and subsequently galvanised, them. *Al-Masry al-Youm* (2011g) similarly noted:

The image became iconic; soon it was everywhere, in the papers, online. The look was kind, with a cocked half-smile, a look of contentment. It had an ethereal quality to it, which might only have been seen retrospectively because all who saw it knew that he had died. The juxtaposition with the other image was shocking—the contorted grimace and the smashed-in face.

The first protests in Alexandria, which were met by further police brutality and filmed by phone, became themselves online triggers for subsequent action through the videos uploaded on Facebook (*al-Masry al-Youm* 2010a), while Facebook, blogs and Twitter were crucial in spreading the word about protests, locations and advice on how to avoid arrest (in this instance, the advice was to stand well apart, read the Qur'an or Bible and do not interact, so as not to fall foul of anti-congregation laws). None of this is to downplay the importance of offline mobilisation. Nor should we forget that previous shocking deaths that became triggers in social protests elsewhere had a similar galvanising effect, without the internet.[14] Nevertheless, Facebook, blogs and Twitter, and the way they were used by the opposition, proved to be significant in broadening awareness of both regime abuses and anti-regime protests, in widening the pool of protesters, in helping to create a collective protest identity and in organising protest events.

Sixth, as during the preceding waves, the 2010 wave saw significant tactical innovations. One such was the move away from stationary protests in front of symbolic buildings. The vigils organised by 'We Are All Khaled Said' were an important departure, as they made demonstrations more visible, baffled the police and lowered the fear threshold by lessening opportunities for direct confrontation. The long lines of people standing with their backs to the traffic, reading holy books, not interacting with each other were both highly visible and difficult to crack down on without losing face. They contributed to the general public's awareness of the protests (especially compared to the small huddles of protesters surrounded by police characteristic of previous protests), and showed that the police were not all-powerful.

Perhaps the most important innovation was the development of flash mobs. Flash mobs are usually associated with groups of people springing into action from different places within a seemingly random crowd, normally in the form of frivolous entertainment. When applied to politics, especially in authoritarian settings, information regarding where to assemble is usually kept secret until the last moment, and then disseminated at the last minute via text message or tweets. According to Maher (Interview 2011), the April 6 movement adopted this tactic from the international Palestinian solidarity activists who accompanied George Galloway to Egypt to protest against Israel's blockade of Gaza.

Flash mob tactics have been used extensively by the Global Justice Movement. The (in)famous 'Battle of Seattle' in November 1999 famously involved 'autonomous but internetworked squads of demonstrators protesting the meeting of the World Trade Organization [using] "swarming" tactics, mobile phones, websites, laptops, and PDAs' (Rheingold 2002: 158). Indeed, April 6 activists studied the film 'Battle in Seattle' to learn from the tactics used there (Maher, Interview 2011; Khalil Saeed, Interview 2011). According to Howard Rheingold (2002: 162):

[These] "swarming" strategies ... rely on many small units like the affinity groups in the Battle of Seattle. Individual members of each group remained dispersed until mobile communications drew them to converge on a specific location from all directions simultaneously, in coordination with other groups. Manila, Seattle, San Francisco, Senegal, and Britain were sites of nonviolent political swarming.

In the hands of April 6, the concept of flash mobs was translated into multiple small demonstrations, starting in Cairo's poorer quarters, where the streets were narrow and the police largely absent, then converging in one place (Maher, Interview 2011; Salah, Interview 2011;

Fouad, Interview 2011). This was in sharp contrast to the earlier practice of issuing a call for a demonstration on Facebook, broadcasting the time and place to the widest audience possible (including the police). It also differed by starting in narrow side streets, rather than the wide boulevards in front of key governmental buildings, where a crowd of 100 would look forlorn and the police could readily surround and dwarf the crowd. This tactical innovation was to prove pivotal to the success of the January 2011 protests (Chapter 5).

A second set of innovations evolved out of an already existing interest in non-violent tactics in groups such as April 6 and 'We Are All Khaled Said.' Building on their increasingly dense connections with transnational movements, activists sought advice on non-violent tactics abroad. They visited Serbia to learn from Otpor! They contacted the Qatar-based Academy for Change, an organisation of Egyptians living abroad, specialising in disseminating non-violent tactics of civil disobedience and received extensive training from the Academy in workshops held in Cairo (the organisers had links with Kefaya going back to 2005) (Stoner 2011). The tactics learned ranged from wearing newspapers under one's clothes to protect against police batons, to always moving in pairs, ensuring protests remain non-violent even in the face of violence, hugging policemen and using slogans to keep the crowds energised (Aljazeera 2011e). Crucially, as Wael Adel, one of the Academy's founders, noted:

Non-violent action is not just about non-violence, but also about joy and happiness ... The festive atmosphere was a key element to drawing the high numbers that Egypt had rarely seen. People felt safe so they came out. They saw in Tahrir what Egypt could possibly be in the future and they wanted to be part of this new Egypt. (quoted in Stoner 2011)

As with the flash mobs, the activists made these tactics their own, adapting them to local circumstances.

Concluding Thoughts

It is clear from Chapters 1 and 2 that the 2011 uprising did not come out of nowhere, but emerged from a decade of intense protest waves which had forged, and been forged by, activists in ever-widening protest networks. The revolt would have taken a very different path without these myriad networks and the experienced protest facilitators they had nurtured.

If we move away from the spectacular, and see the events of January 2011 not as a discrete episode, but as the continuation of a decade of protests, a different picture emerges. To be sure, there are ruptures with the preceding decade. The size of the protests dwarfed anything that had gone before. Apart from a few Brotherhood demonstrations involving more than 100,000 people, the masses had remained largely un-mobilised prior to 2011, and what set January 2011 apart was the sustained convergence of all protest sectors, including the until then not overtly political Ultras.

However, there are as many continuities as there are ruptures. The tactics used had for the most part been experimented with before. The networks providing the organisation behind the uprising were by and large those that had emerged during the preceding protest waves, and the linkages between them, which enabled a high-level of cooperation during the eighteen days, had been forged during the preceding decade. The core themes of regime change and an end to police brutality and emergency law were well rehearsed, as was the use of Facebook and Twitter to mobilise and spread information.

Each wave built on the previous ones, strengthening existing networks, extending network links and bringing in more sectors of society. We have already seen how the pro-Palestinian and anti-Iraq war protests prepared the ground for Kefaya and the various Movements for Change. The workers' movement, taking their cue from Kefaya in a context of increasingly difficult working conditions, took up the baton and instigated an unprecedented wave of industrial strikes, extending the protest culture to all employment sectors (including white-collar workers) and to neighbourhood disputes. By early 2010, hundreds of thousands of people had participated in wildcat strikes, sit-ins or demonstrations, and had overcome their fear of police brutality (even if they did not become activists). During this wave, the seeds were sown for cooperation between the workers' and pro-democracy movements, and the links between human rights NGOs and activists were strengthened.

The fourth wave built on these advances, deepening cross-ideological alliances, reinvigorating the activist networks and creating a unifying frame around police brutality. The arrival of ElBaradei, coupled with the death of Said and the subsequent creation of 'We Are All Khaled Said', significantly broadened the participation of the middle classes, which, together with the ongoing workers' and neighbourhood protests and the increasingly violent police crackdowns, created conditions conducive to an 'autumn of fury'. The youth movements laid the foundations for the 2011 uprising through their experimentation with new protest tactics, both on- and offline, driven on by their confrontations with the police. The Alexandria bombing increased the number of Christians mobilised for protest and, coming only weeks before 25 January, heightened the overall level of mobilisation immediately prior to the uprising. By the time Ben Ali fled Tunisia and Egyptian activists began to call for a mass protest on Police Day, Egypt had experienced a level of mobilisation not seen for decades.

Intriguingly, the Brotherhood played a relatively subdued role in nurturing a domestic protest scene. Although it contributed to creating and sustaining a protest culture, its forays into street protests were usually reactive and later in the protest wave and short-lived. It only began participating in any significant way in 2002–2003, and then primarily in government-sanctioned rallies, which did not critique the regime. During the second wave, it briefly (though very effectively) joined forces with Kefaya, before parting ways and focusing on securing its share of the parliamentary elections. During the workers' wave it was largely absent, focusing instead on *da'wa* activities and institutional politics, with the exception of mass protests against Israel's treatment of Palestinians and in particular its incursion into Gaza in 2008–2009. In the fourth wave, having initially supported ElBaradei's campaign, it went its separate way again, contesting the 2010 election against the wishes of its reformist wing, although its more reformist youth members continued to liaise with the other protest networks.

Much of this behaviour can be explained with reference to the vulnerability of the movement to regime repression. Another key factor was the fact that the movement's leadership was dominated by a risk-averse, conservative old guard, which was strengthened by state repression which weakened the reformists. However, apart from preparing tens of thousands for protest (though not of the domestic kind) through its Palestinian solidarity demonstrations, the main developments preparing the ground for the 2011 uprising occurred among the informal and mostly secular protest networks, which were small and flexible enough to evade repression and experiment with innovation. They were helped in this by their open attitude towards learning from other movements elsewhere, regardless of faith, ideology or circumstance.

3

'DOWN WITH MUBARAK, DOWN WITH THE
MILITARY STATE!'

POLITICAL CONTEXT

Focusing on the networks that provided the organisational backbone
for the protests helps us to understand how the 2011 uprising was
made possible, and how it grew out of the long decade of protests preceding it. What such a focus does not do is situate these networks
within the broader structural changes that shaped the context within
which they emerged. An organisational analysis of the pro-Palestinian
movement shows how this prepared the way for the Movement for
Change in terms of goals, frames, tactics, personnel and institutional
links. It does not tell us how, for instance, socio-economic changes
were creating both new grievances and new opportunities, or how
changes in regime–society relations had alienated large sectors of society, including professional organisations such as the Judges' Club.

In social movement theory terms, where the previous chapter
focused on micro-mobilisational dynamics, this chapter focuses on the
broader political opportunity structure in which the networks operated. Networks need opportunities and resources to organise. Their
protest frames and tactics are influenced by the broader socio-economic and political arrangements of the society they operate in. Their
timing is affected not just by their internal dynamics or by the protest
episodes they have initiated, but by broader structural changes.[1]

WHY OCCUPY A SQUARE?

Delineating Key Structural Factors

There are numerous structural factors which could be said to have played a part. Choosing which factors to single out is complicated by the fact that the relationship between structural changes and protest is seldom direct, let alone self-consciously understood. Although many interviewees described the swarming tactics that made the January 25 demonstration so successful, none explicitly listed the growth of Cairo's crowded 'informal' sector and the flight of lower middle-class families into these sectors as a background factor. A number of people mentioned the shrinking socialist state as a factor; but none linked this directly to a weakening of middle-class loyalty to the regime. The list of factors we focus on below has been drawn partly from the literature on social movements and revolutions, and partly from the factors highlighted by our interviewees and Egyptian internet commentators. Because our focus is on urban opposition networks, we will limit ourselves to discussing factors that primarily affect urban centres.

The classical political opportunity structure literature, as summarised by McAdam (1996: 27), can be boiled down to four sets of structural factors:

1. The relative openness or closure of the institutionalized political system
2. The stability [or instability] of that broad set of elite alignments that typically undergird a polity
3. The presence [or absence] of elite allies
4. The state's capacity and propensity for repression

While these themes are useful (although McAdam has partially abandoned this schema, we still find it helpful in organising our analysis), they need to be adapted to the specificities of the Egyptian case (adaptations which arguably have a broader relevance for studies of politics in the so-called Global South). The first and fourth factors above are directly applicable to Egypt, although the focus of the first should be more on changes in the relationship between ruling party, opposition parties and society and the emergence of a parallel informal oppositional sphere, than on any formal changes in the 'institutionalized political system'.

The third factor is similarly applicable, although 'elite' needs to be understood here in its broadest sense, going beyond the state elite to include professionals, white-collar state employees, and even, we would argue, transnational protest networks, as these provided important resources, from tactical innovation to transnational communication channels.

Besides the presence of (some) elite allies, a crucial factor in the Egyptian case was the increasingly visible disunity among the top echelons of the state elite regarding Mubarak's succession and the regime's neoliberal reforms. This disunity only rarely translated into actual elite alliances with the opposition. Rather, it indirectly affected the opposition's assessment of the stability and popular legitimacy of the regime. As such, elite fissures will be included as a subcategory under 'elite allies'.[2]

The second factor—'the stability of elite alignments undergirding the polity'—is in many ways the most crucial, as the gradual erosion of loyalty to the regime across society created key opportunities for the opposition. The decades prior to January 2011 saw fundamental changes in the relationship between the different classes, the regime and the state, influencing how people perceived the regime's legitimacy, and thus indirectly their appetite for protest. A crucial focus in this section will be the withdrawal of the state from society and the emergence of an autonomous middle class.

Within the classical political opportunity structure literature, political factors are usually differentiated from broader socio-economic changes, such as urbanisation and the rise in tertiary education. The former are obviously affected by the latter. Urbanisation affects the state's capacity for repression just as an expanded tertiary education can erode the elite alignments underpinning a polity. But the distinction is upheld because political and socio-economic factors often affect social movements in different ways. We will therefore devote a separate chapter to socio-economic factors, including both long-term changes and more episodic, short-term changes, such as an increase in food prices or the short-term effects of global recession (which serve more as 'triggers' or 'threats' creating grievances).

The themes developed in the literature on revolutions overlap with those proposed by political opportunity structure theorists, although the focus differs subtly. Among the more Marxist-oriented, the focus is typically on systemic strains creating a revolutionary situation. Declining state capacity (including as a result of international pressures, war or changes in international trade relations); type of regime (e.g. exclusionary authoritarian, neo-patrimonial or semi-open), levels of state repression and regime openness, and strength of civil society; elite fissures resulting from a changing class structure or increasingly exclusive neo-patrimonial arrangements; and broader socio-economic changes giving rise to perceptions of relative deprivation or creating large cohorts of unemployed yet educated youth are all examples of the type of systemic strain covered by this literature (e.g. Skocpol 1979; Goldstone 1991; Goodwin 2001). These themes can be readily absorbed within a political opportunity structure model (although the latter has traditionally underplayed international factors).[3] The main themes we focus on are visually depicted in Figure 3.1.

Changing Elite Alignments and the State: Neoliberal Reforms, Crony Capitalism and the Shrinking State

One of the main factors behind the 2011 uprising was the gradual shrinking of the state as a result of the regime's neoliberal reforms, and the way this affected the relationship between the regime and Egypt's various classes. In a revolutionary studies context, Goldstone (1991: 8) refers to this phenomenon in its extreme as a 'state crisis', when 'elite

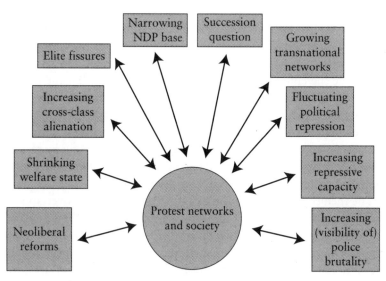

Figure 3.1: Schematic representation of convergence of multiple factors affecting and being affected by the protest networks and broader society.

or popular groups consider the state incapable of performing necessary tasks of governance', causing loss of allegiance. The reforms changed the relationship between state and society and challenged the social contract that had underpinned the Egyptian state. They led to a sharp increase in social inequality and a gradual erosion of the everyday services Egyptians had come to expect. The result was not only an increase in grievances, rendering the opposition's messages more resonant, but also a weakening of the loyalty of the middle classes and the workers to the regime, thus increasing the pool of those who might be mobilised. The reforms facilitated the emergence of, and were driven by, a small, yet blatantly rich and politically influential 'crony capitalist' class, which further alienated Egyptians from the regime. They simultaneously facilitated the emergence of a middle class that was no longer beholden to the state, and thus available for mobilisation.

The welfarist state project, begun amidst much fanfare by Nasser in the 1950s, had been precarious from the start (Rutherford 2008: 135). Already under Sadat, the economic pressures of war with Israel, a growing population and a vast, inert bureaucracy triggered the decision to begin a process of economic liberalisation, called *infitah* [opening up]. It was less a structural reform than an opening of the economy to foreign investment (Rutherford 2008: 135). An attempt to reduce food subsidies was abandoned in the face of mass protests in 1977, the largest of their kind until the protests of the 2000s. By the early 1990s, the Mubarak regime responded to Egypt's spiralling debts by subjecting the Egyptian economy to the structural reforms dictated by the International Monetary Fund, which demanded that the state be scaled back, that interest rates and the exchange rate be liberalised and that public firms be privatised (Niblock 1993: 58–71; King 2009: 121; Rutherford 2008: 137–9). As part of these reforms, international financial institutions encouraged the concentration of power in the hands of the president and a small, technocratic elite to 'reduce structural resistance to policies', thus encouraging a shift from the original 'state–single-party alliance', catering for all sectors of society, to an exclusive 'state–bourgeoisie–private sector' alliance, catering only for top government officials, business tycoons and rich rural landlords (King 2009: 110–11).

Mubarak's programme of neoliberal reforms affected the opposition movement in multiple ways. First, it led to a withdrawal of the welfare state from society, thereby weakening the general population's loyalty to the regime, and in particular the loyalty of the middle and lower classes. Where the Nasserist state had sought to provide welfare, education and employment, Mubarak's state visibly scaled back these services. Employment in the public sector fell from more than 1 million in 1993 to less than 600,000 in 2000 (Rutherford 2008: 198). Subsidised foodstuffs were cut back dramatically, leading to chronic shortages. Public healthcare and education shrunk and deteriorated, welfare provision was privatised and social security disappeared for many of the working poor (Ismail 2006: 71). Illustrative of the extent of the 'withdrawal of the state' is the drop in government expenditure from 30 per cent of GDP at its peak to 12 per cent by the mid-1990s (Blaydes 2011: 44–5).

This process of alienation from the state was exacerbated by the effect of neoliberal reforms on the economy. Liberalisation did not generate the levels of private investment initially envisaged, leading to a shortfall of billions and a dearth of new jobs necessary to keep unemployment down (Rutherford 2008: 204). In addition, it undermined workers' rights. The gradual lifting of import tariffs, one of the conditions of WTO membership, affected the textile industry particularly badly, as did the end of various tariff-free export agreements (Rutherford 2008: 200–1).

Where, before, the spoils of state had been used to 'buy' the loyalty of a broad array of actors, embodied in the Arab Socialist Union and later the National Democratic Party (NDP), now most of the spoils were concentrated in the hands of a small elite, made up of regime apparatchiks, members of the powerful business class that had emerged following Sadat's reforms, and rural landlords (King 2009: 113–24; Blaydes 2011: 36). To illustrate the chasm between this elite and the rest of society, by the early 2000s, 3 per cent of the population was responsible for 'half of all consumer spending'. In 2008, luxury cars made up 50 per cent of all car sales (Blaydes 2011: 45–6). Yet over the period 2000–2006, 40.9 per cent of Egyptians were living on less than $2.70 a day (purchasing power parity or PPP) (UNDP 2009: 114).

By the early 2000s, the NDP had successfully bound the emerging business elite to itself, with businessmen parliamentarians affiliated to the NDP rising to fifty-nine in 1995 and doubling to 120 in 2000 (King 2009: 93–4; Blaydes 2011: 139). By 2005, businessmen controlled 'more than 50 percent of the legislature' (Blaydes 2011: 139). Prominent businessmen, with close ties to Gamal Mubarak, rose through the

NDP's ranks; for instance, Ahmed Ezz (steel magnate) and Ibrahim Kamel (chairman of one of Egypt's largest investment corporations) were promoted to the party's General Secretariat in 2000. In 2004, their rise culminated in what came to be described variously as the 'Businessmen's Cabinet' or 'Gamal's Cabinet' (Diab 2009; S. Mansour 2009: 206).

This alliance came at a price, changing the relationship between the regime and the ruling party, the state bourgeoisie and the middle classes more broadly. By narrowing the circle to this small clique, the regime alienated many of those who had been left out: traditional party bosses whose main source of power, the state, was under threat from neoliberal reforms; the armed forces, whose economic base was similarly threatened by Gamal's business friends; traditional elites who had not benefited from the selling off of state assets; and businessmen who had not succeeded in penetrating Gamal's inner circle.

More broadly, the narrowing NDP base exacerbated the effect of the shrinking welfare state on the middle classes and the workers, who now faced both economic hardship and political exclusion. Where once the NDP functioned as a corporatist party, representing society's key sectors and mediating between them and the state, it had become an alliance between top state officials and 'a new distributional coalition of urban and rural economic elites' (King 2009: 12).

Having increasingly become a neo-patrimonial regime, driven by allegiance to Mubarak, rather than allegiance to some form of legitimating ideology (such as nationalism or Islamism), the already weak 'legitimacy' of the regime was further undermined by a number of elite scandals, brought to public attention by the growing opposition press. Accusations ranged from 'gross negligence' in the 2006 ferry disaster to allegations of monopolistic practices, embezzlement and 'stock market manipulations' (Blaydes 2011: 133–8). Because parliament and the NDP were slow to lift parliamentary immunity, it looked like they provided 'political cover' to corrupt business tycoons to '[use] their parliamentary immunity to plunder banks' (Salama Ahmed Salama, *Al-Ahram* commentator, quoted in Blaydes 2011: 136).

Second, neoliberal reforms, the shrinking state and the rise of a crony capitalist class shaped the context within which opposition networks, tactics and slogans emerged. The fact that the anti-Iraq war protests began to feature slogans such as 'Ahmed Ezz, living in luxury, tell us who is protecting you? Down with the monopoly of the steel mills!' (Moustafa 2004) or 'They wear the latest fashions! ... And we live ten to a room!' (A. Hassan 2003b) was directly related to the effect of neoliberal reforms[4] and the business tycoons' ascent to power in the early 2000s. Similarly, the introduction of slogans likening the regime to the occupation forces in Baghdad and Jerusalem (*Al-Ahram Weekly* 2005a) was facilitated by the withdrawal of the state, the effects of structural reform and the narrowing of the NDP's base to a hated business elite (although other factors, such as the regime's support for Israeli and US policies in the region, were important too).

The rise of the independent workers' movement was similarly a direct response to the neoliberal reforms and the inability (and unwillingness) of the regime to secure the workers' interests. As Sarah (Interview 2011), a labour movement researcher in Mahalla, told us:

Workers are deeply disillusioned by privatisation: factories sold at rock-bottom prices, new owners being corrupt and making a lot of money from these transactions, expensive machinery brought in, workers sacked, Egyptian cotton exported, bad cotton imported for them.

While the General Federation of Trade Unions (GFTU) secured some successes, it was ineffective and largely indifferent in the face of companies circumventing labour laws (Rutherford 2008: 226–7).

Independent workers' strikes have a long history in Egypt. Conservative estimates put the number of strikes between 1984 and 1990 at over 300 (Kassem 2004: 108) and the mid-1990s saw another strike wave as Mubarak's structural adjustment programme began to bite (Stork 2011: 186; Posusney 1997: 230–7, 242). But the jump from hundreds over the course of a decade to hundreds annually in 2004 occurred against the backdrop of a worsening economic situation, a blatantly uncooperative GFTU and an increasingly visibly elite-centric NDP. The main trigger, though, was the second wave of privatisations initiated by the 'Businessmen's Cabinet' of July 2004, with over 70 per cent of the over 260 protests carried out that year taking place after July (Beinin 2011a: 187, 190).

The way workers carried out protests was similarly affected by neoliberal reforms. In the era of Arab socialism, as Beinin (2011a: 187) notes, protests took the form of 'factory occupations (*i'tisam/at*) while production continued, or refusal to accept paychecks rather than strikes (*idrab/at*)', as workers felt a greater sense of ownership. By the 2000s, strikes had become the preferred protest tactic, as workers had lost this sense of ownership.

Finally, the state's withdrawal, coupled to the visible narrowing of the NDP's base, played a role not only in weakening the loyalty of the middle classes to the regime but in facilitating the emergence of an autonomous middle class, as opposed to the state bourgeoisie that had characterised Egypt's class system before. Prior to 2011, a popular argument among students of democratisation was that one of the reasons the Middle East had not experienced the waves of democratisation seen in Latin America and Eastern Europe was the dependence of the middle class on the state (Waterbury 1994; regarding the role of the middle class in democratisation more broadly, cf. Rueschemeyer, Stephens and Stephens 1992). Indeed, during the strikes and demonstrations of the 1970s and 1980s, the middle classes (middle-class students apart) played a relatively minor role (cf. Seddon 1993: 105–7; Baker 1990: 118–32; Hirst and Beeson 1981: 242–6).

By the 2000s, the situation had changed markedly. Employment was no longer guaranteed for university graduates and the private sector was difficult to penetrate, resulting in a decline in social mobility. Those who were employed by the state, meanwhile, found their salaries shrinking (Binzel 2011). The resultant weakening of the middle classes' loyalty to the status quo meant that they could be more readily persuaded to 'withdraw their assent from the existing order', crucial for revolutions (Goldstone 1997: 114). It also facilitated the (limited) alliance with the workers' movement.

Unlike the clear correlation between the timing of strikes and the effect of neoliberal reforms, the link between the 'revolt' of the middle classes in the late 2000s and neoliberal reforms is less clear. The reforms had already begun to bite well before 2000, yet, anti-war and pro-democracy protests aside, large-scale middle-class protests did not become a regular feature until the strikes of the late 2000s, and the middle classes only turned out en masse in 2011. Even though the rise of predominantly middle-class Kefaya was influenced by the establishment of Gamal's 'Businessmen's Cabinet' in July 2004, its emergence was determined by the election cycle and the succession crisis, not the neoliberal reforms. Nevertheless, as Shaaban (Interview 2011), one of Kefaya's founders, argued:

[By 2004] a lot of members of the middle class had been reduced to lower class, with only a very small percentage being very, very rich. The middle classes wanted to reclaim their leadership, their position, and they were against policies destroying the middle class. ... [Through the 2000s] the number of supporters of the system was getting smaller and smaller. Only a very small sector of society supported the regime: businessmen with relations with the regime. When the explosion came [in 2011], lots of people joined.

Elite Fissures and Allies: Changes in the NDP, the Succession Crisis and Transnational Networks

A key factor affecting opposition movements is the extent to which the elite in charge of the state remains united (this is also a focus of revolutionary studies, e.g. Goodwin 2001; Goldstone 1991; Lachmann 1997). The deeper the elite divisions are, the more opportunities that present themselves for opposition activists to form alliances with former regime supporters. Even if such alliances do not materialise, visible fissures among the elite signal to activists and society more broadly that the elite's control is weakening. An additional factor is the presence or absence of transnational support networks, which can change the balance of power between local elites and their challengers.

Two phenomena in particular caused a shake-up in Egyptian elite attitudes: the changes in the NDP discussed above, and the question of Mubarak's succession. Regarding the NDP's changes, what concerns us here is how the shift from a populist party serving broad-based state corporatism to a party serving a small economic elite affected elite attitudes. The combination of changes in the NDP with the very public grooming of Gamal for the presidency profoundly affected the relationship between the regime and key elite sectors, principally the leadership of the armed forces and the judiciary, but also, lower down the 'elite ladder', civil servants, disillusioned NDP members, lawyers, doctors and international figures such as ElBaradei. Indicative of the NDP's crisis—both in terms of its broader legitimacy and its ability to unite and control its members—is the fact that from the mid-1990s onwards, it could only win a minority of seats outright, having to co-opt independent candidates who had run without the party's sanction to secure a majority in the People's Assembly (see Table 3.1).

The crisis in the NDP was in part a result of the changing elite alignments underpinning the party discussed above. Equally significant, though, was the question of Mubarak's succession. Mubarak's response to the disappointing results of the 1995 and 2000 elections was to install Gamal to spearhead efforts to generate 'new ideas' and 'new blood'. Gamal was appointed to the NDP's General Secretariat in 2000, despite having had no previous political appointments. In 2001, he was promoted to the Guidance Committee, the party's inner sanctum, and the following year he became the third ranking NDP official, having been made chair of the newly formed powerful Policies Secretariat (Rutherford 2008: 219).

Divisions between the 'old guard', whose power base was threatened by neoliberal reforms (including the NDP secretary, General Safwat al-Sharif, and presidential chief of staff, Zakaria Azmi), and the 'new guard' around Gamal were already apparent in the early 2000s, when Kefaya emerged. However, they burst to the fore in 2009–2010 when the new elite's control began to wane as a result of the global economic recession of the late 2000s and the increasing protests against neoliberal reform. As Stephen Roll (2010) noted in 2010:

Old guard figures dominated the NDP congress in 2009 much more than other gatherings in recent years ... Regarding policies, old guard NDP leaders have become publicly critical of the Nazif government's reform plans, provoking a slowdown in the government's privatization course.

By 2010, when the fourth protest wave kicked off, the political elite was visibly divided, both on Gamal's planned succession and on neoliberal reforms.

The military leadership was similarly divided over Gamal's leadership. They had strong links with the NDP old guard (Azmi and al-Sharif, for instance, both stemmed from the military) and their economic interests were similarly under threat (Roll 2010; Cambanis 2010).

While the military remained officially neutral, there were increasingly visible signs of dissent. In August 2010, a number of retired military officers 'circulated an open letter criticizing Gamal Mubarak's candidacy', while 'military officials ... expressed reservations in interviews and in the Egyptian news media' (Cambanis 2010). An anonymous blog created in 2009, omarsoliman.blogspot.com, was headed by a banner reading 'la Gamal wa la al-Ikhwan, 'ayzin Omar Suleiman' ['No Gamal and No Brotherhood, We want Omar Suleiman [the (military) head of Intelligence]'] (Hanna 2009). US diplomatic cables at the time similarly quoted sources saying that the military did not support Gamal and would step in if Mubarak died in office, though not if Gamal were elected with Mubarak's blessing (*Guardian* 2011d).

Egypt's presidents have all come from within the armed forces, and their authority has in part been derived from their military legacy. While the role of the military in politics diminished sharply from Nasser's time, when only one of the top republican posts before 1967 was held by a civilian (Hashim 2012), to Mubarak's, with only one active-duty officer among thirty-three ministers by 2009 (not counting minister without portfolio Suleiman), Mubarak continued to bind the military to him by exempting their economic empire from tax, granting them lucrative subsidies and business ventures, and ensuring that retired senior officers were given posts in the civilian bureaucracy (Chams El-Dine 2013: 3; Hanna 2009: 107; *Guardian* 2011d; Cambanis 2010).

However, loyalty to Mubarak was severely tested by Gamal's rise. Gamal was disliked by the army, both for not being 'one of them' and for being associated with the new business elite. Mubarak was the first Egyptian president seemingly contemplating a monarchical transfer of power (although he strenuously denied that this was his intention; A. Aly 2012: 32). In addition, there was rivalry between the military and the police, on which Mubarak had begun to rely progressively.

The re-alignment of the NDP with an increasingly small business and rural elite also contributed to the alienation of other sectors of society, including, crucially, the judiciary. The judiciary had long had an ambiguous relationship with regime. On the one hand, it had sought to limit state power. On the other, it had sanctioned controversial regime initiatives, such as the broadening of the remit of military courts (Rutherford 2008: 52–61). Yet even though the judiciary had acted to limit abuses of state power and to defend its independence, it had largely refrained from overt political activism.

For much of the 1990s, the Judges' Club, one of the most important bodies representing Egypt's judges, had been dominated by a quietist leadership focusing on 'bread-and-butter' issues, such as judges' pensions. In 2001, the Club's elections returned an activist leadership in response to the crisis brought about by the regime's decree that judges oversee elections in an attempt to shore up its waning legitimacy. While the judges welcomed judicial oversight, many were furious at being tasked with overseeing an election where most of the (extensive) fraud occurred outside of their jurisdiction (the election booth). The quietist leadership did little to address their concerns, giving the activist judges who had lost control of the Club in the early 1990s a chance to return to power (Rutherford 2008: 145–63). It was this shift, fuelled by increasing dissonance between the regime and the judges, which paved the way for their joining forces with the Movement for Change in the mid-2000s.

The succession crisis and its concomitant elite fissures profoundly affected the opposition movement. Two of the four protest waves were directly triggered by the succession crisis. Gamal's rapid rise and the 2005 constitutional amendment paving the way for Gamal's succession were two of the main triggers for Kefaya's emergence, bringing together those who had come to call for regime change as a result of the anti-Iraq war protests and those who had long been part of the pro-democracy movement. Gamal's close association with neoliberal reforms and the business elite furthermore facilitated the tentative alliance between the left, the workers' movement and the pro-democracy movement, and the link activists made between constitutional and socio-economic reform.

In 2010, opposition to Gamal's anticipated 2011 presidential bid was one of the key factors driving the ElBaradei campaign. Already in 2008, Ahmed Salah, a leader of the April 6 movement, told US diplomats that 2011 was the deadline for organising a (forced) 'democratic transition' to prevent Gamal from becoming president (BBC2 2012; *Telegraph* 2011), and by 2010, many were galvanised by the fear of having to suffer a further thirty years of Mubarak dictatorship (Chapter 5). The way the succession crisis was intertwined with neoliberal reforms and crony capitalism furthermore influenced which constituencies were mobilised and what frames they adopted.

The emergence of elite fissures more broadly—within the NDP, between the NDP and the military, and between the NDP, the judiciary, civil servants and professionals—created opportunities for the opposition movement, much as the classical social movement literature suggests. If the Lawyers' Syndicate had remained loyal to the regime, rather than becoming a hub of opposition activity during the anti-war protests, the student movement would not have consolidated itself as rapidly, or forged the links with the seasoned activists of the 1970s that were to prove crucial for the Movement for Change. If the Judges' Club had not joined the opposition in 2005, the protests begun by Kefaya would not have maintained the momentum or significance that carried them beyond the elections. If Osama Ghazali-Harb had not resigned and founded the Democratic Front Party, a number of youth activists might not have had the opportunity to join the opposition and play the pivotal role they played in 2011.

The increasing visibility of fissures furthermore highlighted that, at a minimum, the regime's hold on power was under strain. However, although these fissures were known to opposition activists, our inter-viewees insisted that they did not see these as opportunities to be exploited (cf. Shaaban, Interview 2011; Ghazali-Harb, Interview 2011a; Maher, Interview 2011), thus negating a key claim in the social movement literature.[5] We can therefore not draw a direct causal link between awareness of elite fissures and the decision to protest. What we can surmise, though, is that this awareness contributed to an over-all sense that the regime could no longer count on the elite's loyalty, thus increasing the possibility of political change, particularly com-pared to 2005 when these fissures were far less pronounced.

Egyptian activists were furthermore aided by an increasingly dense network of transnational links. During the 1990s, Egyptian human rights NGOs had already begun to benefit from support from human rights activists across the globe. In the 2000s, the transnational Global Justice Movement (GJM) and the Stop-the-War coalition became allies. It is clear from both our interviews and from nascent research that the GJM played a supporting role in both the early evolution of the anti-Iraq war protest wave and in the acceleration of protests in 2010–2011. The early pro-Palestinian networks were in touch with the global Palestinian solidarity movement. Members of the global Stop-the-War coalition, part of the broader GJM movement, came to Egypt in 2002 for the Stop-the-War coalition's first Cairo Conference (stop-war.org.uk n.d.), which became an annual event, cementing links between local Egyptian activists and transnational activists.

Local groups inspired by the GJM, such as the Anti-Globalisation Egypt Group (AGEG), founded in 2002, further strengthened links with the global movement, adopting similar tactics and themes, from a non-hierarchical approach to organisation and an emphasis on cross-ideological networking (Abdel-Rahman in El-Mahdi 2009: 98), to a focus on grassroots education and championing those negatively affected by globalisation (Abdelrahman 2011). The Revolutionary Socialists, another Egyptian protest group, participated in the World Social Forum, attended a transnational Marxist conference in London and maintained contacts with participating Trotskyists in France, the UK, Germany, Canada, South Africa and Tunisia (Saad, Interview 2011). The influence of the GJM transpired in the way anti-Iraq war activists called their occupation of Tahrir Square in 2003 'our Seattle' (Chapter 1) and in the adoption of swarming tactics (Chapter 2). In all this, local factors were more determining, and transnational influences were changed by local dynamics. But these transnational linkages strengthened the Egyptian opposition.

The affinity between (some) Egyptian groups and the GJM was facilitated by the fact that both were responses to neoliberal reforms, the Iraq war, technological innovation and policing practices. In each of these areas, the movements exchanged tactics and learned from each other, a process which was facilitated by globalisation itself.

Changing Levels of Openness of the Political System

A crucial factor affecting the level and shape of opposition activism is the extent to which the political system is open, and responsive to, opposition (in revolution studies, cf. also Goodwin 2001). In a seminal study Herbert Kitschelt showed how, in the case of the anti-nuclear proliferation movement, a closed system encouraged extra-parliamentary and disruptive tactics, while a more open system correlated with less confrontational, more parliament-orientated tactics (Kitschelt 1986). While Kitschelt's findings concerned well-established democracies, the nature and shape of the political system clearly affect both the opportunities and threats opposition movements encounter.

In the Egyptian case, the political system changed subtly, yet significantly, under Mubarak's rule. Formally, Egypt remained a single-party system with regular elections returning the ruling party to power with an overwhelming majority, using any means to buy, coerce and persuade people to vote for the ruling party. Even in 2005, when opposition parties and independent candidates secured 27 per cent of the seats, the NDP still retained 73 per cent—although only after co-opting 172 independent candidates who had run without NDP sanction (Table 3.1, although the precise figures are contested; see footnote 6).

Trade unions continued to function as regime enforcers. Professional syndicates were somewhat more autonomous, particularly during the 1980s, and again in the 2000s when a number became hubs for opposition activity (Kassem 2004: 112–17). But their ability to channel opposition demands effectively remained limited.

This formal façade masked two unfolding processes: one, described above, concerning the narrowing base of the ruling party, the other concerning the openness of the system to challengers, which fluctuated over time. The first process resulted in an erosion of the institutional channels for representing the needs of workers, farmers, the petit bourgeoisie and the middle classes. Although the Egyptian constitution

Table 3.1: Egyptian election results during the Mubarak era.[6]

Party	1984	1987	1990	1995	2000	2005	2010
NDP	390 (87%)	348 (78%)	360 (81%)	417 (94%) (of which 99 independents)	388 (87%) (of which 218 independents)	324 (73%) (of which 172 independents)	420 (83%) (plus 53 independents)
Muslim Brotherhood	8	30	Boycott	1 (served as SLP after election)	17	88	–
New Wafd	50	35	Boycott (14 affiliated independents)	6	7	6	6
Socialist Labor Party	–	27	Boycott (8 affiliated independents)	[See MB]			
Liberal Party	–	3	Boycott (1 affiliated independent)	1	1	–	–
Progressive Unionist Party (Tagammu')	–	–	5	5	6	2	5
Arab Democratic				1	3	–	–
Nasserist Party						2	
Al-Ghad Party						2	1
Al-Karama movement						2	Withdrawn in protest

Party							
Social Justice Party							1
Democratic Peace Party							1
Democratic Generation Party							1
Independents		5	55	13	20 (2 contested later)	8 (12 contested later)	69 (of which 53 pro-NDP)
Total	448	448	444	444	444	444	504 (not counting 4 invalidated)

reserves half of the seats in the People's Assembly for workers and farmers, those who were elected tended to be beholden to the regime or elite figures, not to the actual workers and farmers (cf. *al-Masry al-Youm* 2012). As neoliberal reforms began to hurt, those who had most to lose had less and less recourse to formal channels of making their grievances known, rendering opposition calls for constitutional change more resonant. Reflecting this, however inadequately due to the circumstances in which the polls were taken, the few publicly available polling data from this period (2006 onwards) show a steady drop in satisfaction 'with the way things are going in [your] country today' (Figure 3.2) (Pew n.d.).

The shift from corporatist party to elite cartel also limited the options of those with political ambitions. During Nasser's era, the politically ambitious could find a role in the Arab Socialist Union (the NDP's predecessor), because it was conceived as 'a civic association to mobilise the people' (Kassem 2004: 51). Under Mubarak, as Lisa Blaydes (2011: 48–9) demonstrated, the NDP became a mechanism for binding the elite to the regime through the distribution of rents and promotions. If you or your family were rich enough to buy votes, you could have a career in the NDP. For others, it became all but impossible, as expenditure by electoral candidates became increasingly prohibitive, rising from a reported LE 4 billion in 1995 to LE 10 billion in

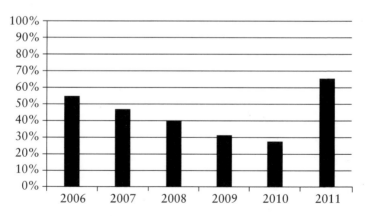

Figure 3.2: Percentage of Egyptians polled by the Pew Research Center answering 'satisfied' to the question 'Overall, are you satisfied or dissatisfied with the way things are going in our country today?' (Pew n.d.).

2000 (Blaydes 2011: 139). Consequently, the number of people available for opposition activism increased.

The progressively narrow nature of the regime similarly affected the growth of the independent workers' movement. The increasingly visible unresponsiveness of the regime-controlled trade unions to the effect of neoliberal reforms pushed workers to organise themselves outside of the official structures (Rutherford 2008: 226–7).

Parallel to this shift, and equally influential, the system oscillated between reluctant experiments with political liberalisation and closing down oppositional space. Regime oscillation between political liberalisation and repression is particularly conducive to oppositional mobilisation as it creates both opportunities for mobilisation during the permissive phases and grievances to be mobilised during the repressive phase (cf. Lichbach 1987). By raising expectations of political participation, it renders any restriction on participation more grievous than before liberalisation was begun.

Over the course of the 1980s Mubarak allowed some formal political opposition, yet political parties remained severely circumscribed. Between 1981 and 2004, only one of over fifty applications to form a new political party was approved (Kassem 2004: 57; Stacher 2004: 221), and the main opposition party, the Muslim Brotherhood, remained illegal throughout, although it was allowed to run independent candidates, affiliated to other parties. Nevertheless, in the 1984 and 1987 elections the NDP secured 'only' 87 and 78 per cent in parliament, and analysts generally agree that these elections were more 'transparent and competitive' than any before (Thabet 2006: 12; Stacher 2004: 221; Kassem 2004: 30); they were accompanied by nascent autonomous civil society and media sectors (Brown n.d.; Wickham 2002: 66).

The 1990s witnessed a sharp reversal of these limited openings, ushering in a period of what Eberhard Kienle called 'political deliberalization'. The law was adjusted to restrict political opposition and press freedom. The use of military courts to try civilians multiplied, and the number of political detainees rose to between 10,000 and 16,000 by 1996. The 1995 elections were billed as 'Egypt's bloodiest elections', with eighty-seven killed and an estimated 1,500 injured. Between 1998 and 2004, the government froze seven of Egypt's sixteen legalised opposition parties, and, leaving aside the Muslim Brotherhood, the few remaining 'active opposition parties' were manipulated or coerced by the state into compliance (Kienle 1998: 221–3; Stacher 2004: 220, 222–33).

In the early 2000s, the regime initiated another round of limited political liberalisation, responding to internal unrest and external pressure (King 2009: 106–9). A faltering economy, popular opposition to structural reform and to Egyptian ties with Israel, particularly following the outbreak of the al-Aqsa Intifada, and the revival of street politics combined with international and regional pressures. The Bush administration pushed for democratic reform in 2003–2004 and between 2003 and 2005 elections were proposed or held in Palestine, Jordan and Saudi Arabia.

The 2000 elections were the first to be overseen by the judiciary, and the NDP's seat percentage dropped back to pre-1990 levels (87 per cent). In 2005, the NDP's percentage fell even further to an unprecedented 73 per cent (with only 34 per cent won by NDP-sanctioned candidates), while the Brotherhood gained eighty-eight seats. The constitution was amended to allow for multiple presidential candidates (although restrictions severely limited who could stand, rendering the competition nominal). The establishment of *al-Masry al-Youm* in 2004 reinvigorated the opposition media, challenging the pre-eminence of the state-owned *al-Ahram* and paving the way for further independently owned media outlets (Brown n.d.). These limited openings were undermined by the continued harassment and arrest of opposition candidates, journalists and human rights activists. Those directly involved in anti-war or anti-succession protests were routinely arrested and tortured (Committee to Protect Journalists 2006; FIDH 2004; US Department of State 2004).

Following the 2005 elections, these half-hearted openings were again shut down. Local elections scheduled for 2006 were cancelled; when they were finally held in 2008, opposition candidates, particularly from the Brotherhood, were severely disrupted. Many opposition candidates were imprisoned, including Ayman Nur, one of the main opposition presidential candidates in 2005, numerous Brotherhood candidates, as well as human rights activists. Parliament was weakened by the regime shifting powers to the more docile Upper House or Shura Council. Police powers were extended in a controversial 2007 constitutional amendment, which also curbed the role of the judiciary in monitoring elections and prohibited the formation of religious parties (Freedom House 2012; Hamzawy 2005; Popham 2007; King 2009: 110).

This oscillation affected the opposition in a number of ways. First, combined with the gradual attrition of the NDP's corporatist function, it further eroded faith in formal politics as a means to address grievances. More prosaically, political repression in the 1990s and 2000s closed down opportunities for opposition activism within the formal party sphere, pushing people to explore other spheres. During the 1980s, human rights NGOs had begun to emerge, a process that accelerated during the 1990s with the growth of human rights networks globally. As parties and trade unions—the two traditional venues for formal politics—became increasingly repressed, human rights NGOs such as the Land Center for Human Rights and the Center for Human Rights Legal Aid (CHRLA) became the principal locus of extra-parliamentary opposition activity.

Illustrating this linkage between the repression of formal politics and the growth of alternative loci of opposition, the Egyptian Organization for Human Rights (EOHR) was founded by, among others, former members of the Communist Workers' Party, which had been suppressed by the government in the early 1980s (Stork 2011: 92). CHRLA was founded by workers in 1996 'when the government prevented them from running in union elections'; the Center for Trade Union and Workers Services was similarly set up by a former leading trade unionist, after he was fired for participating in an 'illegal' strike (Langohr 2004: 188; Solidarity Center 2010: 44). In the words of an early EOHR activist, 'The left underground tried to jump on whatever avenues were left open' (Stork 2011: 92).[7]

The case of Abu al-'Ala' Madi is similarly instructive. He began his political life as a student, before becoming active in the Engineers' Syndicate and the Muslim Brotherhood. Following the 1995 crackdown on the Brotherhood, he left to co-found the explicitly reformist party, Hizb al-Wasat, in an attempt to establish a political platform that would not be repressed. When Hizb al-Wasat repeatedly failed to gain formal approval, he became one of the Islamist leaders in Kefaya (Vairel 2011: 35).

Madi's move towards the non-institutionalised Kefaya movement was indicative of a second shift in opposition activity, away from formal NGOs towards more fluid, informal and seemingly 'leaderless' networks. This shift coincided with a sharp increase in repression against human rights NGOs in the early 2000s (Freedom House 2002–2005; S.E. Ibrahim and Sherbiny 2000). Parties, syndicates and NGOs were

117

all vulnerable to regime repression or co-option in part because they had formal leadership structures and sought formal legal recognition. Those that had a clearly identifiable charismatic leader, such as the Ghad Party, were particularly vulnerable. By contrast, the protest networks of the 2000s were characterised by diffuse leadership, informality and a relative lack of institutionalisation. Kefaya did not have one dominant leader, and its structures were informal and fluid. The various youth movements that followed were even more fluid, facilitated by their particular use of the internet. That this was a conscious choice to avoid repression is clear from statements such as the following by Wael Ghonim, the 'We Are All Khaled Said' administrator, here commented upon by journalist Noha El-Hennawy (2010):

The "We are all Khaled Saeed" page's administrator is fully aware of the advantages of being informal and is determined not to turn his group into a formal political movement or party.

"In order to succeed, we should stay away from becoming an organization, because the government knows how to destroy any organization," he says. "The whole thing is spontaneous and to participate, you simply need to hit the 'like' button on Facebook."

The increasing turn towards internet technology to sustain the opposition movement was similarly influenced by the regime's repressive tactics. In 2005, as Kefaya's Shaaban (Interview 2011) recalls, the security forces were primarily 'concerned with Kefaya and the Muslim Brotherhood, but not with the virtual world. This meant that opposition activists [especially the newly empowered youth] were able to organise themselves through the Internet. Because it was not controlled information could spread quickly.'

Second, oscillation created a potent mixture of opportunities and threats. During the periods of limited liberalisation, opposition activists had a chance to mobilise and expand their organisational structures. The ability of the Muslim Brotherhood to dominate professional syndicate elections in the 1980s and early 1990s, for instance, created opportunities for opposition activists such as Madi to establish themselves as leaders. The relative opening prior to the 2005 elections enabled Nur to found the Ghad Party, which nurtured the early political careers of many of the youth activists behind the 2011 'revolution'.

The ambiguous attitude of the authorities towards Palestinian solidarity protests similarly enabled the protesters to establish themselves and reclaim the street as a site of protest, despite arrests and (growing) police violence (International Palestinian Solidarity Activist, Interview 2012). Despite a ban on demonstrations, criticism of Israeli policies was often 'tolerated', however partially, because of the ubiquity and long history of pro-Palestinian sentiment (Abou-El-Fadl 2012: 6–26). As Shaaban (Interview 2011), one of those involved in the protests, put it: 'Mubarak was happy that we were focussing on Palestine and Iraq [rather than him].' This ambiguity in the regime's attitude towards anti-Israeli protests provided activists with a small window of opportunity to establish activist networks that would form the basis for the next protest wave. The regime's increasingly brutal response to these protests, particularly when they morphed into calls for regime change, in turn fuelled powerful injustice and motivational frames, which sustained the protests and fed into the Kefaya protest wave.

More generally, the repression against workers in the late 1980s drove many to become active in human rights organisations, which had emerged in the period of relative liberalisation.[8] The arrest and trial of leading dissident judges in 2005–2006 following the emergence of the Movement for Change strengthened and sustained the movement beyond its original calls for constitutional change (Vairel 2011: 39–40).

However, the relationship between repression and opposition is not straightforward.[9] In some instances it served (temporarily) to deter, in others it intensified protests. In yet others it encouraged people to modify their goals and tactics. As Vairel (2011: 36) rightly notes, 'high levels of repression made clear [to opposition activists] that any violent attempt to overcome power would lead to a harsh response and a bloody failure'. Indeed, harsh regime repression was a factor in the decision of the revolutionary leftists of the 1970s to adopt a reformist agenda, just as it convinced Brotherhood members of the futility of militancy in the face of government repression in the mid-1990s (Wickham 2013: 89).

The 2010 protest wave occurred at a particularly vulnerable time for the regime. It followed a period of intense mobilisation, facilitated by the (limited) relaxation of controls leading up to the 2005 election, the re-emergence of street politics in the early 2000s, the explosion of strikes from 2004 onwards and the resurgence of a Muslim Brotherhood that was no longer encumbered by a violent 'radical flank' invoking immediate regime repression (as it had been in the 1990s). The government's subsequent turn to heightened repression strengthened the resolve of activists, rather than diminished it, facilitated as they were by strong supportive networks that could be mobilised to broadcast police violence and to campaign for release from prison. Overtly political protests subsided after 2008. But the networks remained intact, enabling them to re-emerge stronger in 2010. As the locus of opposition had by then shifted to informal networks with recourse to social media, formal repression became more difficult for the regime. Leaving aside the Brotherhood, opposition activism had, moreover, spread beyond the small networks of the early 2000s, facilitated by the rapid spread of social media since 2005, the growth of independent youth networks and the expansion of strikes beyond the independent workers' sector. The year 2010 thus saw the classic case of a regime resorting to increasing repression to suppress a burgeoning opposition, yet doing so both indiscriminately and reactively, with an opposition movement greatly strengthened and broadened compared to the early 2000s.

Changing State Capacity and Propensity for Repression: The Expanding Police State

The evolution of protest episodes, as well as longer-term waves, is also profoundly affected by the level of repression meted out by the regime—and how protesters respond to this repression (in revolutionary studies, cf. Goodwin 2001). Of particular importance is whether and how protest policing changes over time, and how these changes affect opposition networks as well as society more generally (cf. della Porta 1995a).

Equally important is the occurrence of violent incidents that become trigger events. Violent deaths have become trigger events for numerous protest waves. In the United States, the (police-tolerated) lynching of Emmett Till in 1955 served to galvanise what came to be known as the 'Emmett Till Generation' among the US Civil Rights Movement (Harris 2006). In Germany, it was the death of a protester at the hands of the police that radicalised student protesters (della Porta 1995a: xiii–xv, 159–60). In the Palestinian Territories, the death of four Palestinians in a road accident, following the killing of an Israeli days earlier, triggered the outbreak of the first Intifada (Aronson 1990: 323). In each case, the deaths came to be interpreted as symbolising broader patterns of repression and injustice and, as such, cannot be separated from their wider context.

In Egypt, police abuses played a central role in the injustice frames of the opposition. The 2011 demonstrations were scheduled for

National Police Day (25 January), with police brutality one of its major targets. The death of Khaled Said in 2010 at the hands of the police was central in mobilising middle-class youth through the 'We Are All Khaled Said' network. Police abuses also featured centrally in many of the protests staged between 2001 and 2011. But beyond this, were there particular changes in the way policing was carried out and how it was perceived that can help us in explaining why the protests developed the way they did, culminating in 2011?

Egyptian police and police practices have undergone dramatic changes over the past four decades. The police had been an instrument of the higher classes to control the lower ones from its inception in the colonial era, but in the first decades of the Nasserist state, the police were not the primary instrument for suppressing political dissent. That task was reserved for the armed forces. Moreover, the police played a symbolic role in the struggle against British rule, which earned them strong nationalist credentials (Naeem 2011; Ahmed Osman 2011).

From 1967 onwards, however, following the State of Emergency, Nasser began to rely increasingly on the police to quell domestic dissent. Sadat, less certain of the loyalty of the army, expanded police powers in his struggle against political dissent in the 1970s. Sadat's 1981 assassination gave Mubarak, his successor, the justification to reinstate the State of Emergency (suspended in 1980), enabling him to further extend police powers and suspend constitutional rights (Ahmed Osman 2011).

Police numbers grew from 150,000 in 1974 to over 1 million in 2002, or 21 per cent of the number of state employees (Samer Soliman in El-Hennawy 2011). By 2006, according to the opposition daily *Eldestour*, $1.5 billion was spent on internal security, trumping the state's budget for healthcare, and the security forces had grown to 1.4 million officers, or one officer for every fifty-six Egyptians, dwarfing the Egyptian army (just over a quarter of this). Of these, an estimated 450,000 belonged to the paramilitary Central Security Forces, or 'riot police' (2009 figures). An additional 250,000 people had reportedly been recruited as police informants. 'Egypt,' *Eldestour* concluded, 'has become a police state par excellence' (S.E. Ibrahim 2007; El-Hennawy 2011; Ismail 2006: 152).

This rise in police numbers went hand in hand with a dramatic rise in prisoners, and in particular political detainees. Although political detention and torture were hallmarks of Mubarak's reign from the start, the Egyptian Organization for Human Rights reported in 2006 that 'while Egypt's population nearly doubled during ... Hosni Mubarak's regime [1981–2006], the number of prisons grew more than fourfold [and] the number of detainees held for more than one year without charge or indictment grew to more than 20,000'. In 2005, Kefaya estimated the number of political detainees to be 30,000 (S.E. Ibrahim 2007; *Al-Ahram Weekly* 2005b).

Mubarak's 'war' on Islamism left a legacy of not just an extended police force but also of the systematisation of torture. During the 1990s, torture, which had been routinely used against political opponents, became widespread in the regime's increasingly indiscriminate 'war' on the Islamists, particularly following the appointment of Habib al-Adly as Interior Minister in 1997 in the wake of the Luxor bombing (the same al-Adly whose resignation the protesters demanded on 25 January 2011) (Ahmed Osman 2011). By the 2000s, torture was used regularly against non-activist citizens (Bradley 2008: 117–45; Human Rights Watch 2004), a trend which was facilitated by the 'War on Terror', extraordinary rendition programmes and the unwillingness of international state officials to pressurise Mubarak on torture (El-Dawla 2009: 132–3; Bradley 2008: 130–4). As Gasser Abdel-Razek of Human Rights Watch noted, 'we have two generations of police who were brought up to use torture against Islamists. But if it's allowed and seen as effective, it spreads' (quoted in El-Dawla 2009: 122).

Illustrating this spread is the number of annual torture cases monitored by one of Egypt's leading human rights NGOs, the Egyptian Organization for Human Rights (Figure 3.3). While these represent only a fraction of the torture that took place, they are indicative of broader trends; by the 2000s, the levels of torture exceeded those seen during the regime's 'war' on militant Islamism.

Besides expanding, the police also became increasingly corrupt. From the late 1990s police salaries had decreased compared to others in the public sector, and to maintain their lifestyles, officers relied progressively on corruption. Under pressure to boost their performance, the increasingly demoralised and under-skilled force began to employ ex-convicts and thugs or *baltagiyya* to help extract information from reluctant witnesses and to suppress dissent, particularly from 2005 onwards (Naeem 2011; Jacinto 2011; Ismail 2006: 144–5).

As a result, non-activist Egyptians were increasingly likely to be arrested, whether to fill officers' arrest quotas, to supplement their

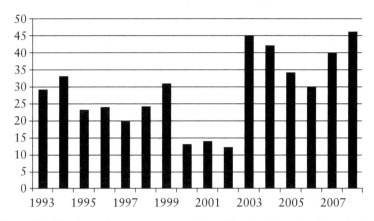

Figure 3.3: Number of torture cases monitored by the Egyptian Organization for Human Rights (EOHR n.d.).[10]

income, to pressure people into becoming informants or simply as a 'technique of establishing control and discipline'. Similarly, the category of who was considered 'suspect' or 'dangerous' widened, both in response to the broadening of political opposition and as part of a regime clampdown on the supposed moral decay of society. During this period police even began to arrest family members, 'especially sisters, mothers, and wives ... to force suspects to turn themselves in', thus further broadening the sectors of society affected by police brutality (Ismail 2006: 145–53, 150, 151). By 2005, according to El-Ghobashy (2005):

the target of state violence [had] shifted from insurgents to ordinary Egyptians. Once tranquil residential side streets in Cairo and Alexandria now serve as permanent parking lots for the ubiquitous trucks of the Central Security Forces, "in case a demonstration breaks out or something," said an idle conscript. Activists and unsuspecting passersby alike have become accustomed to new levels of police brutality.

In addition, the police became progressively involved in enforcing house demolitions in the 'informal areas' of Cairo where the 2011 demonstrations began (ECHR, n.d.). Because the police were largely absent from the narrow alleys of these crowded areas and slow in coming to people's rescue, their presence at house demolitions only served to reinforce the image of a threatening, to some even an 'occupying', force.

From 2007 onwards, following a change in the student charter, State Security Intelligence became more blatantly involved in university life, barring students from running in student elections, vetting promotions and standing guard on campuses. In 2010, the government added insult to injury, refusing to implement a court ruling banning SSI guards from campuses. This move alone triggered a series of anti-police protests on university campuses (Appendix).

Police violence against the Ultras similarly intensified in the late 2000s, although clashes between football supporters and police were nothing new. By the late 2000s, the international anti-police slogan of ACAB ('All Cops Are Bastards') began to appear in Egypt. Chants became increasingly explicitly anti-regime, such as the Al-Ahly Ultras' chant of: 'Regime! Be very scared of us, we are coming tonight with intent.' Supporters began to see themselves in more overtly political terms. In 2007, the leader of the Al-Ahly Ultras told a British football author: 'The two biggest political parties in Egypt … are Ahly and Zamalek', referring to Egypt's two biggest football clubs (Montague 2012; Crimethinc 2012). A watershed moment for the Ultras was the 2009 international match between Algeria and Egypt, which resulted in mass riots (Montague 2012).

The year 2010 saw a rapid succession of particularly violent encounters. The demonstrations commemorating the second anniversary of the April 2008 strike were described by an eyewitness as 'the most violent clashes since 2005' (Ziada 2010). Two months after came the death of Khaled Said and police violence against the explicitly non-violent vigils, and the 2010 elections saw widespread police intimidation, resulting in nine dead (Ikhwanweb 2010b). The protests against the 2011 church bombing in Alexandria similarly resulted in protracted battles between police and protesters.

By the late 2000s, therefore, what united Islamists, leftists, liberals, workers, football supporters, regular youths and inhabitants of informal quarters, was direct or indirect experience of police violence. Activists, workers and football supporters, moreover, learned valuable lessons in how to confront the police. Indeed, the success of the 2011 uprising was due in large part to the tactical innovations activists had developed in their encounters with the police, particularly during 2010 (Chapter 5), as well as to the development of horizontal, fluid, informal networks, enabling activists to avoid suppression.[11]

Police violence contributed to people becoming alienated from the regime. Salah (Interview 2011), for example, cited the police response to the anti-Iraq war demonstration in 2003 as a turning point in protesters' perception of the regime:

[Before 2003] we were not yet sophisticated enough to see the regime as responsible. But after that, because of the brutal dispersion [of protesters by the police], we realised that the regime was the problem. They beat up people until they were bleeding very hard, then they tied them up with their own clothes and put them on a pile in front of the Ramses Hilton. Following this event, there was a meeting in the Syndicate of Journalists to discuss: where is the enemy, and the importance of creating change.

El-Mahdi (2009: 93) similarly quotes a leading Kefaya activist who links the 'especially brutal' response of the police to the March 2003 demonstration with 'different political groups [beginning] to openly think about doing away with Mubarak'.

Crucially, apart from police violence becoming more arbitrary and blatant, awareness of police violence also increased, aided by the cumulative work of human rights NGOs, the reinvigoration of the opposition media and the spread of video phones and internet technology, particularly from 2007 onwards (Chapter 2). Specific instances of police brutality—the treatment of journalist Abdel Halim Qandil; the rape and torture of Emad al-Kabir, the micro-van driver; the death of Khaled Said—became widely known, making people feel increasingly vulnerable to random police violence. The more people could be made to realise that non-activism did not protect them against police violence, the easier it would be for them to overcome their fear of the police and start protesting.

Frame-wise, police brutality increasingly came to be overtly represented as systemic: reflective of the regime, rather than as incidental. During the 1990s, human rights NGOs tended to limit themselves to naming and blaming individual officers for torture abuse (even though torture was already systemic, and said to be so, at the time; cf. EOHR statement quoted in Human Rights Watch 1992: 4). By the early 2000s, they explicitly linked torture to 'those who occupy high political office'. In an important 2003 statement by the Egyptian Association Against Torture, a group of lawyers and human rights activists argued boldly:

When we talk about torture in Egypt we are not talking about a violation here or there. Nor are we talking about the sadism of a number of Egyptian police officers ... Egyptian authorities use torture as a systematic and organized tool to terrorize citizens and to ensure complete submission of the people to the policies of those authorities. (quoted in El-Dawla 2009: 134)

This shift in opposition discourse served both to further undermine the regime's legitimacy and to turn opposition to torture and other police abuses into an explicitly anti-regime activity.

That people protested against abuses by the police was not new in itself, just as police abuse was not new. People had taken to the streets before to protest against illegal detentions, torture or deaths at the hands of the police. Salwa Ismail (2006: 161–4) documents a number of such instances from the late 1990s onwards, particularly in rural areas. What distinguishes those events from the events of 2000 onwards, and particularly post-2005, is the way the latter became channelled into overtly political, organised protests in urban locations where the police had a stronger presence. Of the 175 demonstrations of 100 or more protesters documented by Al-Bura'y (2008) during the period 2005–2007, thirty-seven (21 per cent) specifically concerned police abuses. During 2008–2009, the percentage of protests involving over 500 protesters focusing explicitly on police violence dropped to below 10 per cent, but in 2010 this number soared again to 19 per cent (Appendix). A number of these protests concerned the same police abuses, and were staged at subsequent anniversaries of the original abuse, thus fuelling and intensifying the mobilisation of those involved.

4

'ATEF, THE PEOPLE OF EGYPT ARE FORCED TO EAT BRICKS!'

SOCIO-ECONOMIC CONTEXT

In the previous chapter we looked at the political context within which the protest networks emerged, and how this affected the networks' characteristics, timing and tactics. Here, we continue our analysis by looking at the socio-economic context, and how this interplayed with the protest networks. We will start with an analysis of economic factors impacting people's livelihoods and expectations, before focusing on changes in Egypt's youth ratio, as young people were the backbone of the protesters. We will end with a discussion of changes in Cairo's urban make-up and how this affected the protesters' mobilisation potential.

Our analysis is not exhaustive. There are other factors we could have looked at, such as shifting levels of household debt[1] or changes in crime patterns or patronage networks. However, time and space limit what we can include. The selected topics are thus an example of the type of analysis we propose, while covering some of the key dynamics of the decade(s) preceding the revolution.

Economic Factors Affecting People's Livelihood

Economic factors play a central role in explanations of revolutions and protest movements. We have already discussed the impact of neoliberal reforms on the relationship between the state and the wider population. The focus in this section will be on those economic factors that directly affect people's livelihoods, and thus the way they perceive threats and opportunities. Earlier theories of revolution and protest focused on economic strains, such as a sense of relative deprivation among one population group vis-à-vis another (cf. Gurr 1970; see Buechler 2004 for an overview). One popular classical theory is the J-curve model, describing a situation where a sharp drop in economic well-being follows a period of growth, thus creating a 'revolutionary gap' between expectations and lived experience (James Davies 1969). These theories have since been critiqued for being too deterministic; for assuming that economic strains automatically result in heightened grievances, frustrations and hence protest; for not taking mobilisation and political context into account, and so on (Buechler 2004). We do not adopt such a mechanistic approach. Rather, we take from this earlier literature the notion that economic factors contribute to creating conditions that could fuel protests, if protest networks exist with the capacity and opportunity to mobilise people by interpreting these conditions in a way that galvanises them.

In the case of Egypt, before 2011, most international bodies such as the World Bank and the IMF held Egypt up as an economic success, praising its human development programmes and its solid growth in GDP (cf. World Bank 2009). Indeed, if we look at official indicators such as nominal wage index, the Gini index (measuring inequality), poverty rates and number of people living in slums (Figures 4.1–2), Egypt's economic situation does not look particularly bad. The nominal wage index doubled during the 2000s, while the Gini index decreased. Official figures suggest that poverty, despite rising, remained relatively low, while the numbers of people living in slum areas decreased. With GDP per capita more than doubling within five years, we would thus be hard pushed to explain the events of 2003 (anti-Iraq war protests), 2008 (Mahalla protest) and 2010–2011 using these indicators alone.

Yet a closer look suggests that these figures mask a grimmer reality. Egypt's official data tend to undercount those living in 'informal' or unregulated urban areas, which contain many of Egypt's poor. A vivid illustration of this is Ezbet el-Haggana, an informal area in Cairo. According to Sarah Sabry (2009: 25), Egypt's official database, CAPMAS, list this as having 412 inhabitants. But estimates based on satellite images suggest a figure between 200,000 and 1 million (which

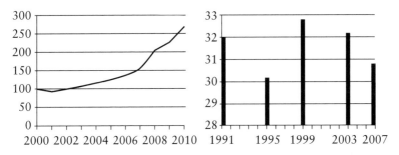

Figure 4.1: Nominal wage index (CAPMAS n.d.) and Gini Index (World Bank n.d.; only intermittent year data available).

would make it the fourteenth largest slum in the world). Sabry also gives numerous other examples, which, when taken together, indicate that poverty is far higher than the official story suggests.

Official figures similarly routinely undercount the unemployed and those working in the informal sector. The number of unemployed is regularly questioned by ethnographic estimates that are at times multiple times higher,[2] largely because only those actively 'seeking work' are included, not the masses who have given up looking for a job, while official employment figures, such as those of the International Labour Organization, typically include the underemployed and 'the hidden unemployed who, for lack of salaried employment, join the ranks of the informal sector's "self-employed" in order to survive' (Achcar 2013: 38–9). The Gini index, meanwhile, measures consump-

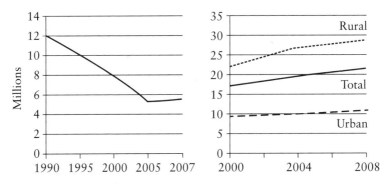

Figure 4.2: Slum population in urban areas (UN MDGI n.d.) and poverty head count ratio (CAPMAS n.d.).

tion inequality, rather than income inequality and inequalities in wealth distribution, and does not take social exclusion into account, which is exacerbated by the increasingly sharp discrepancy between rich suburban zones and slums. If the World Bank's Gini figures are correct, Achcar (2013: 32–4) points out, the richest 10 per cent in Egypt 'spends less than ... $420 (PPP) a month, or $155 at the market rate that prevailed in 2008. That seems highly unlikely.'

Economic Motivations for Protest?

Leaving aside the fact that Egypt's official data downplay key segments of the population, even the official data point to a number of economic strains that could help to explain protest dynamics. That economics played a role is clear when we look at what motivated protesters. One of the few polls available providing data about people's motivations suggests that a majority of respondents (64 per cent) cited low living standards and lack of jobs as the main reason for their support for, or participation in, the January 2011 uprising (Figure 5.3 in Chapter 5). Many of our interviewees similarly cited economic factors as being important drivers (Chapter 5).

The initial protest call included a demand for a higher minimum wage and, although the demonstrations' main instigators were middle class, most of those making up the demonstrations' foot soldiers were from the lower classes, including many from Cairo's informal areas. Anecdotal information suggests that anger at economic inequality played a major part. Take for instance a young former textile worker turned fruit peddler, who was reported to have said during the 2011 uprising, 'These big guys are stealing all the money ... If they were giving us our rights, why would we protest? People are desperate' (*New York Times* 2011c). The *New York Times* continued:

He had little sympathy for those frightened by the specter of looting. He complained that he could barely afford his rent and said the police routinely humiliated him by shaking him down for money, overturning his cart or stealing his fruit. "And then we hear about how these big guys all have these new boats and the 100,000 pound villas. They are building housing, but not for us—for those people up high."

Taken together, some of the key indicators of economic well-being— GDP growth rate, food prices, inflation, poverty, unemployment, vulnerable employment (Figures 4.3–5)—paint a deteriorating situation,

World Bank praise notwithstanding. Poverty (measured by the UN as those living below its definition of the national poverty line)[3] started to rise in 2000 and increased by more than 5 per cent over the decade to around 22 per cent. If, however, we take the upper national poverty line of PPP $2.70 per day, the poverty rate for Egypt for the period 2000–2006 jumps to 40.9 per cent (UNDP 2009: 114), which is explained by the large percentage of Egyptians living just above the UN's poverty line (Achcar 2013: 31). Vulnerable employment or 'unpaid family workers and own-account workers as a percentage of

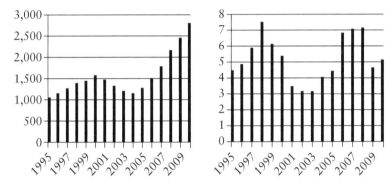

Figure 4.3: Per capita GDP (current prices) and GDP growth rate change (constant prices) (IMF n.d.).

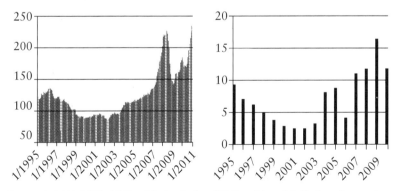

Figure 4.4: FAO World Food Price Index (FAO n.d.) and inflation change (av. consumer prices) in per cent (IMF n.d.).

131

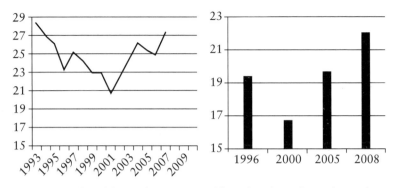

Figure 4.5: Vulnerable employment (World Bank n.d.) and population living below national poverty line in percentages (UN MDGI n.d.).

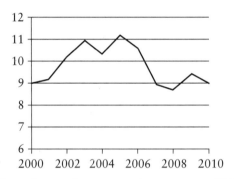

Figure 4.6: General unemployment rate in percentages (CAPMAS n.d.).

total employment' (World Bank n.d.) worsened in 2002, following a period of improvement during the 1990s, and grew by more than 6 per cent. Inflation took off in 2004, rising dramatically towards the end of the decade from less than 5 per cent in the early 2000s to over 15 per cent in 2009. Food prices increased exponentially in 2007, doubling between 2005 and 2008 to an unprecedented peak, then peaked again in January 2011. The exceptions to this trend are GDP, GDP growth rate and unemployment. GDP and GDP growth rate dipped in the early 2000s in response to a mixture of global and domestic factors, picking up again after 2004–2005. Unemployment peaked around 2003–2005, then similarly levelled off. However, both unemployment and GDP growth rate deteriorated towards the end of the decade, thus adding to the pressures created by the other factors. GDP growth rate in particular dipped after the global financial crisis of 2007–2008, dropping by more than a third.

Despite increasing GDP and relatively low unemployment (at least according to official figures), the picture emerging from these graphs is that, for ordinary Egyptians, the economic situation grew substantially worse over the course of the decade, though not necessarily linearly so. By 2011, exceptionally high food prices combined with high inflation (though less than in 2009), rising poverty, an increase in those in vulnerable employment and a significantly decreased GDP growth rate. The gradual rise in economic hardship described by some of these graphs cannot help to explain the timing of the 2011 events. There are, however, two trends that may have some direct explanatory power in relation to the timing of the protest episodes: the steep rise in food prices in 2008 and 2011, and the fluctuations in GDP growth rate between 2001 and 2005 and 2008 and 2010.

Rising Food Prices, Mahalla 2008 and January 2011

The most striking coincidence is between the two extraordinary peaks in world food prices in 2008 and 2011 and the two largest mass protests of the late 2000s (leaving aside the Brotherhood's Palestinian solidarity demonstrations): 6 April 2008 and January–February 2011. That on both occasions there were mass protests suggests that this is more than pure coincidence. A sharp increase in food prices had after all triggered the 1977 bread riots and, globally, the food crisis of 2007–2008 led to an outbreak of food-related protests in at least forty-three countries across the world (Cohen and Garrett 2009: 16).[4] Indeed, many (international) reports of the 2008 Mahalla strike used the idiom of bread riots, rather than a strike (cf. *Telegraph* 2008; *Huffington Post* 2008; *Spiegel* 2008).

According to the FAO Food Price Index (a measure indicating the price of a basket of basic staple foods), the world food price index rose from 140 in April 2007 to 217 in April 2008. Within a year, food prices had grown by a staggering 54 per cent, more than doubling what they had been in April 2005. Because Egypt imports a significant amount of its food (at the time, it was the largest wheat importer in the world), Egyptian food prices are particularly vulnerable to global fluctuations. As a result, between February 2005 and 2008, the cost of a nominal minimum food basket increased by 47 per cent (FAO 2008). With more than half of household income being spent on food, especially among the poor (Sabry 2009: 7), this would have placed a severe strain on not just the poor but also the (lower) middle classes.

By the end of 2008, the food price index had returned to the 140s, reducing the pressure on poor and medium-income households. During 2009, prices began to rise again. The resurgence of the pro-democracy protests of 2010 coincided with an increase in food prices to the 170 mark, around which they hovered for much of the year. By January 2011, food prices had returned to the impossible height of 217.

The rise in food prices was only one factor, and its effect was exacerbated by other economic factors, such as inflation (which doubled from an already high 9.5 per cent in 2007 to 18.3 per cent in 2008), rising poverty levels and erosion of the buying power of wages. In 2011, the peak in food prices was made worse by a drop in GDP growth rate and creeping unemployment. It was further augmented by the wider political situation, including the withdrawal of the welfare state, the narrowing of the regime's class base, police brutality and the ongoing protest episodes in the workers' and pro-democracy movements. Although the state stepped up its food subsidies to mitigate the worst effects, it was incapable of containing the food crisis, with long food lines and daily scuffles for subsidised food underlining the state's incompetence.

The precise relationship between rising food prices and these political protests needs further study.[5] But one thing that is noteworthy in comparison to the 1977 'bread riots' is the different focus and modus operandi of the ensuing protests. In 1977, the demonstrations were largely spontaneous (though in numerous instances, workers reportedly played a part in starting the demonstrations and students joined them). They involved primarily those most affected by the rise in bread prices— the urban poor and workers. Their focus was the rise in food prices, rather than regime change or political reform, with shouts like 'O Hero of the Crossing [reference to 1973 Arab–Israeli war], Where is Our Breakfast' and 'Jihan, Jihan [Sadat's wife], the People are Hungry.' The closest they came to challenging Sadat directly was to invoke his predecessor's name, 'Nasser' (Hirst and Beeson 1981: 242–4; Baker 1990: 124, 128–9; Seddon 1993: 104–7). In 2008 and even more so in 2011, the protests were carefully orchestrated by the main protest networks, although large numbers of the affected general population joined in, especially in 2011. The regime's very legitimacy was called into question and a reduction in food prices was not the main demand in either event (although people did shout slogans demanding an end to price hikes in 2008). The way protests evolve around economic crises is thus profoundly influenced by the shape and form of the networks carrying out the protests, as well as by the broader political context. It was thus arguably the presence of well-established protest networks, with their ready resources, tactics and frames, which enabled activists to channel any anger or fear arising from rising food prices into explicitly political opposition, and sustain it in the face of repression.

Fluctuations in GDP Growth Rate, the Anti-Iraq War Protests and the Pro-Democracy Protest Wave

The second trend that may carry some explanatory power is that of GDP growth rate. Although GDP growth rates halved and then doubled again during the period under consideration, they stayed within the 3–8 per cent range, never dipping below zero. Their effect, therefore, should not be overemphasised. In addition, GDP has fluctuated in the past, without giving rise to phenomena on the scale of 2003, 2008 or 2011. Nevertheless, it is striking that the 2000–2003 protest wave kicked off as GDP growth rates began to drop, culminating in the 2003 anti-Iraq war protests just as GDP growth rate hit rock bottom. Equally intriguing is that GDP growth rate had recovered to almost pre-2000 levels at about the time that the second wave of protests began to wane, while the 2010 protest wave started after a sharp drop in GDP growth rate the year before, with growth remaining lower than during the mid-2000s. Though the precise relationship between the protest waves' trajectories and the broader economy will remain a question of conjecture, it is possible that the slight easing of the economic situation in 2004–2005, coupled with Kefaya's failure to change the political status quo, contributed to this protest wave remaining relatively muted. It is also possible that the drop in GDP growth rate in 2009–2010, following a period of high growth, contributed to creating the beginnings of a 'revolutionary gap', just as it had done in 2001–2003 when a sharp drop followed high growth in the 1990s.[6] A counter-argument would be that the slump in GDP growth rate in 2009 was not severe enough to spur people into action, but sufficiently hard-hitting to divert people from political protests and focus on economic survival (including through protest). The slight rise in GDP growth rate by 2010, meanwhile, would have given people more leeway to act on the drop in GDP growth and refocus on political protest.

The March 2003 demonstration against the Iraq war played out against the backdrop of a sharp decrease in GDP growth rate, coupled with rising unemployment and poverty. GDP growth rate had slumped from over 5.4 per cent in 2000 to 3.5 per cent in 2001, and through 2002 and 2003 it remained just above 3 per cent. Coming after a period of high growth, this was a significant change in the country's economic outlook, felt in particular by the lower middle classes, the working classes and the poor. Reflecting this, even official unemployment figures rose above 10 per cent in 2002—for the first time since 1995—reaching 11.3 per cent in 2003. Per capita GDP similarly fell from $1566 in 2000 to $1209 in 2003, a drop of 23 per cent. Considering the huge discrepancy between the elite and the general population—by 2007, those who owned property assets accounted for 80 per cent of annual GDP, whereas wage earners (the vast majority) accounted for less than 20 per cent (El-Naggar 2009: 49)[7]—this 23 per cent drop would have affected the less well-off, who formed the bulk of the demonstrators in 2003, to a much greater extent. The fact that this downturn coincided with the rich becoming increasingly wealthy and powerful further exacerbated this discrepancy. It is in this context that people at the anti-Iraq war demonstrations shouted 'They wear the latest fashions! ... And we live ten to a room!' and 'Atef, a kilo of beans now costs six pounds! Atef, a kilo of meat is over thirty pounds! Atef, the people of Egypt [are forced to] eat bricks!' (A. Hassan 2003b).

To appreciate fully the effect of a drop in GDP (or indeed a rise in food prices) on society, we need to look more closely at the class make-up of Egypt. Although the African Development Bank (2011: 20, 22) estimated the number of poor (measured as living on less than $2 a day) at 'only' 17.9 per cent in 2008, nearly 50 per cent belonged to the floating middle class (earning between $2 and $4 a day), while a further 20 per cent made up the lower middle class (earning between $4 and $10 a day).[8] Leaving aside that other databases provide different figures, using different algorithms, what concerns us here is that a majority of Egyptians belonged to the lower middle classes and were thus highly vulnerable to changes in GDP growth rate, food prices and inflation, and likely to feel particularly threatened by the prospect of dropping down a class.[9] It is these societal sectors that would have been particularly hit by the rise in vulnerable employment rates and the privatisation of state industries, and its concomitant loss of job security and social benefits.

A second factor was the erosion of the buying power of wages. While wages, in real (official) terms, continued to grow (Figure 4.1), the purchase capacity of people's wages decreased drastically. In 1970, a university graduate's salary could buy 68 kg of beef monthly. By 1977, this had halved to 35 kg. By 2008, it had dropped to a mere 6 kg of beef (El-Naggar 2009: 43). In a country where beef is a core part of the menu, this had a serious impact on people's sense of well-being. In addition, the cost of living had risen as a result of, among other things, escalating educational and health costs following the withdrawal of the state.

Though the 2003 anti-war protests were clearly triggered by the invasion of Iraq and fed off the earlier Palestinian solidarity protest wave, we can conclude that the protests were simultaneously fuelled by economic hardship. This hardship, moreover, was the product of— and increasingly seen as—what Achcar (2013: 95) calls

the peculiar modality of the capitalist mode of production [in the Arab region]—a mix of [(neo-)]patrimonialism, nepotism and crony capitalism, pillaging of public property, swollen bureaucracies, and generalised corruption, against a background of great socio-political instability and the impotence or even non-existence of the rule of law.

That the protesters merged anti-war chants with slogans decrying both the domestic economic and political situation makes this conclusion all the more valid. Rising unemployment, a drop in GDP growth rate and a steady erosion of purchasing power would have given protesters both additional grievances and an imminent sense of threat to their livelihoods. Combined with an increasingly narrow, kleptocratic regime overseeing an accelerating privatisation process, these conditions would have made anti-regime chants resonate more readily with people, as any worsening of the economic situation could be readily blamed on the regime. Crucially, these economic and political changes coincided with a growth in opposition networks, which, for ideological or pragmatic reasons, actively sought to link everyday economic grievances to critiques of the regime.

WHY OCCUPY A SQUARE?

Economic Factors and the Workers' Protest Wave of 2006–2008

One thing that the economic factors discussed here cannot readily explain is the growth of the workers' protest wave in 2006–2008. High unemployment and low GDP growth rate would have contributed to the steep increase in strikes in 2004. But the timing of the 2004 strikes was driven primarily by the arrival of the new 'Businessmen's Cabinet' and the large-scale privatisation drive they championed. If economic factors had been the primary driver, the strikes would have abated when unemployment began to drop and GDP growth rates started to grow again in 2005–2006. Not only did they continue, but when the workers' strikes were at their height (2007–2008), Egypt experienced a high GDP growth rate and the lowest level of unemployment of the 2000s (although rising inflation and food prices would have placed additional strains on the workers).

Apart from the fact that national GDP growth rates are not necessarily a good measure for the economic situation facing textile workers, to explain this seeming anomaly we need to go back to social movement dynamics and look at how the protest wave grew out of the (perceived) success of earlier strikes and the failure of the government to honour the promises it had made in seeking to bring these to an end. The 2008 Mahalla strike, for instance, was the culmination of a dispute that began in 2006 over bonuses (an essential part of workers' income), and was a direct response to the non-fulfilment of previous promises. In addition, by that time, Kefaya and the workers' movement had helped to create a protest culture that made protests acceptable to a far larger part of the workers. By then, a growing number of strikes had succeeded in securing workers' demands, as the government sought to divert the wave of industrial disputes, making strikes ever more attractive. In other words, the 2007–2008 protests were in part a function of the success of the ongoing workers' protest wave, the growth of the organisational capacity of the workers' movement and the government's ambiguous responses, rather than simply a response to worsening economic conditions. However, the bonus dispute came in the context of wages—already among the lowest in the world for textile workers (Beinin 2009: 75)—coming under severe strain from rising food prices and inflation, and of an increasingly visible gap between the rich business elite and workers. As such, economic conditions were exacerbated by an acute sense of relative deprivation and injustice.

Economic strain and volatility can, however, help to explain why the epicentre of the strikes was in the cotton and textile industry, and why the strikes accelerated from 2004 onwards. One of the conditions of WTO membership was the gradual phasing out of import tariffs. With clothes being produced cheaply in Asia, this particularly affected the textile industry, which was also hit by the end of tariff-free export agreements with various European and North American countries (Rutherford 2008: 200–1). In addition, government assistance to cotton producers had fallen from a reported $290m in 1997–1998 to $14m in 2000–2001, although it crept up to $33 in 2002–2003 (Baffes 2004: 70), and in the second half of the decade €80m of EU funding was in fact made available for the modernisation of the cotton and textile industry (Ameinfo.com 2008).

The phasing out of tariffs was somewhat offset by new international agreements providing duty-free access through Qualified Industrial Zones (El-Haddad 2012: 3; just-style.com 2009). Nevertheless, cotton exports began to decline from 2004 onwards, and by 2006 they had halved compared to 2003. Overall cotton production similarly declined steeply from 2005 onwards, halving again in 2008 (Figure 4.7). Textile and clothing exports increased, but a sharp increase in imports resulted in a negative overall trade balance by 2007, particularly in the textile sector (El-Haddad 2012: 3–4). Much of the growth was in the expanding private sector, while the public sector remained in a state of decline (El-Fiqi 2006; Fibre2fashion 2006). The situation was exacerbated by the dynamics of privatisation, with factories in danger of being sold off often becoming sites for strikes due to fears over social security and unemployment (Beinin 2009: 78). The financial crisis of 2007–2008 hit the cotton industry particularly hard, with production halving between 2007 and 2008 (Figure 4.7) and exports dropping from 619,000 to 100,000 bales (USDA 2009, 2010). As a direct outcome of the world financial crisis, USDA (2010) reported, 'many spinning and weaving mils were forced either to shut down or reduce production'.

Changes in tariffs and export quota, the drop in government investment in the cotton industry and the global financial crisis did not usher in the protest wave. This had already begun in 2004, and had been given added momentum by the pro-democracy movement (Beinin 2009: 77). But these economic fluctuations, coupled to an increase in privatisation of the cotton industry, added fuel to the protest wave of 2006–2008 (and beyond). It is thus perhaps of little surprise that,

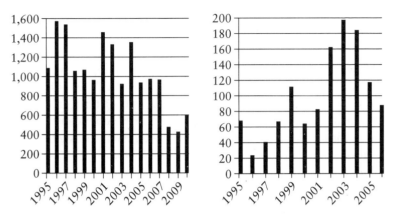

Figure 4.7: Egyptian cotton production (1,000 bales) (IndexMundi n.d.) and exports (1,000 tonnes) (Abu Hatab 2009).

while the pro-democracy wave petered out in 2005, the workers' movement gained in strength from 2005 onwards, with workers' protests tripling in 2007 and spreading beyond the textile and clothing industry (Beinin 2009: 79).

Summary

In summary, there are (at least) three macro-economic dynamics that can be said to have affected the timing and shape of the protest episodes and waves between 2000 and 2010. The first consists of the drop in GDP growth rate and the concomitant rise in unemployment at the start of the decade, which, interacting with the arrival of the 'Businessmen's Cabinet', regional wars and the regime's support for them, and the withdrawal of the welfare state, helped to set the scene for the anti-Iraq war protests, and their morphing into an anti-regime movement. The return to a higher GDP growth rate and lower unemployment, meanwhile, may have contributed to the relatively muted nature of the pro-democracy protest wave of 2004–2006.

The second dynamic concerns the rise in food prices, exacerbated by soaring inflation and, by 2011, another dip in GDP growth rate, which together helped to create volatile conditions in both the spring of 2008 and early 2011. That these were channelled into industrial strikes in 2008 and anti-regime protests in 2011 can be explained with reference

140

to the protest networks that were dominant at the time, and the particular problems besetting specific industries (2008) and the general population (2011).

The third dynamic concerns the gradual worsening of a slew of economic factors, from rising inflation and poverty, to higher unemployment for university and college leavers and an increase in vulnerable employment. By 2011, despite rising GDP and nominal wages, the Egyptian population faced a toxic mix of economic insecurity, which was made worse by the fact that over half of the population earned less than $4 a day according to official figures (and thus likely a higher percentage in reality). When food prices peaked again in January 2011, the convergence of these factors meant that some form of mass protest was a strong probability (though not inevitable). That it turned into a mass revolt against the regime, led primarily by university graduates, but encompassing workers and the lower middle classes, was down to the interaction between economic and political factors, and the existence of an opposition movement channelling any economic grievances into a political reform agenda.

None of this is to suggest that the economic situation alone would have triggered the various protests. The demands and slogans of the mass protests of 2003, 2008 and 2010–2011 were largely political (with the partial exception of the Mahalla strike) and, apart from Mahalla, they were direct responses to political events. The overtly political nature of the protests set them apart from the genre of 'bread riots' (although 'bread riots' are usually both 'an economic and political phenomenon' and should be seen as integral to the process of political contestation; Sadiki 2000: 82). To reduce them to mechanistic responses to economic fluctuations is to miss both the wider context and the meaning that the activists themselves accorded the protests.

In addition, there were other periods without mass unrest when economic indicators were negative—or periods with mass unrest when economic indicators were not particularly alarming. The strikes of the late 1980s, for instance, coincided with official unemployment figures of between 7–9 per cent (Figure 4.8)—well below those of the 2000s—and subsided in the early 1990s, when unemployment rose above 10 per cent. The figures for 'vulnerable employed' (Figure 4.5) were as high in the early 1990s as they were in the mid-2000s, yet there were no comparable mass protests (although the very bloody struggle between Islamist militants and the government was nearing its zenith).

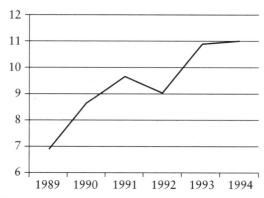

Figure 4.8: Unemployment as percentage of the total labour force (World Bank n.d.).

Nevertheless, given the repeated co-occurrence of economic strains and large protest events, we cannot discard the notion that economics influenced protest dynamics, particularly where political slogans merge with economic ones.

The most striking anomaly in this narrative is the continuing growth in per capita GDP throughout 2005–2011. However, if we take into account the sharp increase in people's daily outgoings as a result of the hike in food prices and rising inflation, and consider that the GDP figures are grossly skewed by the contribution of a very small elite, we can appreciate that per capita GDP figures are not an adequate measure of how daily fortunes fluctuated between 2005 and 2011.

Demographic Factors: Youth Bulge

A factor profoundly affecting the protest waves of the 2000s was the ratio of youth to general population. Pundits made much of the high percentage of youth in the Middle East and North Africa, and their prevalence in the uprisings of what became known as the 'Arab Spring'.[10] While we do not have reliable statistical data on the age profile of Egypt's protesters, a cursory look at the images taken during the revolution shows that the youth played a prominent part in the uprising. Although photos and anecdotal testimonies underline the presence of older Egyptians, youth dominated the activist networks that planned and instigated the protests, just as they did in previous protest waves.

The question we want to address is whether Egypt's demographic changes can help to explain the onset of the various protest waves.

'Youth bulges' feature heavily in the literature on political violence and revolutions. While the Egyptian revolution was largely non-violent, it is nevertheless instructive to consider this literature, as it seeks to explain the conditions that make revolutionary mobilisation possible. Whether this mobilisation turns violent is a separate question, and depends on the specific context within which movements mobilise, and how they frame the conflict.

The presence of a 'youth bulge' is routinely cited as a factor in the emergence of violent unrest, although opinion is divided regarding its importance, its precise role, what constitutes 'youth' and what type of violence results. Some, like Samuel Huntington (1996), take a simplistic and overly deterministic view, suggesting that once a critical mass of youth is reached, political violence is likely to occur. Others, such as Henrik Urdal (2006, 2007), argue that, while the presence of a 'youth bulge' increases the statistical risk of political violence (a 1 per cent youth ratio increase corresponds, according to Urdal, to a 4 per cent increase in the likelihood of conflict), much depends on the political and economic context (see also Achcar 2013:40–43). Within revolutionary studies, Jack Goldstone (1997: 106–15, 1991: 1–62) expands on this by arguing that 'youth bulges' usually lead to political crisis only when they coincide with a decline in state capacity, elite conflicts and widespread economic strains as a result of falling wages, unemployment and over-urbanisation—although he emphasises that 'youth bulges' exacerbate these other factors. Urdal (2006) further distinguishes between different types of violence, suggesting that 'youth bulges' coinciding with educational and economic strains are statistically more likely to lead to terrorism and riots, whereas 'youth bulges' in authoritarian settings are more likely to correspond to armed conflict. Others, such as Lindsay McLean Hilker et al. (2009), caution against using 'youth bulges' as a predictor of violence, noting that there are instances where 'youth bulges' herald periods of growth and innovation, and that, where they do coincide with violence, correlation does not automatically mean causation. Because of its negative connotations, we will not use the term 'youth bulge' and will use 'high youth ratio' instead.

Whichever approach one adopts, it is striking that, historically, revolutions and mass protests tend to coincide with high youth ratios, whether one looks at the revolts and political crises sweeping Eurasia in the seventeenth and nineteenth centuries or the civil wars and revolutions of the late twentieth century in the world's low- to middle-income countries with the highest population growth (Goldstone 1991, 1997: 105–6).

Besides having different definitions of youth and 'youth bulges' (Collier and Hoeffler, for instance, define youth as 15–29 year olds and 'youth bulges' by the ratio of youth to general population; Urdal focuses on the 15–24 age bracket and measures the ratio of youth to adult population), there are also different explanations for why youth are particularly likely to engage in violent activism. Some of these arguments are equally applicable to explaining mobilisation into risky yet non-violent protest tactics. Explanations range from the physiological–psychological characteristics of youth (energy, strength, idealism, impatience, risk-seeking), to the opportunities represented by 'youth bulges' or the grievances felt specifically by youth. The presence of large numbers of youth, especially if they are unemployed and unmarried, lowers the recruitment costs for opposition networks. The unemployed in particular are likely to have less loyalty to the status quo.[11] In addition, 'youth bulges' can create opportunities for mobilisation if their presence contributes to a weakening of state capacity, elite fissures and a greater mass mobilisation potential as a result of worsening economic conditions (Goldstone 1997: 106–15).

Youth share general grievances. But they also experience grievances specific to youth (and exacerbated by high youth ratios), such as youth unemployment, lack of housing for young adults, police repression targeting youth or disempowerment through rigid societal and political hierarchies. Besides the latter grievances, the literature highlights another youth-specific grievance of particular interest to us: the notion of 'waithood', which describes a situation where the transition from youth to adulthood is blocked by economic and societal factors (Singerman 2007; for discussion of young Cairene men's problems of finding housing and a wife, see Ismail 2006: 110–12). For instance, in societies where adulthood is symbolically represented by stable employment, marriage and ownership of a house, un- or underemployment can seriously delay the transition to becoming 'fully recognised' adults, giving rise to grievances and alienation (although the precise relationship between these personal grievances and the political demands of those engaged in protest is not necessarily straightforward). In addition, 'waithood' means that more youths are available for mobilisation until later in life as they remain unencumbered by the commitments that come from marriage and parenthood.

Youth Ratios and Protest Waves

Before discussing youth ratios in Egypt, it is important to emphasise that, contrary to the widespread belief that high youth ratios were a major factor in the 'Arab Spring', populations in the Middle East and North Africa are not particularly young—or as Achcar notes '*no longer* especially young'—but are comparable to those in sub-Saharan Africa, South Asia and South East Asia (Achcar 2013: 41–2).

Because youth ratios are calculated using the same flawed statistics discussed above, the actual youth ratio is likely to be higher than official numbers suggest, given that it is particularly those who live in urban 'informal areas', often in large families, who remain unaccounted for (cf. Sabry 2009: 21). However, if we take these statistics as a rough indicator of population composition, it is striking that, whether we adopt the 15–29 or the 15–24 age bracket definition (Figure 4.9), the ratio of youth to general population peaked twice during the period 1970–2010:[12] once during the 'bread riots' of 1977, and a second time during the Palestinian solidarity protests of the early 2000s that culminated in the 2003 anti-Iraq war demonstration.[13] Prior to 2008 and 2011, these were indeed some of the largest mass protests in recent Egyptian history, although neither was violent in the

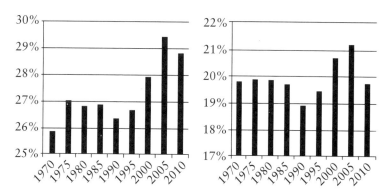

Figure 4.9: Proportion of populations aged 15–29 and 15–24 (UN World Population Prospects 2010).

way suggested by the 'youth bulge' literature (despite many other factors traditionally linked to violence being present).[14] Conversely, Egypt's most violent period, the struggle between militant Islamists and Egyptian security forces during the 1990s, occurred at a time when the ratio of youth to general population was at its lowest. In the case of Egypt, the occurrence of a high youth ratio thus appears to be better at explaining mass protests than political violence (even though 2011 happened six years after the youth ratio peak—we will return to this).

Although the increase in youth ratio is relatively small (3 per cent between the lowest point in 1990 and the peak in 2005 for 15–29 year olds), it is highly significant. As Goldstone notes in his study of historical revolutions, even 'small changes in the age distribution of a population can have a marked effect on popular mobilization' (Goldstone 1991: 137). The key lies in differential perceptions of how widely supported an opposition movement is. To illustrate this, Goldstone presents a simplified model, where, reflecting different levels of risk averseness, each successive age group will need higher assurances of the extent of popular support. If 26–35 year olds join when a quarter of those aged fifteen and over have joined the opposition, and if those over thirty-five join only if more than half has been mobilised, a mere 5 per cent increase in 16–25 and 26–35 year olds would change the situation from stable to unstable, if the starting point was a 25–20–55 per cent division for each of the age groups.

In social movement terms, by the early 2000s, the pool of potential activists with both the time and inclination to go out on the street had grown substantially compared to earlier decades. One (very crude) way to explain the onset of street protests in the early 2000s is to point to this peaking youth ratio. The fact that the only other mass protests in recent Egyptian history occurred at the only other moment in recent times that the youth ratio peaked (mid-1970s) makes this argument all the more persuasive, even though it cannot explain the precise form these protests took, or how the second one was maintained after the youth ratio had peaked, culminating in a far larger protest in 2011, well after the peak had passed. However, a high youth ratio in itself is not sufficient to explain these mass protests.

Both the 1977 and the 2003 mass protests occurred against a backdrop of a sharp increase in grievances, and particularly economic grievances. In 1977, these stemmed from the sudden cut in food subsidies, amidst a turbulent period of economic and political transition. In

2003, the grievances arose from the convergence of a rapidly deteriorating economic situation, coming on the back of socially devastating neoliberal reforms, and the increasingly bloody al-Aqsa Intifada just across the border. Exacerbating the effect of these factors was the growing belief among politically aware Egyptians that the regime cared neither for the Palestinians nor for Egypt's impoverished, as they closed ranks with the business elite and continued to align themselves with US foreign policy. In other words, the high youth ratio itself did not seem to be the primary cause of the protests; rather, the protests were responses to a set of converging strains, affecting both people's livelihoods and their political sensibilities. The bulge served to intensify the pressure on the already strained economy, thus exacerbating the grievances people felt (particularly youth), while at the same time ensuring that there was an unusually large pool of potential recruits, unencumbered by family commitments.

The presence of a high youth ratio in itself does not predict how mobilisation plays out. Here we have to turn to a social movement analysis. In 1977, the protests did not directly emerge out of an ongoing protest wave, although the workers and, less so, the student sectors had both seen sustained protest episodes over the previous years related in part to economic grievances, and their already existing networks played a role in the demonstrations (though not, as far as the literature discusses it, as central a part as in 2003 or 2011). Nor did the protests themselves appear to have played the kind of seminal role played by the 2003 protests in preparing the ground for the next protest wave, although more research on this relationship is needed (Seddon 1993: 98–112; Hirst and Beeson 1981: 242–52; Baker 1990: 118–32; Hinnebusch 1985: 243–53). In 2003, by contrast, the mass protests emerged out of an ongoing protest wave, driven by increasingly experienced and interlinked pro-Palestinian and anti-US foreign policy networks. Experienced activists channelled the mass outpouring, linking economic grievances with regime change, and kept the protest wave alive after the immediate trigger (the invasion of Iraq) had passed (although, unlike the bread riots, which ended when Sadat reinstated the food subsidies, the 'cause' of the protests, the occupation of Iraq, clearly continued, Sadat's mismanagement of the economy likewise remained). The linkage between Iraq and regime change furthermore enabled the protests to morph into the second wave (although by then they had lost their mass character).

Youth Ratios, Youth Unemployment and 'Waithood'

As the 'youth bulge' literature predicts (cf. Urdal 2006: 610–11), the 2003 peak was accompanied by a surge in youth unemployment, affecting both the loyalty of the youth to the status quo and their readiness to protest. However, in the case of Egypt, and indeed the entire region, youth unemployment is exceptionally high compared to other regions. Figures compiled by the ILO suggest that youth unemployment in the Middle East and North Africa is roughly twice as high as in sub-Saharan Africa and almost triple what it is in South and East Asia (Achcar 2013: 40). According to CAPMAS, youth unemployment in Egypt, already high at around 28 per cent in 2000, rose, following a brief drop, to a phenomenal 35 per cent in 2003, and stayed at that level through 2005, before dropping off to the mid-20s from 2007 onwards (Figures 4.10–11).[15] If these figures are correct—according to some reports, youth unemployment was as high as 75 per cent among 15–29 year olds by 2007–2008 (El-Naggar 2009: 42)—the peaking of the youth ratio in 2003–2005 coincided with an unemployment peak. General unemployment peaked in 2003–2005 (Figure 4.6), as a result of low GDP growth, the increasing effects of neoliberal reforms and an adverse global financial environment. But youth were hit particularly hard. During the first and second protest waves, youth unemployment figures were much higher than they had been during the 1990s, while the proportion of 'new entrants among the unemployed' (i.e. school

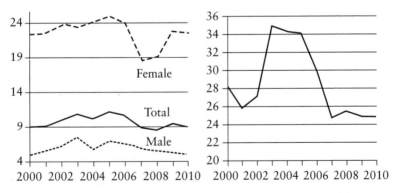

Figure 4.10: General and youth unemployment rate (15–24 year olds) in percentages (CAPMAS n.d.).

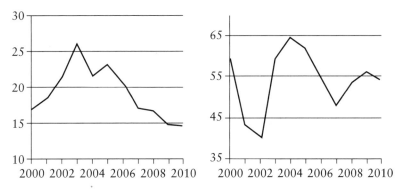

Figure 4.11: Youth unemployment rate for male and female 15–24 year olds (CAPMAS n.d.).

and university leavers) increased from an already high 74 per cent in 1998 to 82 per cent in 2006 (World Bank 2008).[16] With the total number of 15–24 year olds hovering just under 16 million, this meant that (at least) 5.5 million youth were unemployed. Actual figures are likely to have been considerably higher (Van Eekelen, de Luca and Ismail 2002: 21; Sabry 2009: 15–18). In addition, there were the millions who were underemployed or in informal, often very insecure, jobs. According to the Egypt Human Development Report (2010: 6, 83), nearly a third of employed youth were in this position in the late 2000s (others suggest this figure was closer to 72 per cent in 2005; A. Aly 2012).

Significantly, unemployment progressively hit those with a university or technological college education (Figure 4.12)—a phenomenon that is linked to the shrinking of the public sector (Achcar 2013: 50–1). By 2006, according to Assaad (2008: 155–6), 20 per cent of male urban university graduates and 30 per cent of technological high school leavers were unemployed, up from 16 per cent and 20 per cent in 1998 (the figures for urban females were 17 per cent and 27 per cent in 2006 against 10 per cent and 19 per cent in 1998).[17] This is precisely the demographic that was one of the chief engines behind the anti-war and the pro-democracy movements. The fact that they were unemployed meant they had time and a weakened loyalty to the status quo. The fact that they were highly educated meant that they suffered greater 'status inconsistency' (livelihoods incommensurate with educational status and expectations) and were in a better position to analyse their plight.

149

Economic factors also played a role in blocking youths from achieving full adult status. By the early 2000s, the average age at which an Egyptian man married was reported to be around thirty (CAPMAS 2001–2007), although the accuracy of this figure is disputed (Kholoussy 2010). Youth unemployment, the effects of privatisation on the economy and a drop in GDP caused by global factors meant that many families were delayed in gaining the financial means to pay for marriage and a marital home. By the late 2000s, pundits were talking about a 'marriage crisis' (cf. Abdelhadi 2008; Kholoussy 2010). Overall marriage rates are reported to have dropped from an average of 8.2 over the period 1995–1999 to 7.6 in 2001–2005 (CAPMAS 1982–2007; M. Osman and Girgis 2009).[18] In major urban centres, such as Cairo and Alexandria, marriage rates seem to have plummeted even more dramatically over the past three decades, and particularly after 1999 (Figure 4.12). More research is needed to establish whether and how 'waithood' affected people's motivation to protest. What appears to be the case, though, is that 'waithood' has become more pronounced in the 2000s, and given that it has been noted to play a role elsewhere, it is likely to have affected activists' decisions to mobilise in non-violent opposition.

In addition to youth unemployment and delayed marriage, young Egyptian men experienced police repression (women were also increasingly targets as the 2000s wore on, but men bore the brunt of police

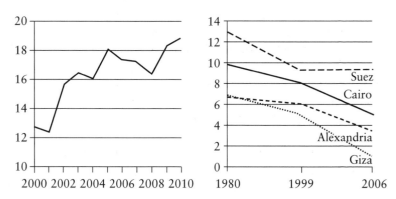

Figure 4.12: Unemployment rate for university leavers (ISCED 5–6) (CAPMAS n.d.) and crude marriage rates in key urban areas (classified by governorate, urban rates depicted only) (M. Osman and Girgis 2009).[19]

abuses). In addition to general police abuse, young men were the target of 'police raids on coffee shops and "campaigns to arrest suspects"' as well as identity card checks and 'suspicion and investigation' procedures in Cairo's informal neighbourhoods (Ismail 2006: 120–1). Because of this, young men from informal neighbourhoods have traditionally been attracted to groups that openly oppose the police. As Ismail found in her ethnographic work among Cairo's young men, '[militant] Islamist groups active in popular neighborhoods [in the 1980s and 1990s] drew support from youths in the market and streets' precisely because this 'offered an opportunity to band together and challenge police incursions into their spaces'. Experiences of humiliation at the hands of the police and particularly slights to their sense of masculinity, which demanded acts of strength, courage and honour in the tradition of *awlad al-balad* [sons of the country], played a central role in these young men's motivations. Acts of humiliation and random abuse became routinised in the late 1990s, for instance through the passing of the law of *baltaga* [thuggery] in 1998, which specifically targeted young males and the practice of *futuwwa*, groups of local youths acting as neighbourhood protectors (but also at times associated with gangs and drug trafficking) (Ismail 2006: 121–4, 113–14). This type of police targeting intensified just at the time that the youth-to-population ratio was increasing, thus creating an added incentive for young men to join anti-regime networks.

Figure 4.12, depicting youth ratios, youth unemployment and marriage rates may be able to offer a partial (and very crude) explanation for the timing of the 1977 and 2003 mass protests. What the graphs do not explain is why the events of 2011 happened when they did. Strikingly, apart from the continuing drop in urban marriage rates, none of the graphs provides clues for why the years 2010–2011 were particularly eventful in terms of youth activism. The graphs can, however, tell us more if we drill down into the 15–29 cohort, disaggregating the 15–19, 20–24 and 25–29 age groups (Figures 4.13–15), and look at the interaction of these demographic factors with the social network dynamics discussed in Chapters 1–2.

Drilling Down Into the Youth Cohort

Percentage-wise, the largest of the three five-year brackets making up the 15–29 cohort consists of those born in 1980–1985, just preceding

Mubarak's fertility interventions (Korotayev and Zinkina 2011: 83–4). The graphs (Figures 4.13 and 4.14) on the following page clearly show how this cohort drives the peaks in the three consecutive age brackets as it ages: they peak in 2000 as the 15–19 category, in 2005 as the 20–24 category, and again in 2010. Particularly intriguing in social movement terms is that this cohort contains the activists who were socialised into street protests as school and junior university students in the early 2000s, graduating to junior leadership roles in the pro-democracy protest wave, and providing the experienced backbone for the 2010 protest wave. They grew up on a diet of human rights discourse with an increasing emphasis on participatory politics and a growing alienation from the state as a result of the political and economic strains described above. Their rise through the ranks of the pro-democracy movement was enabled by—and in turn fuelled—a shift towards increased youth participation in the decision-making of protest networks. This trend was facilitated by the spread of IT-based social media among this new generation.

By 2010, this generation had had a chance to absorb the taboo-breaking tactics of the pro-democracy movement, making them experienced activists by the time of the 2011 uprising. That their absolute numbers had by then dropped below those of the younger cohorts is not significant for this argument, as our concern is with those socialised into activism, rather than with the size of the total cohort. At the same time, the fact that this cohort still faced difficulties with marriage and employment (26.4 per cent of the unemployed in 2010 were in this age bracket) (CAPMAS 2010) and that the ratio of 25–29 year olds peaked in 2010, thus creating extra pressures for this group, underlines that this was a cohort that was likely to have the motivation, the time and, importantly, the experience to protest. This, combined with the political factors discussed above (such as the timing of the expected Mubarak succession, the growing visibility of elite fissures and increased police repression), adds an additional factor to explanations for the timing of the 2010–2011 events. Crucially, because the anti-Iraq war protests, unlike the 1977 bread riots, grew organically out of, and fed into, an organised network of activists, who succeeded in creating structures that could sustain activism over a prolonged period, the drop in youth-to-population ratio after 2005 did not spell an end to this protest wave.

By 2010, when the fourth wave kicked off, the youth cohort outnumbering the others in absolute terms was the 20–24 year cohort. It

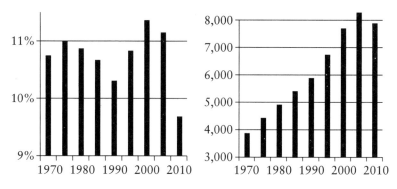

Figure 4.13: Proportion of population aged 15–19 and population aged 15–19 in thousands.[20]

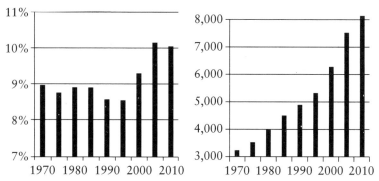

Figure 4.14: Proportion of population aged 20–24 and population aged 20–24 in thousands.

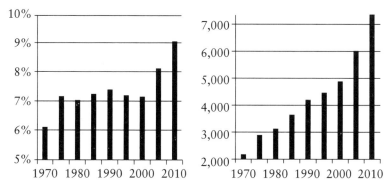

Figure 4.15: Proportion of population aged 25–29 and population aged 25–29 in thousands.

153

is this cohort that could provide the largest number of potential recruits, larger, intriguingly, than the 15–19 year cohort (by some 300,000 or 4 per cent of the latter's total). Besides being the largest cohort, these were youths who had already been exposed to activism, even if from a distance, during their formative teenage years, and who faced a particularly acute uncertain future, exacerbated by their numbers. According to CAPMAS, the percentage of the total number of unemployed aged 20–24 was 49.3 per cent for 2010, compared to 11.4 per cent for 15–19 year olds and 26.4 per cent for those aged 25–29. In other words, someone unemployed was four times more likely to be in this age group than in the age group immediately below, and twice as likely as in the age group immediately above. In addition, those having university degrees made up 43.1 per cent of the unemployed (67.2 per cent for female university leavers, against 32.8 per cent for males), while the total of those having an intermediate or higher level of education stood at 94.8 per cent of the underemployed.[21] In short, this cohort contained a large percentage of unemployed, highly educated youths, facing a blocked transition to formal adulthood: precisely the profile of those found to be ready recruits for opposition groups in the literature. While they had peaked in 2005 in terms of their percentage of the general population, their absolute numbers were still rising by 2010 (unlike those for the 15–19 cohort).

The 15–19 cohort, having peaked as a percentage of the general population in 2000, peaked in absolute numbers in 2005, just when the second wave had reached its zenith and the third wave was starting up (although, being made up of workers, this wave would have had a higher age average). This cohort was thus in a prime position to provide the rank and file for the pro-democracy movement, which by now included leaders from among the 20–24 cohort socialised during the anti-Iraq war demonstrations. Intriguingly, though, it is this period that has the lowest number of active activists, which may have something to do with the increase in GDP growth and the decline in youth unemployment. By 2010, the 15–19 cohort had grown smaller. But it was still large enough to provide protesters for the 2010–2011 events.

None of these explanations can give us a definitive clue for the precise timing of the 2010–2011 protest wave. But, by breaking down the youth cohort into smaller age brackets, we can see how the availability of different levels of different age groups interacted with the growth of opposition networks.

Changing Urban Structures

Changes in Cairo's urban structure, and in particular the growth of informal settlements, were another factor affecting both people's livelihoods and the opportunities available to the protesters. Having occurred over decades, these changes cannot explain why certain events happened when they did. They can, however, provide insight into how they were made possible. The focus in this section is Cairo. Each city participating in the uprising had its own unique socio-spatial arrangements, and what holds for Cairo may not be generalisable across the country. Nevertheless, other large cities, such as Alexandria and Tanta, similarly have a high percentage of informal settlements. According to Soliman and De Soto (2004: 131–3), in 1999–2000, 50 per cent and 25 per cent of these cities constituted informal areas,[22] although in Alexandria their spatial distribution is not as advantageous to the types of concentric swarming tactics deployed in Cairo, as the informal areas are not as centrally located.

One of the key changes in Cairo's urban make-up was the growth of informal settlements, or what has come to be known derisively as *ashwaiyyat* (derived from the word 'haphazard') (Ismail 2006: 1). Starting in the 1960s, but accelerating during the 1970s, land designated as agricultural within the Greater Cairo area began to be used to build cheap houses without planning permission. As a result of the pressures of mass migration, inadequate public housing policies and expensive real estate in 'formal' Cairo, 'informal' housing became the fastest growing sector, constituting 84 per cent of new housing built during the 1970s, fuelled by the remittances sent back from the Gulf following Sadat's *infitah* policy (Séjourné 2009: 18–19). Despite a slowing migration rate into the city and a drop in remittances as a result of the oil price slump in the 1980s, between 1986 and 1996 the informal areas grew ten times as fast as the formal areas. During that same period, migration from Cairo's formal areas into the informal zones reached a peak, with 500,000 inhabitants or 20 per cent of their 1986 populations moving out of Cairo's inner districts. This process continued at a reduced rate over the next decade, with a further 250,000 people moving into the informal settlements (Séjourné 2009: 19; Sims 2010: 55–6). By 2009, 64 per cent of residents of Greater Cairo lived in these settlements, comprising around 40 per cent of Greater Cairo.

Informal areas were both contested and insecure. Three aspects are particularly important for our analysis of the 2011 events. First, these informal areas offered an ideal urban landscape for outmanoeuvring the police, although it was not until 2010 that activists developed the tactics conducive to doing so (underlining how human interpretation shapes how structures are used). Because houses were built right to the edge of the original agricultural plots, the result was a maze of narrow alleyways cut through by wider streets built on former irrigation canals. These alleys were, to use Asef Bayat's phrase, 'streets of discontent' par excellence (Bayat 2009: 164–70). They were different from the headline streets described by Bayat in his spatial analysis of Egyptian and Iranian protests: those in the vicinity of urban university campuses and squares or those containing bookstores, theatres or cafés to attract the intellectuals. They did fulfil some of the same functions as the narrow streets mentioned by Bayat surrounding key squares and thoroughfares: a means to escape the police. But, in addition, they became sites of mobilisation where the demonstrations could start and grow, away from the security forces, until they were large enough to overwhelm the police stationed at the large public thoroughfares and squares. They thus became feeder sites, as well as boltholes, linking the periphery with the centre by making them the epicentre of revolutionary mobilisation (Chapter 7). What made these alleys attractive was their size (they were small enough to make a small crowd look large and powerful, thus lowering people's fear threshold), and the absence of policemen (Sims 2010: 122).

Second, the informal settlements offered a close sense of community and solidarity, facilitating mass mobilisation (once enough people had been persuaded to join). Ismail (2006: 19) found in her study of Cairo's informal areas that:

many [interviewees] stressed the relations of solidarity found in their neighbourhood in contrast to the lack of concern for others that they perceive to be characteristic of the attitudes of residents in the city's more prosperous areas, such as Muhandissin, Zamalek, and Garden City. Solidarity is thought to be evidenced at times of illness, death, or need.

If the goal is to get people on to the street, persuading people to join will be easier if they have a strong sense of solidarity with those already out there. Through arduous networking in these areas prior to the uprising, opposition groups such as April 6 had built up a network of local influential people who could mobilise sections of their neighbourhood (Chapter 5). Ismail provides an insight into the solidarity networks that thrive in Cairo's informal areas, from groups of young men

acting as self-help defence groups (*futuwwa*) to neighbourhood frater-
nities linked to 'work, religious activities, and quotidian practices of
sociability' and religious networks (Ismail 2006: 99–108, 113–14). It
is these existing networks, forged in adversity and close proximity,
which helped to swell the numbers of protesters in a way that would
have been far more difficult to achieve in Cairo's formal areas
(although more research is needed to establish exactly how).

Third, mobilisation was facilitated by the fact that the protest frames
of the opposition (challenging police abuse and calling for an increase
in the minimum wage) would have resonated especially with the inhabitants of these informal areas. While the police were largely absent
from the alleyways, they were very noticeable in the larger thoroughfares and marketplaces, harassing stall owners, extracting bribes and
arresting young men in their 'suspicion and investigation' raids, which
specifically targeted informal neighbourhoods (Ismail 2006: 120–4,
145–60). There were also regular house demolitions overseen by the
police. The inhabitants of these settlements would furthermore have
suffered disproportionately from the various economic crises discussed
above. They would, moreover, have felt particularly distant from the
regime, given the disconnection between their daily lives and the state.
There was no centralised provision of water, electricity and sewerage
services, so inhabitants had to fend for themselves, siphoning off electricity clandestinely from electricity masts for example.

The increasingly visible gap between the lives of inhabitants of these
areas and the inhabitants of Cairo's new formal settlements on the
city's outskirts would have further fuelled people's alienation from the
ruling elite. As the *New York Times* (2011c) observed:

The widening chasm between rich and poor in Cairo has been one of the con-
spicuous aspects of city life over the last decade—and especially the last five
years. Though there were always extremes of wealth and poverty here, until
recently the rich lived more or less among the poor—in grander apartments or
more spacious apartments but mixed together in the same city.

But as the Mubarak administration has taken steps toward privatizing more
government businesses, kicking off an economic boom for some, rich Egyptians have fled the city. They have flocked to gated communities full of big
American-style homes around country clubs, and the remoteness of their lives
from those of average Egyptians has become starkly visible.

It was this chasm that drove the limited looting that took place during
the first days of the revolution (*New York Times* 2011c).

The final factor affecting the protests is that the informal areas
served as social equalisers. Although they contained many poor, they
were far from homogeneous. Rather, they were reflective of the distribution of social classes in urban Egypt generally (Sims 2010: 111–12).
The inflow of members of the lower and middle classes started in the
1970s, and then accelerated with the exodus of inhabitants from formal Cairo as a result of economic pressures. A further incentive came
with the introduction in the late 1990s of 'speculative one-off towers,
… dotting well-located inner fringe areas of Cairo', offering 'large
apartments in central locations at an affordable price' (Sims 2010:
104–5). The result was an increase in opportunities for the poor and
the lower middle classes to mix and experience similar living circumstances, distinct from those experienced by the upper or middle classes
who could afford to buy properties in Cairo's new developments in the
desert. This, in combination with the levelling of opportunities, which
used to be exclusive to the middle class but were now available to the
lower classes, meant that a coalition between members of the lower
and middle classes, so crucial for the success of the revolution, was
made easier. The close proximity and solidarity networks offered by
the informal areas, and the shared experience of living outside of the
state's formal structures, would have facilitated the development of
shared protest and grievance frames.[23] Although more research is
needed to establish the precise dynamics of cross-class interaction, it is
striking that the proliferation of cross-class alliances and networks
began to accelerate in the early 2000s, when the first generation of
those who had been born in the informal areas had come of age. It is
equally intriguing that these cross-class alliances took on a more central role in the late 2000s, as the next generation, more of whom
would have been born there, gained maturity.

Equally important is that the informal areas offered some autonomy
from the state for protest frames and networks to develop. Whether
classical revolutionary movements succeeded in carving out a semi-
autonomous space has been identified as crucial to the success or failure of revolutions (cf. McColl 1969). It was similarly crucial for the
development of Islamist networks in the 1990s (Dorman 2009: 421–2;
although Dorman is right to challenge the notion that informal Cairo
is necessarily oppositional to the state).

Without these areas where state control was patchy and indirect, it
is questionable whether the protesters would have managed to outma-

noeuvre the police. Because they formed an almost perfect circle around Tahrir Square, and were within walking distance, they enabled the protesters to develop the surround-swarming tactics that they used so effectively to outwit the police. Crucial was that the activists did not predominantly reside in the new developments in the desert, far from the city's centre and easily controlled by the security forces, and that there were well-established links with activists in the *ashwaiyyat*.

Concluding Thoughts

Although the relationship between structural changes and protest is ambiguous and indirect, combining a structural analysis with social movement dynamics has enabled us to shed some additional light on the timing of the different protest waves, the frames and tactics adopted, and the make-up of those involved in the protests. Different variables impacted different waves differently at different times. Taken in isolation, none of the factors discussed above would have created conditions sufficiently conducive for networks to act upon to achieve mass mobilisation; rather, it is the confluence of these conditions which created a situation with increasingly revolutionary potential, though at different times and with different intensities over the past decade. The neoliberal reforms on their own would have created fertile ground for strikes. Combined with the emergence of a crony capitalist class, the conditions would have been there for middle-class activists to mobil-ise, once crony capitalism was successfully framed as a remediable ill. But without increasing levels of indiscriminate police violence and trig-ger events such as the death of Khaled Said; without the technology to circumvent the state media and broadcast independently; without the narrowing of the base of the ruling party and the crisis surrounding Mubarak's succession; and without dramatic economic changes result-ing in a sharp decline in living standards, high levels of unemployment (especially among university graduates), a (shifting) youth ratio and the emergence of mixed-class, densely populated 'informal' quarters, the situation would have been largely devoid of revolutionary potential.

By 2010–2011, almost all the factors we consider had worsened, making it tempting to argue that Egypt had reached a tipping point (like the traditional image of a volcano about to erupt; cf. Goldstone 1991: 35).[24] However, without the example of Tunisia shaking off its dictator or if the Mubarak regime had responded differently, it is debatable whether the 25 January demonstrations would have led to a mass uprising. How this volatile situation turned into a mass uprising is the subject of the next four chapters.

PART II

DYNAMICS OF A
REVOLUTIONARY EPISODE

5

A 'LEADERLESS' REVOLUTION?

PLANNING VS SPONTANEITY

The previous chapters told the story of how activists and networks prepared the ground for the revolution through a decade of protest waves and how these waves interacted with broader structural changes. However, if we focus overly on the networks behind the demonstrations—a focus encouraged by the prism of social movement theory—we risk missing the 'spontaneous' nature of much of the January 2011 uprising. This raises the question of to what extent the uprising was in fact spontaneous (in the sense of not being planned), which overlaps with the question of contingency (cf. McAdam, Tarrow and Tilly 2001: 223–5). Moreover, if we concentrate overly on structures and organisations, we risk overlooking agency and the fact that each protester had to make a conscious decision to go out and face the police—and possible death.

Until 25 January, Palestinian solidarity demonstrations aside, the largest street protest had involved 55,000 tax-collectors in 2007 (Said 2009). Most demonstrations, especially political ones directed at the regime, had attracted but a few hundred. On 25 January, there were tens of thousands protesting across Egyptian cities. There were reports of 8,000 protesting in Alexandria, 3,000 in Mahalla, 2,000 in Ismailia and 200 in Aswan, in addition to the estimated 15,000–20,000 in Tahrir Square in Cairo (*al-Masry al-Youm* 2011b; Amir Ahmed 2011; CNN 2011a).

By 28 January (the 'Friday of Rage'), these numbers had swollen to unprecedented levels. Aljazeera (which usually gives higher estimates than other broadcasters) cites reports of 40,000 people demonstrating in Mansoura, 15,000 in Luxor, 50,000 in Beni Sueif (100 km south of Cairo). Eyewitnesses such as Mohammed Rashed (2011) put the number in Cairo at hundreds of thousands, with *al-Masry al-Youm* (2011c) reporting 20,000 on Qasr al-Nil Bridge alone—although international news-providers talked about tens of thousands (BBC 2011a; *Guardian* 2011c). Others set the number at 'hundreds of thousands' nationwide (Dar al-Shuruq in Amr Osman and Samei 2012: 10; retrospectively, AhramOnline 2013). On Tuesday, 1 February, Aljazeera (2011b) reported that the 'march of a million' had succeeded in mobilising 1 million people on Tahrir Square alone, although the intelligence website Stratfor (2011) put the number at a conservative 200,000, based on the Square's physical dimensions and the average space a protester would occupy. By the end, it is estimated (though impossible to verify) that 15–20 million—or 18–24 per cent of the entire population—had participated (Salah, Interview 2011; Al-Aswani 2011; Omar 2011). This figure chimes roughly with the results of a poll conducted in April 2011 in which 28 per cent of people polled claimed to have participated in the revolution (IRI Poll 2011). What accounts for this level of mobilisation?

What further distinguished the January 2011 demonstrations was the fact that they outmanoeuvred the police. On the Tuesday, they succeeded in mobilising thousands without being kettled and in briefly occupying Tahrir Square for the first time since 2003 (as well as many other public spaces across Egypt). On Wednesday and Thursday small-scale demonstrations continued, despite vicious police violence. On Friday, a record number of protesters marched on the row upon row of security forces protecting central areas such as Tahrir Square. As night fell, the police had capitulated across the country. Leaving aside other factors such as rivalries between the regime, the military and the police, and external pressure, how are we to account for this tactical success in mobilisatory terms?

A third distinguishing factor was the way the protesters organised themselves during the subsequent fourteen days, creating autonomous communes where the 'normal rules' of politics were suspended. Islamists and secularists organised the spaces together, even praying together—unthinkable before the revolution. Women could move relatively freely, without the usual harassment. Rubbish was collected efficiently and recycled. The borders of these temporary 'republics' were defended effectively against state thugs.

A fourth theme concerns the role played by Facebook, Twitter and other social media. According to many pundits, this was the Facebook revolution par excellence, led by technologically savvy middle-class youth. Social media have been credited with providing both the space to mobilise, away from the authorities' stifling censorship, and the tools to organise the revolution. Yet when we look at the profile of the protesters and at the tactics deployed, many did not have access to Facebook or Twitter and were mobilised by face-to-face encounters or word-of-mouth communications.

In the next four chapters we will reflect on these dynamics. In this chapter, we look at the relative roles played by activists and non-activists, and in particular the many instances of 'self-help' in which non-activists responded to the needs of the revolution. We then reflect on the motives driving people to join, before concluding with a discussion of the relative roles played by violent and non-violent tactics, and what this means for the centrality of the largely non-violent seasoned activists. In Chapter 6, we focus on perhaps the most vivid theme emerging from protesters' testimonies: the process by which people overcame their fear of the police. The two final chapters focus on the dynamics of the temporary 'republics' and the role of social media in the protests.

The Role of Activist Networks in the Revolution

To what extent were the events of January 2011 planned, and to what extent were they a spontaneous outburst of 'people coming together in concert', to use Hannah Arendt's celebrated phrase? Given the huge numbers of Egyptians with no experience of activism pouring out on to the streets, and the chaotic dynamics of the first few days, one could be forgiven for thinking that this was a spontaneous eruption of pent-up anger and humiliation, unleashed by the ousting of Ben Ali from Tunisia less than two weeks before. Indeed, similar popular 'uprisings', from the 1960s race riots in the United States, to the ousting of Marcos from the Philippines and the 1987 Palestinian Intifada, have often been depicted as spontaneous outbursts.

However, as in these other cases, there is a wealth of evidence suggesting that the protests had been meticulously planned by a small number of activists, and that the activist networks that had evolved over the prior decade formed the core of the organisation on the Square. The tactics adopted had been experimented with before, and the specific locales and modes of protest had been carefully worked out beforehand. Furthermore, one could argue that the activists had prepared the ground for the tens of thousands of non-activists to go out and 'spontaneously' protest by breaking the taboo of challenging the regime and by reclaiming the streets as a site of protest.

Timing of the Protests

That the protests began on 25 January, and not earlier (for instance immediately after Ben Ali's fall) or later, is no coincidence. Various protest groups had already begun to plan a protest for National Police Day (25 January), well before the ousting of Ben Ali. The April 6 movement, having tried (unsuccessfully) to organise mass protests on the same day in 2009 and 2010, had been preparing for a Police Day protest from late autumn 2010 onwards, holding workshops for its activists throughout December (Maher, Interview 2011).

The 'Khaled Said' network was similarly interested in National Police Day, since Said had become a symbol of police violence. As Wael Ghonim (2012: 123), the network's Facebook page's administrator, wrote:

The page's primary concern, after Khaled Said, had evolved to focus on the abuses of the Egyptian police. With every passing day I became more convinced that the police force was the chain that the regime tied around our necks; if the police force could be neutralized, the regime would be paralyzed.

Consequently, the 'Khaled Said' administrators had similarly set their sights on 25 January:

In late December, AbdelRahman Mansour [Ghonim's fellow administrator] suggested that since the police celebrated National Police Day on January 25, then perhaps we should do something on that date. I thought his idea was brilliant. Many people loathe the police force. ... Yet we had no idea how to "celebrate" the day. ... I had an online brainstorming chat with Ahmed Maher, the co-founder of the April 6 Youth Movement, and it turned out that that group had done something similar before. ... I was getting excited about all the possibilities. We agreed to brainstorm further after the new year. Yet on December 30, I posted:

January 25th is Police Day and it's a national holiday … I think the police have done enough this year to deserve a special celebration … What do you think? (Ghonim 2012: 121)

For the other protest groups, from ElBaradei's National Association for Change to Kefaya, the Democratic Front and the various other protest networks, police violence was similarly a focal point, as all had suffered at the hands of the security forces. The same held true for the Muslim Brotherhood and the Ultras, both of which would eventually join the uprising.

Moreover, 2011 was the year that Gamal Mubarak was expected to run for president. Already in 2008, April 6 activists had earmarked 2011 for a democratic transition to prevent Gamal from becoming president (BBC2 2012; *Telegraph* 2011). The sense that 2011 was a pivotal year grew throughout 2010. As Shadi Ghazali-Harb (Interview 2011a), nephew of the founder of the Democratic Front, Osama Ghazali-Harb, and one of the party's leaders, recalled:

I had a strong feeling something was going to happen in 2011. I knew Mubarak would die and there would be chaos. The son wants power [to contain this chaos] and we decided we will not let this happen. So we needed to bring ourselves together for this specific moment … coordinate with the ElBaradei campaign, with April 6, with the Democratic Front, create a network all over Egypt, across different cities.

Illustrating the general sense of urgency, Ghazali-Harb had returned from the UK in 2010 to join the increasing number of experienced local activists in putting together this coalition (cf. also Samer, Interview 2011). The events of 2010, from ElBaradei's return to Egypt to the death of Khaled Said and the fraudulent parliamentary election, had widened the pool of politically engaged and had created a protest momentum. The 2010 election, in particular, had convinced the Muslim Brotherhood and the other political parties, which had opposed boycotting the elections, that opposition within the system was futile and that systemic change was now needed (Wickham 2013: 150). The bombing of the Coptic church in Alexandria in early January 2011 further galvanised the protest movement. Structurally, Egypt was facing a volatile situation (Chapters 3–4). The fall of Ben Ali thus could not have happened at a more opportune time for the protest movement.

Activist leaders themselves credit Tunisia for their eventual success. In the words of Ghazali-Harb (Interview 2011a):

Then came the Tunisian revolution. This was a pivotal point. I don't know if we would have had our revolution [without it] in the first place. We realised it could happen. To reach this point, we tried to set a date for the revolution. I was not very convinced. This was the first time a revolutionary date was set. The police was the symbol of repression, the 'Khaled Said' group was linked to repression, plus there was a public holiday coming up, National Police Day. We decided to plan for it.

Ahmed Maher (Interview 2011), one of April 6's founders, recounted similarly that, before Tunisia, only some 1,000 activists had come to the workshops April 6 had organised in December. 'After Tunisia,' he continued, 'all people wanted to join in. Tunisia did the mobilising for us: 8,000–10,000 joined us every day on Facebook before the 25th.' Within days, 90,000–100,000 had signed up to the Facebook page calling for a revolution, pledging that they would be there (*New York Times* 2011b; Ghonim 2012: 160).

Although the activists could not have foreseen the events that took place in Tunisia, their preparations meant that they were ready to grab the opportunity. The leaders first met on 15 January, the day after Ben Ali's fall, in one of the activist cafés near Talat Harb Square. They met again on 20 January, and this time the meeting included representatives from not only the informal protest networks—the ElBaradei campaign, April 6, the Freedom and Justice Group (a left-leaning spin-off from April 6), the Democratic Front Party—but also the youth wing of the Muslim Brotherhood who had decided to defy their leadership (which eventually acquiesced) and join the protests (Maher, Interview 2011; Salah, Interview 2011; Wickham 2013: 160–1). It was decided that the activists would use the planned 25 January protests to capitalise on the change in public mood, in the hope that the protests would be larger than any before. Yet none of those interviewed foresaw either the mass turnout or the eventual fall of Mubarak. As Maher (Interview 2011) put it, somewhat understatedly, 'It was Police Day. We made a page on Facebook, called it "Thugs Day," and called for a small demo.'

Tactics

The activists' second contribution to the revolution concerned tactics. The tactics used, like the networks and the activists, did not emerge out of nowhere, but had been honed over years of protest. At the two meetings in January it was decided that the activists would employ the swarming flash mob tactics that April 6 and others had experimented with (Maher, Interview 2011; Ghazali-Harb, Interview 2011a; Salah, Interview 2011). It was these tactics that enabled the demonstrators to outwit the police on 25 January and gain access to Tahrir Square. As activist author Ahdaf Soueif (2012: 10–11) underlines:

The Midan [Square] has been our Holy Grail for forty years. Since 1972 ... demonstrations have tried and failed to get into Tahrir. Two years ago we managed to hold a corner of a traffic island ... for an hour. We were fewer than fifty people, and the government surrounded us with maybe 2,000 Central Security soldiers ...[1]

The tactics used during the revolution had been developed throughout 2010, which had seen an acceleration of tactical innovation:

In January 2010, George Galloway came to Egypt with operation Code Pink, to bring aid to Gaza. The people who came with him started a demo, but not Egyptian-like. We made links, learned from them, especially about flash mobs. We had experience with organising sudden demonstrations, then disappearing quickly. They taught us how to make a demonstration from several starting positions, then appear at the same time in the centre. We did this many times, especially in poor places where they would understand [our message]. We practised this lots and in May–June 2010 we studied the films *Battle in Seattle* and *Shields*, to learn about how to protect ourselves against police violence, how to manufacture shields from carton and plastic, and so on. In December [2010] and January [2011], we gave courses in how to protect your body in a demonstration, and published this on YouTube. (Maher, Interview 2011)

The flash mob tactic was adapted to Egypt's local context. Prior to 2010, most protests consisted of small numbers standing in front of a designated building (a ministry or a professional syndicate), surrounded by a police cordon outnumbering the protesters. Police knew where the protests would be from flyers and social media announcements and ensured, through kettling, that the number of protesters remained small. Indeed, it was this sight of small groups of protesters being kettled by police that had put off a number of the non-activists we interviewed, because protest looked futile and dangerous.

To prevent kettling, the activists adopted swarming flash mob tactics, starting unannounced in Cairo's informal neighbourhoods:

Before, we would organise small demonstrations that were easily surrounded. We agreed to change strategy. A few months before January 25th,[2] we began by starting demonstrations in poor, densely populated areas, with people who can be readily mobilised by chants about how oppressive the regime is, and how bad the economy is. People in these areas are more likely to be responsive and turn out in big numbers. We had a pilot demonstration in October 2010 in Imbaba [one of Cairo's poor 'informal' areas], organised by the Democratic Front Party and April 6 (not 'Khaled Said'). It was very successful. Within one and a half to two hours, we had 3,000–5,000 people demonstrating, just inside the area of Imbaba. ... We decided to use the same strategy on the 25th: start outside downtown, in a poor area, Nahia, inside Bulaq al-Daqrur. (Ghazali-Harb, Interview 2011a)

Maher (Interview 2011) explained the new tactics in similar terms:

In 2008, we started in Tahrir Square and Manshiyya Square in Alexandria. But the police easily arrested us as we appeared one by one. Now, if we start in poor neighbourhoods, there will be no media coverage. We published several squares as meeting points for 2pm [on the 25th] on Facebook, but we didn't mention Tahrir. In reality, we started at 1pm in the poor areas to get the poor out on the street. These areas were known to April 6 because we had relations there since a few years, and experience in organising demos fast. Every group has a leader, and knows the location and where to go. Members follow. In Shubra Square, Giza Square, Matariyya Square, Mustafa Mahmoud Square, at 2pm, the police was awaiting us there. We had many groups, each 50 persons, students, middle class. We started at 1pm in the neighbourhoods around the squares. We called: 'join us, for your rights.' People were ready for that. We started with 50, then 100, 200, became 1,000s. The police were surprised by how many arrived. ... From the beginning, the plan was to go to Tahrir. Every 6 April (2008, 2009, 2010) we had tried to reach Tahrir but failed. We didn't expect a revolution but we did expect a big event.

Speaking about 25 January, Ghazali-Harb (Interview 2011a) recalled:

We started in Nahia, and took the bridge into Mohandessin once we were 5,000–7,000. We called early in the morning, around 50 of us in Nahia. We gave a speech, and shouted for people to join us. Riot police were not expecting us there, and were not ready. We then went into Mohandessin, to the decoy areas. We confused the riot police, and the people [who were already there] joined us. We then went to Tahrir Square, with some 20,000–25,000. We decided to stay in Tahrir. The security forces were not ready. We had expected only a few hundred, but we managed to break through all the barriers, with not too much violence. ... We didn't organise the other streams, but we announced them [on the 'Khaled Said' webpage]. There was a group at the High Court, another in Qasr al-Aini, all small, easily dispersed. We knew some of the others, like my father was at the High Court. But we had the biggest group. We weren't at all the demos, for example we weren't in Matariyya. The 'Khaled Said' group was there.

As discussed in Chapter 4, around 40 per cent of Greater Cairo consisted of 'informal areas', home to over 64 per cent of Cairo's population, with houses built illegally, right to the edge of what used to be agricultural plots, leaving room only for narrow alleyways, with no police presence. Informal Cairo provided a perfect recruiting ground as the activists' calls resonated particularly with its inhabitants, who lacked all but the basic services and had extensive experience of police violence. Informal Cairo being residential and crowded, thousands could be mobilised by simply calling up to the balconies overlooking the street. Unlike the wide boulevards of central Cairo, the narrow streets made small crowds look large, lowering people's fear of protesting. As Salah (Interview 2011), one of April 6's former leaders, recounts:

When we asked people about Mubarak [before the revolution], most were negative, apart from a few. Those who said 'I hate Mubarak, he is the problem,' we would ask: 'Would you take part?' They would answer: 'Of course not, it is useless. We are scared, afraid of torture, of becoming disabled. We are afraid of loss of income.' We would then ask: 'Would you ever come out? What would make you go?' The answer: 'If everyone else goes, we will go, if it is a big event.' ... How, then, if we make the illusion that everyone is out? Small numbers in a small room feel like many. If a small number start in a narrow alley, it seems like more, plus it is safe from the police. If we start this everywhere, we go around, encourage more people [to come out], then go to a bigger place. So we talked to many people. ... We decided to start with Nahia. A good rally, but only one. Most of those who approached us were not political activists. We were surprised by the response. So we gave crash courses, handed out flyers, on how not to get caught, how to do graffiti.

Part of this new tactic's success was to keep moving, making it difficult for police to surround protesters (as long as they remained in the small alleys). Equally crucial was that the police were forced to divide forces and given false starting positions. By announcing multiple meeting places, the police were forced to spread out, making kettling more difficult. These meeting places were, furthermore, decoys to distract the police from the real action (although they also served as meeting points for those who only knew the activists online through Facebook):

On Facebook, which had an important role to tell people, we set decoy places on our route. We would join these people later, but they were not the main points for gathering. The points for gathering were only known to six of us. One decoy place was Mustafa Mahmoud Mosque. Some went there, the riot police were there [in force]. People were surrounded. Some of our friends were there to say: stay, and give it some time. (Ghazali-Harb, Interview 2011a)

The physical location of Cairo's informal areas was pivotal. Had they been on the outskirts of Cairo, or concentrated on one side of the city, they would not have been as effective for the tactics adopted.

Their being situated in a large circle around the city's political centre (Figure 5.1) meant that they were ideal for the multiple swarming flash mobs the activists had planned.

Similar tactics were used on 28 January. Unlike 25 January, the police knew what to expect and had hermetically sealed off all roads into Tahrir Square. 28 January was a Friday, the Muslim day of prayer, which meant that people would already be gathered in mosques across the city. In addition, by now—after the government accused it of orchestrating the 25 January demonstration and threatened it with mass arrests—the Muslim Brotherhood leadership had abandoned its neutral position and called on its members to join the demonstrations (Wickham 2013: 162). Nevertheless, the activists employed a similar logic of starting in multiple places, growing crowds by walking through narrow streets and converging on Tahrir Square. As Soueif (2012: 17) recounts:

We walk and the numbers grow. Every balcony is full of people; some just watch passively, some men look uncomfortable. 'Come down from the heights/ Come down and get your rights' ... For more than two hours the protest walks through the narrow residential lanes, cheering, encouraging, instigating.

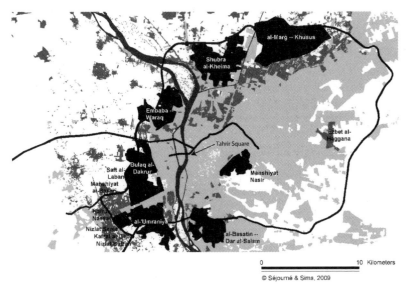

Figure 5.1: Map of Central Cairo indicating key 'informal areas' in black (adapted from Sims 2010: 127: with permission from the author; with thanks).

Maher (Interview 2011) explained:

On Friday, we used the same tactics, but on a larger scale. The MB officially joined (before, the MB youths were there as individuals only). We started in all squares, mosques, because the police was waiting in Tahrir Square. Any 10, 20 people can begin, anybody, not just activists. ... Groups started everywhere, in Imbaba, Maadi, Nasr, etc. We started with 200 in Imbaba, turned into 30,000. We started to march 30–40 km to Tahrir Square. My brother started in Maadi, 20 km [to Tahrir]. ... ElBaradei was in Giza, where there were 15,000. ... From Shubra, from Abdin, from Maadi (via Qasr al-Aini), Nasr City, through Abbasiya, Ramses Street (I was in Bulaq on the 25th, in Imbaba on the 28th; I have links with Imbaba).

Ghazali-Harb (Interview 2011b) highlighted the differences:

The 28th was different from the 25th. People had already been humiliated on the 25th, they were frustrated, they wanted to come back. The general feeling was that the 28th was going to be a big day. We heard by midday [on Thursday] that the phone lines would be down, in addition to the Internet. There was a feeling that there would be a big battle. To arrange the 28th, we got together in a friend's house. Where were the best places to start a demo? On the 28th, it was Imbaba. With no communication on Friday, we had to plan everything: plan A, B, C. Plus we learned tactics from the Tunisians: how to confront riot police, like using lemon juice, onions, using paintballs, throwing them on police shields, empty bags, fill them with paint. Most of our group started in Imbaba. The same strategy [as on the 25th] of getting smaller groups earlier to Tahrir, big one to hold groups together. From Imbaba, we went to Galaa Square with 100,000. There were 100,000 from Giza. These were the two main groups that held everything together. We managed to get to Tahrir by 7pm. It was submerged with teargas. Two died in front of me, shotguns into their bellies. ... On the 28th, the army came down in Cairo. There were some comforting messages [from them], so we welcomed them, assured them that we were not against them. We were against the regime. We were writing 'Down with Mubarak' on the tanks. The 28th was the true revolution.

The largest difference between 25 and 28 January was the use of violence by key elements among the demonstrators, primarily the Ultras and the youth from Cairo's poorer areas. As we will see in the final part of this chapter, these tactics were crucial to the eventual success of the demonstrations and differed fundamentally from the tactics developed by the largely middle-class activists of the various protest networks behind the revolution.

On both days the activists played a central role in orchestrating the events; deciding where to concentrate efforts to start mobilisation, how to converge on Tahrir, and coordinating with other activists and local contacts. Ghazali-Harb (Interview 2011b), for instance, recalled: 'We decided at midnight [of 27 January what to do], as the phones would go down at 11am on Friday. We had people at mosques, specific people [to lead the protests].' Soueif (2012: 16–17) remembers seeing a young man sitting intensely still in a café on 28 January, waiting for the prayers to finish; then seeing him again on top of 'a loose knot of some fifteen young people,' 'his still concentration ... transformed into energy, ... his arm movements ... precise,' shouting 'Al-sha3b yureed isqat al-nizam' ... 'The people—demand—the fall of this regime!' 'Later,' she continues, 'we will learn that similar marches started after prayers in every district of Cairo and many other cities. We will know this young man as one of the three hundred young people who organised these first marches.'

These tactics had been experimented with well before 25 January. We have already heard Maher and Ghazali-Harb describe earlier experiments. The same tactics were used in the protests following the bombing of the church in Alexandria on 1 January 2011. George Ishak (Interview 2011), one of the founders of Kefaya, recalled that 'it was the first time they went out of the Church into the street. They started a demonstration by night, went out from narrow streets, five by five, five by five, then converged to make a very big demo. This tactic was used on the 25th.' Nadim Mansour (Interview 2011), an activist labour lawyer, similarly recounted that:

There were massive demonstrations after the Alexandria bombing. For more than a week, they went on. Massive demos in Shubra and Bulaq. In the poorer areas, for the first time, 1,000s of normal people were marching. ... For the first time, the demo would break through the security forces' rings. The largest two feeders into Tahrir [on 25 January] were both from Bulaq. One came from Shubra, but this was violently attacked. These earlier experiences helped to create a model to feed into the 25th. In Shubra, the neighbourhood came out to fight security forces when attacked.

An employee of the Foreign Ministry, who joined the demonstrations on 28 January, confirmed the novelty of these tactics:

After the January massacres, I saw demonstrations by Copts in front of the Ministry, that were moving. This was very unusual. I was taken aback by this. It took place in big streets, though, not in small alleys. But this was the first time I saw people moving in large numbers, in their 1,000s. (Gamal, Interview 2011)

It is noteworthy that it only took a reported 250 activists to influence the protest pattern of 4,000 protesters in these demonstrations (al-Masry al-Youm 2011a; Elaph 2011).

Besides influencing the choice of tactics on 25 and 28 January, the activists had prepared the ground by building up a network of contacts in the informal areas and familiarising themselves with the areas' layout. As Maher (Interview 2011) stated:

These areas are known to April 6 because we have relations [with people there] since a few years. We have experience in organising demonstrations fast. Every group has a leader who knows the location and knows where to go. The members follow.

Well before 2011, April 6 members had pledged at every gathering to tell two non-activists about April 6, its goals and methods (April 6 Cadres, Conversation 2011). Both April 6 and the Democratic Front Party had furthermore (some) members who lived in the *ashwaiyyat* (Maher, Interview 2013; Ghazali-Harb, Interview 2013). When the small band of Muslim Brotherhood youth joined the protests on 25 January, they brought with them additional *ashwaiyyat* contacts, since many of them lived in the *ashwaiyyat* themselves and the Brotherhood's networks in these areas were far more extensive than anything the secular groups could boast (cf. Sennott 2011; Wickham 2013: 162–3, 263). It is clear from interviews that the Brotherhood's youth knew about the swarming tactics, and that 'the key organizers (secular and Islamist) divvied up the sha'abi [informal] neighborhoods and went there in small groups to mobilize people through direct face to face outreach' (C. Wickham, pers. comm., 2013; also Wickham 2013: 161–3). These local contacts were crucial on 25 January, but even more so on 28 January. When the internet was shut down on 27 January, the activists activated their local contacts, calling them on their mobiles to discuss tactics (Ghazali-Harb, Interview 2011b). By 28 January, moreover, the number of Muslim Brothers had increased from the number of reformist Brotherhood youth who had established contacts with the secular protest groups prior to the revolution[3] to, according to some estimates, over 100,000, mostly in Cairo (Wickham 2013: 162).

Parallel to this, April 6 had run numerous workshops, training activists in non-violent tactics, as part of a long search for alternative ways of protesting. As Maher (Interview 2011) related:

We tried to find a structure, a new vision, a new organisation, different from Kefaya, Youth for Change. We found the Academy of Change [a non-violent training centre run by Egyptian expatriates], the Serbian student movement, Solidarity, Martin Luther King, etc. We started to study things, movies, books. Every week we showed a movie, like *V for Vendetta*, then discussed it afterwards. Gandhi, Martin Luther King, a movie about Otpor! (Serbia), about [the revolution in] Ukraine. We adopted the same symbol as the Serbian student movement. We have a link with them. The Serbian youths are like us, students, three years protesting against Milosevic. We read about non-violence, how to attract people to your movement (for example, using people's language, not politicians' language), using strange [unusual] events, not in Cairo only, but Alexandria, Port Said. We were arrested many times, tortured, kidnapped. In the beginning, political parties refused us, saying 'you're crazy.' We were the most powerful movement for a few months, in nine districts. ... The message: you can do it, stand together, using non-violence.[4]

We already alluded to media reports of training provided by members of the Academy of Change (Chapter 2). Salah (Interview 2011) described having given numerous 'crash courses, flyers on how not to get caught, how to do graffiti', both as part of April 6 and after leaving. One of the April 6 activists we talked to confirmed that he had been on courses, and that he had learned from Serbian activists when they visited Cairo to discuss non-violence (Fouad, Interview 2011). Khalil Saeed (Interview 2011), from the Democratic Front Party, had similarly attended training events organised by April 6:

I didn't join courses. But I joined with April 6, where movies were shown, like *Battle of Seattle*. I heard about some of their tactics. I registered with them, was informed about their activities, especially their 2010 non-violent focus. I saw a brochure about an Egyptian intellectual talking about the importance of non-violence. I believe an article by Dr Nasr Abu Zayd was posted by April 6. I believe in non-violence from the practice of tai kwondo, also through my training with Initiatives of Change [an international grassroots peace movement].

Leaflets on non-violence and how to cope with the police were distributed, both as hard copies and through the internet (*Guardian* 2011b; Bauer and Schweitzer 2012).

In the weeks before 25 January, the protest groups carefully choreographed the events. Ghazali-Harb (Interview 2011a), from the Democratic Front, and Maher (Interview 2011), from April 6, would start in Bulaq al-Daqrur (according to Ghonim (2012:158), Maher had earlier selected Shubra). Mahmoud Samy (April 6) would organise protests from the Arab League Street in Mohandessin (Ghonim 2012: 158). The 'Khaled Said' network would concentrate on Matariyya (Ghazali-Harb, Interview 2011a) (although Ghonim (2012: 177) himself joined the protests in front of the High Court). The lawyers and doctors would start from Cairo University, although that was later changed to the Doctors' Syndicate near Tahrir Square (Ghonim 2012: 158, 176).

Protests were coordinated across Egypt, using the networks established during the previous decade. According to Ghazali-Harb (Interview 2011a):

On the 25th, there were about 10,000 people demonstrating in Mahalla, 10,000 in Alexandria, based on networks established in 2010, more than in 2008 [as a result of the Mahalla strike]. The links with the workers went through ElBaradei and the Justice & Freedom group. Our links were more with Alexandria.

The activists recognised the importance of mobilising Mahalla, given not only the city's central role in the 2006–2008 workers' protests but also the burden it would put on the security forces. Salah (Interview 2011) told us that:

awakening it was a priority. We made a protest on the 21st to alert people to the 25th. We held a big meeting and gave crash courses to people [on non-violence, how to confront security forces]. Mahalla had to rise on the day. Because of the 2008 experience, if it would rise, it would rise strongly. This would help other areas. It took security forces from five governorates [to deal with the Mahalla protests in 2008].

The purpose of organising multiple protests across the country was similar to that of organising swarming flash mobs: to force the police to spread out too thinly to be effective. This is precisely what happened. Beleaguered police forces in provincial cities such as Mahalla and Suez asked for reinforcements from other cities (El-Ghobashy 2011), giving protesters there the opportunity to storm their local police stations and occupy them (Marei, Interview 2011). In Alexandria, police forces capitulated early on 28 January, outnumbered and outmanoeuvred by the protesters. In Cairo, towards the end of the day, police 'soldiers' similarly gave up when they realised the tide had turned (A. Khalil 2011: 177). This would have been far more difficult to accomplish without the national networks of activists built up by the various protest networks.

In addition, the activists reached out to 'non-activist' organisations to maximise numbers. Crucially, attempts were made to get the Ultra football fan clubs on board. According to Maher (Interview 2011):

We tried to get in touch with as many groups as possible. Most important were two groups of football fans: al-Ahly and al-Zamalek. We did this all over the country. We had been trying to do this before in other events, but it didn't work. This time it worked. This year is the year of presidential elections, that the father would give [the reins] to the son. This had to be prevented. We were all hoping for a big demonstration, as the basis for a later revolution at the elections. We got confirmation from the fan clubs. If they came out, they would be strong, because they are sporty and organised. They were the ones charging against the Central Security Forces, charging, counter-charging.

Ghonim (2012: 139) similarly posted a call to the Ultras on the 'Khaled Said' webpage:

To the ultras of Ahly, Zamalek, Ismaili, and Itihad soccer teams ... If you exert the same effort you do for any soccer match on the 25th of January, you will help Egypt change ... Let us all be ultras of Egypt ...

A diplomat (M. Hamdy, Conversations 2011) who joined the demonstrations on the Square confirmed that:

Football supporters were there. If the leaders agree, all 15,000 of the club come. If both clubs agree, there will automatically be 30,000. One of my friends is an Ultra. He is not political, but educated, a university student, middle class. He knew all about Khaled Said, I discussed this with him. This was a turning point for many Ultras, many of whom are middle class. They are a 'natural' opposition to the police. Since the Ultras started, they have been in clashes with the police. They tried to organise events in the stadium, bring in banners, fireworks, like elsewhere [in the world]. This is not allowed, so there would be clashes. Mainstream newspapers usually side with the police, so this creates alienation. But they are not political. Football is their world. My friend was there from the start, as were many others.[5]

It is possible that the Ultras would have joined in any case. Ghazali-Harb (Interview 2011b) suggested that when he talked to them, 'they [already] did have this in their mind. My info is that when the Ultras joined, they announced this over Facebook. The Ahly Ultras felt they had to join as well, they had to do something more than football.' Whether or not this is so, the decision of the Ultras to join was clearly influenced by the planning of the activists.

Organisational Structure

The third major contribution the activists made was to provide an organisational structure. They set up operation rooms. They helped to coordinate emergency services and the provision of medicine and food. Once the Square was occupied, they provided the core of the organisation on the Square, coordinating security, provisions (food, fuel and medicine) and media communiqués. Non-activists played a central role in all of this, and much of what was organised was done on an ad hoc basis, based on non-activists' practical thinking, rather than pre-planning. The activists, nevertheless, brought experience and established networks to the table. According to Maher (Interview 2011):

We organised something new: an operation room in the Hisham Mubarak Center, 12 members with laptops and new SIM cards. We published [the numbers of] 5 lines in Cairo, in Alexandria, etc. All members covered all the news, directed the people: go to Tahrir Square, Matariyya Square (on the 25th, 26th, 27th). On the 28th, they cut down the [mobile] phones. We then used landlines. For Facebook, we used a proxy against being shutdown. We used international lines to connect to the Internet.

The Hisham Mubarak Center was also the base for the Front to Defend Egypt's Protesters, which had been established to offer legal services at every major protest since April 2008. In January 2011, they became a clearinghouse for medical and food supplies, channelling the hundreds of gifts from the public to the demonstrators (Samer, Interview 2011; N. Mansour, Interview 2011).

Once the Square was occupied, the activist networks provided a ready organisational structure. The Square was divided into sections, accommodating each of the political trends, as well as makeshift prisons and hospitals. According to Heba Ezzat (Interview 2011), an Islamist thinker, political scientist and resident on the Square:

People on the Square were mixed, but there were corners: leftists (Tagammu' flag), Salafis (bearded) who were the victims of the Gama'at [al-Islamiyya] crackdown, people from Upper Egypt, 50 people from the Delta in my part of the Square. To the right of my house, there were 40 prisoners of state security; opposite, across the street, the old left, singing songs of Sheikh Imam. Further [down] the Muslim Brotherhood.

Ghazali-Harb (Interview 2011b) described the level of organisation that went into life in the Square:

We organised starting points and routes and made available things we needed: masks, lemon juice, vinegar, onions, paintballs. That was the main organisation. After that, we formed stages on Tahrir Square [for speeches, announcements], a field hospital, especially for people hurt around the Ministry of the Interior, blankets. We tried to direct people; during the protests we directed people to Parliament (with microphones), to the Presidential Building.

The Muslim Brotherhood were reportedly the first to set up microphones and speaker towers on the Square and, fortified by a well-oiled structure and a much larger organisation than any of the other protest networks, they brought in water, tents, blankets and food and helped to organise garbage collection (Wickham 2013: 166; Ezzat, Interview 2011).

In terms of coordination between the different groups, Maher (Interview 2011) elaborated:

We had a committee [on the Square] with one representative from every group. We organised where we got foods, the Square hospital, how to decide, what is our message to the media. The Arab media were against us ... just Aljazeera, BBC Arabic for us, plus the foreign media. *Al-Masry al-Youm* was important. It supported us before the 25th on the 23rd and the 24th. They said: 'Tomorrow will be a great day.' They also supported us during the revolution. On the 26th, *al-Ahram* reported nothing. *Al-Masry al-Youm* and other opposition newspapers called it a revolution.

To handle the media and senior visitors to the Square, a central communication point was organised. Ezzat (Interview 2011) reported:

The Tourist Company on the Square opened [to become a central coordinating point], behind the Aljazeera screen: a small office, where senior elite figures visited the Square, international media would meet. There you could meet the youth of the coalition, the Brotherhood. You could also ask there for someone, they would know where they were.

Although reports on the size of the Brotherhood's presence on the Square differ, it is clear that it did not want to overshadow the secular protest networks who had initiated the demonstrations, as it was acutely aware of the adverse impact this would have on the image of the revolution, both domestically and abroad, and thus how it would be received (Sennott 2011; Wickham 2013). It thus was careful to participate in the organisation of the Square as an equal to the other networks, despite its larger size.

Security was organised centrally, although here too non-activists played a significant part. April 6 deployed activists at various entry points to ensure no government-controlled 'thugs' would enter the Square. According to an April 6 cadre from the Zaytoun area we met on the Square after the revolution, he 'was responsible for securing six entry roads (into Tahrir). Security was provided by groups of "boys and girls." They had a back-up team so that they could relieve each other every hour, so that they stayed fresh' (Gunning, Research Note 2011).[6] During the 'Battle of the Camel' on 2 February, the Muslim Brotherhood and Ultras in particular used their organisational discipline and prior experience to defend the Square, and to teach non-activists how, for instance, to use slingshots (Wickham 2013: 166; Ghazali-Harb, Interview 2011b; Martini, Kaye and York 2012: 11–12).

The workers' movement was responsible for the crucial final phase of the revolution. Nadim Mansour (Interview 2011) noted:

Between the 25th and the 5th/6th, there were no workers involved as workers. [But] they were there. If you look at how people related to the protests, workers' methods were used. The workers' movement was very effective in this, the ideas of striking, marching, occupying. ... Workers were on the Square as citizens, Egyptians. On the Square and everywhere else in Egypt. The regime tried to isolate the Square by opening the factories. But once the factories opened, the workers went on strike, almost reaching a general strike: Suez, Helwan factories (most of them), Mahalla, transportation system, banks (actual strikes or threatening to strike), from roughly the 7th onwards. This sent a very strong message and gave depth to the protesters' demands.

Samer (Interview 2011), the human rights activist, likewise observed that 'labour only really became involved halfway through the revolution. At the beginning, everything stopped, because of the violence. Halfway through, when everything was opening up again—a mistake by the regime—it turned into a strike.' However, workers were there on the Square from the start. Shaaban (Interview 2011), one of Kefaya's founders, reported that 'on the 25th, first the youth went out, via Facebook, the middle class; later on the workers joined'. Maher (Interview 2011) similarly said that he 'saw a group of workers after the 28th, drivers, factory workers'.

Once the factories reopened, the workers came into their own, providing what many agreed was the final blow to Mubarak. Saad (Interview 2011), the leftist journalist, put it most explicitly:

[By the second week] I thought: we're finished, we will lose this fight. But during the last three days: there were 400 strikes in 3 days, three in the Suez Canal. The strongest sector of the working class got involved in the revolution. In the railway section. They cured the revolution. ... I was pessimistic until the 8th when the working class joined.

These strikes, which added pressure on the armed forces to break definitively with Mubarak,[7] would not have been possible without the independent workers' movement, the thousands of strikes they had organised in the years leading up to 2011 and the links that had been built between this movement and the other protest sectors. However, Alexander (2012) is correct to nuance this by noting that:

The existing independent unions were too small in relation to the scale of the movement for their presence as an *organised* force to shape the overall outcome of the uprising, or even influence its direction much. The intervention of strategic groups of organised workers who had not yet formally constituted independent unions, such [as] the Public Transport Authority Workers, the postal workers and Suez Canal Company workers in the strikes during Mubarak's final week in early February 2011 was probably more significant in terms of shifting the balance of forces between the revolutionary movement and the state at a crucial juncture.

Beyond the Activists: the Role of non-Activists

Without the preparations and innovations discussed above, it is questionable whether the uprising would have succeeded in ousting Mubarak. Without the response of the masses, however, the outcome of these preparations would have been the same kind of smallish crowds as had been the norm throughout 2010. Illustrating the extent of non-activist involvement, a survey carried out two weeks after Mubarak's fall found that 'approximately two thirds of people [sampled] ... who had demonstrated in Tahrir Square ... had not been involved in previous protests' (Tufekci and Wilson 2012: 369).

Amira (Interview 2011), a journalist with *al-Masry al-Youm*, gave a poignant illustration of this dynamic:

[My father] had been a protester when he was young, but for 20 years he had not been active. He lives in Maadi. The young in Maadi are famous for being funky guys, going to bars, doing sports. This was the first time that young people were in the streets in Maadi, waving to my father. My father, 76 years old, joined them, walked all the way from Maadi to Qasr al-Aini on the 28th (on the 25th ... he watched everything on TV). He left his car, he didn't think he would walk that far. He didn't know what he was doing, just forgot everything. He arrived here [on Qasr al-Aini Street] felt tired and sick, people offered to take him back. He stopped at the street because it was blocked. My brother [who was with him] was a former policeman, now a public investigator. He started to feel very enthusiastic, shouting slogans. Some people who knew him made it public [that he was a public investigator] (he didn't want people to know). People didn't expect an investigator to be with the people. ... My brother walked to Qasr al-Aini, then walked home again. He didn't go again, except for the last days. ...

Or consider the testimony of Latifa Fahmy (Interview 2011), a childhood friend of Suzanne Mubarak, whose husband had been a minister in Sadat's government:

I went out on the streets of Zamalek to protest on the 25th, despite being a long-term friend of Suzanne Mubarak who was a schoolmate of mine. But I nearly joined the pro-Mubarak protests on Mustafa Mahmud Square on February 2nd because I felt the protesters had achieved their aims, but I didn't in the end. I was shocked at how implicated the Mubaraks were in the corruption. I had thought them above that, just that their entourage was corrupt. I disagreed with the way Gamal was being groomed, rather than letting him make his own way. I was disgusted with the election fraud of 2010 (I had been asked to stand because of the work I did in the countryside and was told that I didn't need to do anything, and I probably would have won; I was very glad I didn't run because of the way the elections were conducted in the end). I thought Suzanne had done many good things as well, felt that people were now maligning her. I had told Suzanne Mubarak about my views about Gamal, that he needed to stand on his own feet and earn the Presidency.

Before we look at how hundreds of thousands with no previous record were mobilised (Chapter 6), it is important to gain a sense of what role non-activists played in the demonstrations. The graph below (Figure 5.2), based on a poll carried out in April 2011, shows the iterative process of people joining the protests. Once started, the demonstrations took on a momentum of their own. Not only did tens of thousands of non-activists join, but thousands began to organise themselves, providing food, medical supplies and security, directing the crowds, organising the Square. In the words of Shaaban (Interview 2011): 'this revolution is unique as for the first time, there is no organisation, or rather, no party in control. ... No one knows who is leading.'

Samer (Interview 2011), who helped with the distribution of food and medical supplies from the Hisham Mubarak Center, recalled that

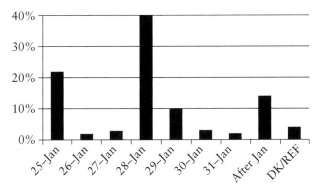

Figure 5.2: First day of participation in 2011 uprising (IRI Poll 2011).

'the volunteers [who helped us distribute medical supplies] were mostly random citizens. People risked their lives with thugs. People insisted they would help with medical aid. People were phoning in to ask what to do. ... Someone who sold ambulances got us one.' Another human rights activist working from the Hisham Mubarak Center (Ahmed, Interview 2011) stated:

[The revolution] was very spontaneous and positive. No one was in control. People were just coming in [to the Hisham Mubarak Center]. ...

[Question: Was there no organisation at all?]

There was collective spontaneity. People organised themselves. Take for example the [earlier] workers' strikes. They were [largely] spontaneous. People managed to feed themselves for six days. On the first day, you had 100 people, then 1,000 came in. They secure the factory, feed themselves. People knew each other. The same on Tahrir, but on a larger scale. Take security: when they think of a thing, they call each other up. Or they use megaphones. They call for volunteers, to defend against thugs. ... The Muslim Brotherhood were organised. But there were very few [of them]. ... For the rest: if you need help, just ask. When people are in danger together, a collective consciousness emerges, with people helping each other. Many came out with their friends. But also Salafis were acting with Christians and even atheists, accepting each other and [practising] self-help. ... This is not something you learn, but you do it spontaneously. It was not like people saying: this is what happened in Mahalla, let's do the same.

While this quotation underplays the role of organisation (for instance, the workers' strikes usually did have a coordinated leadership), Ahmed's observations highlight the role of people 'coming together in concert', using their connections and common sense to solve problems as they occurred. For this to happen, you do not necessarily need pre-existing networks or a Mahalla strike to emulate.

However, as Ahmed (Interview 2011) himself noted, Mahalla and other such protests created an environment in which acting collectively to demand rights became an acceptable path. The 'Khaled Said' web-page, for instance, encouraged people to take responsibility for collective action, even if they had no activist history. According to Ghonim (2012: 73), 'the individual efforts of the page members were extremely valuable, and they spread further to friends who had not subscribed to the page. The page resembled a product being marketed by its loyal users. For this reason, we relied on the members themselves to promote the event.'

Many who did not consider themselves activists had already contributed to spreading political awareness prior to 25 January. Anonymous (Interview 2011), a teacher trainer at the American University in Cairo, is a poignant case in point:

[In the past] I felt politics was dangerous and futile, useless. ... But in 2010, I started writing a lot of stuff on Facebook. ... I wasn't an activist ... I just met an ex-colleague who said: I've been following everything you've written on Facebook.

This anonymous speaker inspired many of those who read her posts to join but she herself did not do so until 11 February.

While the image given by many media reports is that of a middle-class revolution, the bulk of those on the Square appear to have been from the lower classes. All those we interviewed confirmed that the protesting crowds were from different social classes. According to Khaled Barakat (Interview 2011), from *al-Ahram*, 'everybody was at Tahrir. I saw very rich people, I saw people from Imbaba, Bulaq [informal areas in Cairo] ... also from outside Cairo, *fellahin* [farmers].' Amira (Interview 2011), from *al-Masry al-Youm*, similarly 'saw every kind of person on Tahrir. High class, poor, children, Muslims, Christians, journalists, doctors. People who I know were never interested in politics before ... I saw more poor than rich ...' Ezzat (Interview 2011), who lives on the Square, told us that 'people coming from humble areas ... came in massive numbers'. Gamal (Interview 2011) similarly recalled:

Yes, the poor were there. They came later that Friday. They came when they felt this was a watershed. It is from them that the attacks on the police stations came, not from the middle classes. The middle classes respect authority, plus they are cowards. I saw it on Friday, I saw a lot of people who I didn't see in demos earlier. I had to walk for an hour [when walking home], I walked through lower class areas, I saw people chanting, coming later. The demo at Qasr al-Aini was mainly middle class.

Intriguingly, a number of those we interviewed told us that they had not seen the better-known activist leaders in the Square, or that they had seen them in cafés (Saad, Interview 2011; Salah, Interview 2011; Tahrir Square Shop Owner, Conversation 2011; M. Hamdy, Conversations 2011). Some of the more derogatory comments ('they were media lights' or 'they came after it was safe. Ordinary people took the Square. Now the activists take the credit') may have been inspired by post-revolution disagreements among the activists and between activists and the general population. As Gamal (Interview 2011) commented: 'People who criticise the role of activists are criticising the role of activists now, after the revolution. There are disagreements over whether activists should have a say in politics now. People feel they exaggerated their role to get a bigger part of the cake.' Moreover, the fact that the well-known activists were not seen on the Square (leaving aside that it would be difficult to identify people in large crowds) does not mean that they were not coordinating the revolution. April 6, for instance, had an office during the first days of the revolution from where the leadership coordinated events (Aljazeera 2011e).

Whatever the role of well-known activists, these observations do underline that the activists were few, and that they could not possibly organise everything. Following Gamal Eid (Interview 2011), a long-time human rights activist, 'before the revolution, all activists knew each other. They would say: "Can you send lawyers, make a statement?" At demonstrations, we knew each other, met each other.' The 2011 uprising was vastly different in scale, with activists a tiny minority. It is here that we see the important contribution of non-activists, which social movement theory is ill-equipped to see as it overly focuses on organisation and pre-existing networks.

Non-activists played an important role in directing the crowds on 28 January, alongside the experienced activists. When asked who was leading the demonstration he was part of, Hossam (Interview 2011), the owner of a boutique cooking school, said:

There were a few experienced activists who told us what to do, how to break through the line, how to use vinegar [against teargas]. This helped a lot. I was in the front. There were many girls in the front line, going back to the front when beaten. Later in the day, a couple of girls took the lead, ordinary people supervising, not activists (in my opinion). People would say contradictory things [about what to do next], we would divide into two groups if there were two roads.

When the regime withdrew the police and released prisoners to create chaos, non-activists took control of their neighbourhood's security. Following Wynne-Hughes (Interview 2011), 'that night was the night of the lootings. The next night there were *ligan sha'abiyya* [popular committees]. My flatmate got a call from his friend in the building to come and help.' When walking back home on the night of 28 January, Joumanah Younis (Interview 2011), an Iraqi–British language student, recalled that 'checkpoints had been set up by ordinary people. Later people set up committees. I was walking alone, a bit lost, then a man with a big metal bar came up to me and said: can I help you? He walked me to my house.' We will return to this in Chapter 7.

Once the Square was occupied, organisational mechanisms were developed comprising both activists and non-activists. Impending danger was communicated to the masses in the Square by people hitting lampposts with stones (Ezzat, Interview 2011). 'Improvised tents' were constructed, 'with names of the area [where people came from]' (Salah, Interview 2011). Residents of the Square and other volunteers became part of the Square's organising committee, and helped to set up a garbage collection and recycling service with the help of Cairo's Zabbalin network of garbage-collectors (Ezzat, Interview 2011).[8]

Besides taking leadership, non-activists contributed in myriad subtle ways. Wynne-Hughes (Interview 2011) told us how, never having participated in protests before, 'I bought a box of Pepsi for people to wash out their eyes. I saw others do this and volunteered. Others did too. Some announced something about teargas.' Later, she recalled how 'people volunteered to guard houses. ... People came to check we're ok. People knocked on the door, asking for bread for people on Tahrir. I didn't know them, but I helped out.'

Ezzat (Interview 2011) recalled:

Ordinary Egyptians would come with two bags of *kushari* [famous local Egyptian dish], one lady came with 10 sandwiches, people came with cheap biscuits, with very exclusive biscuits. Some [donors] ran away, afraid of getting caught. There was so much food, it attracted all street children. There was safety and so much food. People were so kind. People carrying bags with cotton, Dettol, micro gauze, at a cost of £E20–30. People would say: please give this to the clinics [on the Square]. I had to say: please spread the word: we have enough. We would get small bags with the same components. People would think: what are the basics, then bring them in. Sometimes this was announced on Facebook, sometimes they just came, many times people called: what do you need? People may not have agreed with the revolution, but they helped out. (Khalil Saeed (Interview 2011) told us the same)

Significantly, people helped out in spite of the danger. Salah (Interview 2011), for instance, reported: 'A few [of those who brought supplies] were killed, many were attacked. It was very dangerous.'

Protester Motivation: Grievances, Identity and Emotions

There has as yet been no systematic research on what motivated people, especially non-activists, to participate in the January 2011 revolution. But there are some tentative pointers. One poll, carried out in April 2011, found that low living standards and lack of employment topped the list of grievances at 64 per cent (Figure 5.3). Lack of democracy and political reform came next at 19 per cent. Events in Tunisia and encouragement from friends both scored 6 per cent. The death of Khaled Said only scored 3 per cent.

Our interviewees painted a somewhat different picture. When asked what they thought motivated people, lack of democracy and electoral fraud were cited more often than the economy. Most cited Tunisia as a key factor motivating people and many listed the death of Khaled Said or police violence more broadly. In addition, they mentioned other factors, such as the boat and ferry disasters of 2006 (Chapter 3), the Alexandria bombing and the impending succession of Gamal Mubarak.

The liberals among our interviewees tended to focus on electoral fraud and police violence, as well as trigger events such as the train disaster, the Alexandria bombing and Gamal's expected succession (cf. Group Interview 2011; Anonymous, Interview 2011; Ishak, Interview 2011). Those commenting on the economic situation were either leftists (who typically also pointed to the contribution of previous protest waves, particularly the workers' movement; cf. Samer, Interview 2011; N. Mansour, Interview 2011) or, intriguingly, government employees.

The latter's motivation seems to have come from a mixture of a sense of social obligation and hurt national pride. Consider Abdel-Rahman (Interview 2011), an employee of the Central Bank:

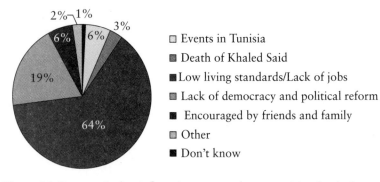

Figure 5.3: Factors cited as influencing support for or participation in January 2011 events (IRI Poll 2011).

I work in a government job, with a double-digit salary, I studied in the US. But what I hated was the lack of opportunities [for ordinary Egyptians]. I come from the countryside. My parents are not poor, they paid for the AUC [American University in Cairo]. But many of my friends have no opportunities; they are very smart, but have no prospects. ... For example, people graduate with a 4.0 from state universities, but have no job after many years. While you can get 4.0 if your father is the chairman of the department. ... I went to Tahrir Square for these people. ... I travelled to many countries, saw their infrastructures. Yet we have zero infrastructure for the old, for the disabled, no street crossings. You can't escape that question: why are people not treated as human beings [here]? You [referring to us, the researchers] are staying in the Shepheard Hotel, one of our top hotels. Compare that to the Champs Elysées, to London. You can't get away from this. I want to claim the same rights as everyone else has, for my friends too. (cf. also Gamal, Interview 2011)

Underneath the political and economic grievances, all interviewees expressed deep contempt for the way the regime dealt with its people. Gamal (Interview 2011), the young diplomat, expressed how he became alienated from the regime he worked for most eloquently:

2005 was the first time I heard the slogan 'down with Mubarak' in Cairo. I went to an event organised by the Bedouin who were brutalised by the police. After the 2004 terror attacks in the Sinai, the Bedouin were subject to huge human rights abuses. Wives, mothers arrested, brutal tactics of investigation. I went to an event at the Journalists' Syndicate, women talking about what happened to them. A woman in a *niqab* told a horrifying story of how state security brutalised her, threatened to send her to Mossad officers. Listening to her testimony, the whole audience started to shout: 'down with Mubarak.' It got me, not easy to hear something like that.

The discrepancy between the poll's findings and our much smaller sample can partly be explained by our interviewees being middle class and active on Facebook. The poll, by contrast, included representatives from all sectors of Egyptian society. In addition, the way the question was phrased ('which of the following factors most influenced you ...?') forced people to choose between competing factors; because the economic situation had worsened since the revolution, this factor was more immediate than the more distant events of Said's death or the fall of Ben Ali.

Significantly, the key factors that both the pollsters and our interviewees listed map remarkably well on to the structural strains discussed in Chapters 3–4. 'Low living standards and lack of jobs' reflect the high unemployment figures, the sharp rise in inflation and food prices and the withdrawal of the state as a result of neoliberal reforms.

'Lack of democracy and political reform' covers the narrowing base of the NDP, the increasingly autocratic behaviour of the regime and widespread election fraud, as well as the impending succession of Gamal. The 'death of Khaled Said' is symbolic of the growing power of the police and the increase in (awareness of) police abuses. What is intriguing is that other underlying factors did not feature. For instance, no one mentioned youth ratios specifically (although many referred to the revolution as a revolution of the youth), nor did any of our interviewees list changes in Cairo's urban make-up or elite fissures. Technology and exposure to transnational networks were mentioned, but not in the context of what motivated people.[9]

Leaving aside grievances and other drivers, people's motivations were also shaped by mundane factors, such as whether they had to go to work on the day. As one of our interviewees pointed out, 'the 25th was a holiday. Most vacations for students started on the 26th' (Group Interview 2011). Ghonim (2012: 134) and Ashraf Khalil (2011: 122) similarly suggest that the regime helped the protesters by making Police Day a national holiday in 2010. Two of our interviewees said they did not attend at first because they had classes or exams on 25 January (J. Younis, Interview 2011; M. Hamdy, Conversations 2011). In addition, the protests were helped by the fact that the regime declared a national emergency, thereby closing the factories and most places of work, enabling workers and Ultras to join the protests unfettered.

Although both the poll and our interviewees focused primarily on macro factors, identity, beliefs and emotions also played a role in motivating people (cf. Klandermans 2004). The emergence of a collective protest identity, centred on a rejection of the Mubarak regime and the construction of a new 'Egyptianness', was crucial to the success of the revolution. Protesters did not agree on what to replace the Mubarak regime with, what Egyptianness meant or even on what their main reasons for protesting were. But they began to identify strongly with the notion of a new Egypt in opposition to Mubarak. Posters and slogans saying 'I used to be afraid, now I'm an Egyptian' (Gribbon and Hawas 2012: 109) or 'lift your head up high, you're Egyptian' (*irfa' rasak fawq, inta masri*) (J. Younis, Interview 2011) encapsulated this coming together under one label, 'Egyptian', regardless of class, gender, religion or ideology. Khalil Saeed (Interview 2011) summarised this as follows:

We found common ground: dropping the regime. Focusing on this common dream, we could transcend whatever differences we had, try to neglect whatever might drive us apart. This is how I understand the word citizenship: find common ground, common values. Common ground: get rid of the regime. Common values: dignity [symbolised by 'bread'], freedom and social justice.

Just like the Global Justice Movement (Clark 2003: 157–9), the activists sought to project an inclusive protest identity that appealed to all Egyptians, regardless of goals, beliefs or identity. When framing the initial call to revolution ('January 25: Revolution Against Torture, Poverty, Corruption, and Unemployment'), Ghonim (2012: 136–7):

... deliberately included poverty, corruption, and unemployment in the title because we needed to have everyone join forces: workers, human rights activists, government employees ... If the invitation to take to the streets had been based solely on human rights, then only a certain segment of Egyptian society would have participated.

The demands of the revolution were similarly inclusive: address poverty by increasing the minimum wage, annul the emergency law, fire the minister of the interior, limit the presidency to two terms (Ghonim 2012: 166–7). This was reflected in the revolution's main slogan: 'bread, freedom, social justice' ('aish, hurriyya, 'adala igtima'iyya') (Khalil Saeed, Interview 2011; Soueif 2012: 17). Here, again, we can see the influence of the activists in shaping the 2011 uprising.

It was this inclusivity of demands, this funnelling into a set of pared-down core demands, beyond ideological divisions, that meant that more people could identify with the protests than ever before. In doing so, the revolution was framed as, to use the famous phrase of Subcommandante Marcos, the leader of the Mexican Zapatista movement, 'one big no and many many yesses' (Clark 2003: 158): 'no' to Mubarak (and what he stood for: police violence, emergency law, unlimited presidential terms), 'yes' to an increase in minimum wage and whatever one believed should replace him. People thus did not have to agree on shared values or what to replace Mubarak with before acting.

Protesters coalesced around a shared 'collective action frame'. They agreed broadly on what was wrong (the economy and the political system), even though views differed on the weight of the different wrongs. They agreed on who the victims were (the people) and who was responsible for these wrongs (the regime). And they (broadly) agreed on what to do to change it (protest and occupy public spaces until the regime agreed to change, although views differed on how long protesters should hold out, what role violence should play and so on). Before January 2011, the different protest sectors had remained divided on what the primary wrongs were. They had similarly been divided on who was responsible; the workers' movement, for instance, was reluctant to link their industrial struggles with regime change. They were also divided on what to do. It was the (temporary) convergence of so many different parts of society around this pared-down collective action frame that enabled the protests to turn into a mass demonstration.

The protest movement also went out of its way to enable people to discover their collective identity and enjoy and celebrate it. The marches through the small alleys of informal Cairo, with its greater sense of solidarity, made it easier for onlookers to identify with the protesters, egged on by the numerous chants. Once Tahrir had been conquered, the collective protest identity was reinforced by chants such as 'welcome, welcome, to revolutionaries' (*ahlan, ahlan, bi'l-thuwwar*), or 'Muslim, Christian, one hand' (*muslim masihi eid wahda*) (Keraitim and Mehrez 2012: 46). Even the chant 'the people demand the removal of the regime' (*al-sha'b yurid isqat al-nizam*) (Keraitim and Mehrez 2012: 27) served to reinforce the identity of 'the people' against the enemy, 'the regime', creating a strong incentive to join the protests, as not joining came to be seen as being complicit with the regime (Chapter 6). Since identification increases feelings of solidarity, defection was thus made more difficult while the benefits of participation were increased.

At an emotional level, feelings of solidarity, outrage and shame played a central part in protesters' motivations. As we will show in Chapter 6, the shame of not participating, of being seen as complicit with the regime, of not being manly enough to face the police, was a pivotal motive, as were feelings of outrage at police violence. Many of these emotional motives only came into play once the demonstrations had begun. Solidarity became a major factor only once non-activists had come out to participate, and had begun to adopt an activist identity as a result of collective action. Outrage became a key driver when the police began their brutal clampdown. Other emotions were already at play before 25 January. Hope had begun to take root following the fall of Ben Ali (for some, with the emergence of ElBaradei as a presidential candidate). Moral indignation (mixed with outrage) at police brutality, corruption and regime incompetence had been growing for years (following Goodwin, Jasper and Polletta (2004: 416, 422), we make a distinction between outrage and long-term moral indignation; the former is classified as a reflex emotion, the latter as a moral emotion). Emotional motives thus augmented instrumental, identity and ideological motives, particularly once the protests were under way.

Violence vs non-Violence

The question of the relative roles of violence and non-violence in the 25 January revolution takes us to the heart of the interplay between activists and non-activists. All the available evidence points to the activists behind the original demonstrations pursuing non-violent tactics. Yet a significant section of the demonstrators used violent tactics, from throwing Molotov cocktails to attacking the police and storming police stations, and this violence seems to have played a crucial part in the security forces' defeat (although more research is needed to validate this conclusion).[10] What role did activists and non-activists play in the pursuit of both violent and non-violent tactics?

Activists and pundits alike have tended to depict the revolution as largely non-violent. The demonstrations indeed began as non-violent events, the tactics developed by the activists were predominantly non-violent, and considerable effort went into keeping the protests non-violent. Once occupied, the occupations of Tahrir Square and other public places across Egypt were similarly largely non-violent (although defending them against attacks involved sustained violence).

There are numerous reports of activists calling on protesters to remain non-violent. Two of the non-activists we interviewed recalled activists asking those who picked up sticks or bricks to put them down (Abdel-Rahman, Interview 2011; Hossam, Interview 2011). There are accounts of demonstrators helping or protecting police 'soldiers' (though not officers) and not attacking them when the crowds surged passed them near the end (Ezzat, Interview 2011; A. Khalil 2011: 172–5, 177). According to journalist Hisham Allam (Interview 2011), when soldiers shouted 'let us go,' 'we told them: "we're not against you, we are attacking the regime"'.

However, whether non-violence was a result of activists controlling the crowds or a calculation (conscious, pragmatic, ethical or otherwise) on the part of the crowd is unclear. As we saw above, many activists had undergone non-violent training workshops and both the April 6 and 'Khaled Said' websites exhorted the virtues of non-violent struggles elsewhere. Quotations from Gandhi frequently appeared on the 'Khaled Said' webpage and Ghonim (2012: 105–7, 107) posted an extensive quotation from the 1982 film *Gandhi* about being prepared to die, but not kill, receive blows and 'through our pain we will make them see their injustice'.

Khalil Saeed (Interview 2011), who himself believes in non-violence, argued that non-violence was a product of both activist leadership and people's 'natural' sympathy with the police's lowly paid foot soldiers:

Some factors helped. People liked [the] April 6 [movement]. On the 25th, they were doing a great job. Before [25 January], I tried to join a demonstration ... near the Lawyers' Syndicate. [Police] soldiers were trying to ban people from going in. There were almost 1,000, 2,000 in the Square. I could see April 6 inside trying to control the crowd. Many were like myself, joining perhaps for the first time, trying to shout. [April 6] were trying to stop individuals from shouting insulting chants, trying to control. On the 28th, they were spread all over the mosques, trying to control. But on the 28th, there was lots of confrontation, for instance the battle on Qasra Nil Bridge. People trying to advance, they didn't have the means, except to throw back gas canisters, or throw them in the Nile. People were just trying to defend themselves. It was not like Gandhi's first line forward, beaten, then second line. But, when people broke the line, they didn't hurt the soldiers. People had sympathy with them, ... they knew they [the soldiers] just took orders. The NDP buildings and police stations were attacked. I'm not sure whether the NDP was attacked by thugs, to get rid of [compromising] papers, or [by ordinary people] to steal weapons. But for me, it is normal [that people react like this] after 30 years. At least it is good that they directed their anger at the police and the NDP.

Ezzat (Interview 2011) put the non-violence down to people sympathising with the lot of police soldiers:

In many cases, youngsters gave onions to [police] soldiers or Pepsi [against the effects of teargas]. [This was] something human; they [the soldiers] are paid a meagre income, live in bad conditions; [this was like saying:] we're doing it for you as well. One protester, who had lost an eye ... told [a soldier]: 'I love you [bahibbuh]. Why are you doing this?'

Hossam (Interview 2011) believed the influence of seasoned activists was crucial:

Any time someone tried to throw a rock, someone would hold their hand and say, 'no this is a peaceful protest.' ... [Non-violence] was the result of a mixture of the general mood and activists keeping people in line. More of the latter, with activists saying: 'We know what happens when we throw stones.' The truck [which was overturned on Qasr al-Nil bridge] was put on fire afterwards, when we had broken through, probably by ordinary people. The mood changes (though not the slogans), but also there was a sense of: you deserved it.

194

Maher, perhaps predictably, credited the central role of activists, who had learned from the Serbian Otpor! movement about the danger of even one protester turning violent, handing the police an excuse to clampdown and destroying the protests' media image (Aljazeera 2011e):

On the 25th, we were insisting on non-violence. If we found any small group of police soldiers, we protected them. On the night of the 25th, it was different. We didn't attack, we withdrew, ran again, tried to move forward. On the 28th, we tried to penetrate [to get to Tahrir Square which was cordoned off], but there were 1,000s of soldiers. We used metal shields, wooden sticks, trees (to overturn trucks), bricks, motorcycle helmets, carton under our shirts [to protect against police batons], plastic bottles squashed then wrapped around our arms, plastic shields, masks with vinegar. We didn't attack soldiers or destroy anything. We did not destroy any building or private car, only police trucks. ... (Maher, Interview 2011)

In sharp contrast, Salah (Interview 2011), who had taught hundreds of activists about non-violence, noted that non-violence was primarily carried out by untrained non-activists:

I saw people doing things, in a disciplined [non-violent] way, without [apparently] having been taught. I had been trying to teach people non-violent tactics, but there was clearly no need here, and those I had taught were too few anyway [compared to these numbers]. I saw incredible examples of sacrifice, altruism—it brought out the best in people.

Activists appear to have played a significant part in steering the protests in a non-violent direction and encouraging de-escalation mechanisms (Bauer and Schweitzer 2012: 10–11). But since the crowds were simply too large to control, tens of thousands of non-activists must have decided to act non-violently of their own accord, whether for pragmatic, cultural (see the *mulid* discussion in Chapter 6), moral or other reasons. The shouts of '*silmiyya*' (peaceful), which dominated the protests on 28 January (A. Khalil 2011: 161; Soueif 2012: 23), came after all from activists and non-activists alike. Moreover, once the military was deployed, popular perceptions of the military (particularly in comparison with the deeply negative perceptions of the police) affected how people reacted to military deployment (Bauer and Schweitzer 2012: 12). That the military ostensibly refrained from putting down the demonstration was another factor critical to the sustained non-violence of the protesters.

Violence, meanwhile, played a crucial part in the struggle to gain access to the Square (and other locations) and in protecting these locations from attacks by pro-Mubarak supporters and thugs.[11] The burning down of police stations was central to the collapse of the security forces' morale, just as the full-scale war between Bedouin fighters and security forces on the Sinai Peninsula played a part in weakening the police's capacity. To overlook these aspects of the revolution, as, for instance, Bauer and Schweitzer (2012) do (they do acknowledge small-scale spontaneous and self-defensive violence), is to romanticise the role of non-violence, even though, compared to other revolutions, the Egyptian revolution was remarkably non-violent.[12]

More research is needed to establish exactly what happened.[13] But two things seem clear from interviews and eyewitness reports. One is that the Ultras played a significant part in confronting, and eventually beating, the police. The other is that the burning of police stations, mostly by inhabitants of Cairo's informal areas and in provincial cities, was a crucial factor. In the words of Saad (Interview 2011):

> The revolution was not just about youth, not just about Facebook, not peaceful; 300 police stations were burned, people were fighting in self-defence, more than a 1,000 [killed]. But, we saved the [police] soldiers. The regime made the soldiers shoot teargas without masks. We saved the soldiers, but not the officers. We arrested them and sent them to the army.

Nadim Mansour (Interview 2011) accorded violence an even more central role:

> Violence was very important in the first days. It didn't escalate because of the very clever move of the regime to remove the police. If it had continued, people would have got more violent. People did fight the police. There was massive violence, for three hours or so. ... There were many chants of 'silmiyya, silmiyya' [peaceful, peaceful]. But when confronted, people would fight. The peaceful chants were very strong on the 25th. People were spreading it out, not April 6, but many more. But the media over-romanticise this. There was no police station where no officers were killed. Protesters specifically targeted people who had tortured them. Some [police] soldiers were attacked, others were protected. I protected some, gave them money to go home. By the end of the 28th, the police were dismantled. ... They had nowhere to go. Some were beaten up, others protected them. But the main part of the revolution was violent.

Numerous media reports documented violence against government buildings, and police stations in particular. On the morning of 27 January, Aljazeera (2011a) reported that protesters torched a police station in Suez, where some of the worst fighting had taken place during the preceding days, and assembled in front of a second police station, demanding the release of people imprisoned during the protests. On 28 January, the city's main police station was burned down. By the end of this date, activist reports suggested that over twenty police stations had been burned down across Egypt (clayclai 2011). According to Human Rights Watch (2011), 'many police stations in [Alexandria alone] were burned down on January 28, and demonstrators tried but failed to burn down the intelligence services building'.

The following description of events in Suez, admittedly amongst the most violent of the revolution, illustrates both that violence was part of the repertoire and that it was a direct response to the violence of regime forces:

On Friday, thousands of Egyptian protesters stormed the main police station in the port city of Suez ... The protesters freed prisoners from the city jail, destroyed armored police vehicles, then sacked the building and looted its contents. The demonstrators emerged from Friday prayers at mosques in Suez and confronted police outside the station. Police fired at the demonstrators, who then surged forward to take over the police station. The protesters dragged fleeing riot police off their motorbikes and seized their batons and equipment, AFP reported. They also set at least a half dozen armored vehicles on fire. After storming the police station, protesters removed its contents—refrigerators, desks, files, and other equipment. (PressTV 2011; see also El-Ghobashy 2011)

Amira (Interview 2011) similarly recalled:

The station in Maadi was burned down, even though it was in a rich area. In the poorer areas, it was revenge, a response to the opening of the prisons. My brother, [a public] investigator, thinks this too. He is still close to the police, knows this from police friends. In Maadi, Dar es-Salaam, a popular area close by, orders were given to the police to open the jails. Criminals spread out, trying to quell the demo of the Maadi youth. When they continued onto the Corniche, people living around police stations saw attacks by criminals. They took revenge, attacked police in their stations. The police ran away. The burning started at that time. One of my brothers' friends hid in a jail in Suez. People started to throw fireballs ... When he saw fire in the office, he ran away, was hunted. They treated him badly. He himself was not a bad person.

In addition to attacks on police stations, there were attacks using handmade weapons such as Molotov cocktails during the battle for Tahrir Square. Joumanah Younis (Interview 2011) told us how a 'swat team' came to use the building where she was hiding on Tahrir Square:

A group of protesters started to use the house I hid in. ... The *bawab* [doorman] played an important role, a community watch role. No one was allowed in unless they lived there. There was an argument at the door. The doorman claimed that the people coming in were security people, looking for protesters. ... A group of protesters was allowed in, they were making Molotov cocktails with bottles and gas canisters. There were two girls with them. They wanted to know if there was a roof to throw cocktails off on the police down in the street. ... It was like a little Swat team.

Ashraf Khalil (2011: 181, 189) also reports seeing Molotov cocktails being used in the Kit Kat district and on the October 6 Bridge.

When asked whether he had heard of groups using Molotov cocktails, Ghazali-Harb (Interview 2011b) answered: 'I saw some groups trying to bomb in return for violence, but they were not organised. It doesn't need much organising. Some people had it ready just in case.' Samer (Interview 2011) responded to the same question, saying:

If there were 'swat cells,' this was the exception. Most protesters did not have Molotov cocktails. There was violence against police stations, in poor areas. But then there was that striking image of a man in Alexandria standing in front of the police cars. There was a determination to remain peaceful. In Suez, there was violence, they shot at the police. But that should not tarnish the general spirit.

Some of this violence, particularly of the defensive kind, was carried out by seasoned activists. But the bulk was carried out by the Ultras and, later, once the Square was occupied, by the Muslim Brotherhood youth (particularly at night, when many protesters left):

We avoided violence on the 25th. But because of the brutal repression at the end, we felt we shouldn't be that peaceful. If under attack, you fight back. You have the right to defend yourself. If we didn't fight back, we wouldn't have got to Tahrir. The other turning point was the Camel attack. We had to fight back and defend Tahrir, to throw back stones. We had to do something. It was one of our darkest days, Egyptians fighting each other in that way. We managed to put all our defences to work. They did have snipers with them, but we still managed to push. ... The Muslim Brothers were there, they were important [in this battle], but not just them. The Ultras were equally important but no one mentioned them, for some strange reason. Both of them were organised, they played a central role. We managed to push back the camel charge during the daytime, there was no Muslim Brotherhood then. The Brotherhood played its role at night. (Ghazali-Harb, Interview 2011b)

Salah (Interview 2011), like Maher, confirmed that the Ultras 'were the ones charging against the Central Security Forces, charging, counter-charging' and that, without them, Tahrir might well not have been occupied. The Ultras, like the Brotherhood, had a long history of battling the police; they had the experience and the stamina that many of the protesters lacked. Thus, though this violence was carried out by others than the activists behind the revolution, it was not spontaneous; rather, it followed well-worn patterns of violent combat, developed through years of confrontations with the police.

A second non-activist group credited with carrying out much of the violence were those living in informal areas. It was these that attacked many of the hated police stations, and played a central role in the assault on the police forces blocking Tahrir Square. According to Nadim Mansour (Interview 2011), this readiness to fight was a product of regular run-ins with the police in Egypt's informal areas and the harshness of people's lives there (see also Bauer and Schweitzer 2012: 11):

Most of the protesters were from the poor neighbourhoods, where you don't just run but fight. When political activists were beaten, they went home. The poor stayed, went back and forth, for 24 hours. Then they went home to their neighbourhood and called for a fight. On the 28th, the police would fire, someone would be killed, people would attack the police and burn the police building.

There have indeed been prior incidents of citizens attacking police stations in the aftermath of police abuse (Ismail 2006: 161–4), including one just days before the revolution (El-Ghobashy 2011). But encounters between the police and the inhabitants of informal Cairo seem more often to be characterised by concealment, trickery, passivity or evasion than by confrontation (Ismail 2006: 160–1). Nadim Mansour (Interview 2011) himself acknowledged that 'Normally, if beaten, people are afraid. This time, it mobilised them.' We will return to the question of how people overcame their fear of police violence (Chapter 6). Suffice it to say here that, whatever the reasons behind the decision of people to fight, much of the violence that played a part in defeating the police was not orchestrated by the activist leaders.

The intensity of the violence, particularly against police stations, was a crucial factor in the demoralisation and eventually the defeat of the police—although the decision to withdraw appears to have been in part tactical, to create conditions of anarchy that could then be blamed on the protesters, in part a reflection of a tug of war between the military and the police (Bauer and Schweitzer 2012: 11). Political commentator Mona El-Ghobashy (2011) put the police's decision to withdraw directly down to the attacks on police stations: 'At 5 pm on the afternoon of January 28, when reports started rolling in of police stations

burning down, one after another, al-Adly [the interior minister] capitulated and ordered the removal of his forces from the streets.' By the
afternoon of 28 January, there were reports from across the country
that the police were pulling back. From Alexandria, there were reports
claiming '"Not a single security officer left in Alexandria", with up to
500,000 protesters forcing them out ... [arresting] the police who did
not pull out' while five minutes later 'Al Jazeera and AFP [reported]
that protestors have set Alexandria City Hall on fire' (Lucas 2011).

Equally important was the fact that the acts of violence happened
nationwide, and that they were complemented by mass nationwide
demonstrations. Cities where reinforcements had been sent, such as
Suez and Mahalla, drained the resources of the cities whose forces had
been depleted by dispatching the reinforcements. Police resources were
drained even further by the armed clashes that took place in the Sinai
Peninsula, where the Bedouin, already engaged in a long-standing battle with security forces, joined the protests. They stormed police stations, kidnapped police officers, freed Bedouin prisoners, and
eventually forced out the security forces from the Peninsula (Omer
2011; McGregor 2011).

The crucial role of violence notwithstanding, what appears to have
defeated the police more than anything was the fact that they were
faced by tens of thousands who had overcome their fear. Tellingly, it
was not the burning police stations that al-Adly referred to in his pre-
trial defence, but the fact that the police were facing millions who had
lost their fear of the police:

The situation was beyond imagination. The faces of the demonstrators showed
how clear they were in challenging the regime and how much they hated it,
how willing they were to resist with their bodies all attempts to divide them
with truncheons and water cannons and all other tools. They outnumbered
security forces by a million or more, a fact that shocked the Interior Ministry
leaders and the president. Those government officials all sat at home watching
the demonstrations on TV. Not one of them devised a political solution to
what policemen were facing—confrontations with angry people and indescrib-
able hatred of the government. All of us were astonished. (El-Ghobashy 2011)

Ashraf Khalil (2011: 177) similarly cites the moment when the
police realised they were outnumbered by people who had lost their
fear as the turning point in the battle for Tahrir:

At about four in the afternoon, the phalanx of Central Security troops broke
ranks and ran, leaving their paddy wagons behind. ... It was a powerful

moment—the exact turning point when the police realized the people weren't afraid of them and that they were badly outnumbered. ... In an instant, the fearsome and hated bullies of the Interior Ministry had become pathetic and irrelevant.[14]

The non-violent character of the demonstrations and the kindness shown by many protesters towards police 'soldiers' may have played a role in the latter's decision to capitulate, just as non-violence and protesters appealing to military conscripts' backgrounds by chanting 'the army and the people are one hand' may have affected the army's decision not to shoot (among other factors such as the army's self-perception or the rift between the army and the regime, reflected in the military leadership's reportedly point-blank refusal of Mubarak's request to put down the demonstrations; Wickham 2013: 164–5). However, this is beyond the scope of this book, as more research is needed to unravel the precise causal relationship between the various violent and non-violent tactics, the police's collapse and its subsequent tactical withdrawal, and the army's decision not to quell the uprising.

6

'I USED TO BE AFRAID, NOW I'M AN EGYPTIAN'

FROM FEAR TO DEFIANCE[1]

One of the striking features of the January 2011 revolution was that hundreds of thousands of non-activist Egyptians broke through their fear barrier. On paper, the Egyptian regime was still as strong as ever in terms of its repressive capacity, and throughout that first week the regime displayed its full panoply of brutal tactics. Thousands were wounded, dozens killed and over 1,000 arrested (*Guardian* 2011c; Aljazeera 2011f). Many choked on teargas, made more vicious by being past its expiry date. Consider this account by Hossam (Interview 2011), the owner of the boutique cooking school, who had never demonstrated before:

We guessed that there would be plenty of people in the main mosque on Tahrir, and that we needed to go there and link up. ... We started moving slowly to Tahrir. So far, the police did not interfere. We were 7,000–8,000, but people kept joining us from [their] houses. Old people were waving Egyptian flags [from the balconies]. We called [on them] to stop watching and come down. I was surprised that people came down. Police were moving parallel to us. Until we got close to Qubri al-Galaa, 1.5 km away from Tahrir, Tahrir Street, a straight line to Tahrir. I saw that something was happening ahead, smelled teargas. Someone started to pull little masks out and distributed them. There were about 12,000–15,000, I saw people all the way to the end of the street. The police was on the bridge, big camions blocking the bridge, about 100 [police] soldiers. I didn't know what teargas smelled like, or its effects. It took

203

us 30–40 minutes to get through. ... Then the first truck was overturned, and put on fire. Walking past the Opera (on the left), [police] soldiers on the other side of the road, we started to get hurt. Teargas breathing problems. It was weird to see scenes like you see on TV. I'd never seen them before. From 1pm to 7pm, we didn't get to Tahrir. We were pushed back, took a second route, a third route. Numbers were starting to decrease. I decided to walk back (6 km) ... because I was hurt on my back and had completely inhaled two teargas bombs.

How did people overcome their fear of this? On previous occasions, police brutality had typically succeeded in suppressing protests, at least in the short term (though often sparking further protests in the future). Police violence may have provoked short outbursts of popular anger, as in the working-class neighbourhood of Warraq days before the revolution (El-Ghobashy 2011). But these outbursts were usually short-lived. The threatening presence of police at demonstrations had furthermore put many off from joining demonstrations in the first place.[2] What was different this time?

One way to explain the mass demonstrations in Egypt is to look into how people overcame their fear. In the words of a political acquaintance of Gamal (Interview 2011), the diplomat: 'If people manage to defeat the fear within, this is going to be the end of the regime.' Intriguingly, despite fear being a key factor determining whether protests succeed, especially under repressive regimes, very little has been written by social movement analysts about how people overcome fear. Before the 'emotional turn' in social movement theory, scholars tended to use a rational choice model, casting people's decisions as clinical cost–benefit calculations. The visceral qualities of emotions such as fear and anger were missing from this analysis (Goodwin, Jasper and Polletta 2000: 70–4). The 'emotional turn' produced a wealth of articles on emotions such as pride and anger, but few on fear as such. A comprehensive analytical framework for understanding how people overcome fear is still lacking.

Encouragement Mechanisms

In one of the few seminal studies of fear in protests, Jeff Goodwin and Steven Pfaff (2001: 285–6) found that in the oral histories they collected from activists in the US Civil Rights and East German democracy movements, fear was cited in 36.9 per cent of the testimonies, far more than anger (10 per cent) and outrage (4.6 per cent) combined. Overcoming fear is thus key to movement success.

Drawing on these two case studies, Goodwin and Pfaff (2001: 286–300) identified eight 'encouragement mechanisms' which helped protesters to neutralise their fears:

1. intimate social networks;
2. mass meetings (including chants and music producing collective effervescence);
3. identification with the movement and a belief in its righteousness;
4. shaming;
5. training in the techniques of civil disobedience;
6. mass-media coverage;
7. having access to arms; and
8. a belief in divine protection (the latter two were only observed in the United States).

Confirming the validity of this embryonic model, we found variations of each of these mechanisms in the Egyptian case. Because the Egyptian events happened in the space of days (at least from the perspective of non-activists), compared to the months and years the East German and US protests took, there are crucial differences. We would further argue that the last two mechanisms, which Goodwin and Pfaff found only in the United States, can be broadened to encompass a greater variety of similar processes, and that there are additional mechanisms at work. Access to protection mechanisms (makeshift shields, face masks, safe houses) seems to have played an equivalent role in the Egyptian case to access to arms in the United States. Belief in the righteousness of the revolution appears to have had a similar effect on protesters to belief in divine protection (although more research is needed to confirm this). Nevertheless, the Goodwin–Pfaff model is a good starting point.

There were a number of mechanisms that activists used to reduce people's fear of joining. We will touch on some of the most salient ones, starting with Goodwin and Pfaff's list, and adding three more: different levels of participation, emulation, and taking part, and strategically chosen start locations. We will discuss shaming and identification with the movement later, and will not discuss access to guns and belief in divine protection. Most of the protesters did not have access to arms; rather, they drew comfort from the protection mechanisms taught by non-violent tactics. The question of belief in divine protection, or rather, divine fate, is an interesting one, and may well have played a part among protesters. However, we did not look into this and none of our interviewees mentioned it.

Intimate Social Networks and Solidarity

Intriguingly, activist or pre-existing networks seem to have played a relatively limited role in persuading non-activists to participate. Classical social movement studies place a high-value on pre-existing networks and subsequent activist networks as facilitating activism (cf. della Porta 1995a, 1995b; McAdam 1982; Morris 1981; Klandermans 2004: 278). Goodwin and Pfaff (2001: 287–8) underscore the role of intimate social networks specifically in helping people to overcome their fears. 'Extremely close personal links were forged between activists,' they observed, 'which encouraged them in their activities and raised the costs of dropping out, of submitting to outside pressure, or of becoming an informant for the secret police.'

Seasoned Egyptian activists drew courage from knowing that they were part of an intimate network of like-minded friends who would nurture them if wounded, and work to secure their release if imprisoned. Human rights activists highlighted the role of networks in providing legal aid and moral support prior to the revolution; during the revolution, these networks, aided by volunteers, helped to provide first aid, as well as legal aid and moral support, all of which would have helped to make fear more manageable (Samer, Interview 2011; N. Mansour, Interview 2011). An Aljazeera documentary on April 6 (2011e) likewise showed the group's solidarity mechanisms in action.

For non-activists, the story is more complex. Numerous interviewees observed that neither social nor activist networks played a large part in their decision to demonstrate. Hossam and Abdel-Rahman did credit friends (activist as well as non-activist) with informing them about the unfolding events and sharing their excitement, but both denied having been pressured by their friends and both seem to have arrived at their decision independently. When asked whether he had many friends who participated in the protests, Hossam (Interview 2011) responded:

Surprisingly, I did have many friends. It was like a big party: 'hey, haven't seen you for some years!' I'm sure many [others] were organised. But this is my experience [becoming involved spontaneously, without being part of an organisation].

Neither Hossam nor Abdel-Rahman nor Hamdy, the diplomat, had strong links to activist networks. The same holds for Latifa Fahmy.

Gamal's situation was more complex. Not only did he use his network of friends to gauge how big the event would be, but he also credits friends with helping him to honour his decision to participate:

I was surrounded by reformists, 'cowards,' conservatives who believed in Edmund Burke. ... There are some activists among my friends, but they are embarrassed about me being a civil servant. ... I was talking to friends beforehand to get a sense of how many would participate. I would run a test: if this guy, who is a coward, participates, it is going to be big. Most told me they were going to participate. But the whole night before the Friday I had nightmares, I could not sleep. Even Friday morning, when I had decided to participate, I was pushed to it by social circles around me. (Gamal, Interview 2011)

Once non-activists had become involved, feelings of solidarity towards other protesters became a factor in overcoming fear. Abdel-Rahman talked about his sense of loyalty to a fifteen-year-old street boy who, having sought his protection, was beaten by the police. Gamal recalled moments of shared solidarity in doorways, taking a break from protesting with complete strangers. The 'anonymous mother' (Interview 2011) of a son who joined the protests during the second week told us that her son decided to stay on the Square 'because he was afraid that if he left at night, the others would be arrested, beaten, removed if too few remained. They needed to stay to protect [each other] through numbers.' Fear of what might happen to his newfound comrades trumped fear of what would happen to him personally.

Mass Meetings, Chants and Festival-Like Atmosphere

In the United States and East Germany, mass gatherings played a crucial part in helping people to overcome fear, giving them 'a sense of security in numbers' (particularly important in high-risk demonstrations; cf. Klandermans 2004: 366), and convincing them that they were not alone in their determination to protest. Quoting a US Civil Rights activist, Goodwin and Pfaff (2001: 289) write: 'part of the way that you get people to buy into oppression is to convince them that they're absolutely alone ... So part of organizing is showing people that that's not true.' Prior to January 2011, there were no mass meetings comparable to those in the United States and East Germany, apart from the regular protests of 2010 and before, which tended to be small affairs. But once the demonstrations were under way, the sheer numbers of people out on the streets played a key role in helping people to overcome their fears. As Khalil Saeed (Interview 2011) observed:

by 2011, you knew you wouldn't be alone [if you went out into the street]. If you see only 100s [demonstrating], you won't do anything. But when you know there will be 1,000s, ... Now people in the streets were shouting: 'Ya ahalina, yandammu ilayna,' 'Our families, join us.' When we were 100s, we shouted this, but people on the other side of the street did not join us. Now all over Cairo, Mahalla, people were joining.

What Goodwin and Pfaff's model cannot tell us, though, is why so many more people responded on 25 January 2011 than before. We will return to this when discussing the change in people's 'emotion culture'.

Goodwin and Pfaff (2001: 89, 290–1) specifically single out communal singing as key in 'produc[ing] something like a Durkheimian "collective effervescence," ' that is, a collective feeling of unusual energy, power, and solidarity'. Protesters in East Germany 'would often encourage one another with shouts, cheers, chants, and songs. The importance of this is especially clear when protesters faced police beatings and arrests ...' More broadly, Jasper (2011: 294) notes that music, chants and collective locomotion produce emotional energy in protest situations.

Groups such as April 6 self-consciously used chants to energise protesters and encourage onlookers to join; they had learned this from their Serbian counterparts, who had similarly used chants in their non-violent struggle with Milosevic (Aljazeera 2011e). Chants were used to encourage bystanders to join ('Come down from the heights/Come down and get your rights') (Soueif 2012: 17). They were used to reaffirm the protesters' revolutionary identity and encourage them to continue ('welcome, welcome, to revolutionaries' [ahlan, ahlan, bi'l-thuwwar] or 'don't forget, come tomorrow' [ma'adna bukra ma ninsa]) (Keraitim and Mehrez 2012: 46). They were even used to contain violence on both sides ('peaceful, peaceful' [silmiyya, silmiyya]) (A. Khalil 2011: 161) and, later on, to bind the army to the protesters ('the army and the people are one hand' [al-gaysh wa'l-sha'b, eid wahda] (Amira, Interview 2011)[3] or, even more poignantly, to humanise both the soldier, and the protester questioning the soldier's loyalty ('You! Soldier with a rifle, are you with me or against me' [ya 'askari yabu bundu'iyya, *inta maʿaya walla ʿalaya*]) (M. Khalil 2012: 263).[4] Chants, such as the famous 'the people demand the fall of the regime' [*al-shaʿb yurid isqat al-nizam*],[5] or 'down, down with Hosni Mubarak' [*yasqut, yasqut Hosni Mubarak*] (Keraitim and Mehrez 2012: 54) validated and channelled people's anger towards the regime. But they also helped people to calm their nerves and keep up morale. Amira (Interview 2011), for instance, told us: 'the more I shouted, the more I relaxed'. Chants like 'we will not leave, he will leave' [*mish ha nimshi, huwa yimshi*] (Amira, Interview 2011; Aljazeera 2011e)[6] or 'my country be strong, rise up strongly, Suez' [*shiddi haylik, ya baladi, shiddi haylik, ya Suez*] (Amira, Interview 2011) kept protesters' morale up, while chants about the revolution's demands ('we want freedom, social justice' [*ayzin hurriyya, ʿadala igtimaʾiyya*]) (J. Younis, Interview 2011) reaffirmed protesters' goals. Chants such as 'lift your head up high, you're Egyptian' [*irfaʿ rasak fawq, inta masri*] (J. Younis, Interview 2011)[7] were both morale-boosting and reclaimed the notion of 'Egyptian' for the protesters, away from the regime's control.

Some likened 25 January to a celebratory march after a victorious football match, involving music, chants and drums. According to Elisa Wynne-Hughes (Interview 2011), the resident British PhD student, the protests 'felt a bit like [after football matches]. That same football energy, directed that way.' Ashraf Khalil (2011: 212) described the 'millioniyya' march of Tuesday 1 February as 'equal parts angry rally and jubilant street party. From every direction came defiant speeches, clever new chants, and infectious bursts of music or drumming.' That this was so was no coincidence. As one of those teaching April 6 and other groups about non-violence explained:

Non-violent action is not just about non-violence, but also about joy and happiness … The festive atmosphere was a key element to drawing the high numbers that Egypt had rarely seen. People felt safe so they came out. They saw in Tahrir what Egypt could possibly be in the future and they wanted to be part of this new Egypt. (quoted in Awad and Dixon 2011)

Sahar Keraitim and Samia Mehrez (2012: 32–7, 44–7) suggest that this festive atmosphere was in part made possible by the fusion of revolution with a popular form of celebration called the '*mulid*' [*mawlid*]:

the general dispositions of the actors in the *midan* [Tahrir Square] bore many traces of the *mulid* celebration, a popular form of carnivalesque festivities that has been celebrated in Egypt for hundreds of years and whose rituals, enacted by multitudes of demonstrators, were marshalled, politicized and revolutionized during the massive protests and sit-ins to sustain and transform the impetus and impact of revolt.

According to Keraitim and Mehrez, it was 'this historic familiarity of the millions of people who came to the *midan* with the extended and elaborate rituals and festivities of the popular *mulid* celebrations' that 'attract[ed] thousands of entire families with children and elderly relatives'. *Mulid* refers to the popular festivities surrounding the celebration of a saint's birth: festive, chaotic, subverting the usual order of authority, taking place in the streets around the site of veneration. Every year between 200 and 2,000 *mulids* are celebrated across Egypt, involving Muslims, Christians and Jews, making its practices instantly recognisable to most Egyptians. It is this familiarity that, according to Keraitim and Mehrez, accounts for the absence of stampeding, harassment, violence and strife, with Tahrir becoming the site of veneration/celebration for Cairo's protesters.

Linking this insight back to our analysis of fear, we would argue that this adoption of the familiar practices of the *mulid* played a significant part in helping people to overcome their fears of protesting. This was so once the Square was occupied (remember that regime violence continued even after the police had collapsed) (cf. Soueif 2012: 52–4, 49–50), but also during the first day when commentators noted the 'almost carnival-like atmosphere' and the 'family-friendly marches' all over the country (Aljazeera 2011e). It was this festival-like spirit that seems to have both attracted and reassured newcomers.

Training and Preparation

For activists, fear was managed through training and preparation. Groups such as April 6 had organised numerous sessions to teach activists about the practices of non-violence. Part of the purpose of these sessions was to teach techniques enabling activists to outwit the police. But they also taught them to protect themselves against police violence, defuse confrontational situations and avoid provoking violence. Each of these techniques helped to manage fear better.

For non-activists, preparation was equally important. Unlike activists, their preparation seems to have come from studying the internet or by word of mouth or example. The non-activists we interviewed told us how they prepared themselves by looking up tips on the internet; during the protests, they learned from more experienced activists by copying. The accounts of Hossam, Gamal and Abdel-Rahman in particular suggest that the acts of researching the internet and kitting themselves out accordingly helped them to manage their fears of police violence. Take Abdel-Rahman's account of what he did when he returned from his first demonstration and encounter with the police:

I went back home, I looked up websites, what to do with teargas, etc. ... I went to work, then went back to look for strikes. I went home, put on my gear (based on Internet search for teargas), went through downtown, to all the locations mentioned on Facebook. ... I saw nothing at those locations [bar a small protest, surrounded by security forces], the whole area was like a military zone. ... I went home, disappointed, to wait until Friday. Everyone I met I told: go on Friday. I talked to every taxi driver, everyone in my street: 'Please go on Friday,' 'Are you going to go?', trying to shame them. Within 5 hours, I had turned into a political activist, without noticing. (Abdel-Rahman, Interview 2011)

Hossam (Interview 2011) similarly came prepared, having never protested before: 'I had plastic bags around my feet against electric prods, I was fully equipped, with goggles.' Or consider Gamal (Interview 2011): 'with the help of Facebook I became an expert on how to deal with teargas, where to go'. Journalist Ashraf Khalil (2011: 162) cites a protester who went to buy 'cheap transparent swim goggles' at the local sporting goods store, to which the store owner replied: 'Oh for the revolution? Well, all your friends bought this kind over here.' Everyone we talked to had become an expert overnight on how to counter the effects of teargas, using onions and Pepsi Cola. Both Abdel-Rahman and Gamal found themselves advising newcomers on 28 January on how to handle teargas, and telling them that it was not as bad as they feared, having gone through the same experience only three days before.

Activists also helped to reduce their fears by preparing meticulously for the protests. Not only did they plan the starting points and the routes that they would take, but they also set up safe houses to enable activists to rest, care for the wounded and communicate (Aljazeera 2011e; *Newsweek* 2011b). Non-activists similarly prepared; as Soueif (2012: 19–20) recounts, when mobile signals were cut off, 'most homes had arranged to have one person stay in by the landline and act as liaison'.

Mass Media

A fourth mechanism activists employed was enlisting the mass media, broadcasting successes and exposing regime violence. Goodwin and

Pfaff (2001: 287) identified mass media coverage of protest events as a crucial 'encouragement mechanism' in the United States and East Germany. In Egypt, activists and newcomers alike used Facebook, Twitter and YouTube to keep the media informed and used the media to 'protect' them. Communication hubs were set up in secret locations, using any means available to connect to the internet in spite of the government's blackout (Soueif 2012: 27). Ways to circumvent the blackout were posted on Twitter and Facebook, and landlines and international mobile phones were used to keep communications with the outside world open (Chapter 8). From the way the media were used it is clear that part of the intent was to provide some level of protection for protesters by exposing regime abuses (cf. Aljazeera 2011e). Ghonim (2012: 183), for instance, writes how, when he ran into a cordon of hundreds of guards, he 'tweeted our location and added that we were about to be attacked'. Similarly, the 'We Are All Khaled Said' website posted a short video on its site, entitled 'The camera is my weapon' (Eaton 2012: 8) (see also Chapter 8).

Different Levels of Participation

Many non-activists managed their fear by hanging back. Ahdaf Soueif (2012: 23), the writer, is up front about this, seeing her task as a middle-aged woman with two young nieces in tow, as minimising exposure to police violence. Describing 28 January, she writes:

We stood. That was our job, the people at the back: we stood and we chanted our declaration of peace: 'Selmeyya! Selmeyya!' while our comrades at the front, unarmed, fought with the security forces. From time to time a great cry would go up and we would surge forward: our friends had won us another couple of meters and we followed them and held our ground. ... [S]eeing nothing up ahead except the gas and smoke and fire that stood between us and our capital, we stood our ground and sang and chanted and placed our lives, with all trust and confidence, in each other's hands.

As the last sentence testifies, even being at the back required bravery. Gas was everywhere and all were exposed to snipers (as Soueif poignantly remarks straight after the paragraph above, 'Some of us died'). But the risk of death, injury and incarceration was less at the back.

Gamal (Interview 2011), who, as a strong, young man, would have been expected to be at the front, handled his fear by self-consciously hanging back, leaving the frontline to more seasoned activists. Having already experienced teargas on 25 January, however, he found himself to be braver than those who had not:

I decided I would be at the back of the demo, to feel more safe. If you feel uncomfortably near the front, you make an excuse to get back to safety, by tying your shoelace. I felt this from people around me. They marched hesitantly, assessed the situation every second. People like me, because of experience of the 25th, were in the middle, because we knew about teargas, that it was not so dangerous. People behind us were new, they didn't have this experience. I tried to encourage them that teargas is not so dangerous.

It is also important to remember that many went home, whether because they feared for their homes, or because they felt they had done their bit. Hossam (Interview 2011) found that 'most of the people I know went back home, fearing for their houses, their kids, their money. Few people stayed.' Gamal and Abdel-Rahman stopped participating after 28 January, because they felt they had done enough.

Emulation and Taking Part

Following the example set by seasoned activists also helped non-activists to overcome their fear, a process referred to as emulation (Tarrow and McAdam 2005: 128–30). Never having been at a demonstration, Gamal (Interview 2011) recalled:

At 12.30/12.40 [midnight 25 January], the crackdown started. A heavy attack. This was the first time I had taken to the streets. During university, I didn't participate in the demos for al-Aqsa Intifada solidarity. I saw it on telly, but did not participate. So when the teargas came, I ran away as fast as I could. I wanted to see the reaction of others. Some were steadfast. The leaders said: 'don't move, don't run, it is not harmful (if you know).' ... That night a number of people broke through the barrier of fear (*kasr hagiz al-khawf*). You think it is there, but at some moment it falls down. It lies in you: if you break it, it is not there.

Later, on 28 January, he was fortified not only by the example of those braver them him, but by taking part in collective action:

I looked to people around me in the doorway, where we hid: a housewife, an elderly guy, a middle class youngster, 16-year old guys. Those who were really brave, a woman, told us: 'You shouldn't rest, we have to struggle. Go, why are you sitting?' This was an eye opening experience. In demos, you lose your fear, you involve yourself in collective action. You feel more secure with people around you.

The act of taking part itself thus augmented the feeling of collective effervescence that the chants sought to induce. The fact that so many had overcome their fears for the first time gave taking part extra poignancy. Abdel-Rahman (Interview 2011) told us about the elation he felt at denouncing Mubarak in public for the first time.

Strategic locations

Finally, the decision to start in small alleyways away from the police was taken explicitly to reduce bystanders' fear of joining in (Chapter 5). People would eventually have to face the police. But starting small, with relatively little risk, enabled bystanders to ease into participation, and once they were confronted by the police, they would be part of a large crowd, diluting the fear police could induce and providing solidarity with others to counter that fear. The small alleys were also chosen because they made small crowds look large, thus lowering the fear threshold of those joining in.

Beyond Encouragement Mechanisms to Changing Emotion Culture

Apart from the decision to start in Cairo's narrow alleys, none of the mechanisms discussed so far were particularly new. Activists had used chants and planning well before 2011. They had prepared protesters through training and enlisted the media, and those who demonstrated had long been part of strong solidarity networks. As such, these mechanisms cannot explain why so many more people overcame their fears in January 2011 than before.

To begin to answer that question we need to look at changes in what Deborah Gould (2004: 172) calls people's 'emotion culture', which is influenced by changes in the broader political opportunity structure, events and the way activists interpret both.

Gould makes three crucial contributions to the study of emotions in protests. First, she argues, following William Reddy, that emotional utterances alter the way people feel. When we say 'I am angry', this affects how we feel by 'nam[ing] and categor[izing] a subjective feeling state.' Because 'language cannot adequately represent ... a subjective feeling state,' 'some components of one's feelings' are amplified, while others are suppressed by not being 'brought into the verbal realm' (D. Gould 2004: 170). Movements can alter the way people feel by

strategically using certain emotional utterances and not others, emphasising anger, for instance, while downplaying guilt, altering the way
protesters respond to external events. However, they can only do so
with a receptive audience.

This is Gould's second contribution: emotions are shaped by the
emotion culture in which people are embedded. Importantly, this emotion culture can change in response to 'moral shocks' and movement
framing. The term 'culture' is here thus used to describe something
more fluid and changeable than is usually the case when we talk about
culture. In the United States, Gould argues, the gay community
(Gould's topic of research) at first did not react to the government's
discriminatory and negligent response to the AIDS/HIV epidemic with
anger, as this was not considered acceptable by either mainstream society or the gay community. It was only after a series of 'moral shocks'
in the context of a rapidly worsening epidemic and increasingly explicit
systemic discrimination against the gay community that anger became
an acceptable emotion, enabling activist groups such as ACT UP to use
anger strategically and link it to militant action against the government. As Castells (2012: 219) rightly notes, 'the trigger [for collective
action] is anger, and the repressor is fear'; legitimising anger is thus one
powerful route to neutralising fear. Of particular importance in this
process are watershed events (a court case in the example of ACT UP)
which, through appropriate framing, can create the moral shocks that
shatter a previously established 'emotion culture'. Equally important is
the effect of a movement repeating certain emotional utterances over
and over to name, amplify and normalise certain feelings while suppressing others (D. Gould 2004: 172).

The notion of 'moral shock', which Jasper and Poulsen develop, is
particularly useful, as it helps to explain both why Egypt's emotion culture changed and how people became involved without having been
part of protest networks. Moral shocks can be 'the first step in the
recruitment of strangers: when an event … raises such a sense of outrage in people that they become inclined towards political action, even
in the absence of a network of contacts'. Activists make use of this
dynamic 'by creating or taking advantage of moral shocks, information or events that … suggest to people that the world is not as they
had thought. Their visceral unease occasionally leads to political action
as a form of redress …' However, 'the most effective shocks are those
embodied in, or translatable into, powerful condensing symbols'. Con-

densing symbols are 'verbal or visual images that neatly capture—both cognitively and emotionally—a range of meanings and convey a frame, master frame, or theme'. When movements succeed in translating moral shocks into powerful condensing symbols with wide resonance, they greatly increase their chances of altering people's emotion culture and mobilising people. A particularly potent form of moral shock concerns the 'violent repression of peaceful protest' (Jasper and Poulsen 1995: 498; Jasper 2011: 292).

Gould's third contribution is to suggest that emotional utterances can be conveyed by the body and through behaviour as well as verbally. Gould tells the story of an HIV-positive gay man's decision to become an activist. Having previously ignored flyers containing emotional utterances, the man was transformed when seeing ACT UP pass by in New York's Gay and Lesbian Pride Parade. Gould (2004: 171–2) speculates that:

witnessing ... ACT UP/New York's anger in the streets altered his own feelings. ... ACT UP's expression of anger may have allowed Braverman to feel anger, by legitimating that emotion but also by naming it and ... suppressing some of the other feelings that Braverman may have previously experienced [shame, guilt].

Thus:

A person's very enactment of anger at a demonstration—through chants and facial and bodily gestures, for example—may suppress her other feelings, making the anger physically legible to herself while displacing the sensation of other emotions that simply are not enacted.

Participation creates an adrenaline rush, leaving participants 'feeling elated' and 'really purposeful', which is part of the reason why taking part helps induce the collective effervescence described above.

With these conceptual tools in hand, we will look at some of the dynamics that helped to change people's 'emotion culture'. In the following, we focus primarily on what Searing (1986), in a different context, calls the 'attentive public'—those among the general public who are politically aware, even if they are not activists, although the dynamics described affected the general public as well, increasing the size of the 'attentive public'.

Riding the Crest of a Wave

Significantly, the 25 January demonstration occurred on the back of the 2010 protest wave. Some of the work of overcoming fear had thus already been done. As detailed in Chapters 1–2, a protest momentum had been building since 2000, and 2010 in particular had seen a sharp increase in momentum. Although Ghonim's (2012: 113–20) account suggests that the newly mobilised Khaled Said protesters lacked focus by December 2010, with no clear idea of how to capitalise on the success of the vigils and demonstrations, 2010 had seen a widening of the pool of people with protest experience and many more were ready to be mobilised than even a year before. The events of early January—the bombing of the church in Alexandria and the subsequent protests—meant that many of the newly mobilised had been recently primed for action.

The previous protest waves profoundly affected the way fear was handled in 2011 by widening the pool of people who had overcome their fear of police violence. Khalil Saeed (Interview 2011), from the Democratic Front Party, told us for instance:

I was raised to be afraid to be in demonstrations. I had this fear [of demonstrations]. During my years in university, I was not involved in any of the demonstrations of people who supported Palestine. It started with me joining a youth organisation ... I got to know real activists. Lots of meetings. ... Lots of energy. I was informed about activities. At the time it was Kefaya. A lot of people joined protests. I still didn't know the taste of this. I started to follow news of Kefaya, but I did not join demonstrations. In 2007, I started to get involved, when Kefaya was fading. In 2008, with April 6, this was my first demonstration. I needed to face my fears. I was 32 years old, quite old then. ... They were always asking me for my opinion. I had the ability to take them to common ground ... When I started getting out in the street, I felt responsible. These kids left alone; the least I could do was be with them. This was my place, to be next to them. If all Egyptians did this, we can make change [happen], if everyone started with himself.

Mostafa Fouad (Interview 2011), an April 6 activist, likewise told us how he had overcome his fears by joining April 6 and going on street protests with other activists. By 25 January, he knew what to do, how to counteract the effects of teargas, how to protect himself from police batons. Gamal Eid (Interview 2011), the human rights lawyer, similarly cited earlier labour demonstrations as helping people to face their fears: 'During that time, people started to cross the red line about Mubarak and state security.'

Even the comparatively peaceful vigils organised by the Khaled Said website helped to widen the pool of those who had overcome the first hurdle of fear of protests. Returning to Fouad (Interview 2011):

The first thing they did was that 'We Are All Khaled Said' made regular people that were scared to go down and protest [go out and protest]. ... Some went to the Corniche, stood quietly, reading the Qur'an, the Bible, more and more. Then protests in downtown, Talat Harb Street, Shaif Street, Midan Talat Harb ... People walking, chanting.

Novices were gradually drawn into street protests, starting with the relatively safe vigils, moving on to demonstrations in downtown Cairo. Ghonim (2012: 67–8) describes how he helped online followers to overcome their fear:

The strategy for the Facebook page ultimately was to mobilize public support for the cause. This wasn't going to be too different from using the "sales tunnel" approach that I had learned at school. The first phase was to convince people to join the page and read its posts. The second was to convince them to start interacting with the content by "liking" and "commenting" on it. The third was to get them to participate in the page's online campaigns and to contribute to its content themselves. The fourth and final phase would occur when people decided to take the activism onto the street. ... People feared the emergency law and the threat it posed to those who opposed the regime or its practices. Yet I was convinced that we could make the leap from the virtual world to the real one. ... The page needed to speak directly to its members and convince them to be active participants, and it was also important to break free from all the barriers of fear that controlled so many of us. So I came up with an idea that served both goals: I asked members to photograph themselves holding up a paper sign that said "*Kullena Khaled Said.*" Hundreds of members did so, and we began to publish their pictures on the page.

Ghonim (2012: 45–6) recognised the importance of identifying one-self publicly from his own experience of overcoming fear when signing ElBaradei's online petition, despite knowing that the security services were watching:

Fear overcame me on the first and second days of the petition. But then I entered all my personal information and signed. I was citizen 368 to do so. My fear turned into excitement when I realized I was beginning a new phase: I now publicly opposed the regime.

The ElBaradei campaign had self-consciously asked people to declare their identity. As Khaled Haal, one of ElBaradei's campaigners, recalls:

At the beginning, many voices in the NAC supported anonymous signatures. I disagreed with them. The issue is what we really want to achieve here. Is it collecting signatures or breaking fear? If it is the former then we should keep signatures anonymous, but if we aim for the latter, then a known identity is a must. (quoted in N. Aly 2011: 62)

The next step was getting people on to the street. Rather than opting for a demonstration, Ghonim and his colleagues decided on a 'silent stand', designed specifically 'to avoid a physical confrontation with security forces. The goal was for members to summon the courage to take positive action to the street, not just to put pressure on the Ministry of Interior':

most of the Silent Stand's participants were young men and women who were not politically active. They had never participated in anything like this before. "The 'Kullena Khaled Said' page has changed my life": these words arrived in several e-mails from the stand's participants. ... They felt strong. They had broken the fear barrier. Most important, they had finally transferred virtual activism into real-world action. (Ghonim 2012: 71, 79–80)

By 25 January, many of these recently mobilised protesters had personal experience of overcoming fear, serving as ready role models for non-activists and the social networks they were embedded in.

Significantly, even among those who had not yet made the step to street activism, there were many who had begun to break through the fear barrier. Ghonim (2012: 100–1, 99) tells of members who overcame 'their fear barrier' by entering into online dialogue with police officers or '[telling] their stories and [distributing] documents and visual material in which they condemned the ministry's treatment of citizens'. Although we do not know how many of these online activists had become street activists, it is a safe guess, given the vast discrepancy between the numbers demonstrating before 2011 and the number of online followers (tens of thousands), there were many who had broken through the online fear barrier, without having made the leap to street activism. The April 6 cadres we met on Tahrir in May 2011, for instance, had never demonstrated before 2011 because of fear of police brutality and arrest. 'We stayed far away,' one said. 'Two km underground,' another added (April 6 Cadres, Conversation 2011). Yet they had already identified themselves as April 6 activists well before 2011. There thus appears to have been a large pool of people who had already begun to overcome their fear online, making the final step on 25 January smaller.

The widening of protests in 2010, both on- and offline, had also affected the wider public's perceptions about protest and government legitimacy. Although we have no data to quantify this impact, a number of our non-activist interviewees implied that the protests of 2010 had made them more aware of the possibility of protest.

Moral Shocks

In parallel, a series of 'moral shocks' had created a more permissive environment in which tens of thousands were not only increasingly aware of their government's incompetence but had begun to feel that something had to change. Moral shocks such as the death of Khaled Said, the rigging of the 2010 elections and the Alexandria bombing had already served to mobilise people with no activist history, reordering their emotional landscape and what they considered (un)acceptable emotions and behaviours.

In the decade leading up to 2011, the 'emotion culture' of increasingly widening sections of the population had changed in response to 'moral shocks' and the way protest networks framed them. During the first two waves, the number of people affected by these shocks and the utterances framing them remained relatively small. During the third and fourth wave, the number increased dramatically. Key political events such as the imprisonment of Muslim Brothers and judges in 2005, the rigging of elections or the arrest and torture of bloggers played a central role. But so did a series of shocking accidents, such as the Qaljoub train collision or the sinking of a ferry, both in 2006, which graphically illustrated the government's incompetence and lack of interest in protecting ordinary people. The acquittal of those accused of causing the ferry disaster, in which over 1,000 died, exposed the profoundly corrupt nature of the system, creating another moral shock. In addition, we would argue that everyday incidences symbolising inequality, injustice, casual police violence and corruption acted as infinitesimal 'moral shocklets', which, taken together, created a 'moral tidal wave' which gradually destroyed people's faith in the regime. Thus rocketing food prices, rising inflation and unemployment combined with regime incompetence, the narrowing of the regime's base to a small crony capitalist elite and growing police violence to change people's emotion culture in subtle ways. Crucial here was the framing work carried out by opposition groups, weaving each individual occurrence into an overarching protest narrative which linked daily feelings of anger, frustration and alienation to the need for regime change. However, though this framing legitimised alienation, anger and outrage towards the regime, it did not (yet) change attitudes to fear in the wider population.

Moral shocks mobilised increasing numbers of people beyond the activist networks, as anticipated theoretically by Jasper. But the events that became moral shocks also affected people who did not immediately become mobilised. Data on how many people were affected do not exist. But our interviewees attested to the impact of each of these events on their emotion culture. Samer (Interview 2011) and Ghazali-Harb (Interview 2011a), for instance, decided to return to Egypt in part in response to the shocks of Khaled Said and the election fiasco (although other factors played a role, such as their having been active politically before, and having participated in vigils for Said in London). Hossam and Abdel-Rahman were similarly shocked by Khaled Said and the 2010 election. These events did not cause them to become activists. But they fuelled their sense of indignation, which helped to prepare the ground for the appeals of 25 January.

For an event to turn into a moral shock, a certain amount of framing needs to take place. Khaled Said's death, by itself, would not have galvanised thousands into taking action; it was the way the various websites framed his death, the way the government tried to cover it up and the way the opposition sites kept the scandal 'live' that turned this event into a moral shock. The powerful juxtaposition of the (middle-class) 'everyman' image of Khaled Said and the picture of his grossly disfigured face acted as a condensing symbol, encapsulating both the profound sense of insecurity many among the middle classes felt and what came to be seen as the regime's criminal carelessness. Most of our interviewees cited the impact of these images on their feelings about the regime (see also Ghonim 2012: 127 and Chapter 8).

The fall of Ben Ali constituted another moral shock that shattered people's previous emotion culture. Jasper reserves the term for events that cause 'outrage' or 'visceral unease'. We would call events that cause a radical reordering of hope equally shocking. More than any other event in Egypt's recent history, the fall of Ben Ali legitimated hope and the public expression of anger.

The Fall of Ben Ali and the Resurgence of Hope

All our interviewees cited the fall of Ben Ali as the key event galvanising the wider population. Events in Tunisia showed Egyptians that it was possible to oust a dictator, that mass protests could overwhelm the security forces. Samer (Interview 2011), for instance, said: 'People who had told me stories of fear before [25 January] went down to Tahrir. Tunisia made people break out of their fear, made them believe that [change] was possible.' Hossam (Interview 2011) similarly suggested that what made people face the police was 'the Tunisia example. I don't want to take away from the 25th organisers, but Tunisia played a big part. A slogan before 25 January was: "*hasil fi Tunis la ma yahsil fi Misr*" [it happened in Tunis but not in Egypt].'

Ghonim (2012: 134) put it even more boldly on his website. On 14 January, the day Ben Ali fled, he posted: 'Today is the 14th … January 25 is Police Day and it's a national holiday … If 100,000 take to the streets, no one can stop us … I wonder if we can?' He later followed this with:

After all that's happened in Tunisia, my position has changed. Hopes for real political change in Egypt are much higher now. And all we need is a large number of people who are ready to fight for it. Our voices must be not only loud but deafening. I swear to God, I'm going to participate in Jan 25 and I'm ready to die to free Egypt from tyranny. (Ghonim 2012: 137)

Protesters going out on 25 January may not have believed that they would succeed in ousting Mubarak, but there was hope that reform was within reach—if only enough people turned out.

Crucially, this shift towards hope had been broadcast on the internet. Countless videos were uploaded of activists calling on people to demonstrate and non-activists pledging to be there (90,000 had pledged to attend the 25 January demonstration). Anonymous (Interview 2011), a teacher trainer at the AUC, when asked why she thought, before 25 January, that it 'would be a big day that would develop into something big,' told us:

Tunis gave everyone a lot of hope. If you had been following Facebook, people had started taking pictures and videos of themselves, saying: 'Protest on the 25th.' People were overcoming their fear. Just anyone, not just activists. All over the country.

Hope had also begun to manifest itself in the many volunteers who helped to distribute fliers calling for a demonstration. The journalist Ashraf Khalil captured this sense of hope in his description of the radical change of tone in a video message posted online by the activist blogger Asmaa Mahfouz. Where her first video was characterised by anger and impatience, a challenge to Egyptian men to prove their manhood and come out and protest (see further), her second video, uploaded on the eve of the demonstration, was characterised by hope:

The angry tough-love Mahfouz of the first video had been transformed. She appeared encouraged by all the grassroots political work she had witnessed in the preceding week, talking about seeing everyone from young children to elderly pensioners distributing fliers and spreading the word about the protests.

> The most beautiful thing about it is that those who worked on this were not politicians at all. It was all of us. All Egyptians, we worked hard. ... (A. Khalil 2011: 133–4)

Thus, by 25 January, not only was hope in the air, but a significant section of the attentive public was aware of this, which in turn intensified hope. As Salah (Interview 2011) put it, 'I suspect people on the 25th came out because deep in their heart they had started to believe in hope and change.'

Because so many had begun to hope, against all reason, that change might be possible, non-activists appeared to be actively looking for signs that this protest might be different. Abdel-Rahman (Interview 2011), the central banker, told us how, even though he did not think this would turn into a revolution, he kept an eye on events throughout the day, watching satellite news reports while in the gym, staying in touch with friends about the unfolding events. Moreover, when he saw April 6, his reaction to the group was different:

> On my way home [from the gym] I saw the April 6 group protesting in black, with their symbol of the hand, protesting against detainees. Two weeks before I remember thinking: they [at least] are doing something ... In the old days, we'd say: what the hell are these crazy people doing. Now we had a different reaction. ... I saw these pictures [of groups marching on Tahrir] and thought: I got to go. I can't stay for dinner with my housemates. I must make a stand, say what I have to say.

Gamal (Interview 2011), the diplomat, similarly followed the news throughout the day, as were the friends calling Abdel-Rahman and Gamal throughout the day.

However, hope alone is insufficient. Throughout history, people have hoped, without necessarily acting. Besides needing direction, it needed additional emotions to push people past their fear barrier.

Hope vs Hopelessness, Jealousy, Joy, Anger

The hope generated by Tunisia was enhanced by numerous other emotions. Two of these were jealousy and hurt pride. Egyptians were used to seeing themselves as the leader of the Arab World. Yet here was Tunisia, a small country, taking the lead. Echoing many of our interviewees, Ghonim (2012: 133) wrote: 'Our pride had now been challenged ... It was a shot in the arm. The psychology of the proud and courageous Egyptian played a major role in enabling our country to follow in Tunisia's footsteps.'

Hope was further fortified by long-standing anger—not the reflex emotion of sudden outrage caused by seeing death, but what Goodwin, James Jasper and Francesca Polletta (2004: 416, 422) term the 'moral emotion' of intense indignation at the injustices and unfairness of life in Egypt. More research is needed to understand the role of this type of deep moral indignation, not only in the revolution, but during the previous decade, when there were numerous opportunities for anger to be expressed. One thing that is striking is how over the decade activists had gradually succeeded in legitimising anger, redirecting anger concerning the injustices and struggles of daily life towards the regime. From the first chants calling on Mubarak to go in 2003, the tape marked 'Enough' covering protesters' mouths in 2004–2005, the judges' challenge to the regime in 2005–2006, to the tearing down of Mubarak's poster in Mahalla in 2008 and the vigils of 2010, opposition activists had been engaged in a decade-long struggle, to use Gould's terminology, to name anger, amplify and legitimise it, and in so doing displace other emotions, such as fear.

Illustrating the importance of the protest networks' giving a voice and direction to people's simmering anger, Ghonim (2012: 125) quotes a message from Khaled Mansour, a member of the Khaled Said webpage, saying:

Thank you to the admin of "Kullena Khaled Said" [We Are All Khaled Said] for directing our anger towards something positive ... The idea is how to manage our anger ... Our anger will make us insist on fighting injustice and attempt to address all problems with positive action. I will not direct my anger at myself again.

This last comment ('I will not direct my anger at myself again') is a crucial shift in moving people from apathy to activism. Social movement scholars have long argued that interaction with other members from a social network helps people to overcome what is called the 'attribution error': namely, to recognise that the cause of what is wrong is not themselves but the system. 'We Are All Khaled Said' helped its followers to redirect their anger away from themselves and towards the regime, and to justify the act of publicly expressing this anger.

Paradoxically, hope was further fortified by hopelessness. Hopelessness by itself can lead to apathy or depression. But juxtaposed with
hope, it can act as what Jasper (2011: 291) calls a 'moral battery':

The tension or contrast between [these two emotions] motivates action or
demands attention. An emotion can be strengthened when we explicitly or
implicitly compare it to its opposite, just as a battery works through the tension between its positive and negative poles.

Alongside the growing sense of hope, many protesters felt themselves to be in an acutely hopeless situation. Ashraf Khalil (2011: 146,
171) describes various encounters with educated young protesters who
had been unemployed for years. 'We've been silent and gone hungry
for a long time,' one of them said, 'If we continue like this [protesting],
we will change things, we just have to commit.' Another put it more
bluntly: 'I expect the government to fall today. There will be dead bodies in the streets. I have nothing to lose anymore. I have a degree in
information technology, and I've been sitting at home for the past
three years.'

We similarly encountered people who cited hopelessness as a key
motivation for the protests (e.g. Saad, Interview 2011). Unemployment, rising food prices and inflation, and an increasingly predatory
police state meant that millions of Egyptians had experienced hopelessness for years. What was different about the events of 25 January was
the juxtaposition of hope and hopelessness: the young men stating in
one breath: 'I expect the government to fall today' and 'I have nothing
to lose anymore.' For the first time in years, people had hope that
things could actually change. Their prior hopelessness gave their newfound hope an edge, knowing that they would sink back into hopelessness if they failed. It is in this 'moral battery' of hope reacting with
hopelessness that people found additional inspiration to confront the
regime and risk death or imprisonment.

Once people had joined the protests, other emotions contributed to
the mix. Joy, particularly 'the sudden joy of victory (especially unex-
pected victory)' (Goodwin, Jasper and Polletta 2004: 418), played a
part, for instance, when the 25 January demonstrations turned out to
be far larger than expected, or when the police were ousted from Alexandria and Suez later that week. Tweets from that period testify to the
intense joy protesters felt at achieving key victories (cf. Idle and Nunns
2011). This joy was offset by outrage and sadness as people saw com-

rades being beaten or shot in front of them, acting as another moral battery. More prosaically, hope contrasted sharply with fear of the regime's revenge, if the protests failed. Hisham Allam (Interview 2011), of *al-Masry al-Youm*, for instance, recalled: 'Our faces are now known; it is risky [to back down now]. We have to succeed, we can't go back. If they could recover, they would seek revenge.'

Shame and Shaming

One of the most potent emotions pushing people on to the streets in addition to hope was shame, or rather, the moral battery that operated on the tension between shame and honour. The honour of being part of a righteous revolution contrasted with the shame of not having the courage to stand up and be part of the revolution. Not taking part came to be interpreted as 'complicity' with the regime, as being a traitor. Gamal and Abdel-Rahman explicitly evoked the sense of shame they would feel when facing their friends or family in future and admit that they had not been there. Ashraf Khalil (2011: 165) similarly quotes a human rights activist, who had 'rarely attended public protests' before, deciding that 'the time has come. It was the defining moment. We were at the point where every citizen who didn't step out would be complicit.'[8] The placard quoted at the top of this chapter—'I used to be afraid, now I'm an Egyptian'—carried by a man on Tahrir Square (Gribbon and Hawas 2012: 109), expresses this same sentiment: fear was no longer an acceptable part of being an Egyptian.

Gamal's description of this dynamic is particularly evocative:

When you hear from or about people who are ready to sacrifice themselves, if you happen to know them personally, first you have a bad feeling about yourself as a coward, particularly as you have the same ideas. ... How come they sacrifice time, security, get into trouble, and you just keep talking, telling people what should happen. This is what pushed me to participate. ... Many people called me on the 25th. They didn't embarrass me, they didn't say: 'You're a civil servant, fear for yourself.' But after the phone call, I would think: 'how am I going to face them afterwards?' You can't deny it. At least be able to face friends with dignity. (Gamal, Interview 2011)

Honour, shame and hope were all interwoven in Abdel-Rahman's account of his change in attitude:

Before I had wanted to make an impact. I had wanted to stand in the metro and say: people, wake up. But I didn't do it. Now I had a chance. If I die, it would be for a cause. I could die in a car accident, die crossing the street. Now, if I die, my nieces will know about their uncle.

[Q: Did you think about this at the time?]

Yes, I thought about this on the way to the Square. Dying, but not being captured. That was worse. ... I don't want to be a dishonour to them [my nieces]. I want them to keep their dignity if I die. (Abdel-Rahman, Interview 2011)

The fact that failure to overcome one's fears came to be seen as complicity with the regime was itself a reflection of the change in Egypt's emotion culture—or at least, the emotion culture of those who decided to take part. Prior to 2011, activists generally accepted that protests would be small. They tried to shame people into joining them, but it was accepted that this would have limited effect.

When Ghonim named the site commemorating Said's death 'We Are All Khaled Said', he did so to galvanise people into action through a mixture of fear, shaming and appeal to duty. His first post on the site was: 'Today they killed Khaled. If I don't act for his sake, tomorrow they will kill me.' He then 'posted an edited video of various acts of torture by members of the police force, in the hope that Egyptians would finally confront the dark side of the regime and realize that any of us could be the next victim' (2012: 60, 63).

However, before 2011, such efforts had a limited effect. The key difference was Tunisia, and the hope this had given rise to. With no hope, non-participation could not be construed as complicity. By 25 January, the hope inspired by Tunisia had encouraged many to believe that not participating would mean being complicit with the regime.

Just as US Civil Rights activists had done in a different era (Goodwin and Pfaff 2001: 295–6), activist bloggers such as Ahma Mahfouz fuelled this belief by appealing to Egyptians' honour:

Four Egyptians have set themselves on fire thinking maybe we can have a revolution like Tunisia. ... We want to go down to Tahrir Square on January 25th. If we want to have honor and want to live in dignity then we have to go down on January 25th.

She went on in her video explicitly to shame Egypt's men into joining, appealing to their sense of manhood, their national pride and their fear of being called traitors:

If you think of yourself as a man, come out. Whoever says that women shouldn't go to protest because they'll get beaten, let him have some honor and manhood and come out in the streets on January 25 ... Anyone who says, 'The numbers will be small and nothing will happen,' I want to say that you are the traitor—just like the president, just like any corrupt official, just like the security officer who beats us. ... Speak to your neighbors, your colleagues at work, your family and friends and encourage them to come. ... Sitting at home following us on the news and on Facebook only leads to our humiliation. It leads to my humiliation. If you have honor and dignity as a man, then come out. Come out and protect me and the other girls at the protest. If you stay at home, you deserve everything that happens to you. And you will be guilty before your nation and before your people. (quoted in A. Khalil 2011: 131–2)[9]

Numerous interviewees mentioned people appealing to the male sense of honour. Gamal (Interview 2011) recalled: 'I saw 16-year olds asking me: are you going to stay? I wouldn't be surprised if some decided to stay to prove they were men. In the Square, people were chanting: "We're going to stay the night and brave men are going to prove themselves and we'll know who the cowards are."'

Convergence of Protest Sectors, Proximity of Activists and Aggrieved, and Internet Shut-down

Tunisia gave people hope. Hope contrasted with hopelessness and anger, and was augmented by jealousy. Within this new context, shaming gave additional motivation, as people did not want to be seen as complicit with the regime. This combination alone would have brought more people out on to the street on 25 January. What increased numbers further were two other factors: the convergence of all protest sectors behind the 25 January calls, and the fact that the demonstrations took place in locations that brought activists and aggrieved non-activists together in close proximity.

The last time the pro-democracy, workers and neighbourhood protest sectors had come together, in April 2008, the police had been able to deal with each sector separately and almost 'serially' (El-Ghobashy 2011). The pro-democracy protest wave had been waning already; the neighbourhood protests had only been in their infancy. By contrast, on 25 January all three sectors were in the middle of a protest wave and had grown stronger nationwide. The Brotherhood, moreover, had reopened discussions with the other protest groups in the wake of the fraudulent elections, paving the way for participation by the Brotherhood youth (initially). Thus when these protest sectors came together, they were able to mobilise far more protesters than in April 2008, and to do so simultaneously across the country. Mass mobilisation was facilitated by the shared grievances (including, crucially, a hatred of the police) and by the inclusive 'framing' of the 25 January demonstration, linking police violence with calls for a higher minimum wage and constitutional reform, without demanding commitment to an overarching ideology (Chapter 5) (identification with a protest movement and its goals was one of the 'encouragement mechanisms' identified by Goodwin and Pfaff (2001: 293–5)).

People were also more readily persuaded to join the protests by the fact that the demonstrations were played out bodily on a far larger scale and far more intimately than on most previous demonstrations. Taking place in the narrow alleys across Cairo and elsewhere, more people were intimately exposed to the activists' emotional utterances than ever before. They were more likely to resonate with these utterances as a result of the changed emotion culture. But a significant additional factor was the proximity of the protests to people's houses, and the demonstration effect of hundreds, and then thousands, of bodies expressing anger, hope, determination and lack of fear. The result was that people's emotional states could be affected more powerfully when anger, hope and determination were amplified, and fear and shame were suppressed.

Once the demonstrations were under way, the sheer numbers of people out on the streets lessened people's fears. As Nadim Mansour (Interview 2011) observed:

The real difference lay in the 25th. This event was larger than people had realistically expected. So we became optimistic, which puts you in a stronger position when hit. ... Normally, if beaten [by the police], people are afraid. This time, it mobilised them, because of their numbers ... If there is such a big demo, people are encouraged to go out. People saw themselves as successful because there was a big demo. Plus they felt you have to defend that. So it continued with everyone coming out on the 28th.

In addition, the spectacle of so many demonstrators made non-activists want to be part of it. Wynne-Hughes (Interview 2011) noted how curiosity made her once sceptical flatmate go: '[Abdel-Rahman] heard that stuff was going on, that lots of people were going to Tahrir. This made him want to check it out. It was all by word of mouth, like school dances: when people think everyone is coming, all come.' Samer (Interview 2011) likewise said that she went out on 25 January 'to see what is happening, [as this was] bigger than anything else before'.

Excited phone calls from friends persuaded Gamal (Interview 2011) to overcome his initial cynicism:

On the 25th, I received five phone calls from different people from 1pm onwards, telling me there were demos downtown, in different places across Cairo. ... The number of people on Tahrir by 3–4pm was almost 10,000. ... Initially I wasn't going to participate. It was not going to succeed. Beginning at 6pm, I got phone calls from friends saying it's like Tunisia. One friend abroad, following Facebook and Twitter, kept calling me: this is different. At 7pm I went down with a friend. At the first glance I knew this was different. Why? There were lots of people whom I didn't know. The usual suspects were not handling the show. We met Osama Ghazali-Harb, Alaa Al-Aswani. But however significant, they were not the main force. I met some old school friends, apolitical, never participated in such events before. Second, people were shouting: '*Al-sha'b yurid, isqat al-nizam*' (the people demand the regime to step down). This was imported from Tunisia, the same rhymes and music. ... I was trying to understand ... where it would lead. Then I heard people deciding to have a sit-in, through the night. The idea of having a sit-in was not new. But if 100,000 stayed for two nights, the regime would fall. Similar events [had happened] in Ukraine and Georgia. This concept reinforced the idea that this was different. Some of us thought: this might be the moment.

Another key moment was the regime's decision to shut down the internet and mobile phone networks. At that moment, people realised that the situation was far more serious than previously believed, paradoxically giving them hope (Hossam, Interview 2011; Gamal, Interview 2011). In Soueif's (2012: 19) words, 'We knew then that this was a regime fighting for its life.' It furthermore forced people to go out on to the street. If they wanted to stay in touch with friends, and keep on top of unfolding events, they had to go where the action was. As Samer (Interview 2011) summarised it:

Shutting down all electronic communication was a mobilising event. There was stubbornness, a sense of no going back. But more so, it actually made people want to go down into the street to see what was happening. An attitude of: 'Go down with a friend and die together. You think you can stop us? We've passed the phase of mobilising by mobile.' (cf. also Maher, Interview 2011; Group Interview 2011)

'Looking back,' Soueif (2012: 6) notes, 'I think this concentrated our minds, our will, our energy: each person was in one place, totally and fully committed to that place ...'

Responding to the Call of History: from Protest to Revolutionary Episode

What turned a large demonstration into a revolutionary episode was the growing belief that this was a historic moment to change the fate of Egypt that, if missed, would condemn everyone to another thirty years of dictatorship. As one interviewee poignantly put it: 'If you can't take freedom today, with all these clashes, we won't have another chance' (Allam, Interview 2011).

Before 25 January, many like Gamal, Mahmoud, Hossam and Abdel-Rahman who sympathised with the opposition had refrained from activism because they did not believe it would achieve anything. Like most, they did not wish to risk death or arrest in ineffective demonstrations. Over the course of the first week of demonstrations, people began to believe that this was a revolutionary moment, a date with history that demanded their total commitment. Consider the following testimony:

I didn't join until 2nd or 3rd February. I didn't want to join the demos and risk being arrested and the consequences that would have had for my job and career, just for a demo, which focuses on small things. January 25th felt to me like it was about jobs, workers' issues. The second Friday felt like this was a revolution. By then, I was prepared to risk everything, be a martyr. I had called friends in the army and asked them whether the army could push Mubarak, but I felt the army was closed, like a stone wall. There was no other option but to push. I normally believe one should change things gradually. But this needed a push, so I went and stayed. (Anonymous Son, Conversation 2011)

Hamdy (Conversations 2011), a young diplomat, similarly realised gradually that this was a revolutionary situation:

I joined the protests on Saturday 29 January. On Tuesday, I had exams. At the time, I and my colleagues and friends thought this would be a new wave of protests but nothing like a revolution. By Thursday 27th, we had begun to realise that this was different. By Friday, many were hoping that Mubarak would step down. By Saturday, we realised that it would not be as easy as that, that we were in it for the longer haul.

We can clearly see the importance of momentum here. The early protests were larger than expected but no one believed this to be a revolution. According to Gamal (Interview 2011):

There was plenty of talk about the possibility of [Tunisia] being repeated in Egypt. But to tell you the truth, I thought it could not be repeated. This was an exceptional event [and Egypt was different from Tunisia]. Lots of analysts, people we trust, repeated this. ... I knew about the event on the 25th. I don't follow Facebook but friends told me: 'It's big. Mobilisation on Facebook is unprecedented.' ... On the 24th I watched a TV talk show, four youngsters interviewed, two for, two against the demonstrations. ... One of the girls mocked the idea of preparing a revolution beforehand. Of course, a revolution cannot be prepared beforehand. We know this. There was a sense of banality about the whole thing. For the past five years, there had been weekly sit-ins, protests. 1.5 million people had participated in collective action. In 2009 alone, there had been almost 2,000 collective actions. Bizarrely enough, that gave us a sense of normality.

Amira (Interview 2011), the *al-Masry al-Youm* journalist, similarly said:

[When I heard about Ben Ali's fall] I was sceptical [about Egypt]. I was very excited about Tunisia, I was congratulating my Tunisian friends in Germany. When the 25th came, I was laughing at people saying: 'We have a rendezvous for revolution.' I thought: you can't have a revolution by appointment. People were chatting on Facebook, saying: 'I need to go to sleep now, because tomorrow I have a revolution.'

Even the activists themselves did not expect a revolution. Ziad al-'Ulaymi, an organiser for ElBaradei's movement, told the *Wall Street Journal*: 'We went out to protest that day and expected to be arrested in the first ten minutes, just like usual' (El-Ghobashy 2011; cf. also Maher, Interview 2011; Ghazali-Harb, Interview 2011a).

By the end of that first day, the sheer size and spread of the demonstrations suggested that this was different. Even though, numerically speaking, this was not the largest demonstration in recent history, it was perceived as such (cf. April 6 webpage, quoted in Amr Osman and Abdel Samei 2012: 8)—confirming Charles Kurzman's (1996) observation that political opportunities are about perceptions, rather than 'objective' facts. The symbolic impact of Tahrir having been occupied contributed enormously to this perception, as did the fearless behaviour of those who protested, as symbolised by the YouTube video of a young man, dubbed 'tank man', refusing to run away from a water cannon (YouTube 2011).

By the end of 25 January, some people already began to say this was a revolution. Asked when he first thought the system could be changed, Fouad (Interview 2011), an April 6 activist, responded: 'On the 25th, when I saw this big group, when so many joined them ...' Samer (Interview 2011) recalled how 'on the 26th and the 27th, my [activist] friend was already very confident [that they would succeed]'. Gamal (Interview 2011) expressed this most evocatively, saying: 'If this is the moment, then [you have to] participate. You don't want your daughter to ask: where were you on the 25th, why didn't you participate?' (cf. also Hossam, Interview 2011; Abdel-Rahman, Interview 2011).

Testament to the perceived extraordinariness of the events is that significant numbers of Egyptians abroad decided to return to Egypt after having seen the events of 25 January (Ezzat, Interview 2011), or when the internet was cut off (Amira, Interview 2011). Soueif (2012: 14) similarly describes seeing Tahrir Square on CNN while at a literary festival in India, deciding to return home immediately, and calling her sister upon arrival, saying 'Where's the revolution? Should I go to Tahrir?' By 28 January, when absolute numbers exceeded all precedents and the police capitulated, it was clear that a revolutionary situation had arrived. This belief was strengthened when the army decided not to suppress the protests.

Once people believed this was a historic moment, calculations, interests and identities changed. As Hamdy (Conversations 2011) put it: 'This was revolution, and under revolutionary circumstances, the normal rules no longer apply. This was about Egypt, not about the ethics of my job.' Gamal (Interview 2011) joined the protests against his convictions as a state employee because he wanted to be on the right side of history:

I felt ambivalence [about joining the demonstrations]. I am not ashamed of being part of the state apparatus. ... I am convinced that state policies, as undemocratic and dictatorial as they are, are more progressive than the main forces in society, in terms of men–women relations, foreign policy, etc. ... But on the 25th, with all those convictions, I could not but be part of this, I had a sense that I was on the wrong side of history. ... What I told myself [on the 25th] is that if some people have the guts to stand up to the system, and say no, ordinary people, my people, then I should be part of this, not against this.

People's identities changed, too, even if only temporarily. When Abdel-Rahman decided to go to the Square on 25 January, he was a mere onlooker. By midnight, having fraternised with the protesters, he felt part of the demonstration. After the police attack, fuelled by feelings of solidarity, revenge, outrage and shame, he was a committed activist, willing to risk injury and even death (cf. also Gamal, Hossam and Hamdy).

This sense of history in the making, of having to be on the side of righteousness, with no option but to participate, is a factor cited in other mass protest movements. Goodwin and Pfaff (2001: 294) quote a US civil rights activist talking about 'the Spirit of History':

> at certain points in life ... this force, this spirit, finds you or selects you, it chases you down, and you have no choice; you must allow yourself to be used, to be guided by this force and to carry out what must be done. To me, that concept of surrender, of giving yourself over to something inexorable, something so much larger than yourself, is the basis of what we call faith ... It's an absolutely selfless thing. ... It is a process of giving over one's very being to whatever role history chooses for you.

This is precisely what appears to have happened in Egypt.

Significantly, we would argue that such a total identification with 'the spirit of history' is different from identifying with the movement, under which heading Goodwin and Pfaff discuss this phenomenon. Identification with a movement can vary from lukewarm interest to total commitment. But even if an individual is wholly committed, this does not necessarily mean that they believe themselves to be part of a historic moment. Moreover, most non-activist protesters did not join a protest network. A typical example is Hossam (Interview 2011), who told us: 'I went back on Saturday [the 29th] and the next few days. A few days I went regularly, then I stopped, and only went occasionally after that.' Identification with the historical moment focuses on the event, not the movement. This is closer to a belief in divine protection (or at least, being on the right side of history) cited by Goodwin and Pfaff, than about movement identification.

Believing that this was a historical moment had the effect of inverting the free-rider problem. Usually, bystanders are reluctant to join, even if they will benefit from the protests, because of the perceived costs of protesting. This is a typical instance of 'the prisoner's dilemma': as long as people doubt that others will join and share the costs of protesting, they are reluctant to join, as the cost of joining without others is higher than the loss in benefit caused by not joining. Until 25 January, the protest networks had to wrestle with this free-rider problem (cf. Ghonim 2012: 75–6). By 28 January, this logic had become inverted, at least for those who joined: if I do not join, I will have failed my country, and will have to live with that shame. Under these circumstances, fear of shame, a sense of social responsibility and a desire to be part of history trumps fear of police abuse. Under these circumstances, protests follow 'an accelerative production function', where 'each contribution makes the next one more worthwhile, and thus, more likely' (Marwell and Oliver quoted in Klandermans 1997:

76). As Klandermans continues, 'there is no free riding in this situation, because participation becomes more attractive with every next participant'. Significantly, hope alone would not necessarily have produced such an inversion.

Moral Outrage at Police Violence

Within this changed emotion culture, police violence encouraged protesters to set aside their fears even further. Consider, for instance, Abdel-Rahman's account (Interview 2011):

One of the things that motivated me to go through with the revolution, whatever it takes, was a street kid, 15 years old, really poor. He came and said: 'Basha, ... all I want is physical protection. You are bigger, I need physical protection.' ... He was physically so weak [he had liver failure and an intravenous drip still in his hand]. I decided to protect him. ... [Then] I saw the 15-year old [who had sought my protection] being hit, really ugly. I took him on my shoulders. The thugs' way was: don't attack big groups, wait till they fall down, then beat, slap in the face, in the back of the neck, really insulting. A lot of girls were falling down, a guy was bleeding on my clothes. ... I escaped into a coffee shop, behind the Société Générale. People were sitting in the café, drinking, smoking shisha [water pipe] and I thought: how can you? I washed my face and the boy's face and I decided not to go home. Maybe it was an adrenaline rush, or maybe the boy on my shoulders. I didn't care about my career, maybe that boy was a symbol of everything I hated about the regime.

Omar Saad (Interview 2011), the leftist journalist, likewise, recalled that when 'we saw scenes of police beating people during prayers, of people being killed by snipers in front of the Ministry of the Interior,' 'We closed our minds: we die in the streets.' Ashraf Khalil (2011: 165) describes a human rights activist with an aversion to demonstrations ('I actually hate demonstrations ... It's just a lot of noise') turning from a non-violent chanter into an active combatant on seeing people being shot by the police at close range: 'The people on my right and my left were all shot with pellets,' he told Khalil. 'At that point, I joined the rock throwers.'

Outrage at police violence thus not only fortified activists in their determination, but it helped onlookers like Abdel-Rahman to overcome their fears and become engaged. A large part of what fuelled the transformation of a non-revolutionary mass demonstration into a revolutionary movement was thus the regime's own response to the protests. The police's brutal put-down during the night of 25 January turned many onlookers into activists. It was witnessing police hit the fifteen-year-old, women and old men that motivated Abdel-Rahman to, first, stay the night, and then to return on 28 January. Solidarity, outrage, revenge, shame (at not being able to help) came to replace his initial curiosity, and he came to identify himself as a protester, urging everyone he met subsequently to join the protest on 28 January.

Police violence triggered mini-protest episodes within the larger revolutionary episode. The deaths and incarcerations in Suez, for instance, steeled activists and non-activists alike in their determination to continue. Political commentator Mona El-Ghobashy (2011) summarised the trajectory of action and reaction in Suez as follows:

The situation in Suez developed rapidly. On January 25, security forces had been especially violent; the fighting resulted in 110 injuries and three deaths, as well as 54 arrests. The next day, hundreds of residents flocked to Suez General Hospital to donate blood, finding it so full that the injured were lying on sheets in hallways. Meanwhile, a large group of incensed relatives and citizens had gathered outside the morgue. The authorities insisted on handing over corpses without forensic reports, and security forces besieged the funerals with a ferocity that further enraged residents. "When you see this, you feel like you're in Palestine and Iraq," said the leftist Tagammu' parliamentarian for the city. "Security uses bullets and tear gas canisters and water hoses, and the residents can only confront this with stones." But residents escalated their tactics, setting fire to a police post and the municipal council building on January 26, and trying to burn down the local NDP office. On January 27, hundreds of residents and detainees' relatives demonstrated outside the Arba'in police station, chanting, "Enough! We want our kids!" Demonstrators hurled petrol bombs at the station and ignited several police cars.

The heavy-handed police response to the demonstrations on 25 January served to anger people. The crowds were then further incensed by the police refusing forensic reports and then besieging the funerals. The escalation of protest tactics, from chanting and throwing stones, to setting fire to the police station and municipal council building, was a direct response to these police actions, and might not have happened if the police had acted differently.

Events in Suez in turn affected protests nationwide. Numerous interviewees cited Suez as a catalyst for the revolution, intensifying the sense that this was a revolutionary moment. One cited the deaths in Suez as catalytic: 'What happened in Suez was key. The first four martyrs of the revolution died in Suez. This started an escalation' (Group Interview 2011). Soueif (2012: 17) similarly recalled: 'Again and again the call goes out [The people—demand—the fall of the regime!], and the crowd responds: Your security, your police—killed our brothers in

Suez.' Samer (Interview 2011) highlighted the impact of the protesters' success in overwhelming the police: 'Suez was the first city that fell. ... What happened in Suez gave confidence that it can actually happen.' Barakat (Interview 2011) similarly noted that the protesters' decision to storm the police station inspired people in Cairo to attack police stations in response to similar police violence.

The 'Battle of the Camel' of 2 February[10] similarly strengthened people's resolve. A number of interviewees told us they faced mounting pressure from their families to return home following Mubarak's speech the night before the Camel attack. 'Here was an old man,' Saad (Interview 2011) recounted, 'who had served his country, looking for sympathy. Many said: let us go home, this is enough. After four hours, thugs came out, there was the Camel scene. This made people turn away again from the regime.' Khalil Saeed (Interview 2011) recalled:

[There was] lots of pressure from our families, saying 'Enough, you have got your demands.' But for us, it was not enough. Six months [before the promised stepping down] is too long, he could easily get rid of all of us. When the attacks came on 2 February, that was it. I had a fight with my mother: for me, this was Egypt being attacked by non-Egyptians' [N.B.: note the description of Mubarak's thugs as 'non-Egyptians'].

That people reacted in this way was to a large extent a function of the changed emotion culture. For many, police and thugs' violence symbolised what was wrong with the regime, and thus resonated with a whole set of pent-up grievances about the state of Egypt. Before 2011, this was not enough to draw them in. Where, before, onlookers such as Abdel-Rahman and Gamal would have sympathised with those attacked without joining the demonstration, now the violence drew them in. The difference was the new constellation of hope, history and shame, motivating onlookers to become participants and act out of a new sense of identity and solidarity. In addition, the sharp juxtaposition between the joy of victories (such as the occupation of Tahrir) and the outrage at loss of life acted as another 'moral battery'.

The revolution's martyrs played a crucial role. Maher (Interview 2011), commenting on the impact of police violence on people's motivation, put it most succinctly: 'If a friend is killed, you can't go home.' Soueif (2012: 39) described this process at a more visceral level:

Our shuhada: Our Martyrs of the Revolution, who walked in peace and died before they could live the lives they dreamed of. Their song becomes our anthem. We march in their funerals and we promise 'We'll get what they died for/Or die as they died'. If we tire or our hope dims, our optimism for a moment falters, we open our hearts and they come to us: their bright faces, their hopes, their lives, their parents, their children. This is now our life's work: we will create the Egypt they died for.

Highlighting again the importance of momentum, the fact that people died, rather than deterring protesters as it had often done in the past, spurred people on because they were already engaged and had developed feelings of solidarity, thus deepening their determination not to stop until the demands their comrades had died for were met. This dynamic has been observed elsewhere (cf. della Porta 1995a, 1995b; Araj 2008).

Concluding Thoughts

Our analysis above is speculative, in need of further corroboration. But the testimonies told by interviewees about the process of losing their fear broadly conform to the mechanisms and dynamics observed in other conflicts.

What is clear from the above is that overcoming fear was an iterative process. The fact that the demonstration on 25 January turned out to be larger than expected encouraged more people to set aside their fears and join in as there was both safety in numbers and a sense of palpable excitement in seeing so many people respond. Once people saw what had been achieved in terms of numbers mobilised and police outwitted, police violence served to mobilise rather than dissuade as protesters became enraged by the violence and sought to protect what had been achieved. Pride, honour and the shame of not participating fuelled people's determination, as giving up became a matter of both pride and fear of the consequences if the protests failed. Once the protests had reached revolutionary proportions, people began to see this as a historic moment, a unique opportunity to change Egypt's fate, demanding total commitment.

Equally important were the changes in people's emotion culture prior to 25 January as a result of the moral shocks of 2010 and before, the growing mobilisation of protesters in 2010 and, crucially, the fall of Ben Ali in early 2011. Within this new sense of nascent hope, the shaming campaigns of the activists resonated far more deeply than before, turning non-participation into complicity. Hope contrasted sharply with people's prior hopelessness, and the fear of returning to that state if they failed. Without these changes, the numbers of novices turning out on 25 January would have been far fewer, which would have prevented the cumulative process described above from taking place.

Once the army had stepped in, and it had become clear that it would not use violence against the protesters, the dynamics of fear changed. Although fear and uncertainty remained as pro-regime thugs continued to attack protesters, protesting became safer. One of the reasons Tahrir Square could become an almost autonomous 'republic', suffused for long periods (especially during the day) with a festival-like spirit, is precisely this changed fear dynamic. Hope similarly became stronger, although it was severely tested right until Mubarak stepped down.

It is clear from the above analysis that the regime's response to the protests helped to mobilise protesters. As Maher (Interview 2011) put it, 'if on the 25th Mubarak had said: Parliament will go, it would have been finished. But he didn't and he killed many.' From the decision to use excessive violence to clear the Square, to the shutting down of the internet, to sending pro-Mubarak supporters and thugs to the Square to retake it, the regime's actions enraged protesters, deepened their feelings of solidarity towards each other and made them more determined to put an end to the regime.

7

TAHRIR AS A REVOLUTIONARY POLITICAL SPACE

Political space is rarely a category that is explicitly addressed (outside political geography), and yet all politics happens in spaces. Indeed, the term revolution has etymological connections to spatial dynamics. Hannah Arendt (1965: 42) reminds us that this term was historically used in regard to planets and astronomy. Contrary to the conception of revolution referring to the creation of something new, she writes that 'the word clearly indicates a recurring, cyclical movement' (Arendt 1965: 42). When the term did eventually fall to earth it was metaphorical, and early political usage tied it to a restoration of a previous order. In this process, the spatial aspect of the term was replaced by a temporal one. Yet this spatial dimension should not be forgotten. For even if a revolution does end up being a restoration, the newness of a revolution is often in how spaces are re-inscribed with new practices and meanings.

The activities and networking of social movements may have led to the January 25 revolution, but it was the creation of a revolutionary space in the centre of Cairo that for many carried the symbolism of what the revolution aimed to achieve. The urban political theorist Warren Magnusson (1996; 2011) has argued that political theory and political research more generally has prioritised a view of political life as if politics is primarily understood according to the discourses of the state. Social movement theory's spatial emphasis has also largely been on understanding political movements that function within the political conditions of the state. Yet the political spaces created by the protesters in Cairo are in many ways radically different from the statist conception of political space. To appreciate fully the significance of the January 25 revolution, we must investigate the new practices and meanings that were inscribed on to Tahrir Square and its environs.

One feature that was genuinely revolutionary about the uprising was the change in Tahrir Square from a traffic hub to a model of a new Egypt, with not only its own infrastructure, security apparatus, borders and healthcare stations but, significantly, also its own form of participatory, devolved self-government. Paradoxically, the new political space that the protesters created was both a demonstration of what a non-state space in Egypt could be, and an idealised version of what the state ought to be. In creating a non-state space they created an idealised state space. However, what was significant was how this political space was, in Arendtian terms, without sovereignty. Here was a radically different political space without the usual trappings of sovereignty, one that has been most recently seen in other Occupy movements, which, like their Egyptian counterparts, have been resisted by the state authorities they challenged. As Castells (2012: 222) notes in his reflections on the numerous anti-austerity protest movements that followed the Egyptian revolution, each of these movements end up occupying and re-inscribing urban space because the autonomy they seek from the state 'can only be exercised as a transformative force by challenging the disciplinary institutional order by reclaiming the space of the city for its citizens'. Yet exploration of this aspect of the Egyptian revolution is still only in its infancy.[1]

In addition, the way the protests unfolded was profoundly influenced by spatial arrangements and the meanings and practices embedded in them. An analysis which ignores how spatial practices and arrangements influenced the protests and how the protests in turn reshaped these practices is incomplete.

Space, like time, is, as Deborah Martin and Byron Miller (2003: 144–5) note, 'not merely a variable or "container" of activism':

it constitutes and structures relationships and networks (including the processes that produce gender, race, and class identities); situates social and cultural life including repertoires of contention; is integral to the attribution of threats and opportunities; is implicit in many types of category formation; and is central to scale-jumping strategies that aim to alter discrepancies in power among political contestants. In short, social relations are spatial as well as historical, and altering the spatial or historical constitution of social processes will likely alter how they play out.

Yet space is far too rarely problematised in political science. Tellingly, there is not one chapter in the *Oxford Handbook of Political Theory* that is concerned explicitly with the question of non-state political spaces. The chapter by Margaret Canovan (2006), 'The People', begins with the words, 'The state.' The chapter on 'Civil Society and the State' (Chambers and Kopstein 2006) indicates some potential avenues of inquiry into a non-state space, but it does so primarily by juxtaposing a potential civil society space in opposition to a state space. Social movement theory, despite being more concerned with bottom-up mobilisation, has by and large also insufficiently problematised space, some key contributions notwithstanding (cf. Castells 1999; Miller and Martin 2003). More broadly, contemporary forms of political theory (Jameson 1998), political geography and urban politics (Davies and Imbroscio 2009; Magnusson 2011) provide theoretical explorations of the concept of space, and do not take the spaces where politics ostensibly happens for granted. Significantly, there also exists research that examines the urban political spaces of Cairo (cf. Ismail 2006; Sims 2010; Bayat 2009).

One reason for the lack of interest in space is that, unlike geographers, political scientists and sociologists are rarely interested in space per se; more usually, the focus is on institutional structure, mobilisation, discourses or the actors involved. In this account, there is nothing special about Tahrir other than the events that went on there.

In addressing space in International Relations, (traditional) political theory or political science, the most direct route for most analyses is to provide alternative theories of the state.[2] Even sociology has had a traditional bias towards state spaces, as the ideal of the state became the model for understanding and evaluating other spaces (Magnusson 1996). State spaces thus too often remain the model of political space in which all other spaces are understood.

There are various ways of thinking about space. Within social movement theory, the small but growing work that has been done so far has focused either on the work of Henri Lefebvre (cf. 1991), who theorised the relationship between space and social practices, or on identifying how 'particular spatial forms shape, galvanize, and accommodate insurgent sentiments and solidarities' (Bayat 2009: 162). In the latter category, Asef Bayat (2009: 161–70), for example, looks at how 'the socio-spatial features' of urban centres have shaped protest dynamics in Cairo and Tehran. In this chapter, we draw on aspects of Lefebvre's work, as it has filtered through into social movement theory, to reflect on the dialectic between space and social practices in the Egyptian revolution, and in particular how public space and its practices were renegotiated.

Arendt and Magnusson offer two different yet complementary approaches to thinking about space. Arendt offers the possibility to theorise about political space differently, without binding political space to the model of nation-state sovereignty. Magnusson's work on urban political space with its multiplicity of authorities and its practices of self-government similarly enables an account of political space that is not the same as the nation-state sovereign model. Using their work we will show how what was perhaps the most revolutionary aspect of the Egyptian revolution was the way Tahrir Square became a political space that did not contain the traditional trappings of a sovereign space, instead displaying the multiplicity and self-governing qualities of urban politics.

In this chapter, we focus on Tahrir Square for pragmatic reasons, even though we are aware that this does an injustice to all those outside Cairo who participated in the revolt against Mubarak. Tahrir was one location among many, and without these other spaces being occupied and re-inscribed, Mubarak would not have fallen. Yet Tahrir became the symbolic epicentre of the revolution, both nationally and internationally, an understanding of which is crucial to understanding the revolution.

Situating Tahrir Square

Midan Tahrir, or 'Liberation Square', is a large traffic rotary in the centre of Cairo. The Aljazeera reporter Ayman Mohyeldin (2011: 1) describes the Square as follows:

In the heart of Cairo, in the shadows of some of the city's iconic buildings, five different roads pour into one hub. At the center of that intersection lies a simple, nondescript roundabout. Patchy grass and a few bushes are all that mark its center. Thousands of people and vehicles pass around it daily in a dizzying and often frustrating frenzy. There are no monuments, no memorials or plaques in sight. There are no benches for ordinary passersby to stop and catch a breath from the chaos of Cairo colliding around them.[3]

While it used to be a cultivated field, Tahrir Square is now an important entry point into many key areas of Cairo. Many of the main hotels are a few minutes' walk from the Square, as is the central bus station. The famous Cairo Museum is located at one end, the Soviet-style Mujamma building at the other, housing part of the government's bureaucratic machinery. The Square is close to some of the most important government buildings, including the former headquarters of the NDP, whose burned out ruins are clearly visible from the Square, the state television building, the interior ministry and parliament, many of which had become central sites of protest over the previous decade. The ironically titled Ministry of Social Solidarity is only a few minutes' walk away, and the original American University campus is adjacent to the Square.

Tahrir Square is in many ways an obvious place to protest. Almost on the bank of the Nile, it is a major artery in Egypt's largest city; its geographical location in the centre of Cairo, along with the numerous ways in and out of the Square, makes it an easily accessible, dynamic congregating centre. Linked by two bridges, it is situated at the gateway between the city centre and the expansion of Cairo to the west of the Nile, including the neighbourhoods of Mohandessin, Imbaba, Giza and affluent Zamalek. To the north is the 6 October Bridge, the major artery leading to north-eastern Cairo, including Shubra al-Kheima, Ramses Square (where Cairo's central train station is located) and Heliopolis (where the Presidential Palace is situated). Immediately to the east is the labyrinth of downtown Cairo, including Talat Harb Square, near which are many of Cairo's historical political cafés. To the south is the long Qasr al-Aini Street, leading past the affluent Garden City to the Old City and, further south, Maadi.

The Square has a long political history. Its current design is a product of a Parisian-style remodelling of the city in the nineteenth century, and was named Midan Ismailia until the 1952 Revolution, when it was renamed Midan Tahrir by Gamal Abdul Nasser to symbolise Egypt's liberation from the British-backed monarchy and the destruction of the British Army barracks that were located on the site. The Square has seen large gatherings of football fans after football victories, and it has been a centre point for key mass protests.

During the popular protests against British rule in 1919, thousands filled the Square to demand independence (an event that was highlighted by a number of our interviewees as a precursor and template for the 2011 uprising). The Square was again a site of popular protests in 1952. It was one of the chief sites of both the 1967 protests, following Egypt's defeat in the 1967 Arab–Israeli war, and of the various 1970s protests against Sadat's policies. In 1972, the Square was briefly occupied—for the first time—by students protesting Sadat's policies, and during the bread riots of 1977 thousands gathered at the Square in protest. In 1999, Tahrir again featured briefly in a tax-collector protest (Baheyya 2008a), just as it did in a protest organised by the PCSPI in 2001 (*Al-Ahram Weekly* 2005a). It did so again in the 2003 protests against the war in Iraq. Perhaps most interesting is the coincidence that exactly sixty-five years before Mubarak stepped down on 11 February 2011, Tahrir Square witnessed a political demonstration against the British presence in Egypt, with police killing two dozen Egyptians on 11 February 1946 (AlSayyad 2011). Indeed, a history of Egypt could be written from the perspective of the Square.

That Tahrir Square became an important location in the demonstrations is, consequently, not surprising. It was targeted as an original congregation point by the protesters for 25 January, and it became a major battleground throughout the revolt, especially in the first few days when the Square resembled a warzone. However, once the Square was occupied and defended, the security forces withdrawn, it came to be seen as a prototype of an ideal Egypt. It was, in the words of one activist who was there, 'The Egypt we had all dreamed of' (Khalil Saeed, Interview 2011). Another activist remembers sleeping in Tahrir, awaking with raindrops falling on his face, and reflecting on how wonderful the experience was (Fouad, Interview 2011). Yet another recalled the experience of being in Tahrir as 'The greatest time of my life' (Salah, Interview 2011). Something remarkable happened in Tahrir, and the purpose of this chapter is to explore how the concept of space is important in understanding the events that came to redefine Tahrir Square into the 'Egypt we had all dreamed of.'

Reconfiguring Tahrir

Space and place clearly mattered in the unfolding of the Egyptian revolution. We have already discussed the changes in Cairo's urban make-up, the mushrooming of the city's *ashwaiyyat* or informal, unregulated areas, and the merging of different classes in these informal areas as a background factor enabling the revolution (Chapter 4). Similarly, it is no coincidence that Tahrir became the centre of the revolution. But to clarify in what ways space and place mattered, it is useful to turn to Lefebvre's conceptualisation of space, and the way this has been deployed in social movement theory.

Lefebvre (1991: 33, 38–41) proposes a 'conceptual triad' to understand space. Space, for him, consists of three, dialectically interacting facets:

1. 'Spatial practices' or 'perceived space': this is space as perceived from outside (rather than lived), produced and inscribed by the social relations of production and reproduction. Spatial practices reproduce dominant social relations, including those of the family and the various social classes, and encompass how one lives (e.g. in social housing or private mansions), how one travels to work, practices of access and exclusion, monuments and buildings embodying power, what practices are associated with certain spaces (e.g. protest, leisure, industrial production) and so on.

2. 'Representations of space' or 'conceived space': this is 'the space of scientists, planners, urbanists, technocratic subdividers and social engineers'. Representations of space are linked to the relations of production and 'the 'order' which those relations impose but they are tied specifically to knowledge and the (verbal) signs of the dominant.

3. 'Representational spaces' or 'lived space': this is 'space as directly lived through its associated images and symbols, and hence the space of "inhabitants" and "users"'. This is 'dominated space', tied to 'the clandestine or underground side of social life' as well as to art, and thus more often expressed through non-verbal signs.

When applied to contentious politics, this conceptual lens helps us to see how space and protest mutually constitute each other. Where 'conceived space' jars with 'lived space' and the latter is graphically inscribed by political inequality—for instance, 'when conceived spaces of order and equal opportunity are contradicted by material geographies of crumbling tenements, graffiti, pot-holed streets, dangerous parks, and resource-strapped schools', particularly when 'juxtaposed against the grand housing, immaculate landscaping, and security apparatuses of privileged neighborhoods'—there is a ready pool of grievances to be tapped into. Particularly important is Lefebvre's (1991: 365) insight that:

Socio-political contradictions are realized spatially. The contradictions of space thus make the contradictions of social relations operative. In other words, spatial contradictions 'express' conflicts between socio-political interests and forces; it is only *in* space that such conflicts come effectively into play, and in doing so they become contradictions *of* space.

These contradictions of space are reproduced and controlled by particular practices associated with the prevailing systems of control. Space, moreover, is inscribed with place-specific practices and meanings. For social movement theorists, this means that 'repertoires of contention ... are forged in the context of place-specific social norms, e.g., notions of place-appropriate social behavior (to be violated), and place-based symbolism (to appeal to)' (Martin and Miller 2003: 146–7, 148).

Applying these insights to the January 25 revolution, we can immediately see the (changing) relationship between physical space and the social practices and conceptions that develop in particular spaces and the relation between neighbouring spaces.

Cairo's *ashwaiyyat* had been expanding since the 1970s (Chapter 4). Yet it was not until the late 2000s that groups such as April 6 began to see them as potential sites for protest, linking them strategically to the centre. The idea of starting in the alleyways of the *ashwaiyyat* to circumvent the police was itself forged in the heat of the spatial security practices associated with Cairo's large boulevards. Once the protesters recognised how space-specific these practices were, they could adapt their tactics by choosing spaces where the police were routinely absent and where the dissonance between perceived, conceived and lived space was intense, thus making it more likely that its inhabitants would be responsive to the activists' calls.

Paradoxically, the ability to take Tahrir and redefine it was possible only by first ignoring Tahrir and focusing on other spaces. It was the genius of moving the focus away from Cairo's main boulevards to the small alleyways that enabled the protesters to outwit the police. In doing so, they changed both the spatial practices associated with these alleys and the public perception of them (even if only temporarily). For a short while, the periphery became the centre. Arguably one of the reasons that so many people joined the protests was because the protests came to their streets, making them and their concerns central to the demonstrations. This was no longer an urban elite challenging the regime in the spaces that were associated with central power and its contestations. This was an urban protest, inviting all to turn their street, however mundane and distant from the official sites of power, into a protest site of central significance. This was in sharp contrast to earlier 'localised' protests in poorer areas in Cairo that did not reach the political 'centre'—leading Bayat (2009: 168) to conclude that 'centrality, proximity, and accessibility ... are crucial features of any street of discontent'. That this inversion was possible in this instance was due to the relative proximity of the selected *ashwaiyyat* to Tahrir Square (Chapter 5), the size and determination of the protests and the eventual return to the political centre. The spatial flows of the protests in turn both reconnected centre and periphery in a new way and re-inscribed the transversed physical spaces with new practices. The tactical innovations described in Chapter 5 were at the core of this re-inscription, as was the configuration of the protesters, encompassing not just middle-class elites but members from across Egypt's classes.

Spatial arrangements also mattered in how the protests evolved differently in different cities. The protest dynamics in Cairo were shaped by the layout of the city and the meanings attached to this layout by the regime and the protesters. Once the regime realised that the goal was to reoccupy Tahrir Square on 28 January, they positioned their security forces around it, strategically occupying the arteries leading into the Square. Thus the battles that took place on the Friday were predominantly battles on the bridges leading into Tahrir and its environs from the west, and in the boulevards feeding into the Square from the south and the east. The northern part of the Square, by contrast, was more difficult to control as, there, numerous major traffic arteries converged, with no clearly bounded, and thus readily defensible, space.

The fighting in Cairo, as Ashraf Khalil (2011: 186–7) notes, took far longer than the short, fierce battle that took place in Alexandria, in part precisely because of the layout of the two cities (and, we would add, the way this layout and associated practices were interpreted):

Cairo is a city of bridges, all of which serve as natural choke points where Central Security could gather and effectively halt the protesters' movement. The bridges neutralized the protesters' superior numbers, hindered their ability to surround the riot police, and enhanced the effectiveness of the Interior Ministry's weaponry. That's why many of the most violent and iconic battles on January 28 took place on bridges. But Alexandria, which sprawls along the Mediterranean coast, contains very few such natural bottlenecks; it was a logistical nightmare. ... On January 28, the police in Alexandria didn't stand a chance—immediately finding themselves surrounded, overwhelmed, and dealing with multiple fronts.

Other factors played a role, such as the particularly acrimonious relationship between police and citizens in Alexandria, following the death and protests surrounding Khaled Said in 2010, and the January 2011 Alexandria bombing and subsequent clampdown, described by locals as 'outside the bounds of even the Emergency Law' (Khalil 2011: 186, 183–7). As a former Muslim Brotherhood parliamentarian told Khalil: 'It's like we've been occupied by a foreign power.' In this context, it is hardly surprising that the clashes in Alexandria were ferocious from the start. But this too points to the mutually constitutive relationship between space and social practice, as particularly harsh security practices were associated with Alexandrian public space.

That the bridges played such a large role was itself in part a function of the spatial layout of Cairo, and the particular relations protest groups had with the areas to the west of the Nile. It is here that Imbaba, Bulaq al-Daqrur and Giza are located, each of which contain densely populated areas where the protesters had prior relationships which facilitated mobilisation on 25 January. It is here also that the main campus of Cairo University is situated, where many activists study or have studied, as well as the professional neighbourhood of Mohandessin, where a number of key activists live.

The choice to converge on Tahrir Square was itself a function of both spatial layout and the meanings and representations associated with the Square. By succeeding in occupying Tahrir Square and hanging on to it, the protesters dealt the Mubarak regime a fatal symbolic blow. Unlike Bahrain, where the central square in Manama, having been occupied and renamed Tahrir, was brutally cleared by the security forces, the continuing presence of the protesters in the symbolic heart of Cairo's public space was a daily reminder to people that Mubarak had lost control.

Even more important than occupying Tahrir Square was the fact that the practices and values associated with it had been profoundly altered through the protests. In this sense, it was literally what Lefebvre (1991: 416–17) terms a 'trial by space':

It is in space ... that each idea of 'value' acquires or loses its distinctiveness through confrontation with the other values and ideas that it encounters there. Moreover—and more importantly—groups, classes or fractions of classes cannot constitute themselves, or recognize one another, as 'subjects' unless they generate (or produce) a space. Ideas, representations or values which do not succeed in making their mark on space, and thus generating (or producing) an appropriate morphology, will lose all pith and become mere signs, resolve themselves into abstract descriptions, or mutate into fantasies.

The vision the protesters had of a different Egypt could only gain traction by producing a public space, in which *their* values, rather than the values of the regime, were inscribed. Previous protests had in part failed to capture the imagination of the wider population because they had not succeeded in making a sufficiently deep and lasting mark on public space. The capturing and holding of Tahrir (and squares elsewhere) and the production of a new type of space on Tahrir, based on different values, left a mark that is still there, however contested, incomplete and re-inscribed in the period since. What is more, the values of the Mubarak regime were found wanting in this 'trial'; and although large elements of the old regime live on, they cannot (wholly) ignore the values made manifest in Tahrir. Conversely, unless the protesters keep those values alive, by regularly re-inscribing them in Tahrir Square, they will become mere 'fantasies'.

At the same time as reclaiming public space, the protesters subverted the sharp distinction between public (prohibited) and private (secluded) space by publicly enacting lived practices that had hitherto been typically confined to the private home. This was partly for pragmatic reasons, as protesters had to conduct their daily routines in public if they were to maintain control of the Square. But there also appears to have been an intentional desire to bring the relative freedom of private space into public space and liberate it.[4] Thus Tahrir became a temporary home, a regular prayer house (yet without the usual political connotations), a festival ground, a commercial hub. As one protester tweeted, 'More tents set up in the square as weather might be chilly/rainy tonight. Tahrir feels more like home everyday' (Idle and Nunns 2011: 155). Tahrir also became the embodiment of a new way of life. Or as a Cairo-based reporter tweeted, 'My camera is stolen, my body is bruised and my eye is still black & blue, but I've never felt better in my life' (Idle and Nunns 2011: 148).

Public space, or at least the main squares, boulevards and arteries of Egypt's main cities, had been predominantly the space where the regime and its agents ruled: the space where security forces were in control, where public gatherings were prohibited, unless they were in the context of street markets or public festivals. Everyday life was

WHY OCCUPY A SQUARE?

allowed to flow, but as soon as people came together politically, whether to protest the closure of a local school, to challenge the regime or to show solidarity with Christians under attack, the police would step in. What the occupation of Tahrir Square achieved was the 'liberation' of these public arteries from the clutches of the Mubarak regime, and their 'restoration' to the Egyptian people.

This process had already begun years before on a much smaller scale, when pro-Palestinian and Kefaya activists self-consciously sought to reclaim the streets (Chapter 1). The neighbourhood protests of 2008–2010 had continued this process, in greater numbers, but still in a piecemeal, ad hoc fashion. What the protest marches of 25 and 28 January did was to spread this challenge across the capital (and Egypt's other urban spaces), subverting the regime's claim to public space by first reclaiming the alleyways of Shubra, Imbaba and so on, and then, when gathered in sufficient numbers, confronting the police in the open, public boulevards and squares, pushing them back, inch by teargas-soaked inch, until Tahrir was reached. As such, it was both literally and symbolically a struggle over the right to public space, a struggle pitting an underground 'lived space' over-inscribed with new, often revolutionary practices against autocratic notions of spatial practices (perceived space) and representations of space (conceived space). By turning Tahrir into a lived revolutionary space, with its own art and symbolic expressions, the protesters changed both the spatial practices associated with Tahrir and other public spaces, and the representations of such spaces (though not with the same level of formal backup by architects, technocrats and so on that the regime could command).

Some of the practices that developed on the Square were reproductions of existing power relations, practices and spatial arrangements outside the Square. The establishment of a group calling itself 'the Mukhabarat' (after the Egyptian intelligence service) within the Square illustrates how the Square could not escape entirely from the state structures they were combatting. Similarly, some of the tent camps were organised according to place of origin, and delegations from different parts of Egypt made their presence known by flying city flags and banners (Salah, Interview 2011; Soueif 2012: 148), thus reproducing the spatial divisions of Egypt writ large.

But there are many instances where practices on the Square differed from established practices. Consider the way Khalil Saeed (Interview

2011), of the Democratic Front, described the Square, a sentiment echoed by most of our interviewees and in tweets:

This was my Egypt, this Square, with the Museum as the border. It was a life and death battle. Tahrir Square was like the Egypt we had always heard about from our parents. All together, in peace, Muslims and Christians, poor and rich, no clashes, no gender violence. We were always hearing about this kind of Egypt; we saw this in Tahrir. We found respect, dignity, freedom.

April 6 member Mostafa Fouad (Interview 2011) described the Square in similar terms: 'Everybody loved everybody, nobody was throwing garbage on the ground, no sexual harassment, regular people started talking about politics.'

Sectarian tensions were suspended, as Christians and Muslims enabled each other's prayer practices, ensuring their mutual safety by forming cordons of people linking hands around those praying (cf. Wael Khairy's tweet in Idle and Nunns 2011: 154). Ideological tensions were transcended, as people of all ideological persuasions prayed together—something that would have been difficult to envision in Egypt's 'normal' highly politicised public space, where public displays of prayer are usually associated with being a member of an Islamist group. According to Heba Ezzat (Interview 2011), Islamist intellectual and Square resident:

More people prayed on the Square than in their normal lives. This became part of the revolution: we can pray, [without this being] a political choice. Because this was the most political spot [in Egypt], praying became freed of politics; it became a religious choice again. If 90 percent were praying on the Friday, it had nothing to do with the Muslim Brotherhood or Islamism.

Thus the practice of prayer took on a new meaning in this 'liberated' Tahrir—a meaning that was tied not only to a particular space, but to a particular time.

Similarly, relations between men and women and between veiled and unveiled women were transformed (albeit temporarily). Remember the story with which we opened this book of Amira (Interview 2011) feeling an instant connection with a group of Muslim women wearing the *niqab*. When she found herself in front of a row of men about to pray, the prayer leader similarly invited her to stay. Thus the secluded and rigidly circumscribed semi-public space of the mosque was reconstituted and re-inscribed on the Square as a public space with altered rules. While these new 'rules' may have been pragmatically arrived at, negotiated in an ad hoc manner, they arguably drew on both private spatial practices (such as the model of the more 'liberal' family home) and public ones (such as the model of the religious festival).

In the same vein, women, who under normal circumstances are not socially permitted to sleep in close proximity to men in public spaces, could sleep on Tahrir Square, amidst the men, without the usual fear of sexual harassment on the Square. This was in sharp contrast to the harassment regularly experienced by women in Egypt. In the words of Ezzat (Interview 2011), 'The body was neutralised.' First-hand reports claimed that there was no sexual harassment in the Square during its occupation. Amira (Interview 2011) recalled:

I felt very safe, for the first time in my life. Harassment always takes place in busy places ... But on the Square there was no harassment. Once I had to go to the other side. I said to a man, 'Please, can I go.' They made a corridor with their hands to prevent any man from touching me. They created a safe passage. I felt like a queen. I felt all of them were my brothers and friends.

A blue-eyed, blond British student who was in Tahrir during the protests likewise told us that she experienced no harassment (Wynne-Hughes, Interview 2011). One young woman told a reporter that: 'Men's perception of us is more equal ... At Tahrir we were all Egyptians' (Gröndahl 2011: 26). Only one of our interviewees, the Iraqi British student resident in Cairo (J. Younis, Interview 2011), challenged this narrative:

I kept going back [to the Square] but never slept there. It didn't feel quite safe. I couldn't smoke there, because women are not supposed to smoke. This was not a social revolution. ... When there were violent stages, we were always told to go to the back. The majority of women were veiled. You would stand out if you were not veiled. Women were leading chants, but this changes nothing. Egyptian women have always been bolshy. As long as they stick to politics, it is ok. But if it is about social mores, it is not tolerated.

Although this suggests that different spatial practices competed, on balance the available evidence indicates that gender relations were so markedly different during those fourteen days on the Square that we can speak of a new political space, with different practices and norms associated with it, bordering on the revolutionary (even if only temporary and not extending to a full-scale social revolution).[5] This subversion of norms and practices seemed to echo practices from the *mulid* religious festival, where it similarly becomes acceptable for women to sleep in the streets. Ezzat (Interview 2011), for instance, told us:

There was no moral censure. There are many precedents [for this]: women in poor areas breastfeeding in public, where her body becomes a mother's body, not a female body. ... Or take the *mulid*, a celebration of saints' birthdays, whether Christian or Sufi. ... On the last night of celebrations, there will be millions on the Square, for example the birthday of Sayyidna Zaynab: the Square is occupied, with women sleeping on the street. This is perfectly accepted. So it is the context of the body, rather than the body itself.[6]

Many of these 'revolutionary' practices had already been practised in the 'spaces' of civil society institutions. Sherine El-Taraboulsi (2011), for instance, documents the role played during the revolution by members of 'youth-led and/or youth-targeted organizations' such as Al Andalus Institute for Tolerance and Anti-Violence Studies, Nahdet El Mahrousa (empowering young professionals) and Alashanek ya Balady (youth helping socially deprived areas). These organisations, El-Taraboulsi (2011: 19) argues, 'provided a space [prior to 2011] for emergent forms of citizenship on both ideational and practical levels' away from 'overt politics and [thus] scrutiny from the Mubarak regime'. In doing so, they 'succeeded in negotiating a space for youth to voice their Egyptian-ness and put it into action on the ground ... [representing] a fresh revived understanding of citizenship that was more progressive than that of older NGOs or officialdom'. These spaces contributed to the new spatial practices inscribed on Tahrir, by infusing the Square with their own practices (such as tolerance between Muslims and Christians).

The colonisation of public space by the protesters was a crucial aspect of the revolution, as it reconstituted both what it meant to be Egyptian and what could be done in public. But even more striking was the blossoming of an urban, non-sovereign politics.

Hannah Arendt, Sovereignty and Political Space

Spaces do not just exist, they are produced (Lefebvre 1991). The traditional political theories of space frame the production of space according to how state sovereignty orders this political space. If we look at the social contract tradition, we find in Hobbes (1996 [1651]) the argument that only under a spatially ordered juridical sovereignty, in which people relinquish some of their rights for the provision of security, is politics possible. The problem of sovereignty, as the liberal tradition sees it, is in how people can be free under conditions of sovereign rule. Rousseau (1997 [1762]) framed this problem as a question about individual will. Locke (1988 [1689]) tried to resolve the problem with the idea of tacit consent.

If we adopt an Arendtian perspective, the fictitious contract that Hobbes, for instance, describes, can be understood not to enable politics, but to destroy it by creating a sovereign body politic that is more tyrannical than it could ever be political because it sets up an 'absolute monopoly of power' (Arendt 1965: 171). Hobbes' prioritisation of the commonwealth and of sovereignty ignores the extent to which political orders do not function at the level of the sovereign alone, but operate in multiple places at the same time. Hobbes ties a sovereign political space to security, yet sometimes security processes are the products of different types of non-sovereign organisations operating in non-sovereign political spaces and the traditional sovereign is a provider of insecurity.

A consequence of a traditional vision of politics is that only certain types of activity can be recognised as political, and this understanding of politics is hard to escape. The long shadow of Hobbes (and others like Locke and Rousseau) influences what constitutes a political space, and thus what should be the concern of political theorists. The temptation is subsequently to think about sovereignty and the state instead of thinking about politics.

In addition, the traditional focus on sovereignty comes with particular methodological assumptions about politics that require revealing. Mary Kaldor, Helmut Anheier and Marlies Glasius (2003: 4) have approached this challenge and labelled the problem 'methodological nationalism', a term they use to identify the tendency to prioritise national politics at the expense of other forms and locations of political life. Within social movement theory, where the focus is on grassroots movements rather than states, movements are nevertheless usually studied within national contexts and state structures feature heavily in these analyses. Even the study of transnational social movements suffers from a level of state bias, although it has been the most successful within the social movement field in moving beyond the state.

Political spaces are the product of complex political relations, and the simplifications that a focus on sovereignty produces mask these complexities (Walker 2010). Politics takes place in different locations according to different logics. Politics is, contrary to conventional wisdom, not about the state even if, as Magnusson (2011: 123) readily acknowledges, 'the most powerful argument for seeing like a state is that the most important of political identities in the modern world are the ones produced at the intersection of nationalism within the state system'. While the Egyptian revolt of 2011 does not bear all the hallmarks of a revolution, it was revolutionary in regard to how the space of Tahrir Square came to be redefined and understood politically.

The revolt in Egypt was an empirical illustration of what can happen when people come together in public and act in concert, non-violently and seemingly without sovereignty. Acting together in public is what Arendt refers to in her definition of power and it describes remarkably well what was happening in Egypt during the revolt. Arendt's account of power, however, also relates in an interesting way to a theory of space. Arendt's largest concern with political space is in her analysis of the distinction between public and private spheres (1958), and with the political councils that she writes about in *On Revolution* (1965). Yet she also provides an interesting critique of the relationship between power and sovereignty that is of direct relevance to a philosophical explanation of the significance of the spatial politics of Tahrir Square.

At stake in this discussion is a twofold problem. On the one hand is the empirical problem about how to understand the meaning of a political space, in this case Tahrir Square, and on the other is a theoretical problem about how to identify political spaces. These problems reinforce each other since it is only by having a theory of political space that one can then identify a space as being political. In Arendt's critique of this twofold problem, she identifies a relationship between the politics of space and violence and she challenges any framing of political space that involves this relationship. This framing of political space can be found in Hobbes, but also in Jean Bodin (1992: 3–4), who writes that 'sovereignty ... is not limited either in power or in function, or in length of time', and that 'a sovereign prince is answerable only to God'. Sovereign in this articulation is clearly singular.

For Arendt, sovereignty has little to do with politics, as politics necessarily involves an acceptance and recognition of the inherent plurality of humankind. This is not the place to digress too far into Arendt's complex political theory,[7] but the importance of plurality for politics and sovereignty is emphasised in her famous phrase, 'No man can be sovereign because not one man, but men, inhabit the earth' (Arendt 1958: 234). For Arendt (1958: 245), sovereignty is always 'spurious if claimed by any isolated single entity'. When sovereignty is not spurious is when it figures in the promise of people bound together not because they all share some kind of identical will, but because they share an agreed purpose (Arendt 1958: 245). As Margaret Canovan (1992: 212) has explained, Arendt does not build her theory of politics on the 'Rousseauian tradition, according to which we are free when we rule ourselves by our general will.' The liberal philosophical tradition that often legitimises sovereignty in this way is antithetical to her political thought. For Arendt, this kind of thinking is non-political because 'it does not take account of human plurality' (Canovan 1992: 212). Rather, Arendt (2006: 163) argues that 'the famous sovereignty of political bodies has always been an illusion, which, moreover, can be maintained only by the instruments of violence, that is, with essentially nonpolitical means'. According to Arendt, the traditional understanding of sovereignty as found in Hobbes and Bodin, for example, suggests that violence is necessary for upholding sovereignty. As such, the account of sovereignty that dominates traditional political thought and practice is an illusion maintained by an acceptance of the need for violence. Consequently, because Arendt (1970) distinguishes politics from violence, there is nothing political about sovereignty.

In *On Revolution*, Arendt provides a challenge to the conception of sovereignty that makes politics possible. She writes that, 'in the realm of human affairs sovereignty and tyranny are the same' (1965: 153). The implication is that it is only by overthrowing sovereignty that people can be free. For Arendt, the point is that politics is a particular form of human activity that cannot take place under conditions of violence. Violence is what takes place under tyranny, and to the extent that sovereignty is conceptualised in the singular it requires violence to support it and is thus tyrannical. In her critique of sovereignty, by redefining it to pertain to the promises of people acting together in concert toward a shared purpose, she connects power, politics and sovereignty in a radically different way. For Arendt, this critical redefinition of politics was influenced by what she saw in the American Revolution, namely the creation of political societies that had power but did not claim sovereignty, at least not in the sense articulated by Bodin. The distinction here is tricky, but Arendt is trying to set up a distinction between sovereignty and politics, with, in her terms, violence being a hallmark of sovereignty and power that of politics.

Arendt provides various contradictory explanations of politics. Nevertheless, one of her insights is to claim that politics is not restricted to government or to domination over others based on the threat or use of force. Rather, in Elisabeth Young-Bruehl's words (2006: 84), Arendt thought of politics 'as the organization or constitution of the power people have when they come together as talking and acting beings. Here her emphasis is on preserving the people's power in a constituted government: *potestas in populo*.' For Arendt, the bureaucratic machinery of the state limited politics, for she saw human beings and their capacity for creation (what she calls natality) (1958) as being primary to the human condition and to any understanding of politics. Nevertheless, she considers the state to remain significant for formulations of political space, since it is within the state that the public/private distinction exists, even though she challenges what this centrality means (Arendt 2005, 2007; Bernstein 1996). This creates a tension because, in Arendt's reading, the sovereign is tied to tyranny and violence.

Arendt's solution to this tension is found in her understanding of the Ancient Greek polis. Originally it was not the state but the city, the polis, that set up the public/private distinction, and while the ancient Greek polis was certainly violent in its external relations it was, in her idealised reading, against violence internally, to such an extent that the citizens were spared the indignity of violence in the execution of criminals by '"persuading" those who had been condemned to death to commit suicide by drinking the poison hemlock' (1965: 12). Politics, and political space, for Arendt (1965: 168), always replicated this idealised understanding of the polis. Political spaces were, thus, never sovereign but were tied to the construction of political societies that did not set up divisions between rulers and ruled, and as such did not require sovereignty. In Tahrir Square, there certainly was no sovereign in the traditional sense, and there was also the absence of a state. People, moreover, came together as 'talking and acting human beings' and constituted a form of government that relied heavily on self-help and common sense initiative, with no single sovereign ruler.

The non-Sovereign Revolutionary Space of Tahrir Square

Tahrir Square was in many ways and for many people a symbol of the revolution. It provided a spatial symbol of the revolution and became a space where the revolution could sustain itself by creating a political community that was political in the Arendtian sense and was also, in this same sense, without sovereignty. Yet a paradox of Tahrir was that this especially political space functioned by replicating many of the trappings of the state, and as an idealised space it was not able to last.

That the political space set up in Tahrir was temporary does not reduce its significance or suggest that a lasting political space has to be a statist one. To explore the social relations of the events in Tahrir and the role that the Square played in the revolt is an opportunity to demonstrate that politics happens in a variety of locations and forms, and that how we understand political space in turn frames the lenses through which politics are understood.

To understand the political order created in Tahrir is to reject the traditional claim that a singular sovereign is necessary for politics to take place. The politics in Tahrir was more about the plurality of Egyptians and a kind of anarchical ordering of political life. In this way the protesters created new 'non-sovereign'[8] political spaces that represented the type of community they sought to create. The usual trappings of the sovereign state were absent, yet it was a political order with its own forms of governance. At the same time, the politics of the Square were a reaction against the existing sovereign order and thus connected to it. However, as Magnusson (2011: 60) observes, although 'the state is always of some importance in relation to [political] issues … it is rarely the case that the crucial battle will be fought on the terrain of the state itself'. Tellingly, the key battle did not take place in the usual spaces associated with the state, such as government buildings, but in a traffic rotary.

The political spaces that the revolt created were part of a revolution that could only make sense in the context of the modern Egyptian state, but it was not a space that reflected the order of that state, and in this regard it was no coincidence that the main political public space of the revolt was in a traffic rotary. Tahrir may be a logical place for mass celebrations or protests, but this is largely because of its open geography, not because there is anything obviously political about it. Tahrir does not represent the apparatuses of the state, but it was used to challenge them (though not the existence of the state itself). This challenge played out in many ways, but that the political order created in the occupation of Tahrir was so different from the authoritarian regime is telling. The politics of Tahrir Square were political in an Arendtian sense precisely because there was no singular sovereign in Tahrir. This character of the Square was especially important for the protesters, as it made it possible for all Egyptians, of different classes, genders, religions and even religiosity, to come together as a people and share in the construction of a new Egypt

The extreme character of the regime was reversed in Tahrir by creating an opposite political space to the one that previously characterised life in Egypt. Nowhere was this divergence more apparent than in the fact that outside the Square, and before the revolt, there were few public political spaces, while during the revolt Tahrir Square became the political space par excellence, and discussing politics in public became the norm.

More specifically, the politics in Tahrir were in many ways an illustration of what Magnusson (2011: 123) describes as urban politics: 'If we see like a state, we can lose sight of the fact that the politically important identities (and politically important interests and values) are not necessarily the ones bound up with the nation-state; nor are they necessarily the ones that can be vindicated by an act of state sovereignty.' Rather, he argues that, 'The moment of the political is one of disruption, when the regular routines of government are challenged by something that does not compute with them' (2011: 133). Magnusson (2011: 168) identifies five political characteristics that become visible when we 'see like a city'. These are that political entities are 'self-organizing'; that there exists a 'multiplicity of political authorities in different registers at different scales'; that 'practices of self-government enable civilized order and produce public benefits both in the presence of sovereign authority and in its absence'; that 'order is always temporary and local'; and that 'transformations are non-linear and hence inherently unpredictable'. By framing the political in this way it becomes clearer what happened in Tahrir Square, and what kind of political space was created, albeit temporarily. In the following, we will discuss the first four characteristics that Magnusson identified.

'Self-Organizing' Political Entities

One of Magnusson's (2011: 23–4) key arguments is that cities encourage self-government:

No doubt, every way of life entails self-government, but the need for self-government is especially apparent in an urban setting. People need to show restraint in this world of strangers, and to a remarkable extent they do. ... it is self-government not "anarchy" that the city has to offer. Urban life has its rules, its conditions of possibility, and those rules have to be well observed if a city is to work. But, the rules have to be understood, accepted, and observed by a myriad of individuals who cannot be effectively watched and regulated by external authorities. Each individual has to assume responsibility for him- or herself, and become self-regulating or self-governing. ... So, what Foucault ... called "governmentality", and what others have described as "government at a distance" or "governing through freedom" ... is implicit in urbanism as a way of life. It is a condition of possibility for urbanism and also a name for many of the practices implicit in urbanism.

For Magnusson, cities are the prime location where sovereign state power is challenged. However, in the context of an authoritarian regime, this challenge may remain largely informal and dispersed, expressed in what Bayat (2009: 43–65) calls 'the quiet encroachment of the ordinary'. What is so striking about the Egyptian uprising was that this type of self-governing urban politics became dominant, at least on Tahrir Square and in the popular committees guarding Cairo.

The key moment was when the regime withdrew the security forces. Intriguingly, this is precisely what Magnusson (2011: 85) implies when he approvingly quotes Richard Sennett's recipe for urban renewal:

What is needed in order to create cities where people are forced to confront each other is a reconstituting of public power, not a destruction of it. As a rule of change, the situations creating survival encounters would be as follows: there would be no policing, nor any other form of central control, of school-ing, zoning, renewal, or city activities that could be performed through com-mon community action, or, even more importantly through direct, nonviolent conflict in the city itself.

In Tahrir Square, and central Cairo more generally, public power was reconstituted in a way that people had to confront each other, to take common community action and work things out themselves, on their own authority, rather than some delegated state authority.

When the police withdrew, Egyptian citizens took control of their neighbourhood's security by setting up *ligan sha'abiyya* [popular com-mittees] (cf. Wynne-Hughes, Interview 2011; J. Younis, Interview 2011). Activist author Ahdaf Soueif (2012: 37–8) describes these instances of self-help evocatively, illustrating the spontaneous and ad hoc nature of these committees:

In every district people came down from their homes and set up neighbour-hood watches, 'Popular Committees'. They invented barricades out of tyres and chairs and lengths of wood and blocks of stone and traffic barriers. The characters of the checkpoints varied with the neighbourhoods: in the villages they were farmers with axes and hoes; in the poorer neighbourhoods they wore galabeyyas and carried sticks; in the posh districts they had walking canes and golf clubs; at one Zamalek checkpoint there was a lady in a camping chair holding a glass of gin and tonic. ... For a week, the city was policed by Popular Committees; they had fun, checking ID and licences and ushering cars through with a theatrical flourish. Everywhere they were courteous and apologised for the inconvenience. And we were courteous right back and thanked them for protecting us, thanked them for giving us our city back.[9]

Khalil Saeed (Interview 2011) shed further light on the workings of these committees:

There was chaos all over Egypt. We had to organise ourselves into our districts. I might go to Tahrir, but my house, my mother could be attacked. That is why we had *ligan sha'abiyya*. We would agree: I go today [to Tahrir], you protect, I go tonight. People helped with logistics: speakers, computers, sleeping bags. We started to organise traffic in the neighbourhood. People tried to help drivers. Necessity is the mother of invention.

Ashraf Khalil (2011: 204) likewise emphasised the 'obvious pride and sense of community' that inspired the committees, quoting one of the leaders as saying: 'We don't need Mubarak. We don't need the army or police to protect us. This is the Egyptian people.'

Remembering the 'March of a million' on 1 February, Mona Abaza (2011) of Cairo University similarly reflected on the way protesters governed themselves, with no police to control them:

Words fail me to describe how more than some 2 million people marched peacefully and in an orderly manner towards one main space: the Tahrir Square. The organization was spectacular. A clear sense of order was masterminded by the young protesters to penetrate and then move through the square in a peaceful way. It was most remarkable. The people were amazing in their care for each other so that nothing would go wrong.

On the Square, security was similarly overseen by volunteers and activists. As an Aljazeera reporter (Aljazeera 2011c) observed on 8 February:

On the perimetre [*sic*] of the square, teams of men—most ranging in age from early 20s to mid-40s—guard barricades made of debris and form checkpoints to ensure identification of guards and give thorough pat-downs to make sure no one brings in weapons. Some wear laminated badges bearing the Egyptian flag, others identify their job—"Security"—with a piece of tape. Such checkpoints sprang up from the beginning of the occupation and now co-ordinate with army troops who mostly stand on the side and observe proceedings.

This brief revolutionary moment in Tahrir and Cairo more broadly perfectly illustrates Magnusson's argument (2011: 119) about the need to reclaim security from the central state:

Cities can scarcely exist without policing in some form ... How this is done has varied a great deal, however: only in the last couple of centuries has the modern system of policing become the norm. Although sovereign authority may have become important in this regard, effective policing still depends on an organic relation between the police and the population, and that usually means keeping the state at a distance and allowing local authorities to assert control. So, the policing function is as much an effect of self-organization as is everything else in the city.

The absence of state security (leaving aside the army which, by and large, stood by, a few interventions notwithstanding) thus had the effect of creating a security system that was self-selecting, self-governing and without overarching authority.

Security aside, the way Tahrir was organised similarly displayed a remarkable level of self-governance. Once the Square was occupied, ad hoc organisational mechanisms were developed. Significantly, these mechanisms comprised both activists and non-activists, thus going beyond the usual domination of governance by political elites. Makeshift hospitals, a water point and a kindergarten were set up, operated by volunteers and stocked by voluntary donations. An artists' space was created to display revolutionary art (Wynne-Hughes, Interview 2011). A 'wall of martyrs' was erected. Electrical points were made available to bloggers and tweeters, by siphoning electricity off the Square's electricity lines. Once the internet had returned, someone 'set up a pair of wireless networks called Revolution 1 and Revolution 2', while 'others assembled a video system and showed movies late at night on an improvised bedsheet screen' (Khalil 2011: 247). A central media office was established (Ezzat, Interview 2011; BBC 2011b). One could even get a selection of basic foodstuffs, as illustrated by a protester tweeting: 'At Tahrir sq. you can find pop corn, couscous, sweet potatoes, sandwiches, tea & drinks! Egyptians know how to revolt!' (Idle and Nunns 2011: 157).

A revolutionary committee (which was later to become the Coalition of the Youth of the Revolution) was established to coordinate the overall organisation and collaboration between activist networks. Yet this committee was dependent on activists and non-activists accepting its authority; its remit was limited; it had no means to coerce anyone into obedience; and it had to negotiate with both the activist networks and the Square's inhabitants, permanent as well as temporary. For instance, Ezzat (Interview 2011) told us how:

[I became] a representative of the local citizens [those living on the Square], part of the committee organising the Square: garbage collection, gas cylinders (how to get them in? When you live on the Square, you need to bring cylinders in). I negotiated with an officer on a tank on Talat Harb. I liaised with the security committee, shifts, how to alert. The number of people living on the Square is not large; 6 out of 38 living in my building, the rest are offices, shops. It was difficult to get cylinders, because the local shop was closed. Many on the Square are old; for example, I live with my mother. ... Some left after Black Wednesday.

When asked how she came to be on the committee, she answered:

I went to the central point of the Muslim Brotherhood and April 6, the coordinators and told them: I live on the Square, we need to sort out things. Who is in charge? Hundreds of kilos of rubbish bags, toilets had very heavy use. We needed hygienic support: soap, toilet paper.

When garbage became a pressing issue, people like Ezzat stepped in, using their own social networks to come up with a solution:

We started to recycle after 10 days. The first piles of garbage were removed by the army. ... After that, the army said: this is none of our business. We had contacts with NGOs, including in the Zebelin area in Moqattam, a central recycling area [an area called colloquially 'garbage city']. Garbage is a fortune for them. They sent trucks. It happened on the spot, organically. Recycling is done by garbage people.

The setting up of a recycling system is another instance of new practices being inscribed on to a specific space. As anyone who has been to Cairo will attest, there is no established system of recycling with bins visible everywhere. An extensive recycling network does exist, but it is managed by those who collect the garbage, and then sorted through at their depots (known as 'garbage city'). The recycling in Tahrir was an innovation to this pre-existing system. The trash and recycling was collected, and to some degree sorted, and then provided to the garbage/recycling collectors who would take it to their depots for processing. A pre-existing and local system was augmented by an ad hoc voluntary process developed not only to keep the Square clean and support the livelihoods of a class of workers, but to create the blueprint for the kind of society the protesters sought (Ezzat, Interview 2011; Wynne-Hughes, Interview 2011). This was another example of 'trial by space', inscribing new values on to a space to challenge the prevailing values inscribed by the existing regime.

In addition to non-activists taking leadership, they also contributed to the uprising in different ways. We already discussed how concerned citizens brought bags of staple food and medicines (Chapter 5). An owner of a travel agency on the Square 'emptied his office and gave permission for doctors to use it as a clinic' (Idle and Nunns 2011: 180). On 9 February, one person tweeted: 'Hundreds of protestors now sweeping the floors of Tahrir, others collecting garbage and some are washing the pavements' (2011: 188).[10] Soueif (2012: 143) recalls how, on 3 February, 'everyone walking to Tahrir is carrying something: blankets, bottles of water, medical supplies. Lots of us are taking mobile charge cards for the people in the sit-in.'

While there were coordinated calls for help from various activist networks, there was no central authority overseeing this process and much of it was spontaneous. A poignant illustration of this is that too many of the same basic items were sent into the Square (Ezzat, Interview 2011). These were ad hoc responses of people taking responsibility for each other, of people acting in concert without overarching authority: it was politics without sovereignty.

While nascent lines of authority were being established on the Square, this authority was not based on a rigidly hierarchical sovereign model, backed up by force, but more along the lines of politics that exists without a singular locus of sovereignty, with multiple centres of political authority negotiating with citizens practising self-government and communal common sense.

Multiplicity of Political Authorities

This leads us to the second aspect of urban politics:

Urban life has a logic of its own, a logic that tends to impose itself on the authorities. Nonetheless, there is another aspect of this: namely, the proliferation of autonomous or semi-autonomous political authorities, whose authorizations are from many different sources. One of Foucault's insights was that sovereign centres tend to be effaced by the proliferation of governmentalities, each of which has its own specific logic. (Magnusson 2011: 24)

This stands in sharp contrast to the hierarchy of authorities typical of state structures. Domestic politics and its corresponding spaces are traditionally understood according to a specific type of hierarchy. Magnusson (2011: 3), writing in direct reference to James Scott's (1998) work, explains:

When I *see like a state*, I see three things immediately:

The world is divided into states, each of which has its own territory and claims to sovereignty in relation to it.

Within each state, there is a hierarchy of authority, so that there is always a final authority with respect to issues in dispute.

Within each state, everything and everyone is ultimately subject to the state's authority; in that sense, the state is sovereign.

The implication of this intellectual framework is that politics exists only to the extent that it revolves around a sovereign claim to central and overarching authority. Moreover, a further implication is that political spaces exist in specific sites, each of which exists in relation to a space above or below it, with generally identifiable boundaries separating the sites. It is in this regard that it becomes possible to isolate economic spaces from political spaces, for example, or to define politics as necessarily hierarchical responses on the basis of hypothetical assumptions about the conduct of rational agents in a presumed state of nature.[11]

On Tahrir, despite being affectionately called 'Republic of Tahrir' by some of the protesters themselves (Aljazeera 2011c), no single political authority was in control, nor was there a clear hierarchy of authorities and political spaces. The revolutionary committee nominally oversaw relations with the external world and provided a focal point for organisation on the Square, as illustrated by Ezzat seeking them out when she wanted something done. But the committee seemed to be relatively peripheral to the organisation of daily life on the Square, and there were multiple other groups, some ad hoc, taking it upon themselves to organise the Square. Consider this eyewitness report from an Aljazeera journalist, posted on 8 February (Aljazeera 2011c):

We are discouraged from filming by a tired-looking protester whose head is wrapped in a black-and-white checkered keffiyeh. He apologises profusely but tells us he does not want the rest of the world to think that the square is some kind of festival. ... The man tells us there is no committee that organises the supply of Tahrir; people simply take initiative. Friends pool money, and those with funds make purchases for the poor. ... Many of the volunteers in the square simply offer food for free. As we sit on unfolded newspapers in the centre of the square speaking with Nasser Abdel Hamid, a member of the new youth negotiating committee, we are handed long bread with La vache qui rit cheese and pieces of grainy, "baladi" bread packed with sweet, peanut butter-style spread. We are approached by a young man who asks if he can interrupt briefly. Seif, a student at the Bahareyya Academy university, offers to help us find blankets, food and medicine if we plan on spending the night. He says he

267

is not a member of a committee, just a volunteer. He and his friends pooled $847 to buy medicine for protesters in the square.

Besides the revolutionary committee, there were the various protest networks with their own, typically diffuse, decision-making dynamics; the popular committees who oversaw security in Cairo's different regions (and further afield as well); and concerned citizens taking communal responsibility. Each of these operated in different, though overlapping spaces, with no clear hierarchy established between them.

In the absence of hierarchy, the 'republic of Tahrir' was closer to the idealised notion of the ancient Greek city republics than to the modern state republics we associate with the term—although even the Greek city-states had more hierarchy. There was neither a centralised authority nor a final authority in Tahrir. The governance system that made Tahrir function largely depended on the absence of systems of rule and on individuals volunteering contributions necessary for life in the Square to continue. Contributions came in from the very start. Yet there was no centralised call for donations of such things. Indeed, there was no authority to make such a call, nor was there (for a few days) even the technological means to communicate it. The absence of a central authority was part of the self-organising character of the new political spaces created by the protesters. For example, on 5 February, the tweeter, monasosh, tweeted, 'Rt now Tahrir sq, a meeting initially started wt 20 has turned into 200 discussion how 2 counter trashing campaign of national media' (Idle and Nunns 2011: 156). Soueif (2012: 160–1) similarly notes how 'everywhere there are circles of people sitting on the ground talking, discussing; ideas flowing from one group to the other until the most popular find their way to one of the four microphones on the stages'.

The makeshift hospitals on the Square appear likewise to have been products of people taking initiative, rather than having been set up by some central authority. A medical student (El-Said, Conversation 2011) told us how he had participated in setting up hospitals on the Square, but that the organisation seemed to have come out of nowhere. He recalled how it appeared to be the creation of a kind of revolutionary forum, although there was no one in particular leading the organising of the hospitals. It was because of this dynamic that the student described the Square as 'a utopian republic'.[12]

This type of non-hierarchical politics was partly a response by people to a vacuum of authority, pulling together in the face of adversity.

But for the activists behind the revolution, it was also an intentional departure from politics as usual. Soueif (2012: 148–9) remembers the Square as 'a space for debate', where the views of the 'older people' who were 'still hopeful for democracy' and 'the representative government they've longed for all their lives' are countered by some of the *shabab* [youth] who 'argue that we're beyond ... the old forms of democracy; that for the last twenty years every movement with energy has come from outside the traditional frameworks, that the static structures of the nation-state and the fluid power of capital cannot coexist without leading to repression'. Soueif concludes that 'what we have in Tahrir is the opposite of vacuum; we have a bazaar of ideas on the ground'. Others similarly commented on the almost utopian, deliberative, non-hierarchical nature of decision-making on the Square (Fouad, Interview 2011; G. Ibrahim 2011). More sceptically, one anonymous (2011) interviewee said that the Square was not necessarily 'a new Egypt'.

The downside of this lack of a clearly circumscribed political authority was that, when it came to negotiating with the regime, there was no mechanism by which to delegate authority. As Soueif (2012: 172) acutely observes:

We're in a catch-22 situation: there is no mechanism for Tahrir to select and mandate a group to talk to SCAF. So separate 'leaderships' are taking it upon themselves to do it. And the talks are private; which means that anyone who talks to SCAF now automatically loses credibility with the Midan.

One of the reasons for the temporary nature of the experiment in Tahrir was arguably this lack of mechanisms by which to authorise a leadership, which carried legitimacy on the Square, to deal with the outside world. For while it was accepted that legitimacy flowed from representing Tahrir—one of the popular chants was, tellingly, '*al-shar'iyya min al-tahrir*' [Legitimacy comes from Tahrir] (Soueif 2012: 148)—no consensus was reached on how to establish who represented Tahrir and what were legitimate ways of engaging the regime. However, this situation was problematic not because the political space of Tahrir was fundamentally flawed because of its lack of hierarchy, but because of the difficulties involved in creating a communicating language for negotiations between this 'non-sovereign' politics and the sovereign politics of the Egyptian state. Ultimately, the state won this negotiation, but Tahrir remains a powerful symbol for a different kind of politics that the state cannot ignore.

Practices of self-Government Enabling Civilised Order

The absence of a singular sovereignty clearly did not inhibit the establishment of civilised order. On the contrary, it seemed to enhance it by enabling self-government. Soueif and Ashraf Khalil both attest to the civilised nature of security provisions during those fourteen days, with volunteers at the numerous road blocks treating passers-by with politeness and good cheer, although Khalil also documents cases of middle-class volunteers roughing up those looking poor, out of fear that they were pro-Mubarak thugs. Khalil (2011: 248), for instance, writes:

The searches of those entering the square were incredibly thorough and exceedingly polite. During that final week of the revolution, Tahrir Square was more secure than most international airports. ... Once you made it through all the security procedures, you were greeted by a clapping and cheering crowd welcoming you to "liberated ground."

Soueif (2012: 159) recalls:

Once you're inside, the Midan is amazing. ... Everyone is suddenly, miraculously, completely themselves. Everyone understands. We're all very gentle with each other. As though we're convalescing, dragged back from death's door. Our selves are in our hands, precious, newly recovered, perhaps fragile; we know we must be careful of our own and of each other's.

The Midan is sparkling clean. The rubbish is piled neatly on the periphery with notices on it saying 'NDP Headquarters'. ... Lamp posts have put out wires so that laptops and mobiles can be charged. The field hospitals provide free medical care and advice for everyone. A placard reading 'Barber of the Revolution' guides you to a free shave and a haircut. A giant transparent wall of plastic pockets has gone up. The shabab sit next to it. People tell them jokes and they draw or write them and slot them into the pockets; a rising tide of jokes and cartoons. ... A man eats fire. There's face painting and music and street theatre and a poetry stand.

This image of a hyper-civilised, almost utopian Tahrir came up repeatedly in our interviews. Whether this retrospective image matched the actual lived experience on the Square is in many ways a moot point; what matters, now that the experience has ended, is the memory, which leads us to the fourth of Magnusson's points.

Order is Always Temporary and Local

Although Magnusson is making a more general point about the fundamental contingency of order, in the case of Tahrir Square the revolutionary order described above was local and temporary in a specific way. On the one hand, it lasted only fourteen days and, in its specifics, was confined to Tahrir Square and its barricaded borders. The recycling service, for instance, was specific to Tahrir Square at the time. Similarly, the public harassment of women resumed the moment the occupation was over. On the other hand, the order of Tahrir both outlasted those fourteen days and influenced the order of spaces not only all across Egypt, but also globally (albeit in very specific temporary and local instances). But because we are talking about practices, representations and lived experiences, and not simply about a physical space, what developed on the Square could travel beyond the Square. But inevitably, once transported, it changed, if only because the physical space and its relation with other spaces, practices and norms changed.

The spatial practices and conceptions of Tahrir were both real and imaginary, and in their imaginary form they encompassed all of Egypt. They did happen, but it was the dream of an idealised Egypt in Tahrir spreading across Egypt that gave it such an important place in both the memory of those there and in the imagination of people elsewhere. The spatial politics in Tahrir were not just about Tahrir, but about spreading the ideal of Tahrir across Egypt. In this sense, the political space of Tahrir was not limited to the boundaries of the physical square but encompassed all Egypt. Emblematic of this sentiment was a placard proclaiming 'All Egypt is Tahrir Square' (Gröndahl 2011: 114). The placard included a picture of the Square with arrows pointing out from each of the exits morphing into people dressed in the colours of the Egyptian flag. In subsequent calls for the continuation of the revolution, Tahrir Square was likewise linked to all Egypt's squares. Consider for example this call, issued later in 2011: 'The youth of the revolution call for all citizens to come to Tahrir Square and all the squares of Egypt to fulfill the demands of the revolution in order to preserve the blood of the revolutionaries spilled for the sake of complete freedom' (Tahrir Documents 2011b). Or a leaflet stating: 'The revolution has returned to all of Egypt's squares and streets yet again to complete its course' (Tahrir Documents 2011a).

Tahrir also became a global symbol of resistance to oppression (see also Ramadan 2013). Pearl Roundabout in Manama, Bahrain, was renamed Tahrir Square (Euronews 2011). The original call to occupy Wall Street in September 2011, posted by the counterculture magazine *Adbusters* from Vancouver, British Columbia, Canada, on 13 July

2011, was sub-headed, 'Are you ready for a Tahrir moment?' (Stack-pole 2011). The 15-M anti-austerity protests in Spain in May 2011 similarly took their cue from Tahrir Square, although in both instances local protest traditions and transnational influences affected how the protests developed (Aljazeera 2011f; DTSG 2011). Moreover, many of those who occupied the Square in February 2011 saw themselves as part of a revolutionary global vanguard, as illustrated by key activists travelling to New York to help the Occupy Wall Street movement (*Wired* 2011; Huffington Post 2011).[13] Thus, while the specifics of Tahrir Square were local, the practices and representations of Tahrir Square have had a global reach, though mediated by local and transnational factors.

The utopian Egypt in the Square did not last in empirical terms, even if it remains in the minds of those who experienced it. Consequently, Tahrir poses a particularly difficult problem to understand in that, what it was, it is no longer, but it represents what could be and what many of the protesters still seek. The politics in Tahrir were real, but fleeting, and in their temporary character have become almost a 'simulacra of [reality]' (Keith and Pile 1993: 26).[14] *That* Tahrir no longer exists, even if the urban geography of Tahrir remains unchanged. In this sense Tahrir represents a kind of 'imagined geography' (Keith and Pile 1993: 18) in both spatial and identity terms, giving rise both to 'revolutionary tourism' and to re-enactments of those revolutionary days in subsequent clashes between different power blocs. To be able to occupy the Square subsequently was to increase one's political legitimacy, to be able to claim to be acting on behalf of the 'real' Egypt.[15] Subsequent demonstrations, moreover, often sought to emulate the practices of the original occupation, from setting up checkpoints around the Square to ensure no weapons entered the space, to erecting tents and stages, to shouting similar slogans and unfurling the same metres-long Egyptian flags.[16]

Concluding Thoughts

As we have seen in the two years since the revolutionary moment of early 2011, the authority of the sovereign state of Egypt has been continuously challenged by protesters who have been invigorated by the example of Tahrir Square and who take their authority from Tahrir, rather than from the state. It is too soon to be able to say where these contestations will lead. But what is clear is that the revolution has created urban spaces and related practices where multiple authorities, however asymmetric, compete with each other and where citizens practise a level of self-government, that however truncated, is limited and inconsistent over time.

While the conclusion of the revolution is still unfolding, the impact of Tahrir is unmistakable. What transpired in this traffic rotary in the centre of Cairo captured the hearts and minds of people worldwide in large measure because it was a political space that was powerful due to the absence inside it of state sovereignty and state power. The events in Tahrir Square should give us pause to think about how political space is understood and especially how it is valued. The overarching tendency is to see politics from the perspective of the state, to privilege the statist ordering of a sovereign that Arendt saw as tyrannical and anti-political, and that Magnusson notes is out of touch with how politics actually takes place. The events on Tahrir challenged this statist view and reveal that political spaces sometimes matter the most precisely when they are without state sovereignty.

8

A FACEBOOK REVOLUTION?

As events unfolded in Tunisia and then Egypt, it became popular to call them 'Facebook Revolutions.' There is of course a long tradition of linking political change to technological innovations. In 1957, for example, the famous sociologist William Ogburn (1957: 12) wrote:

That technological change is considered a cause of social change is indicated by various expressions often heard. Gunpowder destroyed feudalism. Railroads created cities. The steam engine increased divorce. The automobile is moving the department store and the supermarket to the suburbs. The airplane reranked the great military powers.

One might be tempted to add Facebook to this list as having sparked the Egyptian revolution. Wael Ghonim put this most forcefully in an interview with CNN, saying: 'This revolution started on Facebook. ... I've always said that if you want to liberate a society just give them the Internet' (quoted in Smith 2011). Most commentators were more cautious, arguing that social media merely provided a tool enabling activists to act more effectively, accelerating an otherwise already explosive situation (cf. Schenker and Khalili 2011; Gustin 2011). Nevertheless, the term 'Facebook Revolution' has stuck, even warranting its own Wikipedia (n.d.) entry, and the notion that social media inherently empower people while undermining autocracies remains prevalent.

There are two reasons why the notion of a 'Facebook Revolution' is particularly appealing to Western audiences. The first has to do with access. As Facebook and Twitter have grown, they have become the

275

media of choice to communicate mass protests as they unfold. International media rely heavily on Facebook and Twitter for such events, giving these media greater visibility and significance than they may have on the ground in the emergence, organisation and evolution of mass protests. Classic cases are the two 2009 'Twitter Revolutions' in Moldova and Iran. In Moldova, critics pointed out, few people had Twitter accounts, limiting the role Twitter could play in people's mobilisation (Gladwell 2010). In Iran, many Western journalists interpreted the availability of English-language tweets as an indication of the central role of Twitter, leading Mark Pfeifle, a former US National Security adviser, to nominate Twitter for the Nobel Peace Prize, saying that 'without Twitter the people of Iran would not have felt empowered and confident to stand up for freedom and democracy'. This, according to Golnaz Esfandiari, was a fallacy based on a fundamental misreading of the role of Twitter in Iran:

Western journalists who couldn't reach—or didn't bother reaching?—people on the ground in Iran simply scrolled through the English-language tweets post with tag #iranelection ... Through it all, no one seemed to wonder why people trying to coordinate protests in Iran would be writing in any language other than Farsi. (Both quoted in Gladwell 2010)

That a revolution is tweeted or called for on Facebook is not in itself proof of the centrality of these media in organising, let alone causing, the revolution.

The second reason that the term 'Facebook Revolution' appeals to certain audiences, particularly in the West, is that information technology is seen by many as an important tool in the spread of liberal democratic values, a view rooted in a belief in the emancipatory potential of information technology.[1] In a book focused on information technology and political Islam, Philip Howard (2010: 11) wrote how:

Information and communication technology are the infrastructure for transposing democratic ideals from community to community. They support the process of learning new approaches to political representation, of testing new organizational strategies, and of cognitively extending the possibilities and prospects for political transformation from one context to another.

Thus even in literature that is concerned with authoritarian states in the Middle East and elsewhere, there remains this Habermasian association between the spread of information technology and the development of modern liberal democratic states, although Howard (2010: 12) himself cautions that 'technology alone does not cause political change …'. Clay Shirky's article in *Foreign Affairs* displays a similar ambiguity.

While acknowledging that 'the use of social media tools … does not have a single preordained outcome' (2011: 29), the article clearly links information technology to the promotion of freedom in its subtitle. However, information technology is not inherently emancipatory (cf. Murphy 2009). Increases in information technology have enhanced state surveillance capacities. Information technology can similarly be exclusionary or be used to infringe other people's rights by posting inflammatory, discriminatory or terrorising content (see also Murphy 2009: 1137–8).

The internet and social media have certainly given new means of political communication to activists. As Lynch (2011: 307) observes:

The strongest case for the fundamentally transformative effects of the new media may lie in the general emergence of a public sphere capable of eroding the ability of states to monopolize information and argument, of pushing for transparency and accountability, and of facilitating new networks across society.

Tufekci and Wilson (2012: 365) link this back to the problems of collective action in an authoritarian state:

Authoritarian regimes not only discourage individual participation by greatly increasing the punishments for dissent, but also control the communicative infrastructure in ways that make it difficult for citizens to coordinate effective collective opposition or to express their dissent in the public sphere. Social media alter the key tenets of collective action … and, in doing so, create new vulnerabilities for even the most durable of authoritarian regimes.

By facilitating coordination and the expression of dissent, social media are thus potentially corrosive to authoritarian regimes. Yet, they offer a paradox. On the one hand, they encourage instant and interactive communication. On the other, the interaction that they encourage may tend away from physical protests toward staying at home and posting political commentary. Thus while social media facilitate debate, they may at the same time discourage offline activism (McCaughey and Ayers 2003: 4). A 'click' does not necessarily lead to a protester on the street.

In the Egyptian case, both dynamics were in evidence. For many, social media enhanced and increased communication with people they otherwise would not have met (cf. the theoretical point made by McCaughey and Ayers 2003: 5). For others, social media offered a ready-made community and outlet that meant they felt less compelled to go out on to the streets (Anonymous, Interview 2011).

In Egypt, moreover, millions have no access to the internet. Many of those who came down from their balconies in the cities' poorer quarters had no regular internet access. Many of the workers, who dealt the deathblow to Mubarak's rule by bringing the country's industry and transport to a standstill in the final days of the revolution, were similarly not internet users.

The question of the extent to which this was a Facebook Revolution has been much commented upon in the press and in academia. There are indeed many questions about the role of technology in the Egyptian revolt. How was technology used by the protesters? How important was the use of social media to the outbreak of the revolt? To what extent did technology contribute to the development of new networks, identities and frames that were instrumental in the organisation of the revolt? How did the state use technology in its attempts to retain (and regain) authority and control?

Our aim in this section is not to cover this topic exhaustively but to reflect briefly on the various ways in which the use of social media affected the Egyptian revolution from a social movement theory perspective. Our focus is purely on the role of social media in the mobilisation of protesters in January 2011, not on its role prior to 2011, its impact on wider society or the international community, or the question of emancipation (except where these topics relate to the protest's dynamics). Nor will we discuss the way the regime used social media to counter the revolution, from monitoring the internet or shutting it down, to flooding it with counter-information and 'trolls'. Because of a dearth of data on how Egyptians use social media, much of the following is speculative.

When we talk about 'social media' we primarily focus on interactive websites or apps such as Facebook and Twitter. Mobile telephones feature to the extent that they are capable of capturing images and accessing the internet. Our narrow focus is purely pragmatic, for reasons of methodology and space. It is not meant to imply that other forms of information and communication technology are unimportant, or that social media exist in a vacuum. In this, we agree with Tufekci and Wilson (2012: 364–7) that 'the connectivity infrastructure should be analyzed as a complex ecology rather than in terms of any specific platform or device', and that it includes satellite TV, internet-based platforms and mobile phones, and interacts with offline networks.

The Limits of Social Media

Before reflecting on social media's role, it is important to establish how widespread its use was. In 2010, there were a reported 22 million internet users in Egypt, according to the World Bank, or 26.7 per every 100 Egyptians (Figure 8.1). Castells (2011) suggests, on the basis of a study by information company Ovum, that this figure is 40 per cent for Egyptians over sixteen, and 70 per cent for young urban dwellers (taking into account access at cyber-cafés and internet-enabled mobile phones). Merlyna Lim similarly quotes a study which found that 64 per cent of households in Cairo had internet access (Lim 2012: 235). With an estimated 70 per cent of Egyptians living on less than $4 a day, a 40 per cent illiteracy rate (Khamis, Gold and Vaughn 2012: 7), vast swathes of urban populations not accounted for in official statistics and reports from people on the ground suggesting that internet usage was limited, we are somewhat sceptical that these figures reflect regular users accurately. Moreover, the number of registered Facebook users in 2010 was far less, standing at 4.6 million by December according to Facebook data retrieved by Nick Burcher (2012) (Figure 8.2; Lim 2012: 235 puts this figure at 5 million, but his data appear to be over-estimations).

Facebook is only one of the various social media used by Egyptians. But given Facebook's prominence in accounts of the revolution, it is significant that the number of Facebook users was considerably less than the number of people who participated in street protests (15–20 million). The number of Facebook users following opposition pages

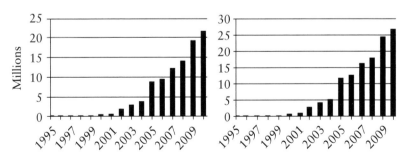

Figure 8.1: Internet users, in absolute numbers and per 100 people (World Bank n.d.).

279

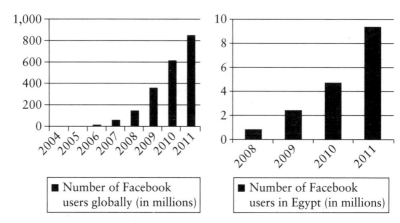

Figure 8.2: Number of Facebook users in millions worldwide and in Egypt (Facebook n.d.; Burcher 2012; all figures in second graph refer to number of Facebook users in December of the relevant year).

was even less. The largest opposition webpage, 'We Are All Khaled Said', for instance, had 365,000–400,000 followers by January 2011 (Ghonim 2012: 142; Eaton 2012: 5), although the call to revolution reportedly reached 700,000 Facebook users (Ghonim 2012: 146).

Illustrating the limited role of Facebook in both communicating the revolution and shaping people's views, a poll conducted in April 2011 found that only 15 per cent of respondents listed Facebook among their three most important sources of information during the revolution, while only 6 per cent listed it as their most important source (Table 10.1). By contrast, television was mentioned by 97 per cent of respondents (with 84 per cent listing it as most important), and word of mouth by 72 per cent (only 6 per cent listed this as most important, but 43 per cent cited it as their second most important source).

Another survey, conducted two weeks after the ousting of Mubarak and focused on protesters, yielded very different results (Table 10.2). According to this survey, 80 per cent of those interviewed had internet access at home and 52 per cent had access via their phones. A more detailed analysis (Table 10.3) suggests that 52 per cent used Facebook in general and 51 per cent used it to communicate about the protests. The figures for e-mail, Twitter and blogs for general use were 83, 16 and 15 per cent, but this dropped to 27, 13 and 12 per cent for protest communication. By comparison, satellite TV and phones scored 92 and 82

Table 10.1: The three most important information sources relied upon during the January 25 events (IRI Poll 2011).

	Single Most Important	Second Most Important	Third Most Important	Total
Television	84%	10%	3%	97%
Word of Mouth from Family/Friends	6%	43%	23%	72%
Facebook	6%	6%	3%	15%
Internet News Sites	2%	7%	4%	13%
SMS	1%	13%	14%	28%
Radio	1%	8%	7%	16%
Newspapers	0%	7%	9%	16%
Email	0%	0%	1%	2%
Twitter	0%	0%	0%	1%

Table 10.2: Sample characteristics of survey carried out by Tufekci and Wilson (2012).

	Males (n=792)	Females (n=258)	Total (N =1,050)
Mean age	29.1 (9.3)	26.6 (7.6)	28.5 (8.9)
Mean education	5.1 (1.6)	5.6 (1.2)	5.3 (1.6)
Percentage with internet at home	77	90	80
Percentage with internet on phone	50	57	52
Percentage present on first day of protests	38	33	36
Percentage who had previously attended protests	34	33	34

per cent for communicating about the protests (94 and 92 per cent for general use), while texts scored 46 per cent (62 per cent for general use).

If these figures are representative of the protesters (the authors note that 'perhaps the best that can be said is that team members believed that the sample was similar in demographic terms to those they had witnessed demonstrating at Tahrir Square') (2012: 368), this would suggest that the protesters were disproportionately drawn from those with internet access, and in particular Facebook access, with the implication that access to the internet was a strong predictor of protest participation (even though satellite TV and phones continued to dominate communication).

Table 10.3: Media usage spread by purpose and gender in percentage points (Tufekci and Wilson 2012).

	Use In General			For Communicating About Protests		
	Male (n=792)	Female (n=258)	Total (N=1,050)	Male (n=792)	Female (n=258)	Total (N=1,050)
Blog	14	18	15	10	16	12
E-mail	83	85	83	25	33	27
Facebook	49	60	52	48	60	51
Phone	92	93	92	80	87	82
Print	64	59	63	59	52	58
Satellite TV	93	94	94	92	93	92
Text	61	67	62	46	49	46
Twitter	15	20	16	11	19	13

Indeed, Tufekci and Wilson (2012: 370–3) find that, while a majority of protesters had first heard about the protests through face-to-face communication (48.4 per cent), the next largest cohort (28.3 per cent) had read about it on Facebook compared to 13.1 per cent via their phones. More strikingly still, they found that 'the early participants in the Tahrir Square demonstrations tended to rely on blogs, Twitter, Facebook, phones, and e-mail for the information about the protests'.

Both these sets of findings are contradicted by what our interviewees told us about the central role played by the poorer, and generally less-connected, sectors of Egypt's urban populations in the revolution, and by the offline tactics the activists employed. We know that much of the mobilisation for the demonstrations of 25 and 28 January took place offline, in Cairo's poorer quarters and elsewhere. Some key protest networks, such as the independent workers' movement and the judiciary, only used social media marginally, whether for economic, habitual or security reasons (Khamis and Vaughn 2011). But even the internet-savvy youth activists spent much of their energy before the revolution on distributing old-fashioned leaflets, and spreading the word through the notoriously garrulous taxi drivers (cf. Lim 2012: 243).[2] To mobilise the masses, those without Facebook access needed to be mobilised.

The numerical discrepancy between the small cohort of 'Facebook youth' and the general population was sharply exposed by the March 2011 referendum on amending the constitution and the results of the first post-revolution election. In both instances, the online youth were wildly out of step with the majority of voters, who were, among other factors, influenced by 'Islamist parties, such as the Muslim Brotherhood's al-Hurriya wa al-Adala (Freedom and Justice) party and the Salafi al-Nour (Light) party—both of which had relatively less online activism but much more on-the-ground organization' (Khamis, Gold and Vaughn 2012).

Many of those living in urban informal areas, which are typically undercounted in the type of statistics Tufekci and Wilson draw on, have no or irregular internet access. Elisa Wynne-Hughes (Interview 2011), the British resident PhD student, told us for instance that:

When talking to some people in poor areas, and mentioning about posting photos on Facebook, they commented 'Do you know about Facebook?' 'She knows about everything here in Egypt.' Many have no access to Facebook or know what is on it, especially before 25 January 2011. So, the Facebook generation is limited. The question is how Facebook spread beyond its users.

Despite the importance of the 'Facebook youth' in organising the revolution, it was the general (urban) population that made this a mass demonstration, and their mobilisation was done mostly offline. We know from groups such as April 6 that they had made a concerted effort during 2010 (and before) to establish face-to-face links with potential allies who did not have an online presence, particularly people living in Cairo's poorer quarters (Maher, Interview 2011; April 6 Cadres, Conversation 2011).

We do not know the precise make-up of the protesters, or how many of the 90,000–100,000 who had signed up to the protest online (BBC 2012a; Ghonim 2012: 160) actually joined. But if the claims youth leaders reportedly made to the leaders of political opposition parties in the aftermath of the Friday of Rage are anything to go by, the youth networks only contributed 20 per cent of the total crowds (Soueif 2012: 47–8). If this is so, and if a significant percentage of the remainder of the crowds was made up of Egyptians with no or irregular internet access, it is likely that only a minority of protesters had in fact been mobilised or informed by social media directly.

In addition, the 'Facebook youth' intentionally avoided the internet when discussing their tactical plans, in the knowledge that the government monitored the internet (Salah, Interview 2011; Maher, Interview 2011; Ghazali-Harb, Interview 2011; Khamis and Vaughn 2011). The very idea of publishing decoy meeting places on Facebook to confuse the police was born out of this knowledge. Leaflets distributed prior to the protests, detailing the protest's goals, how to protest, how to protect oneself against police violence and how to organise, tellingly warned recipients not to distribute them via Twitter or Facebook: 'Please distribute through e-mail printing, and photocopies ONLY. Twitter and facebook are being monitored. Be careful not to let this fall into the hands of the police or state security' (Leaflet 2011). Ghonim (2012: 82, 102–3, 114–16) talks of his constant fear of being found out as the administrator of the 'We Are All Khaled Said' Facebook page, and the advanced technology he used to conceal his computer's IP address. The use of social media was thus self-consciously limited by the core activist leadership.

Crucially, the claim we are making here is different from the claims of others, such as Tim Eaton (2012: 9), who argues that:

Social media was able to reach *enough* people to get significant numbers into the street and the movement into the mainstream. Once it reached the streets, it collected Egyptians from all sectors of society offering an outlet for the widespread latent dissent present among the citizenry. ... Some analysts have suggested that the fact that protests continued without the internet shows that online activism was in fact of little importance. But this misses the point. By getting people into the streets in significant numbers in the first place, the damage had already been done.

The mobilisation of '*enough* people to get significant numbers into the street' seems to have occurred in the narrow streets, away from the decoy meeting points where the 'virtual followers' amassed, involving a significant number of people with little or no internet access who were mobilised through face-to-face calls.

Prior to January 2011, social media had had only limited success in mobilising people for street protests. One of the reasons the 'Khaled Said' Facebook campaign is so remarkable is precisely because it was among the few success stories of social media-driven mobilisation, and even then, it failed to turn its online community into a coherent activist organisation. As Mostafa Fouad (Interview 2011), an April 6 member, put it, 'It's only a Facebook group, not a movement.' Yet even Fouad's own movement was only partially successful in translating online support into offline activism before 2011. Whatever role social media played in 2011, it was thus clearly only one factor among others.

One of the well-known challenges for online campaigns is to translate online support into offline activism—although we recognise that on- and offline is intricately interlinked in what could be termed a 'hybrid' world (Wellman and Rainie quoted in Castells 2012: 232), even for those without internet access.[3] According to Malcolm Gladwell (2010), summarising research by social movement theorists, this difficulty stems from social media facilitating weak links among large, but loose, networks. Weak links with thousands of people are useful for spreading information and increasing low-risk participation. But they do not necessarily produce the motivation and commitment to take high-risk action. From the US Civil Rights Movement and the East German pro-democracy protests to the Italian Red Brigades, strong ties and discipline born from commitment were what sustained protests. Critiquing the social media orthodoxy, Gladwell (2010: 46) writes:

"Social networks are particularly effective at increasing motivation," Aaker and Smith write. But that's not true. Social networks are effective at increasing *participation*—by lessening the level of motivation that participation requires. ... [Social media activism] is simply a form of organizing which favors the weak-tie connections that give us access to information over the strong-tie connections that help us persevere in the face of danger.

Protest dynamics before January 2011 by and large seem to confirm Gladwell's conclusion, a conclusion that is corroborated by research on the transnational Global Justice Movement, which similarly finds weak ties diffused across loose online networks (although in that case weak ties did not prevent mass protests, as the maintenance of multiple weak online ties enabled rapid reactivation of such ties across multiple networks, many of which had strong offline counterparts) (cf. Bennett 2005; della Porta and Mosca 2005: 114–15; Baringhorst 2008: 75–8). That people responded to revolutionary calls on Facebook in 2011 thus seems to have more to do with the context within which these calls were issued, than with the fact that Facebook was used.

Finally, it is important to underline that social media platforms were shut down by the regime during the most crucial days of the revolution. At around 5:20 p.m. on 27 January, internet traffic to and from Egypt dropped from a high usage of over 2500 MBps to just a notch above zero (*Wall Street Journal* 2011). Significantly, rather than strangling the revolution, this had the effect of encouraging people to go out on to the streets, bridging the gap between online and offline communities. As Ahmed Saleh (Interview 2011) noted, it was in part the shutting down of social media that gave the revolution a significant additional impetus:

Pre-revolution, Facebook played a huge role in mobilising the middle class [especially after the death of Khaled Said]. But there is a huge gap between this class and real people. These two communities met when the Internet was shut down. That was a huge government mistake. If you are an Internet activist, you click 'like' and you feel great. But without the Internet, you go out. Then you feel great on the street, and you build momentum. It helped the revolution.

Al-Masry al-Youm (2011d) quoted an activist making the same argument:

"The virtual networks created over social networks like Facebook and Twitter moved into the real world for the first time," explains Saif.

Once people turned to the streets, the process became organic with demonstrators meeting acquaintances and joining groups during their march to Tahrir Square... Word of mouth became the main tool for planning the next steps, confirmed Saif. Demonstrators at Tahrir agreed before they left to convene the next day at 3PM. As they walked home, they spread the word on the street.

The blackout did not wholly stop activists from using social media. Using landlines, international satellite phones, dial-up modems, FTP (file transfer protocol) accounts and 'Speak to Tweet', activists succeeded in bypassing the blackout and keeping the world's media informed of unfolding events in Egypt. Even the stock exchange's network, which the regime kept running, was utilised, with subscribers disabling their passwords to enable protesters to use their accounts (Khamis and Vaughn 2011; Khamis, Gold and Vaughn 2012). But the blackout forced social media users to focus primarily on communicating with the external world, beyond Egypt—which in turn fed into the perception that this was a Facebook Revolution.

Although the above suggests the role played by social media in organising the demonstrations was more limited than is often claimed, this does not mean that social media did not play a significant role.

Beyond the obvious of providing a platform for rapid, effective communication, whether exposing regime abuses, framing moral shocks or providing up-to-date details of protests, social media affected the way the protests evolved in a number of ways.

Communicating the Protests

The most obvious way in which social media influenced the revolution was through the provision of information that was otherwise unavailable, enabling protesters to communicate with each other as well as with the international media. Websites such as 'We Are All Khaled Said' spread information about Police Day, the aims of the revolution, how to protect oneself against police violence and so on. They fed the revolution by providing updates on the success of the protests as they developed, while Twitter provided real-time updates on tactics, locations and threats, such as police charges or sniper fire.

In the lead-up to the protests, the dissemination of text and images had helped in the development and spread of both injustice and action and motivational frames. This cognitive affect cannot be underestimated, both in terms of the attribution of threats and opportunities (crucial in the transformation of an 'objective' threat or opportunity into a subjectively recognised threat/opportunity) and in terms of suggesting ways of creatively responding to these threats and opportunities (cf. McAdam 1982: 48–51). Of particular importance was the way in which social media were used by activists to frame 'moral shocks' (Jasper and Poulsen 1995: 498; Jasper 2011: 292), such as the death of Khaled Said, the 2010 election fraud or the Alexandria bombing, in a way that legitimised anger and channelled it towards the regime (see Chapter 6 for a more detailed discussion of this).

Once the protests were under way, social media offered an instantly accessible source of real-time information about the protests. Heba Ezzat (Interview 2011), for instance, recalled that 'messages were sent round at 3–4 am [26 January] saying: people are still running [dodging the police] ... please put this on Facebook. This started a snowball. I was in Germany on the 25th. When I saw what was happening, I booked a return flight for the 27th.' Of those surveyed by Tufekci and Wilson (2012: 373), nearly half (48.2 per cent) had 'produced and disseminated video or pictures from political protest in the streets', with 'the leading platform for producing and disseminating visuals' being

Facebook (25 per cent), followed by phones (15 per cent). A survey carried out by the Dubai School of Government in March 2011, meanwhile, found 'that Egyptian Facebook users believed that nearly 85 percent of Facebook usage throughout the demonstrations was to organize activism, raise awareness and spread information about events as they happened' (Eaton 2012: 8).

Twitter was even more instrumental in passing on crucial information, ranging from 'practical information on the protests, such as weaknesses in the protesters' lines and instructions on how to deal with a tear gas attack, to defiant messages of commitment to the cause and even notices that they were about to get arrested' (Eaton 2012: 10). Tweets kept people up to date with what was happening, whether it concerned the progress of a street demonstration, a police charge on Tahrir, the tearing down of Mubarak posters in Alexandria or the death of protesters in Suez (cf. Idle and Nunns 2011: 38, 42, 43, 67). Illustrating the intensity with which Twitter was deployed during the protests, the main hashtag used by the revolutionaries, #jan25, had 'nearly 1.2 million tweets in the first quarter of 2011' (Eaton 2012: 10).

It was this avalanche of information from protesters themselves that shaped much of the international media's coverage of the Egyptian revolution and gave it its poignancy. It was also what fed the impression that this was a revolution run and fuelled by social media.

Crucially, just as in the 'offline' world, well-established websites that had been set up for other purposes were mobilised by the opposition networks for their cause. The 'Cairo Scholars' webportal, for example, which had been set up to help expats find housing and local information, came to be used to announce protest details (Wynne-Hughes, Interview 2011).

Informational Cascades and Protest Momentum

Of particular importance is the way social media helped to create a protest momentum among the internet-savvy middle-class youth prior to 25 January. Our anonymous interviewee (Anonymous Interview 2011) told us, for example, that 'even before the 25th, I thought it would be a big day that would develop into something big. ... If you had been following Facebook, people had started taking pictures and videos of themselves, saying: 'Protest on the 25th.' ... Just anyone, not just activists.' The 90,000–100,000 who signed up online for the 25 January protest event helped to create a sense that something big was afoot, as did the thousands who posted messages of support online or uploaded videos pledging they would be there.

Social media thus helped would-be protesters to overcome what social movement theorists call 'the prisoner dilemma' (Chapter 6): people had a much better insight into what others were thinking, and what they were planning to do, lowering the (perceived) risk of joining the protests. They knew that their opinions were shared by hundreds of thousands, and the intensity of online activity suggested that a considerable number of people were motivated to go out and protest (although intentions do not necessarily translate into action).

It was to a considerable extent social media's potential to 'go viral' that facilitated what Marc Lynch (2011: 304) calls, borrowing from the literature on social media and revolutions, an 'informational cascade'. The activists behind the revolution were well aware of this potential. Consider Ghonim's (2012: 43) reflections on choosing a Facebook page as opposed to a Facebook group:

> As an experienced Internet user, I knew that a Facebook page was much more effective in spreading information than a Facebook group. As soon as someone "likes" a page, Facebook considers the person and the page to be "friends." So if the "admin" of the page writes a post on the "wall," it appears on the walls of the page's fans. This is how ideas spread like viruses. ... In the case of groups, however, users have to access the group to remain updated; no information is pushed out to them.

It is this quality of being able to 'push' information to followers, who could then push it to their own networks that made social media so effective in creating an informational cascade that could then be interpreted as proof of protest momentum.

However, this informational cascade was of a particular type. It was more about creating an expectant momentum in the aftermath of Please put full word on one line and a year of deepening protests than about enabling people to realise that they were not alone. Lynch (2011: 304) argues:

> One of the major obstacles to mass protest is ubiquitous preference falsification: individuals who detest the regime refrain from making their views public out of fear of either social or official sanction. On this view, the increased public incidence of oppositional views online helps to encourage others who privately hold such views to express them in public.

In Egypt, the barrier of preference falsification had already been breached by Kefaya, the bloggers' movement, the workers' movement and others, years before 2011. What was needed was a change in 'calculations about the possibility of success' (Lynch 2011: 305)—and, we would add, a change in emotions and levels of identification.

Lynch (2011: 305), paradoxically, concludes that 'while there may have been informational cascades, they seem to have had only a secondary importance'. We would argue instead that cascades did play a role in creating a momentum for activism by flooding those using social media with calls for revolution, pledges of support and information about what was happening and who was participating, thus altering their calculations, emotions and sense of identification with the protesters.[4]

In addition to social media's viral potential, there are two further features that made it particularly useful for this type of mobilisation. One concerns the ability to spread visually captivating images. Ghonim (2012: 58–66, 127) remembered the visceral impact of seeing a picture of the tortured face of Khaled Said and insisted that the 'Khaled Said' page 'was only created as a result of Said's image after he was tortured … If we had not seen it, we would not have cared.' All our interviewees vividly recalled seeing Said's pictures, before and after his death, on the internet. Similarly, the videos that activists uploaded, whether Ghonim's depicting the first successful Silent Stand or Asmaa Mahfouz's plea to the nation to go out and demonstrate, were watched by tens of thousands—and remembered.[5] Images of the tens of thousands of protesters going out on the streets on 25 January constituted a powerful draw for onlookers as well as an effective antidote to the regime's attempts to play down or discredit the revolution. A number of our interviewees specifically mentioned seeing video footage as a key factor in their being moved to go out and investigate (although not necessarily on social media; Abdel-Rahman (Interview 2011) mentioned watching satellite stations).

The second feature that enhances social media's mobilisatory potential is that information can be gathered from multiple sources and posted on one page, eclectically and interactively. Asked about the difference between the response of the print media and social media to Said's death, the anonymous interviewee (Anonymous Interview 2011) commented:

[Said's death] was in the media but Facebook played a [more] vital role. … Some channels did [comment], like DreamZ. But Facebook brought all the details to our attention, the different demos, sit-ins, not just for Khaled Said, but others. ... I was a member of 'We Are All Khaled Said,' I followed events on Facebook. It was also reported in the newspapers, *Dustur, al-Masry al-Youm*, reports on demos. ... But on Facebook I could look at all the pictures, read the comments, read reports of activists, comment myself. ... Very interactive.

Castells (2009: 55) calls this type of communication 'mass self-communication'. What distinguishes it from traditional 'mass communication' is that 'the production of the message is self-generated, the definition of the potential receiver(s) is self-directed, and the retrieval of specific messages or content from the World Wide Web and electronic communication networks is self-selected'. This alters the way users interact with the information, facilitating identification and engagement, as well as reinforcement through seeing multiple sources.

Offline Communication

Although it appears that only a relatively small percentage of the Egyptian population actively used Facebook and Twitter, social media can be said to have had an effect beyond its regular users by changing the perceptions of those who were mobilised from the street (rather than online). One way to think about this is through the concept of a 'textual community'.[6] Developed in the context of medieval studies, amongst others, to think about the relationship between texts and those influenced by the texts (including those who could not read or did not own the text), the notion of a textual community describes both 'an interpretive community' and 'a social entity' (Stock 1996: 150). It revolves around a text, but the community does not necessarily have access to this text: 'what was essential to a textual community was not a written version of a text ... but an individual, who, having mastered it, then utilized it for reforming a group's thought and action' (Stock 1983: 90).

Although the context is vastly different, the concept—of individuals passing on the information they have mastered through a written medium to a much larger group of people who have not had direct access to this medium—is eminently applicable to the context of the January 25 uprising. If every one of the 90,000 Facebook users who had signed up to protest passed on the information, ideas and identities taken from Facebook to fifty friends and family members, the result would be a textual community of 450,000 people knowing about the call to revolution, and the reasons behind it. Given the way internet accounts have historically been shared by an estimated eight Egyptians (at least, prior to the 2002 free internet initiative) (Abdulla 2007: 36), this is not an implausible suggestion.

There is of course no guarantee that all of these 450,000 would go on to the street, or even that the message passed on would have had the same impact as on those using social media. But if these messages are reinforced not only by events in Tunisia (reported far beyond the social media) but also by a few hundred people actually chanting below one's balcony, the impetus to join would have been that much greater. Further research (beyond conjecture) is needed to establish what role such textual communities actually played. However, the fact that earlier in January a reported 250 activists were able to influence the protest pattern of 4,000 protesters in a protest against the bombing in Alexandria (Chapter 5) underlines how influential a small, well-coordinated cadre of activists can be. Similarly, both activists and non-activists told us how they had actively spread the word about the revolution to those beyond the community of social media users, including through talking to every taxi driver they met (Abdel-Rahman, Interview 2011; Waleed Rashed quoted in Lim 2012: 243; monasosh in Idle and Nunn 2011: 57).

Protection through Increasing the Costs of Repression

A third way in which social media played a crucial part was as an attempt to limit regime violence by exposing it to the world. Lynch (2011: 305) describes this function of social media as 'raising the costs to authoritarian regimes of repression ... by documenting atrocities and increasing international attention'. In Chapter 6, we touched on social media being a factor in reducing fear by alerting the global media, as well as local activists, to regime abuses. Social media were used by activists to record or report police violence, upload images of violence, and alert activists to police movements—a practice that had already been well established in the years leading up to the revolution (Chapters 1–2). Ghonim's (2012: 183) immediate reaction to coming under police attack on 25 January was to tweet 'our location and ... that we were about to be attacked'. During the fighting on 2–3 February, tweets were used to alert the world to the violence meted out against protesters (Idle and Nunns 2011: 101–19). Sahar Khamis, Paul Gold and Katherine Vaughn (2012: 17) similarly give examples of activists using tweets to alert their followers that they were being arrested, triggering Twitter campaigns for their release (although their examples post-date the revolution). So widespread has this phenomenon become that it has become known as 'released with a hashtag'.

In his report on the use of social media during the revolution, Eaton (2012: 8) similarly noted that:

From the outset, activists had emphasised the importance of documenting events. Hours before the protest on 25th January WAAKS [We Are All Khaled Said] encouraged its members to become citizen journalists, featuring a short video with the title, 'The camera is my weapon...' For the international viewers, and their governments, [this weapon] ... laid bare the true face of the regime. The walls and hashtags of Facebook and Twitter and the channels of YouTube became the key resources to track events. The result was that the ability of the regime to crush dissent in its traditional manner was greatly constrained. Crucially, unlike in Algeria in 1991 or even Libya in 2011, almost any act of aggression that the Egyptian regime directed against its people found its way on to social media and to TV screens around the world: the ability to bridge the gap between new media and traditional media was vital.

What is beyond doubt is that the protesters used social media extensively to document and broadcast regime violence. What is not as clear is how much this actually impacted the regime. Post-revolutionary Twitter campaigns appear to have played a role in the quick release of famous activists, just as mass social media campaigns before the revolution, such as those surrounding Khaled Said's death or the sodomising of micro-bus driver Emad al-Kebeer, clearly rattled the authorities. But other factors played a part too, including the level of susceptibility of the authorities to reputational risk, the tension between (a section of the) judges and lawyers and the regime and the particular judge in charge of the trial. During the revolution, it is possible that the knowledge that every human right violation would be broadcast imposed a level of restraint on the regime and its security forces. Compared to other revolutions, and in particular the uprisings that subsequently unfolded in Libya and Syria, regime violence in Egypt remained, relatively speaking, limited. For example, the regime never unleashed its air force on the protesters, even though fighter jets were deployed over Tahrir Square. Nor were there any mass executions. However, far more research is needed to establish the exact role social media played in this.

WHY OCCUPY A SQUARE?

Creating Online Communities of Engaged Citizens

Beyond the provision of information, social media provided a platform for non-activists to become politically engaged and to identify with the opposition movement, even if only online at first. As such, it provided an online meeting place, replacing the community halls, cafés and religious buildings of traditional offline social movements. As Mark Surman and Katherine Reilly argue in the context of transnational social movements, online mobilisation is 'much more about relationships and community than about [simply] information' (quoted in Bennett 2005: 217). In the context of social media's contribution to opposition activism in Egypt, Lim (2012: 234) suggests that:

Individuals only participate in collective action when they recognize their membership in the relevant collective ... The degree of group identification appears to be a strong predictor of collective action participation ... Such identification can only grow out of communication between individuals. For angry, unemployed youth to participate in an oppositional movement against Mubarak, she or he first needed to recognize that many other individuals shared the same grievances, the same goals, and a common identity in opposition to Mubarak.

In an authoritarian context, where public meetings and the print media are severely circumscribed, social media can, and in the case of Egypt did, provide a venue for like-minded people to meet, discuss and identify shared grievances and goals, and develop a sense of identification with each other. Illustrating this, our anonymous teacher trainer (Anonymous, Interview 2011) told us:

On Facebook, it was the place where we all met, we all had the same vision, the same dreams. ... I was always angry about Egypt, grumbling. I didn't talk with others so much, but read online. Facebook was an important source of information, a space to express myself, get to know others' opinion, a forum for discussion. My family, my sister (who I live with) are not interested in politics. I found people, as interested as I am, on Facebook.

Despite state surveillance and the threat of arrest, Facebook offered a relatively safe meeting place. As a group of non-activists told us: 'Facebook was more convenient and safer to communicate [than offline]. A greater number of people can express what they want, without fear of being arrested. It is easier [for the authorities] to arrest when people meet [in one place]. On Facebook, you can only arrest one at a time' (Group Interview 2011).[7]

Of particular importance is the possibility social media offers to express oneself (Ghonim 2012: 38). Numerous people told us that the revolution had enabled them to find their voice. Social media facilitated this process by providing an online outlet where people could not just express their thoughts but explore and discover them, in relative safety. Others have highlighted the importance of the emergence of citizen journalists (cf. Tufekci and Wilson 2012: 363–79; N. Hamdy 2009), which would have been difficult without access to social media. Beyond that, social media enabled non-activist people to become engaged citizens. In particular, it offered a place for deeper reflection (for those thus minded). The AUC student (Anonymous Interview 2011) further stated:

I found it easier to have discussions on Facebook [than face to face]. You take your time, you can construct your words. It's not about being safer [than meeting face to face] but a different type of communication, more time and space to think and express yourself. ... I also talked face-to-face with people, but the online conversations were more organised. That's the difference.

Beyond communication and expression, social media enabled people to become identified with the various opposition communities (a process Tarrow and McAdam define as 'attribution of similarity'), whether through brokerage ('linking ... two or more previously unconnected social sites') or relational diffusion ('transfer[ring] ... information along established lines of interaction') (Tarrow and McAdam 2005: 127).[8] The online communities surrounding April 6, 'We Are All Khaled Said' and 'ElBaradei for President', as well as the various Islamist online communities that had proliferated during the 2000s, included people who already identified with the opposition project (in its various guises) and had often already made (some) steps towards becoming an activist. The April 6 activists we met on Tahrir Square in May 2011 had begun to identify online with April 6 long before January 2011. Our anonymous student felt herself to be part of the online opposition community, without having actually demonstrated. Diplomats such as Gamal and Hamdy similarly were sympathetic to the goals of the revolution, just as Abdel-Rahman and Hossam were, without seeing themselves as part of the opposition. Social media played a part in this, although other factors, such as travel abroad, satellite television and offline discussions with friends, also influenced this process.

Social media were also used by activists to prepare followers for street protests through a series of 'commitment-building exercises'

(Bennett 2005: 207, referring to the global anti-war movement). In Chapter 6 we discussed how Ghonim (2012: 71, 79–80) incrementally mobilised people: first he asked them to 'like' the page, then he got them involved by asking them to upload pictures of themselves, which stated their support for Khaled Said; he then followed this up with an invitation to join (relatively safe) vigils, before asking people to join demonstrations. Fouad (Interview 2011) and Khalil Saeed (Interview 2011) described a similar process of gradual induction (although much of this involvement occurred offline). In social movement terms, social media were used to reduce people's 'transaction costs' (see also Lynch 2011: 304), both in terms of their awareness of protest events and in terms of their links with other, like-minded people, both of which tend to lower people's inhibitions to act and increase incentives.

Social media thus enabled the development of both a vibrant online 'public sphere' (Lynch 2011: 306–7; N. Hamdy 2009: 95–6; although the term 'public sphere' is problematic because of its Eurocentric assumptions) and a set of online 'virtual communities',[9] which were susceptible to mobilisation and emulation of existing protest patterns, given the right set of external circumstances. In a country where the public sphere was severely circumscribed, the creation of an alternative, dissenting public sphere, encouraging people not just to become citizen journalists, but also to become engaged citizens more broadly, was crucial to developing a politically aware opposition constituency (even if much of it was online before 2011). Equally important was the creation of like-minded online opposition communities who already identified with the goals of the revolution, knew and trusted the small core of activists and had already at least thought about emulating their example of protesting.[10]

On their own, the creation of online communities and an online public sphere were clearly insufficient for triggering a revolution. One reason for this may well be the supposed weakness of online ties (cf. Gladwell 2010). However, the success of 'We Are All Khaled Said' suggests that it is possible for online followers to create strong enough links (or at least motivations) to become street activists, although more research is needed to determine what role offline networks and other factors played in the conversion of online followers to offline activists. How many of those who responded to online invitations, for instance, were encouraged by offline social networks? What role did offline experiences play in making the online invitations resonate? Similarly, in combination with offline mobilisation, the demonstration effect of Tunisia and the protest momentum of 2010, the presence of online communities was clearly a contributory factor in the mobilisation of protesters on 25 January. Moreover, online relationships can be remarkably strong. Consider the online partnership between Ghonim and AbdelRahman Mansour, his co-administrator, whom he had known through social media since 2009. Their relationship was crucial to the success of both the ElBaradei and 'We Are All Khaled Said' Facebook pages, yet they did not meet offline until much later in their relationship (Ghonim 2012: 43–4).

Both the experience of 2011, and the example of 'We Are All Khaled Said' suggest that Gladwell's argument needs to be researched further, to gain a deeper understanding of what types of links can be created on social media, and how these interact with other, offline factors. In the context of transnational activism, for instance, Bennett (2005: 206–7) notes the importance of being able to move between on- and offline communication:

It is the capacity to move easily between on- and offline relationships that makes [a] scale shift [towards greater mobilization] ... possible. The innovative design and diffusion of communication and information technologies increasingly embeds those technologies in face-to-face experiences such as organizing, meeting, talking with friends, ... coordinating local protest actions in real time as they happen, and reporting them back through digital media channels so they can be recognized by activists themselves, as part of larger-scale developments.

The experiences of 2011 and 'We Are All Khaled Said' also suggests that social movement theory needs to refine its categories, and introduce an intermediate layer between adherents (those who believe in the goals of the movement) and constituents (those who provide resources, such as time or money, to the movement and engage in some level of collective action) (cf. McCarthy and Zald 1977: 1221; Edwards and McCarthy 2004: 141). Many of those identifying with online communities would not have directly engaged in collective action, beyond commenting and reposting (which might just qualify them as constituents). Yet neither were they simply adherents, since they were connected, identified and engaged on a day-to-day basis to an extent that adherents usually are not.

Our small sample of non-activists shows up two different pathways to mobilisation in relation to social media. Some, such as Amira, the *al-Masry al-Youm* journalist, had strong online links with the opposition networks and avidly engaged with them through social media. The fact that she lived and worked in Germany meant that she relied more heavily on social media to stay in touch, and her decision to return to Cairo was strongly influenced by her hearing about, and discussing, the protests on Facebook. However, Amira had been an activist in the past and had long-established offline relations with the opposition networks. Heba Ezzat, who, while being a well-known Islamist intellectual, had not engaged in street activism in recent years, falls into this same category. She too mentioned watching events unfold on Facebook abroad as a factor in her deciding to return early. But, like Amira, Heba had strong offline links with activist networks. Their online links were thus strong, in part, because of the strength of their offline links.

Others, including Abdel-Rahman, Hossam, Gamal and Mahmoud, had weak links with the opposition networks, both on- and offline. Social media informed their understanding of events, but it did not seem to have played a significant role in mobilising them. Rather, they were drawn in after seeing events unfold on satellite TV and hearing about them from friends, whether face to face or via mobile phones. Because social media played such a small part in their mobilisation, it is almost irrelevant to talk about the strength or weakness of their online links. Whether these two patterns were replicated widely across the spectrum of protesters, or whether other patterns prevailed, can only be ascertained by further research. Similarly unclear is whether different levels of relationship developed as a result of different pathways to identification: for instance, Tarrow and McAdam (2005: 126–31) suggest that brokerage in transnational movements typically results in weaker but more widely diffused linkages; while relational diffusion (which tends to have an offline component) encourages stronger, but more limited linkages, making brokerage the more likely mechanism for a sudden growth in protests, or 'scale shift'.

Conclusion: Participatory Culture and Organisation

The interactive potential of social media appears to have facilitated the development of the participatory, non-hierarchical culture prevalent among the informal protest networks. Within the literature on the Global Justice Movement, it is often argued that the non-hierarchic, 'leaderless' character of the Global Justice Movement is facilitated if not shaped by the participative opportunities offered by the internet (cf. Bennett 2005; Clark 2003: 153–4, 158–9; Baringhorst 2008: 75–8). The fact that most internet-based social media offer the possibility to answer back, elicit responses and provide multiple viewpoints simultaneously is held to be a major factor in the development of a less hierarchic leadership structure. Certainly, compared to earlier offline social movements, the Global Justice and other transnational, internet-based movements are remarkably non-hierarchical, although we would caution against overstating its supposed 'leaderlessness'. As with the Egyptian protest networks, there are key facilitators and activists who keep up the momentum of the movement, set the agenda and ensure decisions are made (Bennett 2005: 209–10). What is different from earlier movements is the absence of a centralised leadership structure with clearly visible leaders, and the extent to which constituents and adherents are consulted in decision-making and given a say in the final outcome.

There is a long tradition within the social sciences of seeing technology not simply as a tool, but as constitutive of who we are as human beings. Norman Vig (1988: 9), for instance, argues that 'technology has become so central to our existence and way of life that it must be studied as a fundamental human characteristic'. Castells (2000: 29–30), borrowing from Melvin Kranzberg and Carroll Pursell, similarly suggests that technology penetrates 'all domains of human activity, not as an exogenous source of impact, but as the fabric in which such activity is woven'. This framing of technology has its most famous roots in a short, dense article published in 1954 by Martin Heidegger (2010), in which he argues that technology is part of a particular type of causal process that is related to the question of being.

Put more prosaically, technology can be said to alter our very sense of self. This was, of course, one of Karl Marx's main insights. As Marx wrote in the preface to his *Critique of Political Economy* (2000: 425), 'the mode of production of material life conditions the social, political, and intellectual life process in general. It is not the consciousness of men that determines their being, but, on the contrary, their social being that determines their consciousness.'

Marx's insights can be rephrased to refer to the contemporary politics relevant to an analysis of the Egyptian revolt. First, that there is a crucial link between any individual or group and the technological processes that they become involved with. Second, that people's identities become conditioned or influenced by them. Third, that the involvement with these technological processes are crucial to understanding the self-awareness of those involved and the means by which they participate and interact in politics.

Hannah Arendt similarly explored the relationship between technology and human consciousness. She begins her masterpiece, *The Human Condition* (1958), with a reference to the 1957 space flight, and how it affected human self-understanding. According to Arendt, the technology behind the launch was less important than how this technological event held meaning, enabled new meanings to be created and thus altered humanity's expectations and sense of self. The event encouraged a new sense of what humans are capable of. It was not the rocket but how the rocket was used that captivated the human imagination. Indeed, Arendt's book is heavily influenced by Heidegger's argument that the essence of technology is not what it *is* but how it is used. How we use technology changes how we perceive ourselves and our place in the world.

Within such a framework, it would be persuasive to argue that the way activists used social media profoundly affected the way they thought about themselves, their rights and their relationships to power and organisation. Crucially, though, the argument is not that this new way of non-hierarchical organisation was somehow 'caused' by the characteristics of the internet alone, although the fact that it offered interactive, participative communication tools was important. Rather, this new form of organisation could be said to be a product of the way this new technology was used, a process that was (also) driven by ideological factors and the context within which these movements operated. In both the case of the GJM and the Egyptian protest networks, beliefs about leadership matter. Members of both movements have expressed disillusionment with the hierarchical and exclusive features of traditional forms of political leadership, particularly as it pertains to the state (Bennett 2005: 216–17; Abdelrahman 2013; Soueif 2012: 148–9). Ghonim (2012: 104–5), for example, explicitly endorses participatory democratic methods and 'empowering audience members'.

In addition, there are contextual factors, which could be said to encourage a 'leaderless' organisational structure. One of the reasons the Egyptian opposition networks adopted non-hierarchical leadership structures was arguably the threat posed by the security forces against political organisations with a clearly identifiable leadership

(Chapter 3).[11] One could counter that widespread consultation increases the chances of security forces gaining access to and influencing internal debates. Indeed, there are instances where repression led to isolation and fragmentation, as was the case with the Italian Red Brigades (della Porta 1995b). There are other instances, however, where an increase in repression, among other things, went hand in hand with an increase in consultation, as was the case with the Palestinian Hamas in the early 1990s (Gunning 2007: 40–1). One of the motivations behind Hamas's push for greater consultation was the realisation that maintaining unity in an increasingly heterogeneous movement required greater consultation. A similar dynamic operated among Egypt's opposition networks, making increased consultation an attractive response to the problem of unity and buy-in in a heterogeneous, loosely bound network.

Nevertheless, the tools offered by the internet have appeared to both facilitate consultation and horizontal leadership structures, and to shape users' approach to leadership. Ghonim, for example, was able to make the ElBaradei campaign more responsive to people's views through tools developed by Google and others. More fundamentally, his views on participation were profoundly shaped by his knowledge of, and working with, Google's online tools. When ElBaradei's online signature campaign stalled, for instance, Ghonim (2012: 55) hit upon a tactical innovation as a direct result of his working knowledge of Google products, and how these were applied elsewhere:

As the situation reached this dire point, I got an idea, inspired by a popular Google product that had been utilized by election campaigns in other parts of the world. Google Moderator is a tool that gives the user the ability to solicit questions from an unlimited number of other users and subsequently to rank these questions based on popularity votes so that they can be answered accordingly. ... The initiative was announced on his Facebook page in mid-May 2010. It was called "Ask ElBaradei." The number of fans on the page had now reached 150,000, of whom more than 2,700 participated. They posted 1,300 questions that received about 60,000 votes. It was an astonishing outpouring.

Ghonim (2012: 82–4, 92–3, 95, 104–5, 108) and his co-administrator regularly used online surveys to obtain feedback about the campaigns they were running and to decide on what future strategies to adopt (such as when to hold the third Silent Stand, or what to do on 25 January). These types of participatory online tools change the way brokerage works, 'put[ting] individuals at the center of multiple networks, thus shifting the brokerage process ... from organizational leadership to dense interpersonal relationships' (Bennett 2005: 224).

Castells (2012: 221) similarly argues that it is the freely accessible space of the internet that enables internet-linked protest networks to do away with hierarchy and centralisation:

Because they are a network of networks [existing in the free space of the Internet], they can afford not to have an identifiable centre, and yet ensure coordination functions, as well as deliberation, by interaction between multiple nodes. Thus, they do not need a formal leadership, command and control centre, or a vertical organization to distribute information and instructions. This decentered structure maximizes chances of participation in the movement ... It also reduces the vulnerability of the movement to the threat of repression, since there are few specific targets to repress, except for the occupied sites, and the network can reform itself ...

Castells (2012: 231) goes even further, suggesting that the internet encourages autonomy because autonomy was built into it from the start, from the protocols that were developed to the 'culture of freedom prevailing in the university campuses in the 1970s'. While we agree that the way the internet was developed means it can encourage autonomy, we would caution against making too deterministic a claim.

More research is needed to unpack the exact relationship between how interactive social media platforms are used and the adoption of participative, non-hierarchical organisational structures and a self-understanding that encourages such structures. But, at least at first sight, the interactive facilities of social media and the way they were put to use appear to have been factors encouraging the adoption of a more participative approach. This mirrors our general conclusion: the uprising was clearly not a 'Facebook Revolution' in that hundreds of thousands were mobilised offline and those who were online needed additional triggers to translate their online support into offline participation in street protests. Nevertheless, social media played a significant role in creating online protest communities, facilitating informational cascades about regime failure and protest frames, communicating the protests, and providing (at least the perception of) a level of protection through broadcasting police abuses.

CONCLUSION

As we write this conclusion in June 2013, the streets of Egypt are again the site of intense mobilisation and contestation. On 30 June, a reported 14–17 million people went out on to the streets to demand early elections and an end to President Morsi's rule (Aljazeera 2013), creating conditions not dissimilar to the final days before President Mubarak's ousting by the military in 2011. Earlier in the year, the second anniversary of the January 25 revolution saw tens of thousands gather at Tahrir Square to protest against the Muslim Brotherhood-led government, with reports of hundreds of thousands of protesters across Egypt (cf. Stern 2013). In a macabre echo of the original uprising, five protesters and two police officers were killed in Suez, and over 250 were reported injured across the country (*New York Times* 2013). Since then, protests have continued, fuelled by disagreements over the direction of government, deaths and accusations of terror at the hands of the police, and controversial court verdicts.

The euphoria of the revolution began to fray soon after Mubarak's fall. Within hours, a Western reporter was subjected to a brutal sexual assault by a group of men on the same Tahrir Square that had seen the extraordinary scenes of the Republic of Tahrir (ABC 2011). Sexual harassment became routine again and Muslim–Christian relations were severely tested in the months after the protests. Protesters and citizens did unite to clean up after the protests, in an echo of the festival-like spirit of the revolutionary days, but as time wore on, the protest networks lost their sense of unity, as diverging agendas and beliefs about tactics began to re-emerge. The constitutional referendum became an acrimonious tug of war between the Muslim Brotherhood and the more secular protest networks. The Brotherhood (and numerous emerging rival Islamist parties) won that contest, just as it won the subsequent parliamentary and presidential elections and the second constitutional referendum, leading to accusations that it had hijacked the revolution.

On the one hand, it is clear that the revolution is far from finished. Many of the old elite are still influential. The armed forces retain their privileges, and the political system has not been overhauled (although one could counter that the political system may change as a result of the institution of more genuine elections—if the electoral process is indeed consolidated over the next decades—and a constitutional process that could alter the values underpinning the Egyptian state). Socioeconomic disparities remain stark, and the government is again attempting to curb demonstrations with excessive force. The revolutionary practices of Tahrir Square—participatory self-government, Muslim–Christian and cross-ideological unity, limited sexual harassment—have evaporated or become diluted. More fundamentally, the protest networks did not succeed in translating the mass mobilisation of January–February 2011 into a mass social movement.

On the other hand, the January 25 revolution has been revolutionary in the sense that it has changed people's attitudes towards political debate and public protest. Before, public protest was largely confined to a small group of seasoned activists. The January 25 revolution changed that. Neighbourhood groups have proliferated, and hardly a month has gone by without protests on Tahrir Square. When we visited the Square in May 2011, what struck us most was the level and intensity of public political debate, involving students, workers, villagers and bystanders. Two years on, activists are still managing to collect millions of signatures calling for early presidential elections (al-Masry al-Youm 2013). Although the government is doing its utmost to push the genie back into the bottle, there is no sign that the will to this newfound freedom is waning. In this sense, the original 'trial by space' that characterised the battle over Tahrir Square continues and the protesters are a vivid manifestation of Lefebvre's (1991: 416–17) warning that 'ideas, representations or values which do not succeed in making their mark on space, and thus generating (or producing) an appropriate morphology, will ... become mere signs, resolve themselves into abstract descriptions, or mutate into fantasies'.

CONCLUSION

Summarising the Book's Argument

Our analysis of the January 25 revolution—or rather the mass protests, occupations and strikes that forced members of the ruling elite, primarily the army, to choose between loyalty to the regime and forcing regime change—has thrown up a number of insights. We have shown how by January 2011 a number of structural crises combined with a series of precipitating events and an unprecedented level of activism to create a potentially volatile situation. The ousting of President Ben Ali in Tunisia provided a further trigger by giving Egyptians hope that change might be possible. As Castells (2012: 220–1) has argued, 'social movements do not arise just from poverty or political despair. They require an emotional mobilization triggered by outrage against blatant injustice, and by hope of a possible change as a result of examples of successful uprisings in other parts of the world ...' It was the combination of resurgent hope with long-term outrage at the many injustices in Egypt, channelled by the protest networks, that turned January 2011 into a potentially revolutionary situation.

That it became a full-blown revolutionary episode was by no means inevitable. When the protests started, no one believed that the demonstrations would be as large and sustained as they were. Rather, it was the rapid evolution of events, the momentum they built up, the grievances inflicted by police action and the success of early protests, which turned a situation with revolutionary potential into an actual revolutionary episode. The protests were thus profoundly contingent on people's actions. Had the workers, the Muslim Brotherhood and the Ultras not joined; had more people allowed fear to squash defiance; had Mubarak conceded more, earlier; had the police managed to contain the protests at the start or subsequently not used excessive violence once the protests were underway; had the army not refrained from suppressing the protests, events would have turned out very differently. Any theory focusing solely on structural or organisational tipping points in order to explain the start of such a revolutionary episode is thus unsatisfactory, as part of the explanation has to be found in the evolution of the protest episode itself.

Returning to the questions we posed in the first chapter, our analysis has shown that the events of January 2011 did not come out of nowhere. They had their roots both in the structural changes of the past two to three decades and in the successive protest waves of the 2000s. The revolt of large sections of the middle classes cannot be understood without an understanding of the changes to state–society relations brought about by the regime's neoliberal policies, the narrowing of the NDP's base and the rapid rise of Gamal Mubarak and his exclusive business clique. The mobilisation of the working classes must be seen within the context of neoliberal reforms to Egypt's industry, changes to Egypt's tariff system in the context of fluctuating global trading dynamics and the effect these all had on working conditions— as well as, of course, the mobilising efforts of the workers' movement. The ability of the protesters to reach across class boundaries, crucial to the protests' success, was influenced both by the fact that all classes had become alienated from the regime, and by the growth of mixed-class urban 'informal areas', where inhabitants lived in close proximity while sharing the same everyday hardships that come from living without regulated access to water, sewerage and electricity. Rocketing food prices, rising inflation and unemployment affected all classes, though particularly the poor and the floating middle class, especially by early 2011 when world food prices reached the same impossible height as they had in April 2008, at the time one of Egypt's largest pre-2011 protests.[1] The expansion of the police force and its increasingly indiscriminate violent practices likewise served to fuel grievances— exponentially so as the use of video phones and social media spread among protesters in the late 2000s—and to unite the disparate classes and protest sectors behind one protest frame.

The January 25 revolution can similarly not be understood without a thorough appreciation of the protest networks that emerged over the decade prior to 2011, and the successive protest waves they initiated, each wave mobilising hitherto un-tapped sections of society while developing new tactics and frames. In the early 2000s, the Palestinian solidarity protests reclaimed the street as a site of public protest and created solidarity networks spanning not only the ideological spectrum (unusual at the time), but also students, workers and (some) professional organisations, such as the Lawyers' Syndicate. Between 2004 and 2006, Kefaya, or the Movement for Change, together with (more cautiously and indirectly) the Muslim Brotherhood and others, broke the taboo of explicitly demanding an end to Mubarak's rule, sowed the seeds for a broader protest culture and helped to create a cross-ideological pro-democracy network. Crucially, it broke with tradition by giving youth a greater organisational role, and succeeded in mobilising numerous professional networks and creating an alliance with the powerful and increasingly activist Judges' Club. It began the important 'frame bridging' work of linking everyday economic grievances to regime change, and started to use the internet as a site for mobilisation and alternative information provision. The Muslim Brotherhood briefly threw its weight behind the pro-democracy wave, but its electoral interests and the subsequent regime clampdown persuaded it to refocus primarily on *da'wa* and institutional politics.

The workers' movement consolidated and exponentially expanded Kefaya's protest culture, mobilising an estimated 1.7 million Egyptians in strikes and other protests between 2004 and 2008. The (tentative) alliance between the pro-democracy and workers' movements during the 6 April 2008 Mahalla strike sowed the seeds for the cross-class alliance that enabled the protesters to mobilise the masses in 2011, although the government's violent response set back attempts to link industrial grievances to regime change for another two years. The April 6 Youth Movement, one of the activist networks behind the revolution and a key motor behind the Mahalla strike, emerged out of the youth networks that had been established during the preceding protest waves and built on the contacts established during these waves with workers. The 2010 protest wave grew out of these earlier waves, mobilising people against the fraudulent elections of 2010 and the expected presidential bid of Gamal in 2011, as well as in opposition to specific incidents such as the killing of Khaled Said and the bombing of a church in Alexandria. ElBaradei's presidential campaign, with the initial help of the Brotherhood, helped to consolidate cross-ideological and cross-network links, while the 'We Are All Khaled Said' Facebook network mobilised thousands of middle-class youth, who identified with the life and fate of Khaled Said. Various protest networks, such as April 6, began to experiment with the swarming and flash mob tactics that were to prove pivotal in outwitting the police in 2011, and the youth networks, including reformist Brotherhood youth, maintained the cross-ideological links begun during the previous waves. The outcome of the 2010 election, meanwhile, encouraged a tentative rapprochement between the Brotherhood and the informal protest networks, which facilitated their eventual joining forces in January 2011.

Throughout, we have sought to emphasise that structural changes and networks cannot be separated from each other, as the two co-constitute each other at every juncture. Without the networks interpreting and channelling people's everyday grievances into sustained protests focused on regime change, the strains produced by the various structural crises would at best have given rise to ad hoc protest peaks in response to particular crisis points, as seems to have been the case in 1977. The fact that the 2007–2008 world food price crisis resulted in protests focused on industrial disputes and regime change was down to the alliance between the workers' and pro-democracy movements and their efforts at channelling people's everyday grievances in that direction.

Conversely, without these structural constraints and opportunities (and the way they were interpreted), there would neither have been the kind of protest networks able to carry the revolution, nor the elite fissures and re-alignments necessary to make a revolutionary episode possible. The rapid growth of the Palestinian solidarity and anti-Iraq war protests, for instance, was facilitated by the peaking of 15–24 year olds in 2000–2005 and the impact this had on unemployment at a time of regional and domestic crises, although it took protest networks to galvanise this cohort. Structural changes affect what types of networks, tactics and frames are likely to emerge, and when. Changes in repressive tactics affected the Muslim Brotherhood and the informal protest networks differently, in part because the latter had evolved explicitly as an adaptive response to repression, enabling them to lead where the Brotherhood had to be (or chose to be) more reticent. In addition, key events, such as the death of Khaled Said, serve to crystallise structural strains as networks turn them into 'moral shocks'—although their effect on mobilisation depends on where in a protest wave or structural crisis such events occur. In the language of revolution studies, while structural changes create the 'preconditions' or 'structural shifts in the social foundations of society', events function as 'precipitants'—or what Kimmel defines as 'the shorter-run historical events that allow these deeply seated structural forces to emerge as politically potent and begin to mobilize potential discontents' (1990: 9).

We have also shown how the January 25 revolution was not 'leaderless', but instigated and led by experienced activists, who had learned and developed their tactics in the heat of previous protest waves. Apart from ElBaradei, who had international and national stature but lacked the street credentials and inclination to lead protests, there were no towering revolutionary leaders. Nor was there any political party strong enough to dominate and lead the protests (except for the Muslim Brotherhood, which, controversially, took on this role afterwards). Instead, there were hundreds of seasoned, networked facilitators, from the groups of fifty who began the demonstrations in Cairo's informal quarters, to the activists coordinating medical and relief supplies from offices around the country, to the Revolutionary Youth councils on Tahrir Square and the strike leaders coordinating strikes across Egypt. Without this leadership and the tactics and frames they had developed over the years, there would not have been a coordinated call for a demonstration on 25 January under a carefully crafted, unifying protest frame. Even if, inspired by the success of the Tunisian revolution, people had spontaneously protested on National Police Day, it is unlikely that they would have been able to out-manoeuvre the police and sustain a protest for eighteen days without the activists' tactics and networks. Without the links forged between middle-class liberals, leftists, Islamists and workers, it is questionable whether so many would have turned out, as it was the convergence of all protest sectors and the coordination between them nationwide that made these demonstrations so difficult to contain for a police force that had hitherto had to deal, by and large, with more localised protests.

At the same time, we have argued that the protests would have been unsuccessful if the masses had not answered the call to mobilisation. If the hundreds of thousands with no protest experience had not overcome their fear, if they had not spontaneously taken leadership where needed and practised self-government by volunteering goods, setting up security cordons when the police withdrew and contributing to organising the Square once it was occupied, the demonstration would have been but another chink in the long chain of limited pro-democracy protests.

Central to the success of the mobilisation of 25–28 January was the process by which non-activists overcame their fear. We have detailed various practices by which activists sought to reduce fear, from carefully choosing the location for protests, to training and preparation, chanting, and exposing police violence in the mass media. More fundamentally, what persuaded hundreds of thousands to join was a change in the prevailing emotion culture (at least among those who decided to protest). The ousting of Ben Ali in Tunisia played a central part in this change. But so did the various 'moral shocks' of 2010 and the way the protest networks interpreted them, as did the activists' campaign of shaming in the weeks leading up to 25 January, depicting non-action as treachery and appealing to Egyptian notions of masculinity. Crucially, though, it was the events of that first week themselves which helped to create such a momentum that people began to see this as a historic moment. This sense of being faced by the stark choice of either joining, whatever the consequences, or condemning oneself and one's country to another thirty years of dictatorship, inverted the usual problem of 'freeriding' as the question became 'if I don't join, the revolution will fail'.

Just as we cannot understand the revolution without understanding how people overcame their fears, it is impossible to understand the protests without appreciating how they were shaped by the physical make-up of Egypt's urban spaces and the practices, meanings and social relations associated with them. The decision to start the protests in Cairo's *ashwaiyyat* was a recognition both of the way social inequalities were most starkly manifested there, and the differences between social and policing practices associated with the *ashwaiyyat* and the central boulevards of power. It inverted the relationship between centre and periphery, and brought the revolution to where Egypt's less well-off lived. The battle for Tahrir Square was a quintessential 'trial by space', a contest over the meaning, values and practices associated with public space, and its occupation allowed the protesters to produce a political space that was not sovereign in the usual sense, re-inscribing it with revolutionary practices. By creating space for people to practise self-government through multiple overlapping ad hoc nodes of authority—the politics associated with autonomous cities, rather than the state—the protesters succeeded in rolling back the practices associated with (state) sovereignty, instead enabling people to come together and practise (largely non-violent) politics in an almost Arendtian sense (although violence played a part in the defence of the Square and Cairo's un-policed neighbourhoods).

Technology, finally, was shown to have played a lesser role than assumed in much of the media and academic commentary. Although it had been central in exposing regime abuses, creating online communities prior to January 2011 and facilitating the emergence of non-hierarchical, participatory networks, its role in the January 25 revolution was more limited. Much of the mobilisation was carried out offline in order to evade police attention, and many of those who were mobilised in the *ashwaiyyat* would not have had regular internet access (although the reach of the internet arguably extended beyond actual users through social networks constituting 'textual communities'). Before January 2011, despite the presence of large online communities, the various protest networks had failed to translate online support into

CONCLUSION

offline feet on the ground. What persuaded online adherents to become offline activists was thus something other than the internet, although powerful video appeals such as Asmaa Mahfouz's and thousands of pledges of support played a role.

Egypt in Comparative Revolutionary Perspective

Egypt displayed many of the conditions identified by the literature on revolutions as being conducive to revolutions (especially the more recent literature comparing revolutions during and after the Cold War). It had an exclusive/repressive neo-patrimonial regime with a relatively weak and incompetent infrastructure, lacking ideological legitimacy—precisely the regime type that Goodwin (2001: 27–30) singles out as being most likely to be overthrown by revolutionary movements (see also Wickham-Crowley 1997; Kamrava 1999; Parsa 2000). It combined exclusive neo-patrimonialism with a high-level of intervention in capital accumulation and the market, which Parsa argues makes such regimes especially vulnerable because they become the focus of not just political but also economic discontent, while becoming associated with excessive privilege. The regime had lost the loyalty of large sections of society, including the middle classes and segments of the ruling elite, and it faced various economic crises, which particularly affect neo-patrimonial regimes, with their dependence on patronage networks and lack of effective, meritocratic bureaucratisation. The Egyptian case echoes Goodwin's (2001: 284–5, 287) finding that in exclusive neo-patrimonial regimes tensions between regime and sections of the elite, in particular the armed forces, are likely to emerge in times of crisis as the regime's base narrows. The January 25 revolution also largely corroborates the conventional wisdom that 'revolutions in the twentieth century have occurred only where major social classes succeeded in forming broad coalitions ...' (Parsa 2000: 7; see also Rueschemeyer, E. Stephens and J. Stephens 1992).

However, it is unclear what exactly these similarities between the Egyptian case and general revolutionary theories mean. Many of the structural conditions described above had already been in place for years, yet no sustained mass uprising had occurred prior to 2011. In addition, one could argue that no revolution has in fact taken place, but rather a renegotiation of power between a sector of the incumbent elite (primarily the armed forces) and the strongest, and arguably non-revolutionary, opposition movement, the Muslim Brotherhood. If no revolution has in fact occurred, the fact that Egypt displayed many of the factors identified in the literature on revolutions would call for a re-evaluation of this literature, as one would have to explain why this particular case experienced a revolutionary mass mobilisation yet no revolutionary outcome. In this sense, Egypt resembles Romania or the Philippines, where a revolutionary episode created the conditions for alienated members of the elite to oust the incumbent ruler and redistribute power, while keeping the political system intact, rather than countries such as Iran or Cuba where there was a more radical break with the past.

This leads us back to Goldstone's vectoral model. Rather than looking at all cases defined as revolutionary, it would be more instructive to look at other instances where only the first, second, third and, to some extent, eighth elements of his model occurred, while the fourth, fifth and sixth were largely absent, namely, loss of elite and popular legitimacy, elite revolt against the regime, popular revolt, (relatively) little violence or civil war, no or little change in political institutions, no change in economic organisation and (limited) change in the symbols and beliefs underpinning the distribution of power, status and wealth. One could carry out a comparative study of similar cases, or compare these cases to others where a more radical change has taken place to try and identify factors, actors and processes that differ.

However, such structural comparisons would not be able to explain why a revolutionary episode occurred at a particular time, and not earlier or later, or why latent strains suddenly became operative. For example, in Egypt the regime's weakness and the rifts among the elite only truly manifested themselves once the mass protests were underway. To explain why and when latent fissures become operative, we have to turn to a more processual, network-focused analysis of the way the regime, elites, opposition activists and the general population (or at least the 'attentive public') interacted with each other in the context of a changing structural context, going beyond the type of elite analysis suggested by Richard Lachmann (1997) or the agent- and class-based focus of Mehran Kamrava (1999).

*Social Movement Theory, Revolutionary Studies
and Further Research*

As we have demonstrated throughout, social movement theory can help to bring the interplay between structures, events and agents into sharper focus by looking at the processes of mobilisation. Crucially, it is the focus on protest networks and activists and the tactics, frames and networked relations they develop, which enables us to move beyond the structural focus of much of the revolutionary literature. Without an understanding of the emergence of an explicitly anti-regime frame; of the mobilisation of professional syndicates, student organisations, independent workers' networks and football fan clubs; of the effects of repression on activists and protest networks; or indeed of the adoption of swarming flash mob tactics in poorer areas, it would be difficult to explain how the confluence of exclusion, neo-patrimonialism and neoliberal intervention could have 'produced' the revolutionary episode of January 2011. No structural analysis would be able to capture this.

A poignant illustration of what social movement theory can add to revolutionary theories is how the cross-class coalition, so central to the uprising's success, came about. While students of revolution may point to the importance of class alliances, how they emerge is not typically addressed in this literature. Analysis of protest networks reveals how the Palestinian solidarity networks brought together leftists, liberals, Islamists, students and workers; how Kefaya's youth activists went out into Cairo's poorer quarters and actively linked everyday economic grievances to regime change; how April 6 activists and leftist human rights lawyers linked up with the workers movement and with people living in Cairo's informal areas and vice versa. Without these acts and networks, it is unlikely that a coalition between middle and lower classes would have emerged, strong enough to sustain an eighteen-day-long mass mobilisation.

The framing focus of social movement theory can similarly deepen our ideological analysis. Where revolutionary studies focus on broad-stroke ideologies, social movement theory focuses on the ways particular events are portrayed, and the protest frames around which protesters unite. This more functional, fluid focus is particularly well-suited to the study of the Egyptian revolution, as, the Muslim Brotherhood apart, there were no clear overarching ideological frameworks (and even within the Muslim Brotherhood there were different interpretations of the Brotherhood's ideological beliefs). Protesters united behind a pared down set of beliefs—belief in the culpability of the Mubarak regime, an increased minimum wage and an end to Emergency Rule. The informal protest networks themselves tended to abhor grand ideological statements, regarding these as relics of the ineffective political opposition parties. Thus even within protest networks, let alone between them, there was a great variety of different beliefs. The notion of ideology is too static, homogeneous and reified to be of much use in analysing such a fluid and eclectic set of micro-beliefs (although we agree with Pamela Oliver and Hank Johnston (2000) that the category of ideology must be retained to capture the relationship between structural context and broader belief systems).

Social movement theory also helps us to make sense of subsequent developments. A detailed analysis is beyond the scope of this work. But one can for instance explain the inability of the secular protest networks to secure a slice of power by pointing at their failure to become a mass social movement to counter the influence of the Muslim Brotherhood (although ideological reservations and divisions also played a part). While they succeeded beyond their wildest dreams in mobilising people during the revolutionary episode, they failed to translate this into a permanent mass movement. The non-hierarchical, fluid network structures that enabled them to evade repression and respond quickly to regime threats were ill-suited to formulating a coherent party agenda and mobilising electorates. The proliferation of ideologically eclectic networks, which increased agility under repressive conditions, made it more difficult to move from 'one big no, many, many yesses' to a detailed, unified programme around which all could unite.[2] Conversely, a social movement focus can help to explain why, Palestinian solidarity and youth activism aside, the Muslim Brotherhood remained largely on the sidelines during the preceding decade, and why it succeeded in capturing a share of institutional power after the uprising (cf. Wickham 2013).

Many of the mechanisms and processes identified by social movement theory manifested themselves in the Egyptian case, from the mobilisation of pre-existing networks and the importance of frame bridging, to the impact of the state's repressive mechanisms and changes in the class alignment underpinning the elite arrangement. The specifics of Egypt, such as the early mobilisation of the Lawyers' Syndicate, the peripheral nature of religious institutions in the development of the more secular protest networks, the role played by the Ultras or the importance of culturally specific conceptions of masculinity, may be unique to this case. But many of the key mechanisms and processes identified by the general literature were present, and often in very similar guises, so that the underlying dynamics of mobilisation in

Egypt would be instantly recognisable to a student of, say, the US Civil Rights Movement.

Whether this is a result of our actively looking for these mechanisms, or whether these mechanisms played a significant role separately from our conceptual model, is a question we cannot answer conclusively. Similarly, though we did not find that our conceptual framework imposed uniformity or reified difference vis-à-vis the dynamics we studied, others will have to corroborate our findings. We offer this analysis in the spirit of Ricoeur's judicial model as a springboard for further corroboration, challenge or overhaul.

However, as we have demonstrated, the uprising was not simply the work of protest networks. Its success was to a large extent due to the spontaneous response of hundreds of thousands of non-activists. What was truly striking about the Egyptian revolution was the way non-activists came together and became temporarily self-governing. Social movement theory does not routinely encourage us to think beyond networks. Granted, it spends much time looking at how people are mobilised, and as long as one moves away from the more formal movement organisations favoured by resource mobilisation theorists and includes the types of fluid, informal networks that were the mainstay of the Egyptian revolution, it is possible to map the role played by these networks. But the focal point nevertheless tends to be the networks themselves, rather than the non-networked non-activists, who drift in and out of protests, contributing while they are participating. Here, social movement theory could learn from the framework of 'unruly politics' (Tadros 2012).

Social movement theory also did not help in terms of conceptualising online adherents who had not participated in offline activism, or in theorising what role opportunities played which were not explicitly recognised by participants as opportunities. Although Kurzman already highlighted the tension between opportunity structures and subjective interpretations thereof in 1996, this phenomenon remains under-theorised. Similarly, while scholars studying transnational movements have identified strains between online and offline activism, the role played by purely online adherents needs further reflection.

In our analysis, we focused on headline frames, such as the shift from decrying US foreign policy to calling for Mubarak to go, or the linkage between everyday economic grievances and regime change. Much more detailed research is needed into how frames changed over the past decade and a half, how they changed differently in different protest networks and how each influenced the other, and how frame changes were affected by structural changes and vice versa. Notions of citizenship played a part; tracing how these concepts evolved, and how they came to be linked to protest and regime change, would be illuminating.

We briefly touched on cultural tropes such as notions of masculinity and how they might affect how unemployment is experienced (cf. 'waithood'); the model of local strongmen inspiring neighbourhood youth networks; or the traditions of the *mulid* infusing the practices of revolution. Much more work needs to be done to provide a thick description of the 'deep culture' that informs protesters' frames, tactics and decisions, and how the latter challenge the former.

Parts of what we presented were speculative, due to lack of confirming evidence. The dynamics of fear we postulated need to be corroborated and refined by widening the focus to include other emotions and by, for instance, using larger samples of non-activist interviewees, analysis of Facebook and Twitter accounts and participatory action research. The evolution of the links between workers and pro-democracy activists needs further probing, as does the role played by Muslim Brothers and other Islamists, such as the Salafis, in mobilising the poorer sections of society in the first week of the uprising. The relatively non-violent character of the protests and the differential impact of violence and non-violence on regime behaviour are both worthy of further study. Similarly, exactly how space mattered and what role the internet played in individual protesters' mobilisation and in the development of non-hierarchical organisational structures needs further research.

Finally, given the ambiguities surrounding how these events should be described, a crucial question is why people call it a revolution or otherwise, and what power struggles, identities and interests these framing choices represent. Framing aside, time alone will tell if the protesters who risked their lives will eventually get the political leadership and the Egypt they dreamt of.

Durham, 30 June 2013

APPENDIX

The following figures and tables list the number and type of protests reported by *al-Masry al-Youm* (Arabic) as involving 500 or more people over the period 2008–2010. Although an incomplete snapshot of protest dynamics, a survey of protests of 500 or more reported in this opposition newspaper gives a rough approximation of the number, size and targets of protest events over this period, and thus an insight into overall protest patterns. Smaller protests have not been included in this survey and industrial strikes have only been included if they were reported as protest events. The data have not been triangulated against other news reports. State and international media would not have covered local protests as consistently or faithfully. As one of the main and most respected opposition newspapers, *al-Masry al-Youm* would have covered most significant protests and would have done so with journalistic integrity. However, the number of protesters reported must be taken as rough estimates only as numbers are notoriously difficult to estimate, particularly where large protests are concerned. As the newspaper was pro-opposition, if anything, it is likely to have erred on the side of optimism.

Descriptions of the date, location and type of protests, the identity and number of protesters, and the reasons for the protest have been taken from *al-Masry al-Youm*. Protests have been categorised according to whether they were reported as focusing on economic, political, anti-police, neighbourhood, regional or sectarian issues. Note how often protests focusing on the same grievance are recurring. Where multiple issues are mentioned, we have categorised them under the category we deemed most important. Boundaries between categories are fluid. The 6 April 2008 protest in Mahalla, for instance, was described by *al-Masry al-Youm* as economic, but it was also deeply political; the various solidarity demonstrations held elsewhere that day were described as political. For consistency's sake, we have followed the paper's original description.

Only protests described as numbering 100s or 500 or more have been included. To arrive at a rough calculus of overall numbers, we substituted 500 for '100s', 2,500 for '1,000s', and 25,000 for '10s of 1,000s'. The numbers listed below must be taken as rough estimates only. The data were assembled by Nouran Aly.

Categories:

Economic	e.g. protests against economic hardship, industrial or administrative disputes, removal of subsidies.
Political	e.g. protests against the regime, Gamal Mubarak's succession scenario, election irregularities.
Anti-police	e.g. protests against police brutality, detentions, police authorities within universities, military trials of civilians.
Neighbourhood	e.g. disputes over house demolitions, land evictions, lack of water, school closures, car accidents.
Regional	e.g. solidarity with Palestinians, protests against visits by US or Israeli politicians, World Student Day.
Sectarian	e.g. conversions, general sectarian tensions.

Protests focused on football or 'social' issues, such as female circumcision, have not been included in the list below as only one was reported for each category in the period under investigation (20 Nov. 2009 and 6 Feb. 2010 respectively).

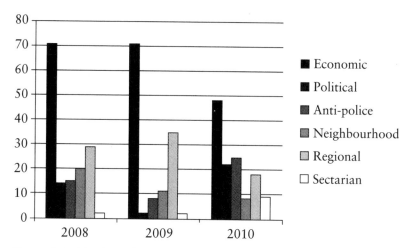

Figure A.1: Number of protests annually, by category, numbering 500 or more, as reported in *al-Masry al-Youm* (Arabic) (2008–2010). This does not include all of the 609, 700 and 584 strikes reported by Abdalla (2012: 2) for the years 2008, 2009 and 2010, unless they were reported as protest events by *al-Masry al-Youm*.

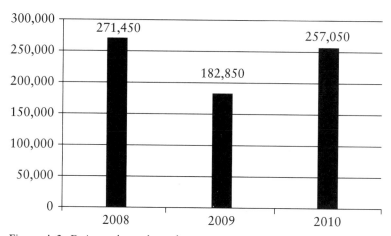

Figure A.2: Estimated number of protesters per year in protests numbering 500 or more, as reported in *al-Masry al-Youm* (Arabic) (2008–2010), excluding the Gaza protests of January-February 2009 (numbering 356,500).

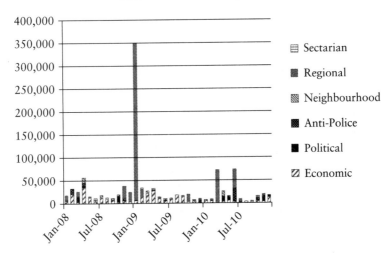

Figure A.3: Estimated number of protesters per category per month in protests numbering 500 or more, as reported in *al-Masry al-Youm* (Arabic) (2008–2010), including the Gaza protests of January–February 2009.

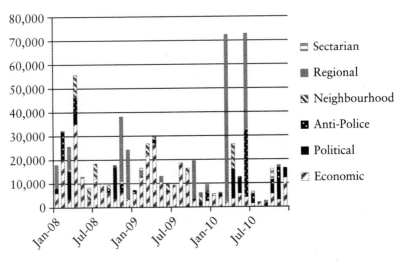

Figure A.4: Estimated number of protesters per category per month in protests numbering 500 or more, as reported in *al-Masry al-Youm* (Arabic) (2008–2010), excluding the Gaza protests of January–February 2009.

APPENDIX

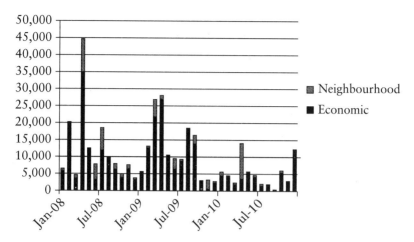

Figure A.5: Estimated number of protesters per month in economic and neighbourhood protests in protests numbering 500 or more, as reported in *al-Masry al-Youm* (Arabic) (2008–2010).

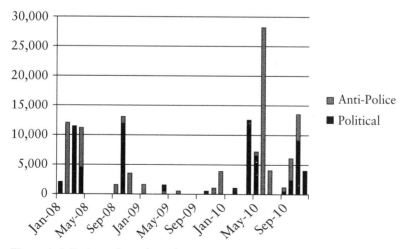

Figure A.6: Estimated number of protesters per month in political and anti-police protests in protests numbering 500 or more, as reported in *al-Masry al-Youm* (Arabic) (2008–2010).

Table A.1: Date, location and type of protest, type and number of protesters, reason for protest and protest category for protests numbering 500 or more, as reported in *al-Masry al-Youm* (Arabic) (2008–2010)

No.	Date	Location	Protesters and their numbers		Type of Protest	Reason for Protest	Protest Category
1	1 Jan. 2008	Qalyubia	Women and children	1,000	Demonstration	Being victims of a rogue investment company	Economic
2	16 Jan. 2008	Cairo	Citizens and lawyers	100s	Demonstration	US President George W. Bush's visit to Cairo	Regional
3	18 Jan. 2008	Gharbiyya	Citizens, political parties, political forces and Kefaya	2,000	Protest	Gamal Mubarak's succession scenario, rising prices and President Bush's visit	Political, economic, regional
4	20 Jan. 2008	Gharbiyya	Citizens and political parties	5,000	Demonstration	Economic hardship	Economic
5	21 Jan. 2008	Cairo	Al-Azhar students	100s	Demonstration	Gaza siege	Regional
6	22 Jan. 2008	Dakahlia	Muslim Brotherhood students and professors at Mansoura University	5,000	Demonstration	Gaza siege	Regional

7	22 Jan. 2008	Cairo	Muslim Brotherhood students and professors at Mansoura University	500	Demonstration	Gaza siege	Regional
8	23 Jan. 2008	Cairo	University students	1,500	Demonstration	Gaza siege	Regional
9	23 Jan. 2008	Damietta	Political parties, professional syndicates, Muslim Brotherhood	1,500	Demonstration	Gaza siege	Regional
10	23 Jan. 2008	Qena	Citizens	500	Road closure	Death of a girl in a car accident	Neighbourhood
11	3 Febr. 2008	Giza	Employees at authority of social affairs	1,000	Sit-in	Economic hardship	Economic
12	6 Febr. 2008	Munifiyya	Workers at Makarem textile factory	2,500	Strike	Economic hardship	Economic
13	9 Febr. 2008	Cairo	Physicians	100s	Rally	Economic hardship	Economic
14	17 Febr. 2008	Gharbiyya	Workers at Mahalla factories, Kefaya, political parties	10,000	Demonstration	Economic hardship	Economic
15	24 Febr. 2008	Cairo	Muslim Brotherhood students at Ain Shams University	2,000	Demonstration	Military trials of civilians	Anti-police

No.	Date	Location	Protesters and their numbers		Type of Protest	Reason for Protest	Protest Category
17	25 Febr. 2008	Dakahlia	Muslim Brotherhood students and professors at Mansoura University	5,000	Demonstration	Military trials of civilians	Anti-police
18	25 Febr. 2008	Cairo	Muslim Brotherhood	2,000	Rally	Military trials of civilians	Anti-police
19	27 Febr. 2008	Toshka	Employees and workers at Ramses company	2,200	Strike	Economic hardship	Economic
20	27 Febr. 2008	Giza	Workers at el-Hwamdiya sugar factory	4,000	Strike	Economic hardship	Economic
21	2 Mar. 2008	Munifiyya	Workers at Munifiyya textile company	750	Protest	Economic hardship	Economic
22	3 Mar. 2008	Munifiyya	Students	2,000	Demonstration	Gaza siege	Regional
23	4 Mar. 2008	Minya	Muslim Brotherhood students at Minya University	1,000	Demonstration	Gaza siege	Regional
24	4 Mar. 2008	Suez	Muslim Brotherhood students at Suez University	1,000s	Demonstration	Gaza siege	Regional

25	4 Mar. 2008	Damietta	Syndicates, political forces and Muslim Brotherhood	1,000	Mob	Gaza siege	Regional
26	5 Mar. 2008	Cairo	Muslim Brotherhood students	3,000	Demonstration	Gaza siege	Regional
27	5 Mar. 2008	Damietta	Citizens	100s	Protest	Proposed location of a factory	Neighbourhood
28	8 Mar. 2008	Kafr el-Sheikh	Muslim Brotherhood	1,000	Demonstration	Local election procedures	Political
29	9 Mar. 2008	Alexandria	Citizens	100s	Sit-in	Administrative decision of Ministry of Awqaf (religious endowments)	Economic
30	9 Mar. 2008	Gharbiyya	Muslim Brotherhood	5,000	Demonstration	Local election procedures	Political
31	10 Mar. 2008	Kafr el-Sheikh	Muslim Brotherhood	2,000	Demonstration	Local election procedures	Political
32	13 Mar. 2008	Sharqiyya	Muslim Brotherhood	3,000	Demonstration	Local election procedures	Political
33	13 Mar. 2008	Alexandria	Muslim Brotherhood	500	Demonstration	Local election procedures	Political

No.	Date	Location	Protesters and their numbers	Type of Protest	Reason for Protest	Protest Category
34	20 Mar. 2008	Qena	Employees at the general authority for protection of the Nile	550	Hunger-strike	Economic hardship	Economic
35	23 Mar. 2008	Alexandria	University professors	500	Strike	Economic hardship	Economic
36	23 Mar. 2008	Cairo	University professors	850	Strike	Economic hardship	Economic
37	27 Mar. 2008	Giza	Workers at el-Hwamdiya sugar factory	100s	Strike	Economic hardship	Economic
38	28 Mar. 2008	Luxor	Citizens	100s	Protest	Forced relocation	Neighbour-hood
39	1 Apr. 2008	Gharbiyya	Muslim Brotherhood	3,000	Demonstration	Local election procedures	Political
40	3 Apr. 2008	Gharbiyya	Workers at Mahalla carpet factories	700	Sit-in	Economic hardship	Economic
41	6 Apr. 2008	Gharbiyya	Citizens	25,000	Demonstration	Economic hardship	Economic
42	6 Apr. 2008	Helwan	University students	500	Strike	Solidarity with 6 April 2008 strike in Mahalla	Political

	Date	Location	Participants	Number	Type	Cause	Category
43	6 Apr. 2008	Cairo	University students (Haqqy or 'My Right' movement)	100s	Strike	Solidarity with 6 April 2008 strike in Mahalla	Political
44	6 Apr. 2008	Cairo	Kefaya movements	100s	Demonstration	Solidarity with 6 April 2008 strike in Mahalla	Political
45	8 Apr. 2008	Beni Sueif	Muslim Brotherhood students and university professors	650	Protest	Detention of a professor	Anti-police
46	9 Apr. 2008	Gharbiyya	Citizens	2,000	Demonstration	Detention of April 6 members	Anti-police
47	9 Apr. 2008	Gharbiyya	Workers at Nasr textile company	1,000	Strike	Economic hardship	Economic
48	9 Apr. 2008	Fayoum	Students	600	Demonstration	Poisoning of students at university dorms	Economic
49	13 Apr. 2008	Gharbiyya	Citizens	100s	Demonstration	Detention of April 6 members	Anti-police
50	13 Apr. 2008	Gharbiyya	Workers at Wabaryat company	1,300	Strike	Economic hardship	Economic
51	14 Apr. 2008	Alexandria	Farmers	1,500	Sit-in	House eviction decision	Neighbour-hood
52	14 Apr. 2008	Alexandria	Workers of Alexandria textile company	3,000	Strike	Economic hardship	Economic

No.	Date	Location	Protesters and their numbers	Type of Protest	Reason for Protest	Protest Category
53	16 Apr. 2008	Cairo	Muslim Brotherhood students at Cairo University	100s	Demonstration	Military trials of civilians	Anti-police
54	16 Apr. 2008	Sharqiyya	Muslim Brotherhood students at Zagazig University	100s	Demonstration	Military trials of civilians	Anti-police
55	16 Apr. 2008	Cairo	Muslim Brotherhood students at al-Azhar University	1,000s	Demonstration	Military trials of civilians	Anti-police
56	17 Apr. 2008	Damietta	Citizens and syndicate members	1,000	Demonstration	Calling for removal of Agriom factory	Neighbour-hood
57	18 Apr. 2008	Al-Wahat al-Baharia	Citizens	2,000	Demonstration	Calling for Wahat to be attached to Minya governorate	Neighbour-hood
58	23 Apr. 2008	Different cities	Physicians	100s	Demonstration	General protest of physicians	Economic
59	26 Apr. 2008	Alexandria	Workers of Alexandria textile company	2,500	Strike	Economic hardship	Economic
60	29 Apr. 2008	Damietta	Citizens	5,000	Demonstration	Calling for removal of Agriom factory	Neighbour-hood

	Date	Location	Who	Size	Type	Reason	Category
61	30 Apr. 2008	Alexandria	Citizens	100s	Demonstration	Removal of milk subsidy	Economic
62	4 May 2008	Gharbiyya	Citizens in Mahalla	100s	Strike	General strike in the city	Economic
63	4 May 2008	Gharbiyya	Workers of Deep Egypt company	500	Strike	Economic hardship	Economic
64	6 May 2008	Cairo	Workers of Shorbagy Textile company	1,000	Strike	Economic hardship	Economic
65	10 May 2008	Cairo	Engineers	100s	Strike	Government control of engineers' syndicate	Economic
66	15 May 2008	Cairo	Lawyers	100s	Demonstration	Anniversary of al-Nakba ('Catastrophe': Arabic term for effects of creation of Israel in 1948 on Palestinians)	Regional
67	18 May 2008	Cairo	Workers of Petrojet and Ebesco companies	3,000	Strike	Calling for permanent employment	Economic
68	25 May 2008	Alexandria	Workers at Amreya textile company	4,000	Strike	Economic hardship	Economic

No.	Date	Location	Protesters and their numbers		Type of Protest	Reason for Protest	Protest Category
69	27 May 2008	Gharbiyya	Lawyers	1,500	Sit-in	Contested lawyers' code of conduct	Economic
70	27 May 2008	Munifiyya	Lawyers	500	Sit-in	Contested lawyers' code of conduct	Economic
71	29 May 2008	Cairo	Lawyers	100s	Demonstration	Government control of lawyers' syndicate	Economic
72	30 May 2008	Ismailia	Workers of Suez Canal Port handling	100s	Demonstration	Economic hardship	Economic
73	1 June 2008	Minya	Copts	100s	Demonstration	Sectarian tension over Malawi events	Sectarian
74	6 June 2008	Damietta	Citizens	100s	Demonstration	Calling for removal of Agriom factory	Neighbour-hood
75	7 June 2008	Kafr el-Sheikh	Citizens	1,500	Demonstration	Economic hardship	Economic
76	8 June 2008	Fayoum	Farmers	100s	Demonstration	Hard living conditions	Economic
77	8 June 2008	Dakahlia	Farmers	100s	Demonstration	Hard living conditions	Economic
78	9 June 2008	Cairo	Workers of the general authority for land reclamation	800	Strike	Economic issues	Economic

79	17 June 2008	Damietta	Citizens	3,000	Demonstration	Calling for removal of Agriom factory	Neighbourhood
80	21 June 2008	Alexandria	Residents of Toson neighbourhood	500	Protest	House demolitions	Neighbourhood
81	22 June 2008	Cairo	Citizens	500	Sit-in	Land evictions	Neighbourhood
82	1 July 2008	Cairo	Workers of Cabo textiles company	6,000	Strike	Economic hardship	Economic
83	5 July 2008	Damietta	Citizens and political forces	1,000	Demonstration	Calling for removal of Agriom factory	Neighbourhood
84	5 July 2008	Gharbiyya	Workers at Tanta oils company	1,000	Strike	Economic hardship	Economic
85	7 July 2008	Alexandria	Workers at Amreya textile company	3,500	Sit-in	Economic hardship	Economic
86	8 July 2008	Cairo	Researchers at Desert Research Center	500	Rally	Against the posting of the Center's head to Washington	Economic
87	14 July 2008	Dakahlia	Residents of three villages	5,000	Road closure	Lack of water provision	Neighbourhood
88	24 July 2008	Alexandria	Residents of Toson neighbourhood	100s	Protest	House demolitions	Neighbourhood
89	28 July 2008	Gharbiyya	Workers at Nile cotton company	1,000	Sit-in	Economic hardship	Economic

No.	Date	Location	Protesters and their numbers		Type of Protest	Reason for Protest	Protest Category
90	7 Aug. 2008	Beni Sueif	Copts	100s	Sit-in	Disappearance of a Coptic citizen	Sectarian
91	10 Aug. 2008	Cairo	Al-Azhar teachers	3,000	Sit-in	Calling for permanent contracts	Economic
92	20 Aug. 2008	Fayoum	Citizens	100s	Rally	Hard living conditions	Economic
93	21 Aug. 2008	Cairo	Teachers	100s	Rally	Professional dispute with the Ministry of Education	Economic
94	22 Aug. 2008	Minya	Teachers	3,000	Demonstration	Professional dispute with the Ministry of Education	Economic
95	23 Aug. 2008	Fayoum	Teachers	500	Demonstration	Professional dispute with the Ministry of Education	Economic
96	24 Aug. 2008	Kafr el-Sheikh	Teachers	500	Demonstration	Professional dispute with the Ministry of Education	Economic
97	28 Aug. 2008	Fayoum	Teachers	100s	Rally	Professional dispute with the Ministry of Education	Economic

98	28 Aug. 2008	Dakahlia	Teachers	900	Rally	Professional dispute with the Ministry of Education	Economic
99	29 Aug. 2008	Red Sea	Citizens working in the Gulf	100s	Protest	Decision to cancel a trip on the Red Sea ferry	Economic
100	2 Sep. 2008	Ismailia	Workers of Suez Canal Port handling	500	Strike	Economic hardship	Economic
101	4 Sep. 2008	Qalyubia	Nurses and employees at Banha University Hospital	650	Strike	Economic hardship	Economic
102	5 Sep. 2008	Aswan	Citizens and lawyers	1,500	Rally	Police brutality	Anti-police
103	7 Sep. 2008	Port Said	Workers at Canal company	850	Sit-in	Economic hardship	Economic
104	10 Sep. 2008	Ismailia	Workers at Ismailia Poultry company	1,600	Strike	Economic hardship	Economic
105	13 Sep. 2008	Aswan	Nurses at Aswan Hospital	500	Sit-in	Calling to be associated with the Ministry of Health rather than the Ministry of Education	Economic

No.	Date	Location	Protesters and their numbers	Type of Protest	Reason for Protest	Protest Category
106	20 Sep. 2008	Munifiyya	School pupils	500	Strike	Protest on the first school day of the year (no obvious reason noted)	Economic
107	22 Sep. 2008	Alexandria	Parents of school pupils	1,000	Sit-in	School closure	Neighbourhood
108	22 Sep. 2008	Munifiyya	School pupils	500	Strike	Construction of mobile communication station near school	Neighbourhood
109	27 Sep. 2008	Suez	Workers at Emco Egypt	600	Sit-in	Economic hardship	Economic
110	28 Sep. 2008	Dakahlia	Employees of the Real Estate Tax Authority	100s	Sit-in	Economic hardship	Economic
111	28 Sep. 2008	Munifiyya	Workers at Munifiyya textile company	700	Sit-in	Economic hardship	Economic
112	7 Oct. 2008	Munifiyya	Workers at Munifiyya textile company	700	Road closure	Economic hardship	Economic
113	8 Oct. 2008	Alexandria	Citizens of a village	1,000	Road closure	Death of a child in a car accident	Neighbourhood

	Date	Location	Actors	Number	Type	Cause	Category
114	11 Oct. 2008	Gharbiyya	April 6, Kefaya and political parties	100s	Rally	Trial of Mahalla workers and April 6 activists	Anti-police
115	14 Oct. 2008	Gharbiyya	Muslim Brotherhood students at Tanta University	500	Protest	Prevention of Muslim Brotherhood students from running in student union election	Political
116	15 Oct. 2008	Fayoum	Citizens	100s	Demonstration	Hard living conditions	Economic
117	18 Oct. 2008	Munifiyya	Workers at ceramic company	1,000	Strike	Economic hardship	Economic
118	18 Oct. 2008	Cairo	Retired citizens	100s	Sit-in	Economic demands	Economic
119	20 Oct. 2008	Cairo	Muslim Brotherhood students at Cairo University	100s	Demonstration	Student union election	Political
120	20 Oct. 2008	Gharbiyya	Muslim Brotherhood students at Tanta University	8,000	Demonstration	Student union election	Political
121	20 Oct. 2008	Cairo	Muslim Brotherhood students at al-Azhar University	3,000	Demonstration	Student union election	Political

No.	Date	Location	Protesters and their numbers		Type of Protest	Reason for Protest	Protest Category
122	22 Oct. 2008	Gharbiyya	Workers at Mahalla hospital	650	Strike	Economic demands	Economic
123	26 Oct. 2008	Cairo	Retired citizens	100s	Sit-in	Economic demands	Economic
124	26 Oct. 2008	Sohag	Lawyers	500	Sit-in	Detention of a colleague	Anti-police
125	1 Nov. 2008	Gharbiyya	Residents of a village	500	Protest	Burial of waste	Neighbourhood
126	3 Nov. 2008	Giza	Parents of school pupils	600	Sit-in	Transfer of children to another school	Neighbourhood
127	4 Nov. 2008	Qalyubia	Students of Banha High Institute of Technology	3,000	Sit-in	Calling to convert institute into a college	Economic
128	11 Nov. 2008	Cairo	Muslim Brotherhood students at al-Azhar University	3,000	Protest	Removal of 270 Muslim Brotherhood students from al-Azhar dorms	Economic
129	23 Nov. 2008	Cairo	Citizens	100s	Demonstration	Disappearance of blogger Mohamed Adel	Anti-police
130	23 Nov. 2008	Aswan	Nubians	3,000	Protest	Police brutality	Anti-police

131	24 Nov. 2008	Cairo	Al-Azhar University students	3,000	Demonstration	Solidarity with Gaza	Regional
132	24 Nov. 2008	Dakahlia	Students and professors at Mansoura University	2,000	Demonstration	Solidarity with Gaza	Regional
133	24 Nov. 2008	Cairo	Muslim Brotherhood students at Cairo University	1,000	Demonstration	Solidarity with Gaza	Regional
134	26 Nov. 2008	Cairo	Muslim Brotherhood students at Cairo University	1,000	Demonstration	Solidarity with Gaza	Regional
135	26 Nov. 2008	Damietta	Muslim Brotherhood, syndicates, and political forces	1,500	Demonstration	Solidarity with Gaza	Regional
136	26 Nov. 2008	Cairo	Students at al-Azhar University	6,000	Demonstration	Solidarity with Gaza	Regional
137	27 Nov. 2008	Luxor	Workers at Alabaster company	500	Protest	Power cuts	Economic
138	28 Nov. 2008	Qena	Muslim Brotherhood	500	Demonstration	Solidarity with Gaza	Regional
139	28 Nov. 2008	Damietta	Political forces	2,000	Demonstration	Solidarity with Gaza	Regional
140	30 Nov. 2008	Gharbiyya	Political forces	10,000	Demonstration	Solidarity with Gaza	Regional
141	1 Dec. 2008	Asyut	Muslim Brotherhood students	4,000	Demonstration	Solidarity with Gaza	Regional

No.	Date	Location	Protesters and their numbers		Type of Protest	Reason for Protest	Protest Category
142	1 Dec. 2008	Cairo	Students of Ain Shams University and the Haqqy ('My Right') movement	100s	Demonstration	Solidarity with Gaza	Regional
143	25 Dec. 2008	Qalyubia	Workers at metal projects company	1,000	Sit-in	Protest against the company's losses	Economic
144	25 Dec. 2008	Asyut	Citizens of a village	100s	Road closure	Contested location of burial site of holy figure	Neighbour-hood
145	27 Dec. 2008	Cairo	Political forces	2,000	Demonstration	Solidarity with Gaza	Regional
146	27 Dec. 2008	Helwan	Workers of Nasr car companies	2,300	Sit-in	Economic demands	Economic
147	29 Dec. 2008	Qalyubia	Tagammu' party	1,000	Demonstration	Solidarity with Gaza	Regional
148	29 Dec. 2008	Sharqiyya	Muslim Brotherhood	5,000	Demonstration	Solidarity with Gaza	Regional
149	29 Dec. 2008	Kafr el-Sheikh	Muslim Brotherhood	5,000	March	Solidarity with Gaza	Regional
150	29 Dec. 2008	Fayoum	Muslim Brotherhood	100s	March	Solidarity with Gaza	Regional
151	31 Dec. 2008	Cairo	Political forces	1,000s	Demonstration	Solidarity with Gaza	Regional
152	1 Jan. 2009	Dakahlia	Muslim Brotherhood women	5,000	Demonstration	Solidarity with Gaza	Regional
153	2 Jan. 2009	Different cities	Citizens	10,000	Demonstration	Solidarity with Gaza	Regional

154	3 Jan. 2009	Different cities	Citizens	1,000s	Demonstration	Solidarity with Gaza	Regional
155	4 Jan. 2009	Different cities	Citizens (mostly Muslim Brotherhood)	10,000	Demonstration	Solidarity with Gaza	Regional
156	5 Jan. 2009	Different cities	Citizens (mostly Muslim Brotherhood)	10,000	Demonstration	Solidarity with Gaza	Regional
157	6 Jan. 2009	Gharbiyya	Lawyers and citizens	4,000	Demonstration	Solidarity with Gaza	Regional
158	6 Jan. 2009	Beni Sueif	Citizens (organized by NDP)	2,000	Demonstration	Solidarity with Gaza	Regional
159	8 Jan. 2009	Kafr el-Sheikh	Muslim Brotherhood women	8,000	Demonstration	Solidarity with Gaza	Regional
160	9 Jan. 2009	Different cities	Citizens and Muslim Brotherhood	200,000	Demonstration	Solidarity with Gaza	Regional
161	12 Jan. 2009	Dakahlia	Muslim Brotherhood	15,000	Demonstration	Solidarity with Gaza	Regional
162	14 Jan. 2009	Port Said	Muslim Brotherhood	3,000	Demonstration	Solidarity with Gaza	Regional
163	15 Jan. 2009	Gharbiyya	Muslim Brotherhood	25,000	Demonstration	Solidarity with Gaza	Regional
164	15 Jan. 2009	Beheira	Muslim Brotherhood	2,000	Demonstration	Solidarity with Gaza	Regional
165	15 Jan. 2009	Dakahlia	Physicians	500	Demonstration	Solidarity with Gaza	Regional
166	17 Jan. 2009	Gharbiyya	Citizens	4,000	Demonstration	Solidarity with Gaza	Regional
167	17 Jan. 2009	Cairo	Muslim Brotherhood	10,000	Demonstration	Solidarity with Gaza	Regional

No.	Date	Location	Protesters and their numbers		Type of Protest	Reason for Protest	Protest Category
168	18 Jan. 2009	Gharbiyya	Muslim Brotherhood youth	1,500	Demonstration	Solidarity with Gaza	Regional
169	18 Jan. 2009	Suez	Citizens	4,000	Demonstration	Solidarity with Gaza	Regional
170	18 Jan. 2009	Port Said	Citizens	1,700	Demonstration	Economic demands	Economic
171	20 Jan. 2009	Cairo	Train drivers	500	Sit-in	Economic demands	Economic
172	23 Jan. 2009	Dakahlia	Muslim Brotherhood	20,000	Demonstration	Solidarity with Gaza	Regional
173	23 Jan. 2009	Asyut	Muslim Brotherhood	5,000	Demonstration	Solidarity with Gaza	Regional
174	27 Jan. 2009	Cairo	Train drivers	700	Sit-in	Economic demands	Economic
175	28 Jan. 2009	Cairo	Workers of Nile Cairo hotel	800	Sit-in	Economic demands	Economic
176	30 Jan. 2009	Gharbiyya	Citizens	2,000	Rally	Economic hardship	Economic
177	31 Jan. 2009	Ismailia	Lawyers	1,500	Sit-in	Detention of a colleague	Anti-police
178	3 Febr. 2009	Beni Sueif	Workers of Kom Abu Rady railway workshops	1,600	Strike	Economic demands	Economic
179	6 Febr. 2009	Beni Sueif	Citizens	5,000	Rally	Solidarity with Gaza	Regional
180	6 Febr. 2009	Minya	Muslim Brotherhood	2,000	Demonstration	Solidarity with Gaza	Regional
181	6 Febr. 2009	Fayoum	Muslim Brotherhood	8,000	Demonstration	Solidarity with Gaza	Regional

	Date	Location	Group	Number	Action	Demand	Category
182	8 Febr. 2009	Cairo	Taxi and microbus drivers	100s	Sit-in	New traffic law	Economic
183	12 Febr. 2009	Kafr el-Sheikh	Citizens	500	Rally	Construction of mobile communication station	Neighbourhood
184	13 Febr. 2009	Different cities	Truck drivers	1,000s	Strike	Abolishment of trucks	Economic
185	16 Febr. 2009	Different cities	Pharmacists	1,000s	Strike	New taxes	Economic
186	18 Febr. 2009	Cairo	Lawyers	100s	Sit-in	New judicial tax law	Economic
187	21 Febr. 2009	Cairo	Students at Cairo, Ain Shams and Helwan universities, as well as Kefaya	1,000s	Demonstration	World Student Day	Regional
188	24 Febr. 2009	Cairo	Lawyers	1,000s	Sit-in	New judicial tax law	Economic
189	24 Febr. 2009	Different cities	Teachers	1,000s	Strike	Professional dispute with the Ministry of Education	Economic
190	27 Febr. 2009	Minya	Copts	1,000	Mob	Sectarian tension	Sectarian
191	2 Mar. 2009	Qalyubia	Students at Banha High Institute of Technology	3,000	Strike	Calling for converting institute into a college	Economic
192	2 Mar. 2009	Alexandria	Microbus drivers	2,000	Strike	Economic demands	Economic

No.	Date	Location	Protesters and their numbers		Type of Protest	Reason for Protest	Protest Category
193	5 Mar. 2009	Munifiyya	Workers in textile company	3,000	Rally	Economic demands	Economic
194	15 Mar. 2009	Dakahlia	Citizens	5,000	Sit-in	House demolitions	Neighbour-hood
195	15 Mar. 2009	Aswan	Students at High Institute of Energy	3,000	Strike	Calling for accreditation of certificates	Economic
196	18 Mar. 2009	Ismailia	Workers of care service company	500	Strike	Economic demands	Economic
197	20 Mar. 2009	Sohag	Employees of local units	600	Rally	Administrative decisions	Economic
198	22 Mar. 2009	Kafr el-Sheikh	Employees of General Authority for Agrarian Reform	1,500	Mob	Economic demands	Economic
199	22 Mar. 2009	Dakahlia	Employees of General Authority for Agrarian Reform	1,200	Mob	Economic demands	Economic
200	28 Mar. 2009	Different cities	Teachers and technicians	1,000s	Strike	Professional dispute with the Ministry of Education	Economic

	Date	Location	Group	Number	Action	Cause	Category
201	29 Mar. 2009	Different cities	Teachers and technicians	1,000s	Strike	Professional dispute with the Ministry of Education	Economic
202	30 Mar. 2009	Cairo	Employees of Workers University	2,000	Sit-in	Economic demands	Economic
203	1 Apr. 2009	Cairo	Families in Sharabiya neighbourhood	100s	Protest	Relocation outside Cairo	Neighbourhood
204	7 Apr. 2009	Minya	Farmers	500	Demonstration	Destruction of crops	Neighbourhood
205	7 Apr. 2009	Different cities	Political forces	100s	Demonstration	Anniversary of 6 April 2008 strike	Political
206	8 Apr. 2009	Different cities	Physicians	10s of 1,000s	Strike	Economic demands	Economic
207	13 Apr. 2009	Fayoum	Muslim Brotherhood students of Fayoum University	100s	Demonstration	Detention of three colleagues	Anti-police
208	14 Apr. 2009	Helwan	Workers of Helwan cement company	100s	Sit-in	Economic demands	Economic
209	15 Apr. 2009	Cairo	Administrative staff at Ministry of Education	100s	Demonstration	Economic demands	Economic

No.	Date	Location	Protesters and their numbers		Type of Protest	Reason for Protest	Protest Category
210	15 Apr. 2009	Fayoum	Muslim Brotherhood students of Fayoum University	100s	Demonstration	Detention of colleagues	Anti-police
211	25 Apr. 2009	Minya	Copts	100s	Rally	Sectarian tensions	Sectarian
212	28 Apr. 2009	Fayoum	Taxi and microbus drivers	100s	Strike	Administrative decisions	Economic
213	28 Apr. 2009	Gharbiyya, Beheira, Minya	Workers of Nile cotton company	100s	Sit-in	Economic demands	Economic
214	5 May 2009	Alexandria	Workers of Amreya pharmaceutical company	2,500	Sit-in	Economic demands	Economic
215	5 May 2009	Munifiyya	Workers of Andorama textiles company	4,000	Sit-in	Economic demands	Economic
216	7 May 2009	Kafr el-Sheikh	Employees at post offices	800	Rally and strike	Economic demands	Economic
217	10 May 2009	Suez	Workers at Egyptian drilling company	500	Sit-in	Protest against being fired	Economic

				1,000s	Demonstration		Regional
218	15 May 2009	Different cities	Muslim Brotherhood	1,000s	Demonstration	Israeli prime minister's visit to Egypt	Regional
219	18 May 2009	Cairo	Employees at the postal authority	100s	Sit-in	Economic demands	Economic
220	18 May 2009	Kafr el-Sheikh	Employees at the postal authority	1,000	Sit-in	Economic demands	Economic
221	31 May 2009	Gharbiyya	Workers of Tanta oils company	1,300	Strike	Economic demands	Economic
222	6 June 2009	Dakahlia	Farmers	500	Rally	Lack of water for irrigation	Neighbourhood
223	11 June 2009	Minya	Copts	1,000s	Rally and Sit-in	Village name change	Neighbourhood
224	17 June 2009	Different cities	Experts at Ministry of Justice	700	Rallies	Administrative decisions	Economic
225	20 June 2009	North Sinai	Bedouins	100s	Road closure	Police brutality	Anti-police
226	22 June 2009	Cairo	Experts at Ministry of Justice	100s	Mob	Administrative decisions	Economic
227	23 June 2009	6th of October (Cairo)	Workers at four shipbuilding companies	100s	Sit-in	Governor's administrative decisions	Economic

No.	Date	Location	Protesters and their numbers	Type of Protest	Reason for Protest	Protest Category
228	24 June 2009	Gharbiyya	Employees of the Real Estate Tax Authority	Sit-in	Economic demands	Economic
229	27 June 2009	Asyut	Citizens	Mob	Governor's administrative decisions	Economic
230	29 June 2009	Luxor	Fresh Graduates	Mob	Elimination from hiring exams	Economic
231	29 June 2009	Munifiyya	Farmers	Mob	Hard living conditions	Economic
232	6 July 2009	Cairo	Employees at the Academy of Scientific Research and Technology	Demonstration	Economic demands	Economic
233	12 July 2009	Gharbiyya	Workers of Aboul Seba company	Road closure	Economic demands	Economic
234	14 July 2009	Cairo	Experts at Ministry of Justice	Demonstration	Administrative decisions	Economic
235	14 July 2009	Gharbiyya	Citizens	Mob and road closure	Car accident	Neighbourhood

236	16 July 2009	Minya	Workers and owners of quarries	1,000s	Road closure	Economic demands	Economic
237	25 July 2009	Ain Sukhna	Workers at Dubai ports company	700	Sit-in	Protest against being laid off	Economic
238	26 July 2009	Alexandria	Workers of Corona company	600	Sit-in	Economic demands	Economic
239	27 July 2009	Fayoum	Workers of Sadat City factories	800	Strike	Economic demands	Economic
240	29 July 2009	Qena	Workers of Sokkar Kos factory	1,200	Sit-in	Economic demands and dispute with management	Economic
241	29 July 2009	Gharbiyya	Citizens	500	Protest	Administrative decisions related to health insurance	Economic
242	8 Aug. 2009	Minya	Truck drivers at quarries	600	Strike	Administrative decisions	Economic
243	10 Aug. 2009	Helwan	Workers of the Egyptian Telephone Equipment Manufacturing Company	500	Sit-in	Early-retirement settlements	Economic
244	11 Aug. 2009	Cairo	Employees of the Real Estate Tax Authority	1,000	Sit-in	Trade union practices	Economic

WHY OCCUPY A SQUARE?

No.	Date	Location	Protesters and their numbers	Protesters and their numbers	Type of Protest	Reason for Protest	Protest Category
245	16 Aug. 2009	Gharbiyya	Workers of Marla textile company	100s	Rally	Economic demands and administrative decisions	Economic
246	18 Aug. 2009	Different cities	Employees at the Public Transport Authority	15,000	Strike	Overvalued traffic fines and unpaid social insurance	Economic
247	22 Aug. 2009	Damietta	Employees at the Ministry of Agriculture	1,000	Demonstration	Administrative decisions	Economic
248	3 Sep. 2009	Sharqiyya	Teachers on permanent contracts	4,000	Sit-in	Cancellation of contracts	Economic
249	8 Sep. 2009	Giza	Residents of Mohamed's Island village	1,000s	Stay at home	Decision not to assign village to Giza governorate	Neighbourhood
250	14 Sep. 2009	Cairo	Employees at water company	1,000	Sit-in	Economic demands	Economic
251	15 Sep. 2009	Alexandria	Workers of Nasr textiles company	7,000	Strike	Economic demands	Economic
252	16 Sep. 2009	Munifiyya	Workers of the Egyptian company for textiles	700	Strike	Economic demands	Economic

	Date	Location	Participants	Number	Form	Description	Category
253	30 Sep. 2009	Helwan	Workers of the Egyptian Telephone Equipment Manufacturing Company	1,200	Sit-in	Economic demands	Economic
254	7 Oct. 2009	Cairo	Al-Azhar University students	700	Rally	Dorm accommodation problems	Economic
255	8 Oct. 2009	Cairo	Lawyers	1,000s	Demonstration	Anti-Israel demonstration	Regional
256	9 Oct. 2009	Cairo	Citizens	1,000s	Demonstration	Anti-Israel demonstration	Regional
257	12 Oct. 2009	Cairo	Students of different universities	1,000s	Demonstration	Anti-Israel demonstration	Regional
258	12 Oct. 2009	Alexandria	University students	5,000	Demonstration	Anti-Israel demonstration	Regional
259	12 Oct. 2009	Fayoum	University students	100s	Demonstration	Anti-Israel demonstration	Regional
260	15 Oct. 2009	Sharqiyya	Workers of Misr-Iran textile company	1,300	Strike	Economic demands	Economic
261	26 Oct. 2009	Cairo	Muslim Brotherhood university students	100s	Rally	Anti-Israel demonstration	Regional
262	26 Oct. 2009	Alexandria	University students	2,000	Demonstration	Anti-Israel demonstration	Regional

No.	Date	Location	Protesters and their numbers	Type of Protest	Reason for Protest	Protest Category
263	26 Oct. 2009	Dakahlia	Muslim Brotherhood university students	Demonstration	Anti-Israel demonstration	Regional
264	27 Oct. 2009	Cairo	Muslim Brotherhood university students	Demonstration	Student union election and anti-Israel demonstration	Political and regional
265	30 Oct. 2009	Cairo	Employees of real estate registration authority	Demonstration	Calling for independence of real estate registration authority	Economic
266	1 Nov. 2009	Minya	University students and the head of the university	Demonstration	Anti-Israel demonstration	Regional
267	3 Nov. 2009	Cairo	Students of al-Azhar University	Rally	Death of twelve students at hands of police	Anti-police
268	14 Nov. 2009	Cairo	Residents of Warraq neighbourhood	Sit-in	Land confiscations	Neighbourhood
269	17 Nov. 2009	Suez	Workers of the Egyptian cement company	Sit-in	Economic demands	Economic
270	23 Nov. 2009	Beni Sueif	Citizens	Protest	Governor's administrative decisions	Neighbourhood

271	1 Dec. 2009	Gharbiyya	Citizens	100s	Mob	House demolitions	Neighbourhood
272	5 Dec. 2009	Cairo	Retired citizens, political forces (Tagammu' and Ghad Party)	500	Protest	New health insurance law	Economic
273	6 Dec. 2009	Cairo	Students at physiotherapy college	100s	Demonstration and sit-in	Administrative decision transforming college into an institute	Economic
274	7 Dec. 2009	Cairo	Workers of the Egyptian Telephone Equipment Manufacturing Company	600	Sit-in	Economic demands	Economic
275	18 Dec. 2009	Damietta	Citizens	1,000s	Rally	Prevalence of police bullying and illegal drugs	Anti-police
276	24 Dec. 2009	Aswan	Citizens	100s	Mob	Police brutality	Anti-police
277	26 Dec. 2009	Cairo	Lawyers	800	Sit in	Police insulting a colleague	Anti-police
278	28 Dec. 2009	Sharqiyya	Citizens	100s	Mob	Hard living conditions	Economic

No.	Date	Location	Protesters and their numbers		Type of Protest	Reason for Protest	Protest Category
279	29 Dec. 2009	Dakahlia	Muslim Brotherhood university students and professors	1,000s	Rally	Gaza border wall	Regional
280	31 Dec. 2009	Dakahlia	Citizens	100s	Sit-in	Administrative decision to sell their land	Economic
281	1 Jan. 2010	Gharbiyya	Citizens	100s	Mob	Hard living conditions	Economic
282	5 Jan. 2010	Cairo	Workers at Honeywell Company	2,000	Strike	Economic hardship	Economic
283	25 Jan. 2010	Sharqiyya	Citizens	100s	Protest	Administrative decisions of housing minister	Neighbourhood
284	26 Jan. 2010	Beheira	Physicians and nurses at National Medical Institute	100s	Strike	Administrative decision	Economic
285	27 Jan. 2010	Kafr el-Sheikh	Farmers	100s	Sit-in	Confiscation of livestock	Neighbourhood
286	30 Jan. 2010	Cairo	Members of Commerce Syndicate	1,600	Sit-in	Economic hardship	Economic

	Date	Location	Group	Size	Type	Cause	Category
287	3 Febr. 2010	Dakahlia	Microbus drivers	800	Strike	Economic hardship	Economic
288	10 Febr. 2010	Sharqiyya	Nurses and technicians at Zagazig University hospital	1,500	Strike	Economic hardship	Economic
289	18 Febr. 2010	Cairo	Political opposition forces	1,000	Demonstration	ElBaradei's arrival at airport	Political
290	18 Febr. 2010	Munifiyya	Workers at Andorama company	2,300	Strike	Economic hardship	Economic
291	28 Febr. 2010	Different cities	Students at Zagazig, Cairo and al-Azhar universities	100s	Demonstration	Solidarity with Palestinians and al-Aqsa Mosque	Regional
292	2 Mar. 2010	Nationwide	University students	1,000s	Demonstration	Solidarity with Palestinians and al-Aqsa Mosque	Regional
293	6 Mar. 2010	Different cities	Employees at Local Development Ministry	100s	Demonstration	Economic hardship	Economic
294	12 Mar. 2010	Cairo	Muslim citizens at al-Azhar Mosque	2,000	Demonstration	Solidarity with Palestinians and al-Aqsa Mosque	Regional
295	12 Mar. 2010	Dakahlia	Muslim Brotherhood	20,000	Demonstration	Support for Hamas	Regional

WHY OCCUPY A SQUARE?

No.	Date	Location	Protesters and their numbers		Type of Protest	Reason for Protest	Protest Category
296	12 Mar. 2010	Different cities	Muslim Brotherhood	1,000s	Demonstration	Solidarity with Palestinians and al-Aqsa Mosque	Regional
297	15 Mar. 2010	Nationwide	Muslim Brotherhood students in 18 universities	30,000	Demonstration	Solidarity with Palestinians and al-Aqsa Mosque	Regional
298	15 Mar. 2010	Gharbiyya	Workers at Tanta company	800	Protest	Economic hardship	Economic
299	16 Mar. 2010	Nationwide	Students at different universities	1,000s	Protest	Solidarity with Palestinians and al-Aqsa Mosque	Regional
300	16 Mar. 2010	Fayoum	Students and the head of Fayoum University	2,500	Protest	Solidarity with Palestinians and al-Aqsa Mosque	Regional
301	17 Mar. 2010	Dakahlia	Muslim Brotherhood students at Mansoura University	2,000	Protest	Solidarity with Palestinians and al-Aqsa Mosque	Regional
302	17 Mar. 2010	Sohag	Muslim Brotherhood students at Sohag University	1,000	Protest	Solidarity with Palestinians and al-Aqsa Mosque	Regional

303	19 Mar. 2010	Cairo	Muslim citizens at al-Azhar Mosque	1,000s	Protest	Solidarity with Palestinians and al-Aqsa Mosque	Regional
304	19 Mar. 2010	Gharbiyya	Muslim citizens	1,000s	Protest	Solidarity with Palestinians and al-Aqsa Mosque	Regional
305	28 Mar. 2010	Gharbiyya	Workers at Tanta company	600	Sit-in	Economic hardship	Economic
306	30 Mar. 2010	Cairo	Residents of Manshiyat Naser neighbourhood	100s	Sit-in	Prevention of house demolitions	Neighbourhood
307	2 Apr. 2010	Dakahlia	Citizens	1,000	March	Support for ElBaradei	Political
308	3 Apr. 2010	Cairo	Workers and political activists	500	Demonstration	Calling for higher minimum wage	Economic
309	5 Apr. 2010	Cairo	Residents of Manshiyat Naser neighbourhood	100s	Protest	Prevention of house demolitions	Neighbourhood
310	6 Apr. 2010	Gharbiyya	University students	10,000	Demonstration	Anniversary of 6 April 2008 strike	Political
311	6 Apr. 2010	Beni Sueif	University students	500	Demonstration	Anniversary of 6 April 2008 strike	Political

No.	Date	Location	Protesters and their numbers	Type of Protest	Reason for Protest	Protest Category
312	6 Apr. 2010	Asyut	University students	1,000	Demonstration	Anniversary of 6 April 2008 strike	Political
313	10 Apr. 2010	Cairo	Employees at Al Hussein Hospital	100s	Protest	Economic hardship	Economic
314	18 Apr. 2010	Munifiyya	Workers at steel company	500	Protest	The firing of a colleague	Economic
315	21 Apr. 2010	Qena	Workers at aluminium factory in Nag Hammadi	2,000	Sit-in	Economic hardship	Economic
316	28 Apr. 2010	Sohag	Citizens	10,000	Mob	Conflict with governor	Neighbourhood
317	2 May 2010	Cairo	Workers, farmers and political activists	1,000	Demonstration	Calling for higher minimum wage	Economic
318	2 May 2010	Nationwide	Employees at national real estate registration offices	100s	Strike	Economic hardship	Economic
319	8 May 2010	Minya	Workers at sugar factories	100s	Strike	Economic hardship	Economic

320	12 May 2010	Cairo	Supporters of Mostafa Bakry (prominent independent parliamentarian)	100s	Mob	Parliamentary election	Political
321	14 May 2010	Gharbiyya	Citizens	100s	Mob	Emergency law	Political
322	15 May 2010	Cairo	Supporters of Mostafa Bakry (prominent independent parliamentarian)	100s	Mob	Parliamentary election	Political
323	21 May 2010	Beheira	Muslim Brotherhood	1,000	Demonstration	Parliamentary election	Political
324	21 May 2010	Kafr el-Sheikh	Muslim Brotherhood	1,000	Demonstration	Parliamentary election	Political
325	24 May 2010	Helwan	Lawyers	100s	Sit-in	Police violence	Anti-police
326	25 May 2010	Kafr el-Sheikh	Muslim Brotherhood	3,000	Sit-in	Parliamentary election	Political
327	25 May 2010	Qalyubia	Banha University students	100s	Demonstration	Administrative decisions	Economic
328	26 May 2010	Gharbiyya	Workers at Tanta company	700	Protest	Economic hardship	Economic

No.	Date	Location	Protesters and their numbers	Type of Protest	Reason for Protest	Protest Category
329	30 May 2010	Gharbiyya	Pharmacists	Strike	Government control over pharmacists' syndicate	Economic
330	31 May 2010	Cairo	Lawyers	Demonstration	Calling for head of syndicate to step down	Economic
331	1 June 2010	Munifiyya	Workers at steel company	Strike	Economic hardship	Economic
332	4 June 2010	Alexandria	Citizens, Muslim Brotherhood, political forces and professional syndicates	Demonstration	Solidarity with Palestinians	Regional
333	4 June 2010	Gharbiyya	Muslim citizens	Demonstration	Solidarity with Palestinians	Regional
334	4 June 2010	Suez	Citizens, Muslim Brotherhood, political forces	Demonstration	Solidarity with Palestinians	Regional
335	4 June 2010	Asyut	Citizens and Muslim Brotherhood	Demonstration	Solidarity with Palestinians	Regional

	Date	Location	Group	Number	Action	Cause	Category
336	4 June 2010	North Sinai	Citizens and political forces	100s	Demonstration	Solidarity with Palestinians	Regional
337	4 June 2010	Cairo	Citizens	100s	Demonstration	Solidarity with Palestinians	Regional
338	5 June 2010	Suez	Citizens	500	Protest	House demolitions	Neighbourhood
339	8 June 2010	Gharbiyya	Lawyers	1,000s	Mob	Dispute with judges and calls for release of detained colleagues	Anti-police
340	8 June 2010	Fayoum	Lawyers	4,000	Strike	Dispute with judges and calls for release of detained colleagues	Anti-police
341	8 June 2010	Suez	Lawyers	100s	Strike	Dispute with judges and calls for release of detained colleagues	Anti-police
342	9 June 2010	Gharbiyya	Lawyers	10,000	Demonstration	Dispute with judges and calls for release of detained colleagues	Anti-police
343	9 June 2010	Cairo	Air hosts	500	Sit-in at EgyptAir	Economic hardship	Economic

No.	Date	Location	Protesters and their numbers	Protesters and their numbers	Type of Protest	Reason for Protest	Protest Category
344	12 June 2010	Dakahlia	Lawyers	100s	Sit-in	Dispute with judges and calls for release of detained colleagues	Anti-police
345	12 June 2010	Minya	Lawyers	1,000s	Strike	Dispute with judges and calls for release of detained colleagues	Anti-police
346	12 June 2010	Suez	Lawyers	700	Demonstration	Dispute with judges and calls for release of detained colleagues	Anti-police
347	12 June 2010	Fayoum	Lawyers	100s	Mob	Dispute with judges and calls for release of detained colleagues	Anti-police
348	13 June 2010	Alexandria	Lawyers	100s	Demonstration	Dispute with judges and calls for release of detained colleagues	Anti-police

	Date	Location	Participants	Number	Type	Grievance	Category
349	13 June 2010	Dakahlia	Employees at the General Authority for Water Resources and Irrigation	500	Sit-in	Economic hardship	Economic
350	14 June 2010	Fayoum	Lawyers	100s	Demonstration	Dispute with judges and calls for release of detained colleagues	Anti-police
351	15 June 2010	Gharbiyya	Lawyers	100s	Demonstration	Dispute with judges and calls for release of detained colleagues	Anti-police
352	21 June 2010	Nationwide	Administrative staff at Ministry of Education	1,000s	Sit-in	Economic hardship	Economic
353	24 June 2010	Qalyubia	Lawyers	100s	Demonstration	Dispute with judges and calls for release of detained colleagues	Anti-police
354	25 June 2010	Alexandria	Citizens, political activists	1,000s	Demonstration	Murder of Khaled Said by police	Anti-police
355	26 June 2010	Different cities	Lawyers	1,000s	Sit-in	Dispute with judges and calls for release of detained colleagues	Anti-police

No.	Date	Location	Protesters and their numbers	Type of Protest	Reason for Protest	Protest Category
356	1 July 2010	Sinai	Bedouins	Demonstration	Calling for fulfillment of security and economic demands	Anti-police and economic
357	10 July 2010	Different cities	Facebook activists and political forces	Rally	Khaled Said	Anti-police
358	12 July 2010	Cairo	Employees of Amonisto Company	Sit-in	Economic demands	Economic
359	17 July 2010	Suez	Citizens	Mob	Hard living conditions	Economic
360	20 July 2010	Ismailia	Workers of Suez Canal Port handling	Sit-in	Economic demands	Economic
361	22 July 2010	Cairo	Copts	Protest	Conversion of a Copt	Sectarian
362	24 July 2010	Tanta, Beni Sueif, Asyut	Political activists from Kefaya and April 6 and Muslim Brotherhood	Demonstration	Khaled Said	Anti-police
363	25 July 2010	Minya	Copts	Sit-in	Refusal to grant permission to build a new church	Neighbourhood

	Date	Location	Group	Number	Action	Cause	Category
364	27 July 2010	Alexandria	Political activists	500	Mob	Khaled Said	Anti-police
365	8 Aug. 2010	Cairo	Engineers and workers of power stations	500	Protest	Economic hardship	Economic
366	15 Aug. 2010	Gharbiyya	Nurses and employees at various hospitals	1,000	Protest	Economic hardship	Economic
367	23 Aug. 2010	6th of October (Cairo)	Citizens	500	Protest	Hard living conditions	Economic
368	3 Sep. 2010	Gharbiyya	Lawyers	100s	Protest	Dispute with judges and calls for release of detained colleagues	Anti-police
369	6 Sep. 2010	Cairo	Muslim citizens	500	Mob	Conversion of a Copt	Sectarian
370	10 Sep. 2010	Cairo	Muslim citizens	100s	Mob	Conversion of a Copt	Sectarian
371	14 Sep. 2010	Cairo	Employees at Local Development Ministry	100s	Sit-in	Economic hardship	Economic
372	21 Sep. 2010	Cairo	Political activists from Kefaya and April 6	600	Rally	Gamal Mubarak succeeding his father	Political

No.	Date	Location	Protesters and their numbers		Type of Protest	Reason for Protest	Protest Category
373	1 Oct. 2010	Cairo	Muslim citizens	2,000	Demonstration	Conversion of a Copt	Sectarian
374	4 Oct. 2010	Damietta	Nurses and employees at al-Azhar hospital	700	Strike	Economic hardship	Economic
375	4 Oct. 2010	Fayoum	Muslim Brotherhood students	100s	Mob	Against police authority within university	Anti-police
376	8 Oct. 2010	Alexandria	Muslim and Salafist citizens	1,000	Mob	Conversion of a Copt	Sectarian
377	11 Oct. 2010	Cairo	Employees at Local Development Ministry	100s	Protest	Economic hardship	Economic
378	12 Oct. 2010	Gharbiyya	Muslim Brotherhood students	1,000s	Demonstration	Student union election	Political
379	19 Oct. 2010	Giza	Parents of school pupils	100s	Mob	School closure	Neighbourhood
380	19 Oct. 2010	Cairo	Employees at Local Development Ministry	100s	Sit-in	Economic hardship	Economic

381	22 Oct. 2010	Cairo	Muslim citizens	100s	Demonstration	Conversion of a Copt	Sectarian
382	22 Oct. 2010	Alexandria	Muslim citizens	100s	Demonstration	Conversion of a Copt	Sectarian
383	23 Oct. 2010	Gharbiyya	Employees at power distribution company	800	Sit-in	Economic hardship	Economic
384	24 Oct. 2010	Cairo	Students of Al-Azhar University	1,000s	Rally	Against police authority within university	Anti-police
385	26 Oct. 2010	Cairo	Employees at Local Development Ministry	1,000s	Road closure	Economic hardship	Economic
386	27 Oct. 2010	Helwan	Muslim Brotherhood students at Helwan University	100s	Demonstration	Calling for release of detained colleagues	Anti-police
387	31 Oct. 2010	Kafr el-Sheikh	Teachers on temporary contracts	100s	Rally	Calling for permanent employment	Economic
388	3 Nov. 2010	Sharqiyya	Al-Azhar University students in Zagazig	1,000s	Demonstration	Against police authority within university	Anti-police

No.	Date	Location	Protesters and their numbers		Type of Protest	Reason for Protest	Protest Category
389	4 Nov. 2010	Alexandria	Muslim Brotherhood	2,000	Protest	Parliamentary election (not permitting their candidates to run)	Political
390	9 Nov. 2010	Gharbiyya	Al-Azhar University students in Tanta	2,000	Demonstration	Against police authority within university	Anti-police
391	10 Nov. 2010	Munifiyya	Workers at Petrotrade company	1,500	Sit-in	Economic hardship	Economic
392	10 Nov. 2010	Cairo	Employees at Local Development Ministry	100s	Mob	Economic hardship	Economic
393	13 Nov. 2010	Dakahlia	Citizens	500	Protest	Parliamentary election	Political
394	13 Nov. 2010	Suez	Employees at a textile company	500	Sit-in	Economic hardship	Economic
395	24 Nov. 2010	Giza	Copts	500	Demonstration	Sectarian tension	Sectarian
396	25 Nov. 2010	Beni Sueif	Muslim Brotherhood	3,000	March	Parliamentary election	Political
397	25 Nov. 2010	Different cities	Copts	100s	Sit-in in Churches	Sectarian tension	Sectarian

398	25 Nov. 2010	Toshka	Employees and workers at South Valley Company	500	Strike	Economic hardship	Economic
399	25 Nov. 2010	Munifiyya	Supporters of an NDP candidate	1,500	Demonstration	Parliamentary election	Political
400	25 Nov. 2010	Minya	Supporters of an NDP candidate	1,000	Demonstration	Parliamentary election	Political
401	25 Nov. 2010	Qena	Supporters of an independent candidate	1,000	Demonstration	Parliamentary election	Political
402	1 Dec. 2010	Different cities	Muslim Brotherhood students in seven universities	1,000s	Demonstration	Election fraud	Political
403	5 Dec. 2010	Minya	Citizens	1,000	Mob	Election fraud	Political
404	11 Dec. 2010	Nationwide	Truck drivers	1,000s	Strike	Tax laws	Economic
405	11 Dec. 2010	Cairo	Political opposition forces	100s	Mob	Election fraud	Political
406	26 Dec. 2010	Cairo	Employees at Abasseya Hospital	100s	Demonstration	Hospital demolition decision	Economic
407	26 Dec. 2010	Cairo	Employees at National Health Insurance Organisation	100s	Strike	Calling for permanent employment	Economic

No.	Date	Location	Protesters and their numbers		Type of Protest	Reason for Protest	Protest Category
408	26 Dec. 2010	Cairo	Workers at textile company	800	Sit-in	Against laying off workers	Economic
409	27 Dec. 2010	Cairo	School pupils	3,000	Protest	Against changing school's educational system	Economic
410	31 Dec. 2010	Cairo	School pupils	5,000	Protest	Against changing school's educational system	Economic

Table A.2: Estimated number of protesters per category per month in protests numbering 500 or more, as reported in *al-Masry al-Youm* (Arabic) (2008–2010).

	Economic	Political	Anti-Police	Neigh-bourhood	Regional	Sectarian	Total
Jan. 2008	6,000	2,000	0	500	9,500	0	18,000
Feb. 2008	20,200	0	12,000	0	0	0	32,200
Mar. 2008	3,650	11,500	0	1,000	9,500	0	25,650
Apr. 2008	35,100	4,500	6,650	9,500	0	0	55,750
May 2008	12,500	0	0	0	500	0	13,000
June 2008	3,300	0	0	4,500	0	500	8,300
July 2008	12,000	0	0	6,500	0	0	18,500
Aug. 2008	9,900	0	0	0	0	500	10,400
Sep. 2008	6,400	0	1,500	1,500	0	0	9,400
Oct. 2008	3,850	12,000	1,000	1,000	0	0	17,850
Nov. 2008	6,500	0	3,500	1,100	27,000	0	38,100
Dec. 2008	3,300	0	0	500	20,500	0	24,300
Total (2008)	122,700	30,000	24,650	26,100	67,000	1000	271,450
Jan. 2009	5,700	0	1,500	0	341,500	0	348,700
Feb. 2009	12,600	0	0	500	17,500	1,000	31,600
Mar. 2009	21,800	0	0	5,000	0	0	26,800
Apr. 2009	27,000	500	1,000	1,000	0	500	30,000
May 2009	10,600	0	0	0	2,500	0	13,100
June 2009	6,450	0	500	3,000	0	0	9,950
July 2009	8,800	0	0	500	0	0	9,300

	Economic	Political	Anti-Police	Neigh-bourhood	Regional	Sectarian	Total
Aug. 2009	18,600	0	0	0	0	0	18,600
Sep. 2009	13,900	0	0	2,500	0	0	16,400
Oct. 2009	3,000	500	0	0	16,000	0	19,500
Nov. 2009	1,000	0	1,000	2,500	1,500	0	6,000
Dec. 2009	2,600	0	3,800	500	2,500	0	9,400
Total (2009)	132,050	1000	7,800	15,500	381,500	1,500	539,350
Jan. 2010	4,600	0	0	1,000	0	0	5600
Feb. 2010	4,600	1,000	0	0	500	0	6100
Mar. 2010	1,900	0	0	500	70,000	0	72400
Apr. 2010	3,500	12,500	0	10,500	0	0	26500
May 2010	5,700	6,500	500	0	0	0	12700
June 2010	4,150	0	28,200	500	40,000	0	72850
July 2010	1,500	0	4,000	500	0	500	6500
Aug. 2010	2,000	0	0	0	0	0	2000
Sep. 2010	500	600	500	0	0	1,000	2600
Oct. 2010	5,500	2,500	3,500	500	0	4,000	16000
Nov. 2010	3,000	9,000	4,500	0	0	1,000	17500
Dec. 2010	12,300	4,000	0	0	0	0	16300
Total (2010)	49,250	36,100	41,200	13,500	110,500	6,500	257,050
TOTAL	30,4000	67,100	73,650	55,100	559,000	9,000	1,067,850

NOTES

INTRODUCTION

1. Cf. Tony Blair's comment that Mubarak was 'immensely courageous and a force for good' at the height of the revolution (McGreal 2011).
2. As Diani and McAdam rightly note, McCarthy and Zald have since come closer to Tilly's definition.
3. Although this distinction is important in thinking about social versus political movements in the thought of Hannah Arendt, for example (cf. Arendt 1986).
4. Diani and McAdam (2003: 10) make the useful distinction between a 'movement network', rooted in 'a shared identity', and a 'coalition network', which is purely tactical.
5. Social movement theory is not strictly speaking a 'theory', but rather a series of conceptual approaches. Its intent, however, is to be a 'theory' in the sense of not just describing a phenomenon but also offering an explanation for its emergence and its behaviour (R. Gould 2003: 233–5). The danger of having multiple conceptual approaches is that, following Roger Gould (2003: 234–5), 'occasionally we do treat movement theory as if it is a laundry list: 'mobilization occurs when groups have identifiable grievances, when they have material and organizational resources, when they perceive an opportunity for success, and when ...' etc. But in our better moments we demand of our theories that they say a bit more about the interrelation of these factors, their etiology, and their contingent effects. When we do that, we are using the term 'theory' in the ... sense ... described [above].' It is the latter approach that we pursue.
6. As with Diani and McAdam, we adopt a broader cultural approach to networks, seeing social networks as 'network[s] of meanings' (White in Diani and McAdam 2003: 5), rather than the more conventional empiricist one.
7. McAdam, Tarrow and Tilly (2001: 25–8) call this 'environmental mechanisms' and 'social change processes'.
8. Within social movement theory, there are those who decry the structuralist bias of social movement theory as a whole, and especially the political process model we borrow from (cf. Goodwin and Jasper 1999: 27).

9. Note on transliteration: where Arabic names/words have a common English transliteration, which diverges from standard transliteration schemes, we have adopted this; we have similarly opted to be faithful to local pronunciations where slogans are concerned (e.g. 'g' instead of 'j'). For simplicity's sake, we have not depicted hamza or ta marbuta.

1. MOBILISING PROTEST NETWORKS I (2000–2006)

1. Using dates as markers always involves somewhat arbitrary dividing lines. There were, for example, important protests prior to 2000. The 1990s saw a number of protest waves. But these were of a different quality in that they did not typically employ street protests, except during elections. The main actors were severely circumscribed political parties and civil society organisations. The latter focused on either providing social welfare or on human rights. There was no equivalent set of increasingly dense networks organising public protests, although some tentative protests had begun in the late 1990s (such as the tax-collectors' protest of 1999) (Baheyya 2008a).
2. The blogger-analyst Baheyya (2008b) gives a similar list of protest categories: 'electoral, rural, industrial, sectarian, cost-of-living, and democracy protests'.
3. See also Oliver and Myers' (2003: 175) distinction between 'diffusion' and 'cycles': 'Diffusion processes tend to generate waves or cycles of events, but not all waves of events arise from diffusion processes. Waves of protest can also arise from rhythms and from common responses to external events. A major event such as a disaster or an act of war may trigger independent responses in many locales.'
4. Not counting demonstrations involving participants that may well have been Muslim Brothers (e.g. 'Muslims citizens' or 'students from al-Azhar').
5. One focused on both student elections and on Palestine.
6. In social movement theory terms, a mixture of 'frame extension' and 'frame bridging' (Snow et al. 1986).
7. Interestingly, the activists' target moved from the 'far enemy' (the United States and/or Israel) to the 'near enemy' (the Egyptian regime), in stark opposition to the shift in militant jihadi circles (cf. Gerges 2005).
8. Labelled by some 'the culture wars' (cf. Mehrez 2008).
9. The Brotherhood does not fit neatly into a 'civil society' category, as it is simultaneously a political organisation (though not a party).
10. Almost all activist interviewees referred to this event.
11. Protests in Morocco arguably drew larger crowds, with estimates ranging between 35,000 and 1 million in Rabat and between 50,000 and 100,000 in Casablanca (cf. Agence France Presse 2003; Deutsche Presse-Agentur 2003; *Guardian* 2003).
12. The leftists already had links with the workers' movement, but Kefaya helped to extend these links to Egypt's liberals.
13. To the extent that people had to be made aware of the importance of certain issues, this process would also have involved 'frame amplification'. One could

also argue that 'frame extension' was involved in the sense that Kefaya's frames were extended to cover people's daily concerns.

2. MOBILISING PROTEST NETWORKS II (2007–2011)

1. Others set the number of strikes in 2009–2010 lower (cf. MENA Solidarity Network 2011).
2. The name of the group signing the statement appears on the original Arabic statement on the Egyworkers blog (http://egyworkers.blogspot.com/2007/04/blog-post_17.html).
3. Significantly, though, 'most strike leaders do not belong to a political organization, and regard political parties with suspicion' (Beinin and el-Hamalawy 2007).
4. For much of the early 2000s, the middle-class left had focused on the Palestinian cause. Only when the workers' strikes became more frequent and visible did the middle-class left, important exceptions apart, become more closely involved with the workers' struggle (Agbarieh-Zahalka 2008).
5. One Palestinian solidarity protest focused simultaneously on student elections.
6. In social movement terms: frame bridging, frame amplification and frame extension. Frame transformation would have taken place if previously sceptical individuals were persuaded of the need for activism.
7. There were only around 3,000 users in the entire Middle East (Radsch 2011).
8. Unlike the others quoted, Gamal was not galvanised into action by Said's death. It took January 25 to make him believe protest would be effective. Said's death fortified his negative view of the regime, though.
9. We met various ex-pats who had returned home, and numerous ex-pats tweeted about their return in Jan. 2011 (Gunning, personal observation, 2011).
10. The remainder focused on economic/industrial (forty-eight), neighbourhood/local (eight), regional (eighteen) and sectarian issues (nine).
11. Where *al-Masry al-Youm* provides concrete numbers, we have used those. Where it says 'hundreds', we have substituted '500'; for 'thousands', we have substituted '2,500' to arrive at a rough estimation of numbers. As an opposition newspaper, *al-Masry al-Youm* is furthermore likely to err on the side of optimism.
12. This was also observed by Samer (Interview 2011).
13. By mid-2010, the number of Twitter users across the Middle East had grown to over 40,000, up from 3,000 in 2008 (Radsch 2011).
14. Cf. Emmett Till's lynching in 1955, giving rise to the 'Emmett Till Generation' within the US Civil Rights Movement (Harris 2006); Benno Ohnesorg's death at the hands of the police radicalising the protest movement from which the Baader–Meinhof Group grew (della Porta 1995a: xiii–xv, 159–60).

3. 'DOWN WITH MUBARAK, DOWN WITH THE MILITARY STATE!': POLITICAL CONTEXT

1. While we use the 'political opportunity structure' framework, we are conscious of its shortcomings (cf. the seminal critiques in Goodwin and Jasper 1999, 2004). There is fundamental disagreement over what constitutes key structures and the term can come to mean anything, collapsing structures and strategies (we focus on both while recognising the distinction). The model has a tendency to overemphasise state structures and formal institutions (while the locus of opposition in Egypt lay in informal networks). It often neglects threats and sees structures as constraining/enabling, rather than also producing/channelling (e.g. repression often produces resistance). It implies a clearly identifiable set of opportunities, understood to be opportunities by activists themselves, yet opportunities are not always self-consciously noted, let alone acted upon, and change as a result of the protests themselves. More fundamentally, behaviour is not necessarily 'rationally calculated' but may be 'instinctive', carried out in the immediacy of the moment. Both calculations and instinct are influenced by pre-existing 'scripts' of habitual and cultural behaviour which actors broadly have to follow for fear of becoming '"dramatically" irrelevant if their scripts do not fit the play that is unfolding at the moment' (Johnston 2008: 322). Activists called for street protests and workers went on strike in part because those were the modes of protest they had developed and were familiar with. More broadly, protesters went out in part because of culturally shaped notions of, for instance, what it means to be a man. These types of 'structures of habit' are not usually included in political opportunity structure analyses. To counter some of these shortcomings, we focus on the interplay between structures, changing strategic uses thereof, trigger events and moral shocks, the interpretation of structures, strategies and events by movement actors (influenced by culture, habits, network dynamics, personal experience) and movement behaviour (including framing).

2. Tarrow and Brockett list 'divisions within the elite' and 'elite fragmentation and conflict' as separate factors (McAdam 1996: 27); within McAdam's model, this aspect is somewhat lost as it neither fits the second category nor the third.

3. Not all of the literature on revolutions is directly relevant to our case. For instance, Skocpol, one of the main theorists, underplays the role of urban workers, focusing more on rural revolutionaries, and places a great emphasis on the role of wars against more advanced capitalist states (Goldstone 1991: 19). Studies of historical revolutions (e.g. Goldstone 1991) focus on states and societies that were often markedly different from Egypt's state and society in the 2000s.

4. Made worse by the regime's decision to float the Egyptian pound's exchange rate in 2003.

5. Ahmad Shaaban (Interview 2011), for instance, said: 'There were some expectations that the army would be against ... Gamal, because he is not an army guy. But we still thought that the army would follow the regime.'

6. The information in this table is drawn from King (2009), Stacher (2004), Inter-Parliamentary Union (n.d.), Carnegie (n.d.), ICEM (2005), IRI (2005), Aljazeera

(2010) and Wikipedia. The precise number of seats differs between sources because many candidates are either associated with illegal parties or run without the official sanction of their party. In both cases, affiliations can be ambiguous, leading to divergent interpretations by different sources. In addition, some sources include election results from later re-runs.

7. This view is not shared by all. EOHR's first secretary-general, Bahey el-Din Hassan, for instance, argues that 'There wasn't a direct link between the decline of the parties and the move to human rights, and human rights was never a cover for political activity. Every day that goes by their political motivations count for less and less and human rights ideals are the governing factor' (Stork 2011: 92). However, this does not negate our argument that the closing down of party space meant that those who sought to oppose the regime began to look for alternative venues.

8. For example, Kamal 'Abbas became a founder of the Center for Trade Union and Workers' Services following his arrest and torture during the 1989 Helwan strike (Stork 2011: 92); Aida Seif el-Dawla, founder of the Nadim Center for the Rehabilitation of Victims of Violence, stated similarly that the torture of 'Abbas and others is 'what got me into human rights work' (Stork 2011: 92).

9. For a critical discussion of this relationship, see Dalacoura (2006).

10. The entry for 2008 includes data for Jan.–Feb. 2009.

11. See also discussion of the impact of police violence on the Italian and German left (della Porta 1995a).

4. 'ATEF, THE PEOPLE OF EGYPT ARE FORCED TO EAT BRICKS!': SOCIO-ECONOMIC CONTEXT

1. The Tunisian case suggests that rising household debt may have been an important factor (Gana 2012; Benoit-Lavelle 2012).

2. For instance, El-Naggar (2009: 41–2) estimated unemployment in 2007–2008 to be 26.3 per cent, three times the official figure of 9.1 per cent, and suggested that youth unemployment was 'over three times that figure [of 26.3 per cent]'. Similarly, the figure given by the Egypt Human Development Report (2010: 6, 83) for youth employed in the informal sector (a third) is countered by Abdel Monem Said Aly (2012: 27) who sets it at 72 per cent.

3. Due to differences in methodology, poverty figures differ between databases. Because the number of Egyptians living close to the various poverty lines adopted is large, 'small differences in methodology could have very large effects on the numbers of poor people in Egypt' (Sabry 2009: 10).

4. Lagi, Bertrand and Bar-Yam (2011) list fourteen major protests in 2007–2008, and fifteen in 2011.

5. We are suspicious of deterministic models, such as that adopted by Lagi, Bertrand and Bar-Yam (2011), who 'identify a specific food price threshold above which protests become likely', regardless of local context, presence/absence of protest networks, the state's repressive capacity, etc.

6. A. Aly (2012: 36) makes a similar observation.

7. In the late 1980s, just over 50 per cent of GDP was produced by property asset owners. By the mid-1990s, their share had risen to 71.4 per cent. Wage earners saw their contribution drop from 48.5 (1980s) to less than 20 per cent (2007).
8. The upper middle class ($10–$20) consisted of just 11 per cent.
9. For instance, when poverty rates returned to their pre-1996 levels in the early 2000s, analysts speculated that this increase was caused by those having escaped poverty in the late 1990s falling back into it (Kheir-El-Din and El-Laithy 2008: 20). Similarly, the 2008 food crisis was estimated to have pushed 6 per cent of the population into extreme poverty, the highest level since 1990 (FAO 2008: 4).
10. Cf. 'The Middle East's Excess of Youth', *Investors Chronicle*, 9 Feb. 2011; 'Out With the Old, in With the Young', *The Times*, 19 Feb. 2011; Mona El-tahawy, 'All Egyptians are Being Liberated from the Burden of History', *The Age*, 31 Jan. 2011.
11. In the civil war literature, there is an additional focus on the rewards offered by membership in armed rebel groups (for instance, through looting or regular salaries) (cf. Urdal 2006: 609). In the Egyptian case, this is less relevant as the bulk of opposition networks did not offer material rewards, beyond access to legal services and solidarity networks in case of arrest (the Muslim Brotherhood is the exception, with its extensive charitable services) (Wickham 2002). Material reward would thus be more in the form of achieving stated goals, such as a reintroduction of bread subsidies (as was the case in 1977). Yet these rewards would be for the general affected population, not just those taking part in the protests.
12. These peaks occurred against the backdrop of a fast-growing population. Between 1970 and 2003, Egypt's population doubled, from just over 35 to over 70 million, increasing pressure on society and the state. However, even though large populations have been linked statistically to a greater likelihood of conflict, population growth in itself is not what concerns us here. Growth continued apace during the 1990s, when the youth ratio was relatively low. It continued during years of economic growth. What concerns us here are those moments when an increase in youth-to-population ratio put additional strain on the system while increasing the pool of potential young activists relative to the general population.
13. Because the UN database only provides age-specific census data in five-year intervals, the actual peak may have occurred a few years before or after 1975 and 2005 respectively.
14. In both instances, high youth ratios overlapped with economic and educational strains, high dependency ratios (less so in 2003; UN World Population Prospects 2010), a semi-authoritarian setting (although opinion is divided over the relationship between semi-authoritarian settings and political violence). Urbanisation, one of Urdal's other factors, only played a role in that large numbers were already assembled within dense urban centres. The percentage of those living in urban centres did not change significantly between 1980 and 2010,

although absolute numbers increased (UN World Urbanization Prospects 2011).

15. The UN (UN MDGI n.d.) gives similar figures for the unemployment rate of 15–24 year olds: 23 per cent (1998), 20 per cent (1999), 28 per cent (2001), 27 per cent (2002), 34 per cent (2005), 30 per cent (2006), 25 per cent (2007).

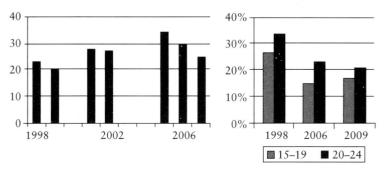

The Egypt Human Development Report (2010: 150) disaggregates the unemployment rates for 15–19 and 20–24 year olds and gives them as 26/34, 15/23 and 17/21 per cent for the years 1998, 2006 and 2009. These figures suggest that unemployment was higher in the late 1990s than the UN figures suggest. M. Hassan and Sassanpour (2008: 6) give figures of 40, 31 and 34 per cent for 20–24-year-old unemployment in 1995, 2000 and 2005. None of these sets covers the peak years of 2003–2005.

16. Assaad (2008: 163) sets this at 71 and 80 per cent.

17. Total female youth unemployment is far higher than total youth unemployment (Figure 4.11).

18. The year 1999 was an outlier at 9.3, possibly because of the impending millennium.

19. Port Said and Ismailia duck this trend, according to M. Osman and Girgis (2009), because they are 'frontier cities'.

20. Source for all graphs on this page: UN World Population Prospects (2010).

21. The Egypt Human Development Report (2010: 152) painted a different picture for 2009, with over 50 per cent standard unemployment rate for males with a university or technical high school education or higher, compared to less than 50 per cent for those classified as illiterate, capable of reading and writing or having completed elementary school. According to this report, this difference was even more pronounced in 2006 when the figure for male university leavers was over 60 per cent, compared to less than 40 per cent for those with only an elementary school education.

22. The figure given for Greater Cairo by Soliman is 52.7 per cent; Sims (2010: 69) sets this figure at 62 per cent in 2000, thus possibly indicating that Soliman's figures are conservative.

23. The proximity of rich and poor in formal Cairo would not have facilitated this type of interaction in the same way, as more rigidly observed social divisions

would have limited interaction, and people did not share the experience of living outside the state's formal structures.

24. Cf. Achcar (2013: 149) already made dire predictions in 2009 about the 'explosive potential of the [Arab] region', which 'can put Egypt and, consequently, the whole region, on the road to major change'.

5. A 'LEADERLESS' REVOLUTION?: PLANNING VS SPONTANEITY

1. The tactical innovations described here focus on Cairo. They played out in different ways across the country.
2. Ghazali-Harb was in the UK until July 2010 so would not have participated in earlier experiments with this new tactic.
3. Although the number of Brotherhood youths joining is likely to have been larger, the core reformist Brotherhood youth leadership (who were the ones with links to the secular protest networks) numbered in their own assessment 'maybe a hundred people' (Wickham 2013: 143). Martini, Kaye and York (2012: 9–10) set the overall number of Brotherhood Youth (reformist and other) at 210,000–245,000.
4. According to Maher (Interview 2011), '*Viva Vendetta* inspired Mahalla. *The Battle of Seattle* inspired 25 January.'
5. See also Ghonim (2012: 184); El-Ghobashy (2011).
6. When we visited the Square on 27 May 2011 during what was billed as 'the Second Revolution', security was similarly well organised: '[Designated security guards] checked our ids and bodies. People willingly submitted to this ... Whenever someone tried to sneak past (e.g. through a separate alleyway, behind the mosque), a group ran after them and checked them. The metro exits were checked as well. All very good-natured, and lots of friends (guards) seeing friends at the entry points, with jovial greetings, then body checks.' As during the revolution, 'there were different stages on the Square, different corners with different groups (socialists towards the Museum on the KFC side, "April 6" towards Qasr al-Nil Bridge, by the statue). Speakers from different stages were speaking simultaneously. Women were very prominent. Islamic prayers were sung from the main stage, in between the political demands ... Groups would form, carrying placards and megaphones, and shouted their demands (e.g. "the people demand a new constitution" [*al-sha'b yurid, dustur gadid*])' (Gunning, Research Note 2011).
7. Castells (2012: 67) cites reports suggesting that 'fear of the [protest] movement extending to the industrial labor force was a factor in influencing the business-wary Army generals to sacrifice the dictator on the altar of their own profits'.
8. While Ezzat, the Square's resident on the Committee, was plugged into the social movement around the Muslim Brotherhood and was well known for her role in setting up Islamonline.net, she was not a street activist and had never before taken on the role of representing the Square. This is therefore still an instance of volunteers responding to the needs of the situation, utilising whatever skills and social networks they have.

9. Although one non-activist cited 'alternative media' as a reason for the demonstrations (Group Interview 2011).
10. Our focus here is on violence perpetrated by demonstrators, not on the role state-sanctioned violence played in the dynamics of the revolution. We briefly discuss this in Chapter 6.
11. See also Ashraf Khalil (2011: 161ff.).
12. By violence, we mean 'behaviour involving physical force intended to hurt, damage, or kill someone or something' (Oxford Dictionaries n.d.). This includes throwing stones, although some of our interviewees disputed that this was violence when faced with a heavily armed police force (e.g. Ezzat, Interview 2011).
13. For instance, there are still competing accounts of who torched the NDP headquarters, and who was behind the looting.
14. Hossam (Interview 2011) made a similar point.

6. 'I USED TO BE AFRAID, NOW I'M AN EGYPTIAN': FROM FEAR TO DEFIANCE

1. Poster seen on Tahrir Square (Gribbon and Hawas 2012: 109).
2. Some social movement scholars have suggested that 'targets and bystanders alike are less impressed by low cost/low risk collective action than by high cost/high risk collective action. This may—paradoxically—make the expectations of the behaviour of others less pessimistic for more strenuous forms of participation' (Klandermans 1997: 90). In situations of severe repression, this logic does not appear to apply, at least initially, because the fear barrier is too high. However, once this barrier is broken, the high-risk aspect of protests against authoritarian regimes may indeed be one factor encouraging bystanders to join. More research is needed to confirm this.
3. Translation by M. Khalil (2012: 251). 'Eid' is the local version of 'yad'.
4. Arabic transliteration adapted.
5. Translation by M. Khalil (2012: 250).
6. Translation by Keraitim and Mehrez (2012: 54).
7. See also M. Khalil (2012: 260).
8. Jasper (2011: 289–90) similarly highlights the importance of reputation, pride and avoiding shame in motivating people to protest.
9. Numerous people told us they had seen this video and Ashraf Khalil likewise testifies to its influence.
10. While the regime was held widely responsible for this attack at the time, the acquittal of regime figures in a subsequent trial brought out accusations that 'some Muslim Brotherhood elements' had been involved as well (BBC 2012b). At the time of writing, it remains unclear who exactly was behind this attack.

7. TAHRIR AS A REVOLUTIONARY POLITICAL SPACE

1. Cf. Gerhart Center (2011); Ramadan (2013); Trombetta (2013); Feigenbaum,

Frenzel and McCurdy (2013 forthcoming). Most of these only touch on space as one factor.

2. An example of this in regard to Egyptian politics is N. Fahmy (2002). For a survey of different theories of state see Held (1989).

3. There used to be 'an empty plinth in the middle of the garden of the central roundabout, ... around which the students gathered in 1972' (Soueif 2012: 13). This plinth was removed during the construction of the Metro.

4. Relative in comparison to tightly controlled public space. Within a conservative, patriarchal society, the freedom of, for instance, women and youth, is still restricted, even at home.

5. Shortly after Mubarak stepped down, CBS reporter Lara Logan was sexually assaulted on the Square (ABC 2011). When protesters marched to celebrate International Women's Day not long after, the demonstrators were attacked (J. Younis, Interview 2011; *Christian Science Monitor* 2011). See also Aljazeera (2012).

6. See also Keraitim and Mehrez (2012) for a discussion of the *mulid* [*mawlid*] tradition and how it informed the protests.

7. For more on Arendt's account of politics see, Benhabib (2003); Calhoun and McGowan (1997); Canovan (1992); Villa (1999, 2000).

8. The term 'non-sovereign' is problematic if one sees sovereignty as existing in different forms. Some of the main IR literature on sovereignty provides some gestures in this direction. In this regard, Jackson (2007) provides an introductory overview of sovereignty. A more critical take from a non-IR perspective is Magnusson and Shaw (2003). In the context of our argument, we will use the term to denote 'not sovereign in a traditional state-centric sense'.

9. Ashraf Khalil (2011: 204) highlights a darker side of these committees, suggesting there was a 'class-based hysteria fueling things' as a result of overblown rumours of looting and fear of agents provocateurs.

10. Ashraf Khalil (2011: 245–6) similarly recalls that Tahrir was 'cleaner than the street outside my apartment in Giza has ever been'.

11. For a critique of theories based on assumptions about human nature and rationality see Schwartz (1986).

12. See also reports on makeshift volunteer 'hospitals' in and around the Square in Soueif (2012: 31–4); Shenker and Khalili (2011); Aljazeera (2011e).

13. See also the barrage of commentary by Egyptian activists on Twitter on the 2011 riots in London (Lede Blog 2011; CNN 2011b).

14. See Baudrillard (1994).

15. Cf. a typical leaflet entitled: 'The Revolution First and Legitimacy for Tahrir' (Tahrir Documents 2011b).

16. E.g. when we visited the Square during a mass demonstration in May 2011, we saw many of the same practices that we had seen on television during the Feb. occupation.

8. A FACEBOOK REVOLUTION?

1. The classic text in this vein is Jürgen Habermas's *The Structural Transformation of the Public Sphere* (1992 [1962]), in which he argues that the printing press was important for the democratisation of Europe (although another important part of his argument focused on the development of capitalism and how it altered the relationship between private and public spheres).

2. Lim (2012: 243) quotes Waleed Rashed, a co-founder of April 6: 'Every time I was in a cab, I would call Ahmed [Maher] on my cell phone and talk loudly about planning a big protest in Tahrir Square for January 25th, because I knew that they couldn't stop themselves talking about what they'd overheard. Eventually, on January 23rd, a cabbie asked if I'd heard about this big demonstration that was happening in two days.'

3. We nevertheless uphold the distinction analytically, to be able to specify different forms of interaction.

4. Informational cascades also played a significant role in mobilising international support for the revolution. Lynch (2011: 306) highlights the potential for social media to affect international attention and alliances, and in the case of Egypt, social media certainly affected international attention (Gunning and Baron, personal observation 2011). To what extent international alliances were affected by the activists' use of social media is a question that falls outside the scope of this book.

5. Mahfouz's video came up, unsolicited, in a number of our interviews.

6. We are indebted to Janet Gunning for bringing this concept to our attention.

7. Awareness of the danger of being monitored on Facebook was widespread, although not all took it as seriously. Ghonim (2012: 46–7, 52) recounts how he had to warn the administrators of the 'ElBaradei President of Egypt 2011' group not to use their real names on the internet. However, while the Egyptian regime harassed those posting critical messages, it did not clamp down as harshly as other Arab countries. Ghonim suggests that this was because 'the Egyptian regime needed to be seen as a progressive, welcoming country to the outside world. Its economy depended in part on tourism ...'

8. Bennett (2005: 206) calls this 'virtual brokerage' and 'hyperlinked diffusion' in the context of social media activism.

9. We use the term 'community' to denote the sense of identification many followers appear to have developed towards a network's Facebook page or associated Twitter feeds. However, these networked individuals did not necessarily constitute a community in the traditional, offline sense of the word.

10. For a discussion of the concept of 'virtual emulation', see Bennett (2005: 206ff.).

11. In the case of the Global Justice Movement, the 'necessity born of the desire to form sustainable relationships with distant others' was a contextual factor (Bennett 2005: 217).

CONCLUSION

1. If we take into account the many who stayed home in protest.
2. One can also deploy this model to explain differences in the trajectories of the Arab Spring in Tunisia, Libya, Syria, Bahrain, Jordan and Yemen.

BIBLIOGRAPHY

Abaza, Mona (2011), 'Revolutionary Moments in Tahrir Square', *Global Dialogue*, 1:4 (3–5), p. 3 (http://www.isa-sociology.org/global-dialogue/newsletters4/GD%201.4%20English.pdf; accessed 7 Dec. 2012).

ABC (2011), 'CBS Reporter Lara Logan Opens Up About Tahrir Square Attack', 2 May (http://abcnews.go.com/Health/MindMoodNews/cbs-reporter-lara-logan-opens-tahrir-square-assault/story?id=13492964#.UMYEvqne Nll; accessed 10 Dec. 2012).

Abdalla, Nadine (2012), 'Egypt's Workers—From Protest Movement to Organized Labor', *SWP Comments*, 32, Berlin: German Institute for International and Security Affairs.

Abdel Fattah, Esraa (2011), 'The New Youth Activism', *Cairo Review*, 1(1): 74–8.

Abdelhadi, Magdi (2008), 'Spotlight on Egypt's Marriage Crisis', BBC News, 12 Aug. (http://news.bbc.co.uk/1/hi/7554892.stm; accessed 26 June 2012).

Abdelrahman, Maha (2011), 'The Transnational and the Local: Egyptian Activists and Transnational Protest Networks', *British Journal of Middle Eastern Studies*, 38(3): 407–24.

——— (2013), 'The Egyptian Opposition: From Protestors to Revolutionaries?', openDemocracy, 22 Apr. (http://www.opendemocracy.net/5050/maha-abdelrahman/egyptian-opposition-from-protestors-to-revolutionaries; accessed 25 June 2013).

Abdulla, Rasha (2007), *The Internet in the Arab World: Egypt and Beyond*, New York: Peter Lang Publishing.

Abou-El-Fadl, Reem (2012), 'The Road to Jerusalem through Tahrir Square: Anti-Zionism and Palestine in the 2011 Egyptian Revolution', *Journal of Palestine Studies*, 41(2): 6–26.

Abu Hatab, Assem (2009), 'Performance of Egyptian Cotton Exports in International Market', *Agricultural Economics Research Review*, 22(2): 225–35.

Achcar, Gilbert (2013), *The People Want: A Radical Exploration of the Arab Uprising*, London: Saqi Books.

African Development Bank (2011), 'The Middle of the Pyramid: Dynamics of the Middle Class in Africa', *Market Brief*, Tunis-Belvedère, Tunisia: African Development Bank.

Agbarieh-Zahalka, Asma (2008), 'Egyptian Workers Impose a New Agenda', *Challenge*, 109 (May/June) (http://www.challenge-mag.com/en/article__212; accessed 23 Feb. 2012).

Agence France Presse (2003), 'Moroccan King Condemns "Dangerous Turn of Events" in Iraq', 20 Mar.

Ahmed, Amir (2011), 'Thousands Protest in Egypt', CNN, 26 Jan. 2011.

AhramOnline (2011), 'Egypt's Muslims Attend Coptic Christmas Mass, Serving as "Human Shields"', 7 Jan.

———— (2013), 'Protests Monday on "Friday of Rage" Anniversary to Press Opposition Demands', 27 Jan.

Al-Ahram Weekly (2003), 'An Uphill Battle', no. 629, 13–19 Mar.

———— (2005a), 'A Chronology of Dissent', no. 748, 23–9 June.

———— (2005b), 'Enough is Still Enough', 8–14 Sep.

———— (2010), 'A Partial Account', no. 1005, 1–7 July.

Al-Anani, Khalil (2008), 'Brotherhood Bloggers: A New Generation Voices Dissent', *Arab Insight*, 2(1): 29–38.

Al-Aswany, Alaa (2011), 'Standing Firm to Defend Egypt's Revolution', *World Affairs*, 22 Dec. (http://www.worldaffairsjournal.org/blog/alaa-al-aswany/standing-firm-defend-egypts-revolution; accessed 15 Jan. 2013).

Al-Bura'y, N. (2008), '*Ala muqarriba min al hafa: hurriyat al ta'bir fi masr 2004–2007* [Close to the Edge: Freedom of Expression in Egypt 2004–2007] (Arabic), Cairo: The United Group.

Alexander, Anne (2012), 'The Egyptian Workers' Movement and the 25 January Revolution', *International Socialism*, 133, 9 Jan. (http://www.isj.org.uk/index.php4?id=778&issue=133; accessed 24 Feb. 2012).

Aljazeera (2010), 'Has Egypt's Ruling Party Grown Fat', 22 Nov.

———— (2011a), 'Protesters Torch Egypt Police Post', 27 Jan.

———— (2011b), 'Protesters Flood Egypt Streets', 1 Feb.

———— (2011c), 'Anger in Egypt: The Different Shades of Tahrir', 8 Feb.

———— (2011d), 'Egypt Protesters Gain Ground', 9 Feb.

———— (2011e), 'Egypt: Seeds of Change' (Video), 9 Feb.

———— (2011f), 'Timeline: Egypt's Revolution—A Chronicle of the Revolution that Ended the Three-Decade-Long Presidency of Hosni Mubarak', last modified 14 Feb.

———— (2011g), 'Spain's Tahrir Square Keeps Up Its Struggle', 22 June.

———— (2012), 'Sexual Violence Rises in Egypt's Tahrir', 5 July.

———— (2013), 'Egypt Opposition to Continue Mass Protests', 1 July.

Al Malky, Rania (2007), 'Blogging for Reform: The Case of Egypt', *Arab Media & Society*, 1.

al-Masry al-Youm (2010a), 'Alexandria Policemen Beat Young Man to Death, Says Rights Group', 11 June.

—— (2010b), 'Brotherhood Collects Half Million Signatures for ElBaradei's Reform Demands', 18 Aug.

—— (2011a), 'Protest against Alexandria Bombings in Shubra', 2 Jan.

—— (2011b), 'Rubber Bullets Fail to Break Up Massive Demonstration in Alexandria', 25 Jan.

—— (2011c), 'BREAKING: 20,000 Protesters Take Over Qasr al-Nil Bridge', 28 Jan.

—— (2011d), 'Activists, Protesters Work around Internet Outage in Egypt', 30 Jan.

—— (2011e), 'ElBaradei Campaign Aims to Repair Image', 5 Apr.

—— (2011f), 'Police Reform: Getting it Right', 24 Apr.

—— (2011g), 'Commemorating Khaled Saeed: The Revolution's First Martyr?' 7 June.

—— (2012), 'Constituent Assembly may scrap workers' and farmers' quota in Parliament', 26 Aug.

—— (2013), 'Tamarod Approaches 15 Million Signatures', 10 June.

AlSayyad, Nezar (2011), 'A History of Tahrir Square', Harvard University Press Blog, 1 Apr. 2011 (http://harvardpress.typepad.com/hup_publicity/2011/04/a-history-of-tahrir-square.html; accessed 17 Jan. 2013).

Al-Shorfa.com (2010), 'Egyptian Opposition, Pro-Government Groups Battle on Facebook', 25 May (http://alshorfa.com/cocoon/meii/xhtml/en_GB/features/meii/features/main/2010/05/25/feature-02; accessed 1 Mar. 2012).

Aly, Abdel Monem Said (2012), 'State and Revolution in Egypt: The Paradox of Change and Politics', *Crown Center for Middle East Studies Essay* 2, Jan., Waltham, MA: Brandeis University.

Aly, Nouran (2011), 'The Journey to Tahrir Square: Egypt's Social Movement for Political Change', MA Thesis (unpublished), Durham, UK: Durham University.

AmeInfo.com (2008), 'Egypt's Textile Industry on Growth Path after €80m EU Funding', 21 Feb. (http://www.ameinfo.com/147691.html; accessed 5 July 2012).

APN (2008), 'Rumours of a Facebook Block Persist in Egypt', 27 Aug. (http://www.arabpressnetwork.org/articlesv2.php?id=2609&lang=; accessed 24 Feb. 2012).

Araj, B. (2008), 'Harsh State Repression as a Cause of Suicide Bombing: The Case of the Palestinian–Israeli Conflict', *Studies in Conflict & Terrorism*, 31(4): 284–303.

Arendt, Hannah (1958), *The Human Condition*, London and Chicago: Chicago University Press.

—— (1965), *On Revolution*, New York: Penguin Books.

—— (1970), *On Violence*, London: Harcourt Brace.

—— (1986), *The Origins of Totalitarianism*, London: André Deutsch.

—— (2005), *The Promise of Politics*, ed. Jerome Kohn, New York: Schocken Books.

—— (2007), *Jewish Writings*, ed. Jerome Kohn and Ron H. Feldman, New York: Schocken Books.

Aronson, Geoffrey (1990), *Israel, Palestinians and the Intifada: Creating Facts on the West Bank*, London: Kegan Paul.

Ashour, Omar (2010), 'ElBaradei and the Mobilisation of the Egyptian Diaspora', *Sada*, Carnegie Endowment for International Peace, 29 Sep. (http://carnegieendowment.org/2010/09/29/elbaradei-and-mobilization-of-egyptian-diaspora/6bwg; accessed 3 Mar. 2012).

Assaad, Ragui (2008), 'Unemployment and Youth Insertion in the Labor Market in Egypt', in Hanaa Kheir-El-Din (ed.), *The Egyptian Economy: Current Challenges and Future Prospects*, Cairo: The American University in Cairo Press, pp. 133–78.

Awad, Marwa and Hugo Dixon (2011), 'Inside a Revolution: Tahrir Square, 2011', in 'After Tahrir: Egypt Post-Mubarak', Reuters *BreakingViews* (http://www.breakingviews.com/Journals/23/Files/2011/8/17/Egypt%20after%20Tahrir.pdf; accessed 8 Feb. 2013), pp. 9–15.

Azimi, Negar (2005), 'Egypt's Youth Have Had Enough', *openDemocracy*, 31 Aug. (http://www.opendemocracy.net/democracy-protest/enough_2794.jsp; accessed 19 Sep. 2011).

Baffes, John (2004), 'Cotton: Market Setting, Trade Policies, and Issues', *World Bank Policy Research Working Paper*, 3218, Washington, DC: World Bank.

Baheyya (2006), 'The Games Regimes Play', 10 Aug. (http://baheyya.blogspot.com/2006/08/games-regimes-play.html; accessed 15 Sep. 2011).

—— (2008a), 'The Organiser', 1 Jan. (http://baheyya.blogspot.com/2008/01/organiser.html; accessed 15 Sep. 2011).

—— (2008b), 'Four Myths about Protest', 16 May (http://baheyya.blogspot.com/2008/05/four-myths-about-protest.html; accessed 15 Sep. 2011).

Baker, Raymond (1990), *Sadat and After: Struggles for Egypt's Political Soul*, London: IB Tauris.

Baringhorst, Sigrid (2008), 'Political Protest on the Net', *German Policy Studies*, 4(4): 63–93.

Baudrillard, Jean (1994), *Simulacra and Simulation*, Ann Arbor, MI: University of Michigan Press.

Bauer, Patricia and Bertold Schweitzer (2012), 'The Egyptian Revolution 2011: Mechanisms of Violence and Non-Violence', in State of Peace Conference & Peace Report 2012 'Democracy in Crisis: The Dynamics of Civic Protest and Civic Resistance', Schlaining, Austria: Friedensburg (http://www.friedensburg.at/uploads/files/Bauer_Schweitzer_StoP2012_paper.pdf; accessed 29 June 2013).

Bayat, Asef (2007), *Making Islam Democratic: Social Movements and the Post-Islamist Turn*, Stanford, CA: Stanford University Press.

—— (2009), *Life as Politics: How Ordinary People Change the Middle East*, Cairo: The American University in Cairo Press.

BBC (2009), 'Egyptian Police Stifle Protests', 6 Apr.

BIBLIOGRAPHY

—— (2010a), 'Mohammed ElBaradei Welcomed Home by Egypt Crowds', 19 Feb.

—— (2010b), 'Egypt Riot Police Break Up Pro-Democracy Rally', 6 Apr.

—— (2011a), 'Egypt Protests Escalate in Cairo, Suez and Other Cities', 28 Jan.

—— (2011b), 'Egypt Unrest' ['Tour of Camp' button], 11 Feb.

—— (2012a), 'Egypt's Revolution: 18 Days in Tahrir Square', 25 Jan.

—— (2012b), '"Battle of the Camels" Acquittals Shock Egypt', 11 Oct.

BBC2 (2012), 'Wikileaks: The Secret Life of a Superpower; Episode 1', 21 Mar.

Beinin, Joel (2007), 'The Militancy of Mahalla al-Kubra', *Middle East Report Online*, 29 Sep. (http://www.merip.org/mero/mero092907; accessed 13 Oct. 2011).

—— (2008), 'The Egyptian Workers Movement in 2007', in Hadjar Aouardji and Hélène Legeay (eds), *Chroniques Égyptiennes 2007*, Cairo: CEDEJ, 2008, pp. 219–40.

—— (2009), 'Workers' Struggles under "Socialism" and Neoliberalism', in Rabab el-Mahdi and Philip Marfleet (eds), *Egypt: Moment of Change*, Cairo: The American University of Cairo Press, pp. 68–86.

—— (2011a), 'A Workers' Social Movement on the Margin of the Global Neoliberal Order, Egypt 2004–2009', in Joel Beinin and Fréderic Vairel (eds), *Social Movements, Mobilization and Contestation in the Middle East and North Africa*, Stanford, CA: Stanford University Press, pp. 181–201.

—— (2011b), 'Egypt's Workers Rise Up', *The Nation*, 7–14 Mar. (http://www.thenation.com/article/158680/egypts-workers-rise#; accessed 13 Oct. 2011).

Beinin, Joel and Hossam el-Hamalawy (2007), 'Egyptian Textile Workers Confront the New Economic Order', *Middle East Report Online*, 25 Mar. (http://www.merip.org/mero/mero032507; accessed 13 Oct. 2011).

Benford, Robert and David Snow (2000), 'Framing Processes and Social Movements: An Overview and Assessment', *Annual Review of Sociology*, 26: 611–39.

Benhabib, Seyla (2003), *The Reluctant Modernism of Hannah Arendt*, new edn, Lanham, MD: Rowman & Littlefield.

Bennett, W. Lance (2005), 'Social Movements beyond Borders: Understanding Two Eras of Transnational Activism', in Donatella della Porta and Sidney Tarrow (eds), *Transnational Protest and Global Activism*, Lanham, MD: Rowman & Littlefield, pp. 203–26.

Benoit-Lavelle, Mischa (2012), 'Consumer Debt Trap Brings Suffering to Tunisian Families', *Tunisia Live*, 15 Mar. (http://www.tunisia-live.net/2012/03/15/consumer-debt-trap-brings-suffering-to-tunisian-families/; accessed 11 Jan. 2013).

Bernard-Maugiron, Nathalie (2008a), 'Introduction', in Nathalie Bernard-Maugiron (ed.), *Judges and Political Reform in Egypt*, Cairo: The American University in Cairo Press, pp. 1–4.

—— (2008b), 'The Relationship between Judges and Human Rights Organizations during the 2005 Elections and the Referendum', in Nathalie Bernard-Maugiron (ed.), *Judges and Political Reform in Egypt*, Cairo: The American University in Cairo Press, pp. 244–5.

Bernstein, Richard (1996), *Hannah Arendt and the Jewish Question*, Cambridge, MA: The MIT Press.

Beyerle, Shaazka and Arwa Hassan (2009), 'Popular Resistance against Corruption in Turkey and Egypt', in Maria Stepan (ed.), *Civilian Jihad: Nonviolent Struggle, Democratization, and Governance in the Middle East*, New York: Palgrave Macmillan, pp. 265–79.

Binzel, Christine (2011), 'Decline in Social Mobility: Unfulfilled Aspirations among Egypt's Educated Youth', *Discussion Paper*, 6139, Bonn: IZA (http://ftp.iza.org/dp6139.pdf; accessed 30 June 2013).

Blaydes, Lisa (2011), *Elections and Distributive Politics in Mubarak's Egypt*, Cambridge: Cambridge University Press.

Bodin, Jean (1992), *On Sovereignty: Four Chapters from the Six Books of the Commonwealth*, ed. Julian Franklin, Cambridge: Cambridge University Press.

Booth, Ken (2007), *Theory of World Security*, Cambridge: Cambridge University Press.

Bradley, John (2008), *Inside Egypt: The Land of the Pharaohs on the Brink of a Revolution*, New York: Palgrave Macmillan.

Breuer, Anita (2012), 'The Role of Social Media in Mobilizing Political Protest: Evidence from the Tunisian Revolution', *Discussion Paper*, 10, Bonn: German Development Institute.

Brown, Nathan (n.d.), 'Can the Colossus be Salvaged? Egypt's State-Owned Press in a Post-Revolutionary Environment', *Sada*, Carnegie Endowment for International Peace (http://egyptelections.carnegieendowment.org/2011/08/22/can-the-colossus-be-salvaged-egypt%E2%80%99s-state-owned-press-in-a-post-revolutionary-environment; accessed 20 Apr. 2012).

Brown, Nathan and Hesham Nasr (2005), 'Egypt's Judges Step Forward: The Judicial Election Boycott and Egyptian Reform', *Policy Outlook: Democracy and Rule of Law*, Washington, DC: Carnegie Endowment for International Peace.

Brownlee, Jason (2007), *Authoritarianism in an Age of Democratization*, Cambridge: Cambridge University Press.

Buechler, Steven M. (2004), 'The Strange Career of Strain and Breakdown Theories of Collective Action', in D.A. Snow, S. Soule and H. Kriesi (eds), *Blackwell Companion to Social Movements*, Oxford: Blackwell, pp. 47–66.

Burcher, Nick (2012), 'Facebook Usage Statistics by Country Dec 2008–Dec 2011', 4 Jan. (http://www.nickburcher.com/2012/01/facebook-usage-statistics-by-country.html; accessed 30 June 2013).

Calhoun, Craig and John McGowan (eds) (1997), *Hannah Arendt & the Meaning of Politics*, Minneapolis: University of Minnesota Press.

Cambanis, Thanassis (2010), 'Succession Gives Army a Stiff Test in Egypt',

New York Times, 11 Sep. (http://www.nytimes.com/2010/09/12/world/middleeast/12egypt.html?pagewanted=all; accessed 19 Apr. 2012).

Canovan, Margaret (1978), 'The Contradictions of Hannah Arendt's Political Thought', *Political Theory*, 6(1): 5–26.

——— (1995), *Hannah Arendt: A Reinterpretation of her Political Thought*, Cambridge: Cambridge University Press.

——— (2006), 'The People', in John Dryzek, Bonnie Honig and Anne Phillips (eds), *Oxford Handbook of Political Theory*, Oxford: Oxford University Press, pp. 349–62.

CAPMAS (n.d.), 'Statistics' (http://www.capmas.gov.eg/database.aspx; accessed 22 June 2012).

——— (2001–2007), 'Average Age at Marriage & Divorce (2001–2007)', Vital Statistics (http://www.sis.gov.eg/newVR/egyptinnumber/egyptinfigures/englishtables/57.pdf; accessed 30 June 2013).

——— (1982–2007), 'Number of Marriages and Divorces and Their Rates (1982–2007)', Vital Statistics (http://www.sis.gov.eg/newVR/egyptinnumber/egyptinfigures/englishtables/53.pdf; accessed 30 June 2013).

——— (2010), 'CAPMAS Labour Force Search Result for the Third Quarter 21 November 2010' (http://www.capmas.gov.eg/news.aspx?nid=503&lang=2; accessed 22 June 2012).

Carnegie (n.d.), 'Representation in Egypt's People's Assembly: 1976–2010' (http://egyptelections.carnegieendowment.org/wp-content/themes/sandbox/swf/partyRep_en.htm; accessed 30 June 2013).

——— (2010), 'Kifaya (The Egyptian Movement for Change)', *Guide to Egypt's Transition*, Washington, DC: Carnegie Endowment for International Peace (http://egyptelections.carnegieendowment.org/2010/09/22/the-egyptian-movement-for-change-kifaya; accessed 25 Feb. 2012).

Carr, Sarah (2009), 'April 6 2009 Protests, Egypt', demotix.com, 6 Apr. (http://www.demotix.com/news/april-6-2009-protests-egypt; accessed 25 Feb. 2012).

Castells, Manuel (1999), 'Grassrooting the Space of Flows', *Urban Geography*, 20(4): 294–302.

——— (2000), *The Rise of the Network Society*, The Information Age: Economy, Society, and Culture, vol. I, 2nd edn, Oxford: Blackwell.

——— (2004), *The Power of Identity*, The Information Age: Economy, Society, and Culture, vol. II, 2nd edn, Oxford: Blackwell.

——— (2009), *Communication Power*, Oxford: Oxford University Press.

——— (2011), 'The Popular Uprisings in the Arab World Perhaps Constitute the Most Important Internet-Led and Facilitated Change', Interview by Jordi Rovira, 'Current Events', Universidad Oberta de Catalunya, Feb. (http://www.uoc.edu/portal/en/sala-de-premsa/actualitat/entrevistes/2011/manuel_castells.html; accessed 20 Nov. 2012).

——— (2012), *Networks of Outrage and Hope: Social Movements in the Internet Age*, Cambridge: Polity.

Chambers, Simon and Jeffrey Kopstein (2006), 'Civil Society and the State', in

John Dryzek, Bonnie Honig and Anne Phillips (eds), *Oxford Handbook of Political Theory*, Oxford: Oxford University Press, pp. 363–81.

Chams El-Dine, Chérine (2013), 'The Military and Egypt's Transformation Process: Preservation of the Military's Reserve Domains', *SWP Comments*, 6, Berlin: German Institute for International and Security Affairs (http://www.swp-berlin.org/fileadmin/contents/products/comments/2013C06_ced.pdf; accessed 25 June 2013).

Chick, Kristen (2011), 'Egypt Protesters Want Freedom, But Can They Organize to Get It?' *Christian Science Monitor*, 26 Jan.

Chitty, Alex (2011), 'Social Media and the 2011 Egyptian Revolution', alexchitty.wordpress.com, 9 May (http://alexchitty.wordpress.com/2011/05/09/247/; accessed 1 Mar. 2012).

Christian Science Monitor (2011), 'In Egypt's Tahrir Square, Women Attacked at Rally on International Women's Day', 8 Mar.

Clark, John (2003), *Worlds Apart: Civil Society and the Battle for Ethical Globalization*, London: Earthscan.

clayclai (2011), 'Mubarak Refuses to Step Down', *WL Central* (the #1 unofficial WikiLeaks resource), 28 Jan. (http://wlcentral.org/node/1119; accessed 6 June 2012).

Clifford, James and George E. Marcus (eds) (1986), *Writing Culture: The Poetics and Politics of Ethnography*, Los Angeles: University of California Press.

CNN (2011a), '3 Dead After Thousands Protest in Rare Egypt Outpouring', 26 Jan.

—— (2011b), 'Egyptian Bloggers Try to Make Sense of UK Riots', 9 Aug.

Cohen, Marc and James Garrett (2009), 'The Food Price Crisis and Urban Food (in) Security,' *Urbanization and Emerging Population Issues*, no. 2, Human Settlements Working Paper Series, London: International Institute for Environment and Development.

Committee to Protect Journalists (2007), 'Attacks on the Press 2006: Egypt', 5 Feb. (http://cpj.org/2007/02/attacks-on-the-press-2006-egypt.php; accessed 20 Apr. 2012).

Cox, Robert (1986 [1981]), 'Social Forces, States and World Orders: Beyond International Relations Theory', in Robert Keohane (ed.), *Neorealism and its Critics*, New York: Columbia University Press, pp. 204–54.

Crimethinc (2012), 'Live from the Streets of Cairo', *Counterpunch*, 6 Feb. (http://www.counterpunch.org/2012/02/06/live-from-the-streets-of-cairo/; accessed 16 Feb. 2012).

Cunliffe, Ann (2003), 'Reflexive Inquiry in Organizational Research: Questions and Possibilities', *Human Relations*, 56(8): 983–1003.

Daily Beast (2011), '"We Are All Khaled Said": Will the Revolution Come to Egypt?' 22 Jan. (http://www.thedailybeast.com/articles/2011/01/22/we-are-all-khaled-said-will-the-revolution-come-to-egypt.html; accessed 1 Mar. 2012)

Daily News Egypt (2010), 'Public Statements on Mubarak's Health Fail to Allay Worries', 8 Mar. (http://www.thedailynewsegypt.com/archive/public-statements-on-mubaraks-health-fail-to-allay-worries.html; accessed 2 Mar. 2012).

Dalacoura, Katerina (2006), 'Islamist Terrorism and the Middle East Democratic Deficit: Political Exclusion, Repression and the Causes of Extremism', *Democratization*, 13(3): 508–25.

Davies, James (1969), 'The J-Curve of Rising and Declining Satisfaction as a Course of Some Great Revolutions and a Contained Rebellion', in Hugh Davis Graham and Ted Gurr (eds), *The History of Violence in America*, New York: Praeger, pp. 690–730.

Davies, Jonathan and David Imbrosco (eds) (2009), *Theories of Urban Politics*, 2nd edn, London: Sage.

della Porta, Donatella (1995a), *Social Movements, Political Violence, and the State: A Comparative Analysis of Italy and Germany*, London: Cambridge University Press.

——— (1995b), 'Left-Wing Terrorism in Italy', in Martha Crenshaw (ed.), *Terrorism in Context*, University Park, PA: Pennsylvania State University Press, pp. 105–59.

della Porta, Donatella and Mario Diani (1999), *Social Movements: An Introduction*, Oxford: Blackwell.

della Porta, Donatella and Lorenzo Mosca (2005), 'Global-Net for Global Movements? A Network of Networks for a Movement of Movements', *Journal of Public Policy*, 25(1): 165–90.

Deutsche Presse-Agentur (2003), 'Moroccan Police Clash with Anti-War Demonstrators', 20 Mar.

Diab, Osama (2009), 'Egypt: Power Has Already Been Transferred', Worldpress.org, 2 July (http://www.worldpress.org/Mideast/3374.cfm; accessed 19 Sep. 2011).

Diani, Mario and Doug McAdam (2003), 'Introduction: Social Movements, Contentious Actions, and Social Networks: "From Metaphor to Substance"?' in Mario Diani and Doug McAdam (eds), *Social Movements and Networks: Relational Approaches to Collective Action*, Oxford: Oxford University Press, pp. 1–17.

Dorman, W.J. (2009), 'Informal Cairo: Between Islamist Insurgency and the Neglectful State?' *Security Dialogue*, 40(4–5): 419–41.

DTSG (2011), 'Egypt, Bahrain, London, Spain? Tahrir Square as a Meme', Deterritorial Support Group, Editorial, 21 May 2011 (http://deterritorial-supportgroup.wordpress.com/2011/05/21/egypt-bahrain-london-spain—tahrir-square-as-a-meme/; accessed 11 Dec. 2012).

Eaton, Tim (2012), 'Online Activism and Revolution in Egypt: Lessons from Tahrir', *New Diplomacy Platform*, 25 Jan. (http://ww.newdiplomacyplatform.com; accessed 25 Nov. 2012).

ECHR (n.d.), 'The Policy of Forced Eviction and House Demolitions in Egypt',

Report, Cairo: The Egyptian Center for Housing Rights (http://www.echr. org/en/asd/02/rep1.htm; accessed 16 Feb. 2012).

Edkins, Jenny (2005), 'Ethics and Practices of Engagement: Intellectuals as Experts', *International Relations*, 19(1): 64–9.

Edwards, Bob and John McCarthy (2004), 'Resources and Social Movement Mobilization', in David Snow, Sarah Soule and Hanspeter Kriesi (eds), *The Blackwell Companion to Social Movements*, Oxford: Blackwell, pp. 116–52.

Egypt Human Development Report (2010), 'Youth in Egypt: Building our Future', Report, New York: United Nations Development Programme/Cairo: Institute of National Planning.

El-Amine, Rami and Mostafa Henaway (2011), 'A People's History of the Egyptian Revolution', *Left Turn*, 7 July (http://www.leftturn.org/peoples-history-egyptian-revolution; accessed 1 Mar. 2012).

El Amrani, Issandr (2002), 'The Monster in Egypt's Box', Salon, 4 Apr. (http:// www.salon.com/news/feature/2002/04/04/egypt/index.html; accessed 19 Sep. 2011).

———— (2003), 'All Hell Breaks Loose in Cairo', Salon, 22 Mar. (http://www. salon.com/news/feature/2003/03/22/cairo/index.html; accessed 19 Sep. 2011).

Elaph (2011), 'Four Thousand Egyptians Demonstrated against Terrorism in "Shubra"', 1 Jan. (in Arabic) (http://www.elaph.com/Web/news/2011/1/ 622220.html; accessed 3 Mar. 2012)

ElBaradei Association for Change (2010), 'ElBaradei Meets Leftist Supporters', 11 Oct./2 Nov. (http://www.changeegypt.com/index.php?option=com_ content&view=article&id=126:elbaradei-meets-leftist-supporters-&catid=5 4:englishnews&Itemid=240; accessed 25 Feb. 2012)

El-Dawla, Aida Seif (2009), 'Torture: A State Policy', in Rabab el-Mahdi and Philip Marfleet (eds), *Egypt: Moment of Change*, Cairo: The American University of Cairo Press, pp. 120–35.

El-Fiqi, Mona (2006), 'A Makeover for the Textile Industry', *Al-Ahram Weekly*, 823, 7–13 Dec. (http://weekly.ahram.org.eg/2006/823/ec3.htm; accessed 5 July 2012).

El-Ghobashy, Mona (2005), 'Egypt Looks Ahead to Portentous Year', *Middle East Report Online*, 2 Feb. (http://www.merip.org/mero/mero020205; accessed 19 Jan. 2012).

———— (2011), 'The Praxis of the Egyptian Revolution', *Middle East Report Online*, 258 (http://www.merip.org/mer/mer258/praxis-egyptian-revolution; accessed 19 Jan. 2012).

El-Haddad, Amirah (2012), 'Effects of the Global Crisis on the Egyptian Textiles and Clothing Sector: A Blessing in Disguise?' ISRN Economics 2012 (http://www.hindawi.com/isrn/economics/2012/941695/; accessed 28 June 2013).

El-Hamalawy, Hossam (2007), 'Comrades and Brothers', *Middle East Report*

Online, 242: 40–3 (http://www.merip.org/mer/mer242/comrades-brothers; accessed 30 June 2013).

——— (2008a), 'Egyptian Strikes: More than Bread and Butter', *Socialist Review*, May (http://www.socialistreview.org.uk/article.php?articlenumber= 10388; accessed 24 Feb. 2012).

——— (2008b), 'Revolt in Mahalla', *International Socialist Review*, 59, May– June (http://www.isreview.org/issues/59/rep-mahalla.shtml; accessed 23 Feb. 2012).

El-Hennawy, Noha (2010), 'We are all Khaled Saeed: Redefining Political Demonstration in Egypt', *al-Masry al-Youm*, 4 Aug. (http://www.egyptindependent.com/news/we-are-all-khaled-saeed-redefining-political-demonstration-egypt; accessed 6 June 2012).

——— (2011), 'The Making of a Police State: From the Battle of Ismailiya to Khaled Saeed', *al-Masry al-Youm*, 27 Jan. (http://www.egyptindependent. com/news/making-police-state-battle-ismailiya-khaled-saeed; accessed 6 June 2012).

El-Mahdi, Rabab (2009), 'The Democracy Movement', in Rabab el-Mahdi and Philip Marfleet (eds), *Egypt: Moment of Change*, Cairo: The American University of Cairo Press, pp. 87–102.

El-Naggar, Ahmad (2009), 'Economic Policy: From State Control to Decay and Corruption', in Rabab el-Mahdi and Philip Marfleet (eds), *Egypt: Moment of Change*, Cairo: The American University of Cairo Press, pp. 34–50.

Elshaheed.co.uk, 'We Are All Khaled Said' (n.d.), 'Background Story' (http:// www.elshaheeed.co.uk/home-khaled-said-full-story-background-truth-what-happened-torture-in-egypt-by-egyptian-police/; accessed 2 Mar. 2012).

El-Taraboulsi, Sherine (2011), 'Spaces of Citizenship: Youth Civic Engagement and Pathways to the January 25 Revolution', in 'Youth Activism and Public Space in Egypt', John D. Gerhart Center Report, Cairo: American University in Cairo, pp. 10–19.

EOHR (2009), 'When Will the Crime of Torture Stop?' Report, Cairo: Egyptian Organization for Human Rights (http://en.eohr.org/2009/03/11/when-will-the-crime-of-torture-stop/; accessed 6 June 2012).

Euronews (2011), 'Bahrain Protesters Look to Emulate Egypt Revolt', 16 Feb. (http://www.euronews.com/2011/02/16/bahrain-protesters-look-to-emulate-egypt-revolt/; accessed 11 Dec. 2012).

Facebook (n.d.), 'Newsroom' (http://newsroom.fb.com/content/default. aspx?NewsAreaId=20; accessed 27 Feb. 2012).

Fahmy, Ninette (2002), *The Politics of Egypt: State–Society Relationship*, London: RoutledgeCurzon.

FAO (n.d.), 'FAO Food Price Index', Rome: Food and Agricultural Organization of the United Nations (http://www.fao.org/worldfoodsituation/food-pricesindex/en/; accessed 22 June 2012).

——— (2008), 'Initiative on Soaring Food Prices: Mission Findings and Recommendations, Inter-Agency Assessment Mission', Report, Nov.–Dec., Rome: Food and Agricultural Organization of the United Nations.

Feigenbaum, Anna, Fabian Frenzel and Patrick McCurdy (2013 forthcoming), *Protest Camps*, London: Zed Books.

Fibre2fashion (2006), 'Textile Industry in a Gloomy State', 1 Dec. 2006 (http://www.fibre2fashion.com/news/textile-news/egypt/newsdetails.aspx?news_id=26944; accessed 5 July 2012).

FIDH (2004), 'Arrest of Two Human Rights Activists', 30 July (http://www.fidh.org/Arrest-of-Two-Human-Rights,1695; accessed 20 Apr. 2012).

Fouad, Hesham (2010), 'ElBaradei Seeks the Support of the Workers without Accepting their Demands for Change', *Ekraa*, 13 Sep. (http://arabicforread.blogspot.com/2010/09/elbaradei-seeks-support-of-workers.html; accessed 25 Feb. 2012; Arabic original available from: http://www.e-socialists.net/node/6131).

Freedom House (2002–2005), 'Egypt: Freedom in the World', Freedom in the World Reports, Washington, DC: Freedom House (http://www.freedom-house.org/country/egypt; accessed 7 June 2012).

——— (2012), 'Egypt: Freedom in the World 2012', Freedom in the World Reports, Washington, DC: Freedom House (http://www.freedomhouse.org/report/freedom-world/2012/egypt-0; accessed 7 June 2012).

Gana, Alia (2012), 'The Rural and Agricultural Roots of the Tunisian Revolution: When Food Security Matters', *International Journal of Sociology of Agriculture & Food*, 19(2): 201–13.

Gerges, Fawaz (2005), *The Far Enemy: Why Jihad Went Global*, Cambridge: Cambridge University Press.

Gerhart Center (2011), 'Youth Activism and Public Space in Egypt', Cairo: American University in Cairo.

Ghonim, Wael (2012), *Revolution 2.0*, London: Fourth Estate.

Giddens, Anthony (1986), *The Constitution of Society: Outline of the Theory of Structuration*, Cambridge: Polity.

Gladwell, Malcolm (2010), 'Small Change: Why The Revolution Will Not Be Tweeted', *The New Yorker*, 4 Oct.

Goldstone, Jack (1991), *Revolution and Rebellion in the Early Modern World*, Berkeley, CA: University of California Press.

——— (1997), 'Population Growth and Revolutionary Crises', in John Foran (ed.), *Theorizing Revolutions*, London: Routledge, pp. 102–20.

Goodwin, Jeff (2001), *No Other Way Out: States and Revolutionary Movements, 1945–1991*, Cambridge: Cambridge University Press.

Goodwin, Jeff and James Jasper (1999), 'Caught in a Winding, Snarling Vine: The Structural Bias of Political Process Theory', *Sociological Forum*, 14(1): 27–54.

——— (eds) (2004), *Rethinking Social Movements: Structure, Meaning and Emotion*, Lanham, MD: Rowman and Littlefield.

Goodwin, Jeff and Steven Pfaff (2001), 'Emotion Work in High-Risk Social Movements: Managing Fear in the U.S. and East German Civil Rights Movements', in Jeff Goodwin (ed.), *Passionate Politics: Emotions and Social Movements*, Chicago: University of Chicago Press, pp. 282–302.

Goodwin, Jeff, James Jasper and Francesca Polletta (2000), 'The Return of the Repressed: The Fall and Rise of Emotions in Social Movement Theory', *Mobilization*, 5(1): 65–84.

——— (2004), 'Emotional Dimensions of Social Movements', in David Snow, Sarah Soule and Hanspeter Kriesi (eds) (2004), *The Blackwell Companion to Social Movements*, Oxford: Blackwell Publishing, pp. 413–32.

Gould, Deborah (2004), 'Passionate Political Processes: Bringing Emotions Back Into the Study of Social Movements', in Jeff Goodwin and James Jasper (eds), *Rethinking Social Movements: Structure, Meaning and Emotion*, Lanham, MD: Rowman and Littlefield, pp. 155–76.

Gould, Roger (2003), 'Why Do Networks Matter? Rationalist and Structuralist Interpretations', in Mario Diani and Doug McAdam (eds), *Social Movements and Networks: Relational Approaches to Collective Action*, Oxford: Oxford University Press, pp. 233–56.

Gray, Chris Hables (1997), *Postmodern War: The New Politics of Conflict*, London: Routledge.

Gribbon, Laura and Sarah Hawas (2012), 'Signs and Signifiers: Visual Translations of Revolt', in Samia Mehrez (ed.), *Translating Egypt's Revolution: The Language of Tahrir*, Cairo: The American University in Cairo Press, pp. 103–42.

Gröndahl, Mia (2011), *Tahrir Square: The Heart of the Revolution*, Cairo: The American University in Cairo Press.

Guardian (2003), 'Threat of War: Protests around the World', 3 Mar.

——— (2011a), 'Protests in Egypt and Unrest in Middle East—As it Happened', News Blog, 25 Jan.

——— (2011b), 'Egypt Protest Leaflets Distributed in Cairo give Blueprint for Mass Action', 27 Jan.

——— (2011c), 'Egypt Protesters Defy Curfew as Tanks Roll into Cairo', 28 Jan.

——— (2011d), 'US Embassy Cables: Egyptian Military's Influence in Decline, US Told', 3 Feb.

Guidry, John (2003), 'Trial by Space: The Spatial Politics of Citizenship and Social Movements in Urban Brazil', *Mobilization*, 8(2): 189–204.

Gunning, Jeroen (2007), *Hamas in Politics: Democracy, Religion, Violence*, London: Hurst.

Gurr, T. (1970), *Why Men Rebel?* Princeton, NJ: Princeton University Press.

Gustin, Sam (2011), 'Social Media Sparked, Accelerated Egypt's Revolutionary Fire', *Wired*, 11 Feb. (http://www.wired.com/business/2011/02/egypts-revolutionary-fire/; accessed 15 Nov. 2012).

Habermas, Jürgen (1992 [1962]), *The Structural Transformation of the Public Sphere*, Cambridge: Polity.

Hafez, Mohammed and Wiktorowicz, Quintan (2004), 'Violence as Contention in the Egyptian Islamic Movement', in Quintan Wiktorowicz (ed.), *Islamic Activism: A Social Movement Theory Approach*, Bloomington, IN: Indiana University Press, pp. 61–88.

Halliday, Fred (1999), *Revolution and World Politics: The Rise and Fall of the Sixth Great Power*, Basingstoke: Palgrave Macmillan.

Hamdy, Naila (2009), 'Arab Citizen Journalism in Action: Challenging Mainstream Media, Authorities and Media Laws', *Westminster Papers in Communication and Culture*, 6(1): 92–112.

Hamzawy, Amr (2005), 'The Continued Costs of Political Stagnation in Egypt', Carnegie Endowment Policy Outlook, Feb. (http://www.carnegieendowment.org/files/Hamzawy_Final.pdf; accessed 20 Apr. 2012).

Hanna, Michael Wahid (2009), 'The Son also Rises: Egypt's Looming Succession Struggle', *World Policy Journal*, 26(3): 103–14.

Harris, Fredrick (2006), 'It Takes a Tragedy to Arouse Them: Collective Memory and Collective Action during the Civil Rights Movement', *Social Movement Studies*, 5(1): 19–43.

Hashim, Ahmed (2012), 'The Egyptian Military, Part One: From the Ottomans through Sadat' *Middle East Policy Council Journal Essay* (http://www.mepc.org/journal/middle-east-policy-archives/egyptian-military-part-one-ottomans-through-sadat?print; accessed 14 Apr. 2012).

Hassan, Abdalla (2003a), 'Police Outnumber Antiwar Protesters in Cairo', Worldpress.org, 30 Jan. (http://www.worldpress.org/Mideast/922.cfm; accessed 16 Sep. 2011).

——— (2003b), 'As War Continues, Tensions Rise in Egypt', Worldpress.org, 31 Mar. (http://www.worldpress.org/Mideast/1029.cfm; accessed 16 Sep. 2011).

Hassan, Mohammed and Cyrus Sassanpour (2008), 'Labor Market Pressures in Egypt: Why is the Unemployment Rate Stubbornly High?' in Conference Paper, International Conference, 'The Unemployment Crisis in the Arab Countries', 17–18 Mar., Cairo (http://www.ilo.org/dyn/travail/docs/437/Hassan%20and%20Sassanpour%202008%20'Labor%20Market%20Pressures%20in%20Egypt'%20API.pdf; accessed 10 Feb. 2013).

Heidegger, Martin (2010 [1954]), 'The Question Concerning Technology', in Craig Hanks (ed.), *Technology and Values: Essential Readings*, Oxford: Wiley-Blackwell, pp. 99–113.

Held, David (1989), *Political Theory and the Modern State: Essays on State, Power and Democracy*, Cambridge: Polity.

Hinnebusch, Raymond (1985), *Egyptian Politics under Sadat: The Post-Populist Development of an Authoritarian-Modernizing State*, Cambridge: Cambridge University Press.

Hirst, David and Irene Beeson (1981), *Sadat*, London: Faber and Faber.

Hobbes, Thomas (1996 [1651]), *Leviathan*, ed. Richard Tuck, rev. student edn, Cambridge: Cambridge University Press.

Horkheimer, Max (1992), *Critical Theory: Selected Essays*, New York: Seabury Press.

Howard, Philip (2010), *The Digital Origins of Dictatorship and Democracy*, Oxford: Oxford University Press.

Huffington Post (2008), 'Egypt Grants Bonuses After Deadly Food Riots', 8

Apr. (http://www.huffingtonpost.com/2008/04/08/egypt-grants-bonuses-afte_n_95685.html; accessed 13 July 2012).

——— (2011), 'Occupy Wall Street: Egyptian Activist Goes "From Liberation Square to Washington Square"' (Video), 8 Oct. (http://www.huffingtonpost.com/2011/10/08/occupy-wall-street-washington-square_n_1001775.html; accessed 11 Dec. 2012).

Human Rights Watch (1992), 'Behind Closed Doors: Torture and Detention in Egypt', A Middle East Watch Report, New York: Human Rights Watch (http://www.hrw.org/sites/default/files/reports/Egypt927.pdf; accessed 25 June 2013).

——— (2004), 'Egypt's Torture Epidemic', Human Rights Watch Briefing Paper, 25 Feb. (http://www.hrw.org/legacy/english/docs/2004/02/25/egypt7658_txt.pdf; accessed 7 June 2012).

——— (2011), 'Egypt: End Use of Live Fire at Peaceful Protests—Dozens Killed in Cairo and Alexandria', Human Rights Watch News, 29 Jan. (http://www.hrw.org/news/2011/01/29/egypt-end-use-live-fire-peaceful-protests; accessed 6 June 2012).

Huntington, Samuel, *The Clash of Civilizations and the Remaking of World Order*, New York: Simon & Schuster, 1996.

Ibrahim, Gigi (2011), 'Fear No More: Power of the People', Interview by Phil England, *New Internationalist*, 442, May (http://www.newint.org/features/web-exclusive/2011/04/20/egypt-revolution-gigi/; accessed 24 Feb. 2012).

Ibrahim, Saad Eddin (2007), 'Egypt's Unchecked Repression', *Washington Post*, 21 Aug.

Ibrahim, Saad Eddin and Naiem Sherbiny (2000), 'A Reply to My Accusers', *Journal of Democracy*, 11(4): 58–63.

ICEM (2005), 'A Testimony for History. Monitoring the Egyptian 2005 Parliamentary Elections', The Independent Committee for Elections Monitoring, Final Report (availablefrom http://aeamisr.org/news/a-testimony-for-history-monitoring-the-egyptian-2005-parliamentary-elections/; accessed 30 June 2013).

Idle, Nadia and Alex Nunns (eds) (2011), *Tweets From Tahrir: Egypt's Revolution as it Unfolded, in the Words of the People who Made it*, London: OR Books.

Ikhwanweb (2010a), 'MB and NAC's Online Petition 7 Demands for Change, Approaches 1,000,000 Signatures Target', 5 Oct. (http://www.ikhwanweb.com/article.php?id=26638; accessed 2 Mar. 2012).

——— (2010b), 'Egypt's Farcical Election', 29 Nov. (http://www.ikhwanweb.com/article.php?id=27350; accessed 2 Mar. 2012).

IMF (n.d.), 'World Economic Outlook Database: By Countries (Country-Level Data)', (http://www.imf.org/external/pubs/ft/weo/2010/02/weodata/weoselgr.aspx; accessed 23 June 2012).

IndexMundi (n.d.), 'Egypt Cotton Production by Year' (http://www.indexmundi.com/agriculture/?country=eg&commodity=cotton&graph=production; accessed 5 July 2012).

Internet World Stats (n.d.), 'Africa' (http://www.internetworldstats.com/africa.htm; accessed 27 Feb. 2012).

Inter-Parliamentary Union (n.d.), 'Egypt: Majlis Al-Chaab (People's Assembly)' (http://www.ipu.org/parline-e/reports/2097_arc.htm; accessed 9 Jan. 2013).

IRI (2005), '2005 Parliamentary Election Assessment in Egypt', Washington, DC: International Republican Institute (http://www.iri.org/sites/default/files/Egypt's%202005%20Parliamentary%20Elections%20Assessment%20Report.pdf; accessed 30 June 2013).

IRI Poll (2011), 'Egyptian Public Opinion Survey April 14–April 27, 2011,' Survey Report, Washington, DC: International Republican Institute (http://www.iri.org/news-events-press-center/news/iri-releases-egypt-poll; accessed 9 Jan. 2012).

Ishani, Maryam (2011), 'The Hopeful Network', *Foreign Policy*, 7 Feb. (http://www.foreignpolicy.com/articles/2011/02/07/the_hopeful_network?page=full; accessed 1 Mar. 2012).

Ismail, Salwa (2006), *Political Life in Cairo's New Quarters: Encountering the Everyday State*, Minneapolis: University of Minnesota Press.

Jacinto, Leela (2011), 'Enter the "baltagiya": Egypt's Repression Spills Out of the Torture Chambers', France24, 9 Feb. (http://www.france24.com/en/20110207-egypt-torture-human-rights-repression-spills-out-torture-chambers-baltagiya-police; accessed 8 June 2012).

Jameson, Frederik (1998), *The Cultural Turn: Selected Writings on the Postmodern, 1983–1998*, London: Verso.

Jasper, James (2011), 'Emotions and Social Movements: Twenty Years of Theory and Research', *Annual Review of Sociology*, 37: 285–303.

Jasper, James and Jane Poulsen (1995), 'Recruiting Strangers and Friends: Moral Shocks and Social Networks in Animal Rights and Anti-Nuclear Protests', *Social Problems*, 42(4): 493–512.

Johnston, Hank (2008), 'Ritual, Strategy, and Deep Culture in the Chechen National Movement', *Critical Studies on Terrorism*, 1(3): 321–42.

just-style.com (2009), 'Egypt's Clothing Fortunes Mirror Global Downturn', 27 July (http://www.just-style.com/analysis/egypts-clothing-fortunes-mirror-global-downturn_id104834.aspx; accessed 28 June 2013).

Kaldor, Mary, Helmut Anheier and Marlies Glasius (2003), 'Global Civil Society in an Era of Regressive Globalization', in Mary Kaldor, Helmut Anheier and Marlies Glasius (eds), *Global Civil Society 2003*, Oxford: Oxford University Press, pp. 3–33.

Kamrava, Mehran (1999), 'Revolution Revisited: The Structuralist–Voluntarist Debate', *Canadian Journal of Political Science*, XXXII(2): 317–45.

Kassem, Maye (2004), *Egyptian Politics: The Dynamics of Authoritarian Rule*, Boulder, CO: Lynne Rienner.

Keith, Michael and Steve Pile (1993), *Place and the Politics of Identity*, London: Routledge.

Keraitim, Sahar and Samia Mehrez (2012), '*Mulid al-Tahrir*: Semiotics of a Revolution', in Samia Mehrez (ed.), *Translating Egypt's Revolution: The*

Language of Tahrir, Cairo: The American University in Cairo Press, pp. 25–67.

Khalil, Ashraf (2011), *Liberation Square: Inside the Egyptian Revolution and the Rebirth of a Nation*, New York: St Martin's Press.

Khalil, Menna (2012), 'The People and the Army are One Hand: Myths and their Translations', in Samia Mehrez (ed.), *Translating Egypt's Revolution: The Language of Tahrir*, Cairo: The American University in Cairo Press, pp. 249–75.

Khamis, Sahar and Katherine Vaughn (2011), 'Cyberactivism in the Egyptian Revolution: How Civic Engagement and Citizen Journalism Tilted the Balance', *Arab Media and Society*, 14.

Khamis, Sahar, Paul Gold and Katherine Vaughn (2012), 'Beyond Egypt's "Facebook Revolution" and Syria's "YouTube Uprising": Comparing Political Contexts, Actors and Communication Strategies', *Arab Media and Society*, 15 (http://www.arabmediasociety.com/peer_reviewed/index.php?article= 791; accessed 19 July 2012).

Kheir-El-Din, Hanaa and Heba El-Laithy (2008), 'An Assessment of Growth Distribution, and Poverty in Egypt: 1990/91–2004/05', in Hanaa Kheir-El-Din (ed.), *The Egyptian Economy: Current Challenges and Future Prospects*, Cairo: The American University in Cairo Press, pp. 13–52.

Kholoussy, Hanan (2010), 'The Fiction (and Non-Fiction) of Egypt's Marriage Crisis', *Middle East Report Online*, Interventions, Dec. (http://www.merip. org/mero/interventions/fiction-non-fiction-egypts-marriage-crisis; accessed 30 June 2012).

Khorshid, Sara (2005), 'A Cry of Distress: The Egyptian Movement for Change—Kefaya', OnIslam.net, 25 Aug. (available from: http://www. onislam.net/english/politics/africa/410329.html; accessed 24 June 2013).

Kienle, Eberhard (1998), 'More than a Response to Islamism: The Political Deliberalization of Egypt in the 1990s', *Middle East Journal*, 52(2): 219–35.

Kimmel, Michael (1990), *Revolution: A Sociological Interpretation*, Cambridge: Polity.

King, Stephen (2009), *The New Authoritarianism in the Middle East and North Africa*, Bloomington, IN: Indiana University Press.

Kitschelt, Herbert (1986), 'Political Opportunity Structures and Political Protest: Anti-Nuclear Movements in Four Democracies', *British Journal of Political Science*, 16(1): 57–85.

Klandermans, Bert (1997), *The Social Psychology of Protest*, Oxford: Blackwell.

——— (2004), 'The Demand and Supply of Participation: Social–Psychological Correlates of Participation in Social Movements', in D.A. Snow, S. Soule and H. Kriesi (eds), *Blackwell Companion to Social Movements*, Oxford: Blackwell, pp. 360–79.

Koopmans, Ruud (2004), 'Protest in Time and Space: The Evolution of Waves of Contention', in David Snow, Sarah Soule and Hanspeter Kriesi (eds), *The Blackwell Companion to Social Movements*, Oxford: Blackwell, pp. 19–46.

Korotayev, Andrey and Julia Zinkina (2011), 'Egyptian Revolution: A Demographic Structural Analysis', *Middle East Studies Online Journal*, 5(2): 57–95.

Kurzman, Charles (1996), 'Structural Opportunity and Perceived Opportunity in Social-Movement Theory: The Iranian Revolution of 1979', *American Sociological Review*, 61(1): 153–70.

Kymlicka, Will (2007), *Multicultural Odysseys: Navigating the New International Politics of Diversity*, Oxford: Oxford University Press.

Lachmann, Richard (1997), 'Agents of Revolution: Elite Conflicts and Mass Mobilization from the Medici to Yeltsin', in John Foran (ed.), *Theorizing Revolutions*, Abingdon: Routledge, pp. 73–101.

Lagi, Marco, Karla Bertrand and Yaneer Bar-Yam (2011), 'The Food Crises and Political Instability in North Africa and the Middle East', NECSI Publication, Cambridge, MA: New England Complex Systems Institute, 10 Aug. (http://www.necsi.edu/research/social/foodcrises.html; accessed 13 July 2012).

Langohr, Vickie (2004), 'Too Much Civil Society, Too Little Politics: Egypt and Liberalizing Arab Regimes', *Comparative Politics*, 36(2): 181–204.

Leaflet (2011), 'Kaif tuthawwir bihada'a [How to Protest Intelligently]' (http://www.indybay.org/uploads/2011/01/29/egyptianrevolutionaryguide_9pages.pdf; accessed 24 June 2013).

Lede Blog (2011), 'Egyptian Bloggers Parse London Riots in Real Time', *New York Times*, 8 Aug. 2011 (http://thelede.blogs.nytimes.com/2011/08/08/egyptian-bloggers-parse-london-riots-in-real-time/; accessed 11 Dec. 2012).

Lee, Eric and Benjamin Weinthal (2011), 'Trade Unions: The Revolutionary Social Network at Play in Egypt and Tunisia', *Guardian*, 10 Feb.

Lefebvre, Henri (1991 [1974]), *The Production of Space*, Oxford: Basil Blackwell.

Leupp, Gary (2003), 'What Democracy Looks Like: The Streets of Cairo', *Counterpunch*, 25 Mar. (http://www.counterpunch.org/2003/03/25/the-streets-of-cairo/; accessed 12 Jan. 2012).

Libcom.org (2007a), 'Kafr el-Dawwar Workers are in the Same Trench as Ghazl el-Mahalla', 18 Apr. (http://libcom.org/library/kafr-el-dawwar-workers-are-same-trench-ghazl-el-mahalla; accessed 24 Feb. 2012).

——— (2007b), 'Statement from Ghazl el-Mahalla's "7th of December Movement—Workers For Change"', 24 June (http://libcom.org/news/statement-ghazl-el-mahallas-7th-december-movement-workers-change-24062007; accessed 24 Feb. 2012).

Lichbach, Mark (1987), 'Deterrence or Escalation? The Puzzle of Aggregate Studies of Repression and Dissent', *Journal of Conflict Resolution*, 31(2): 266–97.

Lim, Merlyna (2012), 'Clicks, Cabs, and Coffee Houses: Social Media and

Oppositional Movements in Egypt, 2004–2011', *Journal of Communication*, 62(2): 231–48.

Locke, John (1988 [1689]), *Two Treatises of Government*, edited by Peter Laslett, Cambridge: Cambridge University Press.

Lucas, Scott (2011), 'Egypt (and Beyond) LiveBlog: Black Hole or Another Day of Revolution', EAWorldview (Enduring America), 28 Jan. (http://www.enduringamerica.com/home/2011/1/28/egypt-and-beyond-liveblog-black-hole-or-another-day-of-revol.html; accessed 3 Oct. 2012).

Lynch, Marc (2011), 'After Egypt: The Limits and Promise of Online Challenges to the Authoritarian Arab State', *Perspectives on Politics*, 9(2): 301–10.

Magnusson, Warren (1996), *The Search for Political Space*, Toronto: University of Toronto Press.

——— (2011), *Politics of Urbanism: Seeing Like a City*, London: Routledge.

Mansour, Sherif (2009), 'Enough Is Not Enough: Achievements and Shortcomings of Kefaya, the Egyptian Movement for Change', in Maria Stepan (ed.), *Civilian Jihad: Nonviolent Struggle, Democratization, and Governance in the Middle East*, New York: Palgrave Macmillan, pp. 205–18.

——— (2010), 'Egypt's "Facebook Revolution", Kefaya, and the Struggle for Democracy and Good Governance (2008–Ongoing)', *ICNC Conflict Summary*, Washington, DC: International Center on Nonviolent Conflict (http://www.nonviolent-conflict.org/images/stories/pdfs/mansour_egypt.pdf; accessed 20 Apr. 2012).

Marston, Sallie (2003), 'Mobilizing Geography: Locating Space in Social Movement Theory', *Mobilization*, 8(2): 227–33.

Martin, Deborah and Byron Miller (2003), 'Space and Contentious Politics', *Mobilization*, 8(2): 143–56.

Martini, Jeffrey, Dalia Kaye and Erin York (2012), *The Muslim Brotherhood, Its Youth, and Implications for U.S. Engagement*, Santa Monica, CA: RAND.

Marx, Karl (2000), *Karl Marx: Selected Writings*, ed. David McLellan, 2nd edn, Oxford: Oxford University Press.

McAdam, Doug (1982), *Political Process and the Development of Black Insurgency, 1930–1970*, Chicago: University of Chicago Press.

——— (1996), 'Conceptual Origins, Current Problems, Future Directions', in Doug McAdam, John McCarthy and Mayer Zald (eds), *Comparative Perspectives on Social Movements*, Cambridge: Cambridge University Press, pp. 23–40.

McAdam, Doug, John McCarthy and Mayer Zald (1996), 'Introduction: Opportunities Mobilizing Structures and Framing Processes', in Doug McAdam, John McCarthy and Mayer Zald (eds), *Comparative Perspectives on Social Movements*, Cambridge: Cambridge University Press, pp. 1–20.

McAdam, Doug, Sidney Tarrow and Charles Tilly (2001), *Dynamics of Contention*, Cambridge: Cambridge University Press.

McCarthy, John and Mayer Zald (1977), 'Resource Mobilization and Social

Movements: A Partial Theory', *The American Journal of Sociology*, 82(6): 1212–41.

McCaughey, Martha and Michael Ayers (2003), *Cyberactivism: Online Activism in Theory and Practice*, London: Routledge.

McColl, R.W. (1969), 'The Insurgent State: Territorial Bases of Revolution', *Annals of the Association of American Geographers*, 59(4): 613–31.

McGreal, Chris (2011), 'Tony Blair: Mubarak is "Immensely Courageous and a Force for Good"', *Guardian*, 2 Feb.

McGregor, Andrew (2011), 'Hot Issue—Has Al-Qaeda Opened A New Chapter In The Sinai Peninsula?', Washington, DC: The Jamestown Foundation, 17 Aug. (http://www.jamestown.org/single/?no_cache=1&tx_ttnews%5Btt_news%5D=38332; accessed 3 Oct. 2012).

McLean Hilker, Lyndsay, Seema Khan, Sarah Ladbury and Jeroen Gunning (2009), 'A Scoping Study for Developing a Research Agenda on the Drivers of Radicalisation and Violent Extremism', Final Report prepared for DFID Research and Evidence Division, London: DFID.

Mehrez, Samia (2008), *Egypt's Culture Wars: Politics and Practice*, Abingdon: Routledge.

MENA Solidarity Network (2011), 'Egypt: Strike Statistics for 2009–2011', 9 Aug. (http://menasolidaritynetwork.com/2011/08/09/egypt-strike-statistics-for-2009-2011/; accessed 1 Mar. 2012).

Miller, Byron and Deborah Martin (eds) (2003), 'Special Issue: Space, Place, and Contentious Politics', *Mobilization*, 8(2).

Mohyeldin, Ayman (2011), 'Foreword', in Mia Gröndahl, *Tahrir Square: the Heart of the Revolution*, Cairo: The American University in Cairo Press.

Montague, James (2012), 'Egypt's Politicised Football Hooligans', Aljazeera.com, 2 Feb. (http://www.aljazeera.com/indepth/opinion/2012/02/20122215833232195.html; accessed 16 Feb. 2012).

Morris, Aldon (1981), 'Black Southern Student Sit-In Movement: An Analysis of Internal Organization', *American Sociological Review*, 46(6): 744–67.

Moustafa, Tamir (2004), 'Protests Hint at New Chapter in Egyptian Politics', *Middle East Report Online*, 9 Apr. (http://www.merip.org/mero/mero040904; accessed 16 Sep. 2011).

Murphy, Emma (2009), 'Theorizing ICTs in the Arab World: Informational Capitalism and the Public Sphere', *International Studies Quarterly*, 53(4): 1131–53.

Naeem, Mohamed (2011), 'Behind the Lawlessness', *al-Masry al-Youm*, 15 May (http://www.egyptindependent.com/node/437711; accessed 2 Mar. 2012).

Newsweek (2011a), 'Is Egypt Next?' 23 Jan. (available from: http://www.thedailybeast.com/newsweek/2011/01/22/the-revolution-comes-to-egypt.html; accessed 8 Feb. 2013).

——— (2011b), 'Egypt Revolution: Inside a Cairo Street Protest', 28 Jan. (available from: http://www.thedailybeast.com/newsweek/2011/01/28/egypt-revolution-inside-a-cairo-street-protest.html; accessed 8 Feb. 2013).

New Tactics in Human Rights (2010), 'Egyptian Activists' Use of Mobile Phones to Alert their Networks of Harassment or Arrest by Police', 17 May (no longer available at http://www.newtactics.org/node/9344; accessed 1 Mar. 2012; shortened version at http://www.kabissa.org/blog/egyptian-activists'-use-mobile-phones-alert-their-networks-harassment-or-arrest-police; accessed 30 June 2013).

New York Times (2008), 'Day of Angry Protest Stuns Egypt', 6 Apr.

—— (2011a), 'Clashes Grow as Egyptians Remain Angry After an Attack', 4 Jan.

—— (2011b), 'Violent Clashes Mark Protests Against Mubarak's Rule', 25 Jan.

—— (2011c), 'Rich, Poor and a Rift Exposed by Unrest', 30 Jan.

—— (2011d), 'Mubarak Family Riches Attract New Focus', 12 Feb.

—— (2011e), 'A Tunisian–Egyptian Link That Shook Arab History', 13 Feb.

—— (2013), 'Deadly Riots Erupt Across Egypt on Anniversary of Revolution', 25 Jan.

Niblock, Tim (1993), 'International and Domestic Factors in the Economic Liberalization Process in Arab Countries', in Tim Niblock and Emma Murphy (eds), *Economic and Political Liberalization in the Middle East*, London: British Academic Press, pp. 55–87.

Ogburn, William (1957), 'The Meaning of Technology', in Francis Allen (ed.), *Technology and Social Change*, New York: Appleton-Century-Crofts.

Oliver, Pamela and Hank Johnston (2000), 'What a Good Idea: Frames and Ideologies in Social Movements Research', *Mobilization*, 5(1): 37–54.

Oliver, Pamela and Daniel Myers (2003), 'Networks, Diffusion, and Cycles of Collective Action', in Mario Diani and Doug McAdam (eds), *Social Movements and Networks: Relational Approaches to Collective Action*, Oxford: Oxford University Press, pp. 173–203.

Omar, Mostafa (2011), 'Egypt's Unfinished Revolution', *International Socialist Review*, 77, May–June (http://isreview.org/issues/77/feat-Egyptunfinished.shtml; accessed 13 Jan. 2013).

OMCT (2003a), 'Egypt: Arrests, Torture and Threats of Rape against Anti-War Demonstrators', World Organisation Against Torture, 27 Mar. (http://www.omct.org/urgent-campaigns/urgent-interventions/2003/03/d16229/; accessed 24 June 2013).

—— (2003b), 'Egypt: Hunger Strikes Launched to Protest against the Detention and Torture of Demonstrators', *World Organisation Against Torture*, 23 Apr. (http://www.omct.org/urgent-campaigns/urgent-interventions/2003/04/d16256/; accessed 11 Dec. 2012).

Omer, Mohammed (2011), 'Revolution Spreads to Egypt's Deprived Sinai', *The Electronic Intifada*, 1 Feb. (http://electronicintifada.net/content/revolution-spreads-egypts-deprived-sinai/9208; accessed 3 Oct. 2012).

Osman, Ahmed (2011), 'Egypt's Police: From Liberators to Oppressors', *al-Masry al-Youm*, 24 Jan. (http://www.egyptindependent.com/node/304946; accessed 16 Feb. 2012).

BIBLIOGRAPHY

Osman, Amr and Marwa Abdel Samei (2012), 'The Media and the Making of the 2011 Egyptian Revolution', *Global Media Journal* (German Edition) 2(1).

Osman, Magued and Hanan Girgis (2009), 'Marriage Patterns in Egypt', Conference Paper (unpublished), XXVI International Population Conference, Marrakech, 27 Sep.–2 Oct. (http://iussp2009.princeton.edu/papers/91490; accessed 22 June 2012).

Oxford Dictionaries (n.d.), 'Oxford Dictionaries Online', Oxford: Oxford University Press (http://oxforddictionaries.com; accessed 16 Jan. 2013).

Parsa, Misagh (2000), *States, Ideologies, & Social Revolutions*, Cambridge: Cambridge University Press.

Pew (n.d.), 'Pew Global Attitudes Project—Key Indicators Database—Egypt', Washington, DC: Pew Research Center (http://www.pewglobal.org/database/?indicator=3&country=64; accessed 5 June 2012).

Popham, Peter (2007), 'Protesters Claim Egypt Has Become Police State', *The Independent*, 17 Mar.

Posusney, Marsha Pripstein (1997), *Labor and the State in Egypt*, New York: Columbia University Press.

PressTV (2011), '13 Killed in Suez in 4 Days', 28 Jan. (http://edition.presstv.ir/detail/162480.html; accessed 6 June 2012).

Radsch, Courtney (2011), 'The Revolutions Will Be Hashtagged: Twitter Turns 5 as the Middle East Demands Democracy', Huffington Post, 29 Mar. (http://www.huffingtonpost.com/courtney-c-radsch/the-revolutions-will-be-h_b_839362.html; accessed 1 Mar. 2012).

Ramadan, Adam (2013), 'From Tahrir to the World: The Camp as a Political Public Space', *European Urban and Regional Studies*, 20(1): 145–9.

Rashed, Mohammed Abouelleil (2011), 'The Egyptian Revolution: A Participant's Account from Tahrir Square, January and February 2011', *Anthropology Today*, 27(2): 22–7.

Reuters (2010), 'Egyptians Protest Parliamentary Vote Results', 12 Dec.

——— (2011), 'Egypt Church Blast Death Toll Rises to 23', 4 Jan.

Rheingold, Howard (2002), *Smart Mobs: The Next Social Revolution*, Cambridge, MA: Basic Books.

Ricoeur, Paul (1981), *Hermeneutics and the Human Sciences: Essays on Language, Action and Interpretation*, Cambridge: Cambridge University Press.

Roll, Stephen (2010), 'Gamal Mubarak and the Discord in Egypt's Ruling Elite', Sada, 1 Sep. (http://carnegieendowment.org/2010/09/01/gamal-mubarak-and-discord-in-egypt-s-ruling-elite/6bcv; accessed 14 Apr. 2012).

Rousseau, Jean-Jacques (1997, 2004 [1750–1754]), *The Discourses and Other Early Political Writings*, edited by Victor Gourevitch, Cambridge: Cambridge University Press.

——— (1997, 2006 [1762]), *The Social Contract and Other Later Political Writings*, translated by Victor Gourevitch, edited by Peter Gourevitch, Cambridge: Cambridge University Press.

Rueschemeyer, Dietrich, Evelyne Stephens and John Stephens (1992), *Capitalist Development & Democracy*, Cambridge: Polity Press.

Rutherford, Bruce (2008), *Egypt after Mubarak: Liberalism, Islam, and Democracy in the Arab World*, Princeton, NJ: Princeton University Press.

Sabry, Sarah (2009), 'Poverty Lines in Greater Cairo: Underestimating and Misrepresenting Poverty', *Working Paper*, 21, Poverty Reduction in Urban Areas Series, London: International Institute for Environment and Development (http://www.iied.org/pubs/display.php?o=10572IIED; accessed 17 Feb. 2012).

Sadiki, Larbi (2000), 'Popular Uprisings and Arab Democratization', *International Journal of Middle East Studies*, 32(1): 71–95.

Said, Atef (2009), 'Egypt: The Rise of the Working Class', Workers' Liberty, 22 Oct. (http://www.workersliberty.org/story/2009/10/22/egypt-rise-working-class; accessed 24 Feb. 2012).

Schemm, Paul (2002), 'Sparks of Activist Spirit in Egypt', *Middle East Report Online*, 13 Apr. (http://www.merip.org/mero/mero041302; accessed 19 Sep. 2011).

——— (2003), 'Egypt Struggles to Control Anti-War Protests', *Middle East Report Online*, 31 Mar. (http://www.merip.org/mero/mero033103; accessed 19 Sep. 2011).

Schenker, Jack (2010), 'Khaled Said Death Protests Renewed as Trial of Egyptian Police Officers Begins', *Guardian*, 24 Sep.

Schenker, Jack and Mustafa Khalili (2011), 'Cairo's Biggest Protest Yet Demands Mubarak's Immediate Departure', *Guardian*, 4 Feb.

Scheuerman, William (2011), *The Realist Case for Global Reform*, Cambridge: Polity.

Schwartz, Barry (1986), *The Battle for Human Nature: Science, Morality and Modern Life*, New York: Norton.

Scott, James (1998), *Seeing Like a State: How Certain Schemes to Improve the Human Condition have Failed*, New Haven, CT: Yale University Press.

Searing, Donald (1986), 'A Theory of Political Socialization: Institutional Support and Deradicalization in Britain', *British Journal of Political Science*, 16(3): 341–76.

Searle, John (1996), *The Construction of Social Reality*, London: Penguin.

Seddon, David (1993), 'Austerity Protests in Response to Economic Liberalization in the Middle East', in Tim Niblock and Emma Murphy (eds), *Economic and Political Liberalization in the Middle East*, London: British Academic Press, pp. 88–113.

Séjourné, Marion (2009), 'The History of Informal Settlements', in Regina Kipper and Marion Fischer (eds), *Cairo's Informal Areas: Between Urban Challenges and Hidden Potentials. Facts. Voices. Visions.*, Chapter 1: 'About Cairo and its Informal Areas', Cairo: GTZ Egypt, pp. 17–19 (available from: http://www.citiesalliance.org/node/591; accessed 6 July 2012).

Sennott, Charles (2011), 'Inside the Muslim Brotherhood: Part 1&2', Globalpost, 21 Feb. (http://www.globalpost.com/dispatch/egypt/110220/inside-the-muslim-brotherhood; accessed 28 June 2013).

Shapiro, Samantha (2009), 'Revolution, Facebook-Style', *New York Times Magazine*, 22 Jan. (http://www.nytimes.com/2009/01/25/magazine/25bloggers-t.html?pagewanted=all; accessed 25 Feb. 2012).

Shirky, Clay (2011), 'The Political Power of Social Media: Communication Technology will Help Promote Freedom—But it Might Take a While', *Foreign Affairs*, 90(1): 28–41.

Sims, David (2010), *Understanding Cairo: The Logic of a City out of Control*, Cairo: The American University in Cairo Press.

Skocpol, Theda (1979), *States and Social Revolutions: A Comparative Analysis of France, Russia, and China*, Cambridge: Cambridge University Press.

Smith, Catharine (2011), 'Egypt's Facebook Revolution: Wael Ghonim Thanks the Social Network', Huffington Post, 11 Feb. (http://www.huffingtonpost.com/2011/02/11/egypt-facebook-revolution-wael-ghonim_n_822078.html; accessed 15 Nov. 2012).

Snow, David (2004), 'Framing Processes, Ideology, and Discursive Fields', in D.A. Snow, S. Soule and H. Kriesi (eds) *Blackwell Companion to Social Movements*, Oxford: Blackwell, pp. 380–412.

Snow, David, E. Burke Rochford, Steven Worden and Robert Benford (1986), 'Frame Alignment Processes, Micromobilization, and Movement Participation', *American Sociological Review*, 51(4): 464–81.

Snow, David, Sarah Soule and Hanspeter Kriesi (2004), 'Mapping the Terrain', in David Snow, Sarah Soule and Hanspeter Kriesi (eds), *The Blackwell Companion to Social Movements*, Oxford: Blackwell, pp. 3–16.

Solidarity Center (2010), 'The Struggle for Worker Rights in Egypt', Report, Washington, DC: Solidarity Center.

Soliman, Ahmed Mounir and Hernando De Soto (2004), *A Possible Way Out: Formalizing Housing Informality in Egyptian Cities*, Lanham, MD: University Press of America.

Soueif, Ahdaf (2012), *Cairo: My City, Our Revolution*, London: Bloomsbury.

Spiegel (2008), 'The Daily Struggle for Food', 18 Apr. (http://www.spiegel.de/international/world/crisis-in-egypt-the-daily-struggle-for-food-a-548300.html; accessed 13 July 2012).

Stacher, Joshua (2004), 'Parties Over: The Demise of Egypt's Opposition Parties', *British Journal of Middle Eastern Studies*, 31(2): 215–33.

Stackpole, Thomas (2011), 'Meet the Ad Men Behind Occupy Wall Street', *New Republic*, 12 Nov. (http://www.tnr.com/article/politics/97353/adbusters-kalle-lasn-occupy-wall-street; accessed 18 Jan. 2013).

Stern, Johannes (2013), 'Mass Protests against Mursi Mark Second Anniversary of Egyptian Revolution', *World Socialist Web Site*, 25 Jan. (http://www.wsws.org/en/articles/2013/01/26/egyp-j26.html?view=print; accessed 4 Feb. 2013).

Stirk, Peter (2009), *The Politics of Military Occupation*, Edinburgh: Edinburgh University Press.

Stock, Brian (1983), *The Implications of Literacy*, Princeton, NJ: Princeton University Press.

———— (1996), *Listening for the Text: On the Uses of the Past*, Philadelphia, PA: University of Pennsylvania Press.

Stoner, Eric (2011), 'The Role of the Academy of Change in Egypt's Uprising', Waging Nonviolence, 19 Apr. (http://wagingnonviolence.org/2011/04/the-role-of-the-academy-of-change-in-egypts-uprising/; accessed 3 Mar. 2012).

stopwar.org.uk (n.d.), 'Stop the War Coalition: Timeline of Events 2001–2011' (http://stopwar.org.uk/index.php/about/timeline-of-stop-the-war-events-2001–2011; accessed 19 Sep. 2011).

Stork, Joe (2011), 'Three Decades of Human Rights Activism in the Middle East and North Africa: An Ambiguous Balance Sheet', in Joel Beinin and Fréderic Vairel (eds), *Social Movements, Mobilization and Contestation in the Middle East and North Africa*, Stanford, CA: Stanford University Press, pp. 83–106.

Stratfor (2011), 'Update on the Size of Protests in Cairo', 1 Feb. (http://www.stratfor.com/sample/analysis/update-size-protests-cairo; accessed 17 July 2012).

Tadros, Mariz (2012), 'Introduction: The Pulse of the Arab Revolt', *IDS Bulletin*, 43(1): 1–15.

Tahrir Documents (2011a), 'Let us Return to the Squares to Complete our Revolution', 26 Nov. (http://www.tahrirdocuments.org/2011/11/let-us-return-to-the-squares-to-complete-our-revolution/; accessed 11 Dec. 2012).

———— (2011b), 'The Revolution First and Legitimacy for Tahrir', 16 Dec. (http://www.tahrirdocuments.org/2011/12/the-revolution-first-and-legitimacy-for-tahrir/; accessed 11 Dec. 2012).

Tarrow, Sidney (1998), *Power in Movement: Social Movements and Contentious Politics*, 2nd edn, Cambridge: Cambridge University Press.

Tarrow, Sidney and Doug McAdam (2005), 'Scale Shift in Transnational Contention', in Donatella della Porta and Sidney Tarrow (eds), *Transnational Protest and Global Activism*, Lanham, MD: Rowman & Littlefield, pp. 121–47.

Telegraph (2008), 'Egyptians Riot over Bread Crisis', 8 Apr.

———— (2011), 'Egypt Protests: Secret US Document Discloses Support for Protesters', 28 Jan.

Tessler, Mark, Jodi Nachtwey and Anne Banda (1999), *Area Studies and Social Science: Strategies for Understanding Middle East Politics*, Bloomington, IN: Indiana University Press.

Teti, Andrea (2007), 'Bridging the Gap: International Relations, Middle East Studies and the Disciplinary Politics of the Area Studies Controversy', *European Journal of International Relations*, 13(1): 117–45.

Thabet, Hala (2006), 'Egyptian Parliamentary Elections: Between Democratisation and Autocracy', *Africa Development*, XXXI(3): 11–24.

Theoharis, Jeanne (2006), '"Alabama on Avalon": Rethinking the Watts Uprising and the Character of Black Protest in Los Angeles', in Peniel Joseph (ed.), *The Black Power Movement: Rethinking the Civil Rights–Black Power Era*, London: Routledge, pp. 27–53.

Tilly, Charles (1978), *From Mobilization to Revolution*, New York: Random House.

Trombetta, Lorenzo (2013), 'More than just a Battleground: Cairo's Urban Space during the 2011 Protests', *European Urban and Regional Studies*, 20(1): 139–44.

Tufekci, Z. Zeynep and Christopher Wilson (2012), 'Social Media and the Decision to Participate in Political Protest: Observations From Tahrir Square', *Journal of Communication*, 62(2): 363–79.

Tully, James (2008), *Public Philosophy in a New Key: Democracy and Civic Freedom*, vol. I, Cambridge: Cambridge University Press.

UNDP (2009), 'Arab Human Development Report 2009', New York: United Nations Publications.

UN MDGI (n.d.), 'Millennium Development Goals Indicators: Egypt' (http://mdgs.un.org/unsd/mdg/Data.aspx; accessed 5 July 2012).

UN World Population Prospects (2010), 'World Population Prospects, the 2010 Revision', New York: United Nations Department for Economic and Social Affairs, Population Division (2010 revision no longer available; for 2012 revision: http://esa.un.org/unpd/wpp/index.htm; 30 June 2013).

UN World Urbanization Prospects (2011), 'World Urbanization Prospects: The 2011 Revision', New York: United Nations Department of Economic and Social Affairs.

Urdal, Henrik (2006), 'A Clash of Generations? Youth Bulges and Political Violence', *International Studies Quarterly*, 50(3): 607–30.

——— (2007), 'The Demographics of Political Violence: Youth Bulges, Insecurity and Conflict', in L. Brainard and D. Chollet (eds), *Too Poor for Peace? Global Poverty, Conflict and Security in the 21st Century*, Washington, DC: Brookings Institution Press, pp. 90–100.

USDA (2009), 'Egypt: Cotton and Products Annual', GAIN Report EG9007, 19 Apr., Washington, DC: US Department of Agriculture.

——— (2010), 'Egypt: Cotton and Products Annual', GAIN Report, 19 Apr., Washington, DC: US Department of Agriculture.

US Department of State (2004), 'Country Reports on Human Rights Practices: Egypt 2003', 25 Feb., Washington, DC: Bureau of Democracy, Human Rights, and Labor, US Department of State.

Vairel, Fréderic (2011), 'Protesting in Authoritarian Situations: Egypt and Morocco in Comparative Perspective', in Joel Beinin and Fréderic Vairel (eds), *Social Movements, Mobilization and Contestation in the Middle East and North Africa*, Stanford, CA: Stanford University Press, pp. 27–42.

Van Eekelen, Willem, Loretta de Luca and Nagwa Ismail (2002), 'Youth Employment in Egypt', *EMP/Skills Working Paper*, 2, Geneva: ILO.

Villa, Dana (1999), *Politics, Philosophy, Terror: Essays on the Thought of Hannah Arendt*, Princeton, NJ: Princeton University Press.

———— (ed.) (2000), *The Cambridge Companion to Hannah Arendt*, Cambridge: Cambridge University Press.

Walker, R.B.J. (2010), *After the Globe, Before the World*, London: Routledge.

Wall Street Journal (2011), 'Egypt Shuts Down Internet, Cellphone Services', 29 Jan.

Washington Times (2010), 'Egyptian Leader's Health on Radar of U.S.', 18 July.

Waterbury, John (1994), 'Democracy without Democrats? The Potential for Political Liberalization in the Middle East', in Ghassan Salamé (ed.), *Democracy without Democrats? The Renewal of Politics in the Muslim World*, London: IB Tauris, pp. 48–83.

'We Are All Khalid Said' (n.d.), 'About' (http://www.facebook.com/elshaheeed.co.uk?sk=info; accessed 1 Mar. 2012).

Whitfield, Philip (2011), 'All for 10 Pounds Life is Cheap and Costly', *Daily News Egypt*, 17 Aug. (http://dailynewsegypt.com/2011/08/17/all-for-10-pounds-life-is-cheap-and-costly/; accessed 19 Jan. 2013).

Wickham, Carrie (2002), *Mobilizing Islam*, New York: Columbia University Press.

———— (2013), *The Muslim Brotherhood: Evolution of an Islamist Movement*, Princeton, NJ: Princeton University Press. References are to the uncorrected proofs. Pagination may differ in the published edition.

Wickham-Crowley, Timothy (1997), 'Structural Theories of Revolution', in John Foran (ed.), *Theorizing Revolutions*, Abingdon: Routledge, pp. 38–72.

Wikipedia (n.d.), 'Facebook Revolution' (http://en.wikipedia.org/wiki/Facebook_Revolution; accessed 15 Nov. 2012).

Williams, Joan (1991), 'Dissolving the Sameness/Difference Debate: A Post-Modern Path beyond Essentialism in Feminist and Critical Race Theory', *Duke Law Journal*, (1): 296–323.

Wired (2011), 'Egypt's Top "Facebook Revolutionary" Now Advising Occupy Wall Street', 18 Oct. (http://www.wired.com/dangerroom/2011/10/egypt-occupy-wall-street/; accessed 11 Dec. 2012).

World Bank (n.d.), 'Egypt, Arab Rep.' (http://data.worldbank.org/country/egypt-arab-republic; accessed 5 July 2012).

———— (2008), 'Youth Unemployment, Existing Policies and Way Forward: Evidence from Egypt and Tunisia', Presentation (http://info.worldbank.org/etools/docs/library/243377/day9EgyptTunisia%20Presentation.pdf; accessed 29 June 2013).

———— (2009), *Egypt: Positive Results from Knowledge Sharing and Modest Lending*, Washington, DC: World Bank.

Young-Bruehl, Elisabeth (2006), *Why Arendt Matters*, New Haven, CT: Yale University Press.

YouTube (2011), 'Egyptian Tank Man', uploaded by MFMAegy, 25 Jan. 2011 (http://www.youtube.com/watch?v=kWr6MypZ-JU; accessed 3 Oct. 2012).

Ziada, Dalia (2010), 'April 6 Demonstration Exposes the Weak-Points of Egyptian Opposition Elite', bikyamasr, 7 Apr. (http://bikyamasr.com/11086/

BIBLIOGRAPHY

april-6-demonstration-exposes-the-weak-points-of-egyptian-opposition-elite/; accessed 25 Feb. 2012).

Zirakzadeh, Cyrus (2006), *Social Movements in Politics: A Comparative Study*, expanded edn, Basingstoke: Palgrave Macmillan.

Interviews and Conversations

Abdel-Rahman (2011), Employee of Central Bank, Cairo, 23 May.

Ahmed (2011), Lawyer with ElBaradei's National Association for Change, Cairo, 22 May.

Allam, Hisham (2011), Journalist with *al-Masry al-Youm*, Cairo, 24 May.

Amira (2011), Journalist with *al-Masry al-Youm*, Cairo, 24 May.

Anonymous (2011), Teacher Trainer at the American University in Cairo and Facebook Blogger, Cairo, 22 May.

Anonymous Mother (2011), Mother of non-activist who participated in the demonstrations, Cairo, 21 May.

Anonymous Son (2011), Non-activist who participated in the demonstrations, Cairo, 21 May.

April 6 Cadres (2011), Conversation on Tahrir Square, Cairo, 27 May.

Barakat, Khaled (2011), Journalist with *al-Ahram*, Cairo, 22 May.

Bowker, Robert (2011), Australian Ambassador to Egypt 2005–2008, Durham, 15 Nov.

Eid, Gamal (2011), Director of the Arabic Network for Human Rights Information, Cairo, 26 May.

El-Said, Sameh (2011), Medical Student, Cairo, 21 May.

Ezzat, Heba Raouf (2011), Islamist Academic and Intellectual, Cairo, 26 May.

Fahmy, Latifa (2011), AUC Professor, childhood friend of Suzanne Mubarak and widow of former minister in Sadat's government, Cairo, 26 May.

Fouad, Mostafa (2011), Activist, April 6 Youth Movement, Cairo, 20 May.

Gamal (2011), Young Diplomat at Ministry of Foreign Affairs, Cairo 23 May.

Ghazali-Harb, Shadi (2011a), Activist Leader, Democratic Front Party, Cairo, 24 May.

———— (2011b), Telephone Interview, Cairo, 26 May.

———— (2013), Follow-Up Interview, Cairo, 10 Mar.

Group Interview (2011), Group interview with thirteen affiliates of Egyptian Moral Re-Armament, an informal grassroots NGO, 26 May.

Hamdy, Mahmoud (2011), Young Diplomat at Ministry of Foreign Affairs, Cairo, 20 and 23 May.

Hossam (2011), Owner of a Boutique Cooking School, Cairo, 25 May.

International Palestinian Solidarity Movement Activist (2012), London, Mar.

Ishak, George (2011), Co-Founder of Kefaya, Cairo, 23 May.

Maher, Ahmed (2011), Activist Leader and Co-Founder April 6 Youth Movement, Cairo, 26 May.

———— (2013), Follow-Up Interview, Cairo, 13 Mar.

Mansour, Nadim (2011), Leftist Workers' Rights Lawyer, Cairo, 23 May.

Marei, Fouad (2011), PhD Student at Durham University, Durham, 16 May.

Saad, Omar (2011), Leftist Journalist, Cairo, 20 May.

Saeed, Khalil (2011), Democratic Front Party, Cairo, 20 May.

Salah, Ahmed (2011), Co-Founder and Former Member of April 6 Youth Movement, Cairo, 22 May.

Samer, Sally (2011), Human Rights Activist with ElBaradei's National Association for Change, Cairo, 22 May.

Sarah (2011), French Academic Researcher in Mahalla, Cairo, 24 May.

Shaaban, Ahmed (2011), Leftist Co-Founder of Kefaya, Cairo, 24 May.

Taema, Mohammed (2011), Media Coordinator, Kefaya, Cairo, 25 May.

Tahrir Square Shop Owner (2011), Cairo, 22 May.

Wynne-Hughes, Elisa (2011), British PhD Student resident in Cairo, Cairo, 19 May.

Younis, Joumanah (2011), British Languages Student resident in Cairo, Cairo, 21 May.

INDEX

413